MW01285778

BLACK SOLDIERS, WHITE LAWS

BLACK SOLDIERS, WHITE LAWS

The Tragedy of the 24th Infantry in 1917 Houston

John Haymond

Atlantic Monthly Press
New York

FIRST EDITION

Printed in the United States of America

First Grove Atlantic hardcover edition: July 2025

Library of Congress Cataloging-in-Publication data is available for this title.

ISBN 978-0-8021-6475-9
eISBN 978-0-8021-6476-6

Atlantic Monthly Press
an imprint of Grove Atlantic
154 West 14th Street
New York, NY 10011

Distributed by Publishers Group West

groveatlantic.com

25 26 27 28   10 9 8 7 6 5 4 3 2 1

CONTENTS

FOREWORD

Once again we are standing at the crossroads of our collective history, viewing a treatise that represents the convergence of the old and the new. This is a story of the past that is told in such a way that the reader cannot help but see its impact and relevance for today.

As a direct descendant of Private First Class Thomas Coleman Hawkins, a member of the 24th Infantry Regiment who was one of the first thirteen men unjustly hung by the Army on that fateful day of December 11, 1917, this story is dear to me. This book not only reveals the forgotten military history of this case but also delves into the personal stories of some of the soldiers of the 24th Infantry. It tells of the slow cadence of their families' journey to justice. It took 106 years to loosen the grip of "denied justice" effectuated by the tightening of the hangman's rope for those executed and the clanging of iron prison gates for those men condemned to rot in confinement. Yet the journey would not be complete until the soldiers who were in life the 24th Infantry finally had their honor restored and received their long-overdue justice in November 2023.

How this story is told is related to how we see our nation and our hopes and dreams for the future. It is a testament to where we stand when our faith is tested and whether we could accept the audacity of the dishonor unjustly foisted upon the 24th Infantry. The legacy of these soldiers, their patriotism, and their service to our nation—protecting freedoms that they themselves could not enjoy in that era of racial segregation—must be told in an unabashed fashion. As the life of PFC Hawkins personified, "The body can be taken, but the eternal spirit shall forever rise."

We stand on their shoulders, on their sacrifice, on their suffering, and revel in the poetic justice revealed in the pages of this book, knowing that our belief in brighter tomorrows has been immortalized. And yes, it is the culmination of decades of work by many individuals, families, and organizations—folks who may have taken different approaches, from advocacy under the Military Code of Justice and in our civilian courts to just plain grassroots activism.

Read this American story of injustice, hope, and redemption. Return to 1917 through the eyes of today and embrace the timeless impact of this tragic point in our history. Judge the stark reality for yourself.

Now rise!
Jason Holt, Esq.
East Orange, New Jersey

A Note on Language and Terminology

In writing a book dealing with the racism of the early twentieth century and using primary sources to tell the story, it is impossible to avoid the highly offensive language that litters the historical record. In 1917 racial slurs appeared in newspaper articles, in court transcripts and official records, and in the sworn statements of witnesses and participants.

It might soothe our modern sensibilities to censor the problematic language of the past and modify every quoted passage where an offensive word appears, especially that one particularly loathsome slur, "nigger." As a historian, I believe that doing so would be an injustice to the men whose story this is. History, if it is to be effective and honest, must confront the full range of offenses and injustices exactly as they occurred, and truth is poorly served by censorship even if it is well intended. The African American soldiers in Houston in the summer of 1917 were not offended by white southerners' use of impolite euphemisms; they were infuriated by the blatant racism and deliberate insult of that specific word, the bigotry it represented, and the physical abuse that often accompanied it. If we today attempt to sanitize the record, we will lose the full picture of the verbal abuse and violent oppression those men endured. If we want to understand them and try to explain their actions, we must first understand what they experienced because that was at the heart of their justifiable outrage. The racism of their time was at the core of it all, and so the pages ahead contain the words spoken and written in 1917 exactly as they were used at that time.

While the current stylistic preference in the twenty-first century is to capitalize the word "Black" when referring to African American people, that word appears here in lowercase when that was how it was originally written in direct quotations or excerpts. It is interesting to note that the word "Negro" in 1917 was almost always capitalized when used by African American writers and almost always written in lowercase when used by white writers. The word "colored," which was then commonly used by both African American and white commentators, seems to have been much less consistently used as a proper noun by everyone—some Black writers capitalized it, and some did not. The phrase "the race" often appeared in Black newspapers to refer to African Americans broadly.

The stylistic rules for how to refer to American military units and soldiers' ranks in writing have also changed repeatedly in the century since this story began, but one rule is constant. Infantry units are always referred to by both their battalion number and their regiment, never solely by the battalion. Thus, the infantry unit at the center of this story, the 3rd Battalion of the 24th Infantry Regiment, should properly be referred to by that full designation or by the shortened descriptor "3-24 Infantry." Infantrymen who speak a common language would say "Third of the Twenty-Fourth" in conversation with each other. Its sister battalion, the 1st Battalion of the 24th Infantry Regiment, would be "1-24 Infantry," or "First of the Twenty-Fourth." The problem is that using the abbreviated forms can be confusing to some readers, and the full designation quickly becomes tedious and repetitious even to readers familiar with the Army's peculiar language. To simplify the narrative in the pages ahead, the 3rd Battalion of the 24th Infantry Regiment will most often be referred to simply as "Third Battalion" and its sister unit as "First Battalion," without the regimental designation. When units of other regiments occasionally appear in the story, they will be referred to by their full conventional designations to distinguish them from elements of the 24th Infantry. For clarity's sake, the four rifle companies in Third Battalion will be referred to by their modern phonetic forms: "India Company" for Company I, "Kilo Company" for Company K, "Lima Company" for Company L, and "Mike Company" for Company M.

The terms used for military installations convey specific meanings and are not freely interchangeable. A "fort" is a permanent military installation (as in Fort Sam Houston), while a "camp" is temporary (even if it exists for decades), but all Army installations can be referred to as "posts." It is also common to refer to military property as a "reservation," which in that context has no connection with Native American territories.

Military ranks also have their own protocols, and the abbreviations used by civilian commentators in 1917 varied greatly, so in this text military ranks will usually be written out in full to avoid confusion and needless jargon. Additionally, while the Army today is meticulous in distinguishing between the different noncommissioned officer ranks, especially the senior grades of sergeant first class, first sergeant, and sergeant major, such distinctions were not always observed at that time, so in the primary sources one often sees NCOs of all grades referred to as simply "sergeant" or "corporal." Those designations are repeated here when they appear in quotations, even though they might appear incorrect to any reader familiar with modern military customs.

Finally, during that era of military segregation the U.S. Army had four all-Black regiments: the 9th and 10th Cavalries and two infantry regiments, the 24th and 25th. In the infantry units, all the enlisted men—soldiers and noncommissioned officers—were African American, and all the commissioned officers—lieutenants, captains, and so on—were white. Thus, whenever "soldiers" or "NCOs" of Third Battalion are mentioned in this text, it should always be understood that those are Black men.

The men at the center of this story were soldiers of the U.S. Army, just as I was for more than twenty years, and I approached my study of this case from a soldier's perspective. Relegated as they so often are to the role of pawns in a game in which they are not always valued as individuals, soldiers have a keen sense of fair play, and perhaps no one feels more keenly the wrongs done to a soldier than does another soldier. For that reason, and because of the respect in which I hold the men of 3-24 Infantry, this book is a direct, unflinching discussion of a disturbing history that should still haunt us a century after it occurred.

PREFACE

Fort Sam Houston is a U.S. Army post situated on a low hill completely surrounded by the modern urban sprawl of San Antonio, Texas. These days, the installation serves as the training center for all soldiers who serve in the Army's medical field and is home to the headquarters of U.S. Army South and U.S. Army North. It is a small post by modern standards, small enough that a person can walk around the main post area in less than an hour if they keep to an infantryman's pace of four miles an hour.

On the northern section of the post, downhill from the big Spanish-style buildings with their red-tiled roofs that form the old Infantry and Cavalry Post parts of the military cantonment, the much newer expanse of the post golf course wraps itself around the lower perimeter of the Fort Sam Houston National Cemetery. Golfers playing their rounds tee off at regular intervals from the fifteenth-tee box, just a couple of hundred yards down Nursery Road from the Fort Sam Houston Elementary School.

If you stand on the fifteenth tee today, nothing tells you that on that spot, in the predawn darkness of December 11, 1917, thirteen Black men were hanged there on a single gallows. It was the largest mass execution of American soldiers in the Army's history. On the other side of Nursery Road, a narrow path disappears down into the thick brush that grows up along the banks of Salado Creek, and nothing in that thicket with its sand spurs and ticks indicates that until 1936 nineteen men were buried there—the thirteen hanged on that cold December morning in 1917 and another six who were hanged at the same spot in September 1918.

That former burial plot, now overgrown by the Texas brush, and the nearly forgotten spot where gallows once marred the carefully manicured flat of the fifteenth-tee box, were the tragic culminations of a night of violence in Houston in August 1917. Three trials followed that incident, the first of which was the largest murder trial in American history. It was an episode of appalling injustice, provoked and compounded by a culture of malevolent racism.

On the sweltering, rainy night of August 23, 1917, more than a hundred African American soldiers of the 3rd Battalion, 24th Infantry Regiment took their weapons and marched into the San Felipe District of the city of Houston under the leadership of their company NCOs. By dawn the next morning, sixteen people were dead. Over the next few days, four more people died of wounds sustained in the chaos. It was the most serious incident of violence between American soldiers and civilians during the First World War. Allegations of injustice inflamed public debate about the incident and its aftermath, especially after the Army court-martialed 118 Black soldiers in trials that were tainted by procedural irregularities and racial bias.

The 1917 Houston Incident and the military courts-martial that followed it are a story of systemic racism, oppression, abuses of power, police brutality, and a legal process marred by a rush to judgment and a lack of due process. This is much more than just a military history. It is the story of a failure of justice that transcends the years, even though for decades it was largely unknown outside of the immediate region where those events took place.

It is important to understand this event in its wider historical context. The Houston Incident was preceded and to some degree influenced by clashes between white civilians and Black soldiers in other Texas towns such as El Paso, Brownsville, Del Rio, and Waco. It occurred just weeks after one of the worst race riots in American history, when more than a hundred African American citizens were murdered by white mobs in East St. Louis; and it foreshadowed the "Red Summer" of 1919, when Black soldiers returning from service in France were the targets of racist violence in cities across America. In many respects the Houston Incident and its aftermath were unique, but it was not an isolated incident.

Something terrible happened in Texas a little over a century ago. The lives forever impacted by this event, the individual stories nearly lost to history, and the account of a long struggle to achieve some measure of restorative justice, are what this book is all about.

1. HANGMAN'S SLOUGH

They came for Jesse Ball in the dark hours before dawn on a cold December morning in 1917.* His mother, home in West Feliciana Parish, Louisiana, had had a dreadful premonition that something like this would happen to him. African American mothers in southern states knew this fear all too well as they watched their sons grow to manhood and venture out into a dangerous world, young Black men in a society where Jim Crow overshadowed every aspect of their lives. A Black man could be lynched for the slightest reason or for no reason at all, and parents could do little to protect their sons from that peril. Jesse's mother told him she had dreamed something terrible would happen to him if he left home for another hitch in the Army. Somewhere out there, she feared, something dreadful was lying in wait for her boy.

However, Jesse loved being a soldier because he had already been one. At seventeen he had enlisted in the 24th Infantry Regiment, one of the U.S. Army's "Buffalo Soldier" regiments of Black soldiers in that era of a racially segregated military. Serving in that famous unit with its proud history gave him a sense of purpose and new opportunities and sent him farther away from the cotton fields of east Louisiana than he had ever thought he could go. He traveled by train out west, sailed across the Pacific, and served three years in the Philippines. When that first enlistment was up, he took his discharge and went back home, but like many other young men he soon realized that home had lost much of its appeal. Home was still the same,

---

* All personal details of Jesse Moore [Ball] are taken from interviews conducted with Professor Angela Holder in Houston, Texas, August 2018. Professor Holder is Jesse Moore's great-niece.

but he was different. He had seen the world beyond Jim Crow's oppressive shadow. He missed the adventure and rough comradery of Army life.

When Jesse announced his intention to reenlist, his mother begged him not to do it. She told him about her premonition, but nothing she said could change his mind. Jesse loved his mother, just as fiercely as she loved him, but he knew his own mind. All the same, he could not bring himself to defy her directly, so in the end he reenlisted without telling her. He used his uncle's surname and signed the enlistment papers as Jesse Moore, reentering the Army under a name his mother never gave him so that she could not petition the government to send him home.

Now here he was in Texas, far from home, and white men with guns had come out of the night and laid their hands on him. At least he was not alone. Twelve other young Black men were hemmed in with him in a feebly lit room. William Nesbit, Charles Baltimore, Thomas Hawkins, and the others; Jesse knew them like brothers, had soldiered and fought and risked everything with them. They were shackled with chains on their wrists and ankles and taken out into the cold darkness. Their captors lifted them up into the back of trucks and drove them away into the night.

Texas in 1917 had a reputation for horrific racist violence. Lynch mobs terrorized African American citizens in almost every county in the state, and a gathering of armed white men in the night usually meant only one thing. With that in mind, one might naturally have assumed that the activity a few miles outside of San Antonio in the predawn darkness that December morning was another lynching in progress. After all, many of the elements familiar to Texas lynchings were evident. A crowd was assembled, though most of them were invisible in the darkness. From the clinking of bridle chains and the stamping of horse hooves it was apparent that the place was surrounded by a cordon of mounted men. Light from a large bonfire glinted on the rifles held by men gathered around a hastily erected wooden scaffold a hundred yards from Salado Creek. Anyone standing at the right spot could see the outline of a row of thirteen nooses draped over a crossbar, silhouetted against the lesser darkness of the eastern horizon.

The clandestine nature of it all, especially the darkness of the hour and the remote location, suggested that the perpetrators wanted to keep what was happening from public view. But other things about this scene did not fit the familiar script of a lynch mob in action. For one thing, all the armed men who ringed the scaffold wore khaki. An orderliness marked this event that one never saw at a lynching—there were no shouts, no confusion. None of these men looked angry, and no one was drunk. A grim solemnity overshadowed the scene.

As the sky tinted with the first hues of the approaching dawn, a faint glow of electric headlights appeared in the distance. The trucks carrying Jesse Ball and his companions bounced and rattled over the rough dirt track that led out to this desolate spot near an old bridge spanning Salado Creek. This was no motley cavalcade of vehicles, as was usually used by hastily assembled lynch mobs. These trucks were all identical, new-model Packards, all painted the same dull green color.

The trucks pulled up a short distance from the bonfire-lit scaffold, and the armed men closed in around them. Jesse and his twelve companions were lifted down from the trucks' cargo beds. They could not climb down by themselves, with their hands manacled behind them, and the shackles hobbled them, so they could only manage short, halting steps as they were led to the waiting gallows. Jesse's friend William Nesbit had always been a leader in this group; now he led them one last time. "Not a word out of any of you men, now," Nesbit said.[1] There would be no pleas for mercy, no protestations of innocence, no displays of fear as they faced the rope. Whatever had brought them to this end, these men were determined to die with their dignity intact.

Clearly, this was not the work of night riders or "white-caps." A purpose-built gallows stood there, not a looming live oak chosen as an expedient hanging tree. The spectators gathered were not a disorderly mob, and the arrival of the men who were about to die did not prompt shouts or jeers from the armed men who surrounded them. The social forces of law and church were also present—several men in civilian clothes wearing silver stars on their coats stood off to one side, along with a Black clergyman. The minister with his Bible approached the condemned men, but the lawmen remained apart, watching. They had no authority in this affair, other than as silent witnesses. If this proceeding was a matter of law, then it was a law in which they were not a part.

Jesse and the other twelve men were taken up the steps of the gallows. Thirteen chairs were arranged on the long trapdoor, six on one side and seven on the other, and there they were seated. A uniformed chaplain mounted the scaffold to stand by them. As the nooses were adjusted around their necks, the condemned men began to sing a hymn, quietly but without a tremor in their voices.

From his position below the scaffold, the man in charge looked at his watch, then at the eastern sky, where the horizon was tinted saffron with the approaching dawn. He spoke to the prisoners, who sat noosed and waiting, and they got to their feet in a jangle of chains. The chairs were removed from the scaffold.

"Goodbye, boys of Company C," one of the doomed men said. He was speaking not to his companions but to the white men who had brought him to his death.

According to the almanac for that year, 7:17 a.m. would be the exact moment of sunrise. The officer below the scaffold, whose uniform epaulettes bore the silver eagles of a colonel's insignia, kept his eyes on the face of his watch. In the stillness of the early morning the men surrounding the scaffold could hear the chaplain praying quietly, his appeal to the Almighty punctuated by the songs of early-rising mockingbirds and the snorting of restless horses.

The colonel raised his arm, held it for several seconds, then dropped it. The long trap fell open with a crash and all thirteen men dropped simultaneously. One witness later claimed that he clearly heard the snapping sound as the nooses broke their necks. After nearly thirty long, silent minutes, a medical officer examined each of the hanged men for signs of life. They were all dead.

Their bodies were taken down from the gallows. Then an unexpected delay interrupted the grim process. Several of the hangman's knots had locked tight from the force of the drop. Nearly twenty minutes of effort were needed to work the nooses loose before the bodies could be placed in rough-sawn pine coffins. Slips of paper written with each man's name and the phrase "Died December 11, 1917, at Fort Sam Houston" were placed inside glass soda bottles that were laid on their corpses before the lids of the coffins were nailed shut. The caskets were loaded onto wagons and taken down the slope to a wooded spot a few yards from the creek bank, where they were lowered into thirteen waiting graves dug in a single row. Jesse Ball was buried as Jesse Moore, the alias he carried to his death. He was twenty-seven years old, a long way from home, and his mother was never able to learn where her boy was buried.

As a crew of Mexican laborers began shoveling dirt into the graves, the sounds of hammers and crowbars sounded through the morning. The gallows were disassembled, and the timbers were piled into trucks and carried back to Fort Sam Houston. By noon, nothing but mounds of ashes and hoof marks in the grass remained to mark the spot where thirteen men had died. Just as the hanging was carried out under cover of darkness and secrecy, all evidence of the act was quickly erased from the site as soon as the execution was over.

Down by Salado Creek, however, a row of thirteen mounds of freshly turned dirt remained in view. In other cases, the graves of executed men had been despoiled by people seeking to add a personal measure of vengeance to the punishment of death, or by macabre souvenir-hunters. A rumor spread that some local people were talking of digging up the bodies of the hanged men and burning them. That sort of desecration would not be tolerated here. An armed guard was placed at the graves day and night for several weeks, until the morbidly curious lost interest and sought other diversions. In the long, dark hours of the winter nights, alone at their posts among the new graves, the soldiers whose duty it was to keep that vigil later admitted they were unsettled by the graves of the thirteen men whom they had seen die at the first light of dawn. They called the burial ground "Hangman's Slough," and they did not like going there.

The hanging that morning was not an extrajudicial lynching, no matter how many incidental similarities it might seem to have shared with the long list of racial murders that stained Texas's collective soul in that era. It was a formal military execution, and Jesse Ball and the other men hanged that morning were soldiers of the U.S. Army who were tried and convicted by a military court-martial on a charge of mutiny after an outbreak of violence in Houston, Texas, on the night of August 23, 1917. It was and remains the largest mass execution of American soldiers ever conducted by the U.S. Army in its entire history.* Two additional trials

* During the Mexican-American War, sixteen former soldiers were hanged on September 10, 1847, and another thirty on September 13. All members of the Batallon de San

over the next four months sent another six Black soldiers to their deaths at that same desolate spot, adding six more graves to the thirteen that the grass was slowly covering down by Salado Creek.

Despite the veneer of legal propriety in those proceedings, however, the execution of these nineteen men and the trials that condemned them are a lingering, festering canker in America's troubled history of racism and judicial inequality. The trials are also a disturbing reminder that the U.S. military's application of law and punishment has too often fallen short of fairness or the equal protection of law. Sometimes the law itself has been the source of the worst injustice; for generations Jim Crow segregation sought to use the force of law to restrict and oppress an entire race. This was also true of official military policies that for almost ninety years segregated and separated American soldiers based on the color of their skin, demonstrating that Black soldiers were not regarded as equal when they stood accused before the law.

Civil authorities in Texas called the Houston Incident a "riot." The Army called it "mutiny." Neither description is completely accurate, but what is certain is that the causes of the tragedy run much deeper than the incident itself. This is a story of concentric rings. Houston lies at the center of it all, with Texas beyond it; it is surrounded by the American South and, still further beyond that, by America as a country during the First World War. It is the story of a city, a state, and a nation, all riven by racism. It is a story of laws and the points at which justice begins and ends or never even existed at all. It is also a story of individual men and the converging paths that brought them to a point of fatal collision on a sweltering, stormy night in the City on the Bayou.

For more than a century, neither the people who died in the violence that August night nor the men who were punished for their alleged part in it received any redress or resolution. Nor did the descendants who still remembered their names. No measure of restorative justice would come until November 2023.

Patricio, they were former U.S. soldiers accused of deserting from the U.S. Army and then fighting against the United States with Mexican forces. The thirteen men executed on December 11, 1917, constituted the largest mass execution of American soldiers in the Army's history because they were still in the military service of the United States and never repudiated that affiliation.

A hundred years and more after this incident, it is clear that the men who were convicted by the three courts-martial at Fort Sam Houston were denied the due process of law. The executions that followed their trials were not the culmination of justice. The Army charged them with joining in a mutiny, and nearly every commentator since then, even those who passionately defend those soldiers' actions and criticize the flawed legal process that sent nineteen of them to the gallows and ninety-one others to prison, has assumed that a mutiny actually occurred. But newly discovered evidence and a deeper examination of the historical record leads to a surprising, disturbing conclusion.

There never was a mutiny in Houston that hot summer night in 1917. Something else occurred, an altogether different crime, and the story of that tragedy has never been told before.

2. LYNCH MOBS AND NIGHT RIDERS

Texas was born in violence. There is nothing unique in that; most countries have their origins in struggles for independence or wars of revolution, just as many nations have had to repeatedly fight for their continued survival. In Texas, however, a grim thread runs through the historical violence that is an indelible part of the state's creation and maturation.

Texas fought itself into existence as an independent republic during the Texas Revolution of 1836 when it tore itself away from Mexico. Though Mexico had explicitly abolished slavery when it gained its independence from Spain in 1821, the new Texas Republic not only specifically wrote legal slavery into its constitution but also barred "Africans, the descendants of Africans, and Indians" from ever becoming citizens in the new country.[1] Throughout the frontier period, Texans were both victims and aggressors in conflict with the Comanche, Kiowa, Kickapoo, Apache, and other Indian tribes whose traditional territories covered parts of the region. Texas was a sovereign nation for nearly ten years before it joined the United States of America in 1845 as the twenty-eighth state, only to attempt to divorce itself from that union during the conflagration of the Civil War. The defeat of the Confederacy and occupation of the state by federal troops during Reconstruction saw the emergence of a new strain of racial violence as Texas resisted every effort to make it repent of its slaveholding past or reform its secessionist soul. "Before the Civil War had fairly ended," one historian noted in 1910, "incidents occurred indicating that, if freedom came to Negroes as a result of the war, it would be resisted by southern whites, who would advocate a 'return to compulsory labor which will make the Negro useful to society and subordinate to the white race.'"[2]

For hard-line southern segregationists determined to keep African Americans in a state of tightly controlled subordination, that goal was suddenly made easier by political machinations at the national level. The presidential election of 1876 ended with the Republican candidate, Rutherford B. Hayes, and the Democratic contender, Samuel J. Tilden, locked in a virtual tie. Amid contested electoral votes and instances of fraud by both parties, the vote tallies from three southern states (Florida, Louisiana, and South Carolina) hung in the balance. Republican and Democratic party leadership agreed to a politically expedient compromise.

The Democrats conceded the election to Hayes in exchange for a promise that the new administration would remove federal troops from the South and the federal government would no longer prevent the election of Democratic governments in the "unredeemed" states of the former Confederacy. It marked the beginning of the end of Reconstruction. To secure the presidency, the party of Abraham Lincoln betrayed Black southerners whose freedom had been won by blood. All that was lacking to mark the ignominy of the deed was an exchange of thirty pieces of silver, the traditional price of betrayal.

Hayes took the oath of office as president of the United States on March 3, 1877. Before the end of April, he ordered U.S. Army units posted in southern states to withdraw from their civil enforcement role. Six years later the last vestiges of Reconstruction died when the United States Supreme Court, in an 8–1 decision, declared key elements of the Civil Rights Bill of 1875 unconstitutional. The federal government essentially stepped away from involvement in racial issues and, as a consequence, left the South free to enforce its own racist policies.[3] This completed the federal government's abandonment of Black southerners, leaving them to suffer under a system of legalized oppression that would persist for almost another ninety years.

With removal of federal and military restraint, the racial violence that had festered since 1865 took on a new, more overtly vicious form. Lynching was perhaps the most savage expression of that violence, and the incidence of this crime increased sharply, particularly during in the 1890s. Lynching was not a new problem in America—it had marred the republic since its founding—but in the post-Reconstruction South, it began to change in both its targets and its methods. During the earlier frontier period, people of all races were lynched when communities resorted to vigilante justice, and in areas without formal law enforcement a white man accused of murder was just as likely to be lynched as was a Black man accused of the same crime. After Reconstruction, however, lynching changed into an undeniably racial crime that almost exclusively targeted African Americans and became indelibly associated with the South. "The implication was that things were different in the North, as undoubtedly they were," one social historian notes; "between 1889 and 1918, 96 per cent of the 2522 African Americans killed by lynch mobs died in the former Confederate states."[4]

In Texas a political majority of white citizens was determined to keep control over every aspect of society in the state, and lynching was a brutally effective weapon in that campaign. Masked bands of marauding night riders known as "white-caps" for the hoods they wore terrorized Black citizens and targeted anyone who transgressed the unwritten social strictures that governed all matters of race. Homes were attacked, farmsteads burned out, schools, churches, and businesses destroyed. Black men and women were murdered on the spot or abducted to be later found shot to death or hanged from a tree. If local authorities ever bothered to investigate these crimes, the inquest was invariably cursory. County coroners could usually be counted on to quickly return the expected verdict, that the victim had died "at the hands of persons unknown," and there the matter would end as far as the authorities were concerned. The purpose of lynching was brutally simple and straightforward—"to teach the Negro that in the South he has no rights that the law will enforce," as Ida B. Wells-Barnett wrote in 1900.

African American people in the South lived under an ever-present threat of violence, never for a moment forgetting the risks they endured as people of color. The writer Richard Wright recalled of his childhood, "The white brutality that I had not seen was a more effective control of my behavior than that which I knew. The actual experience would have let me see the realistic outlines of what was really happening. . . . [I]t remained something terrible and yet remote, something whose horror and blood might descend upon me at any moment."[5] As a Black southerner of the Jim Crow era recalled, "In those days it was 'Kill a mule, buy another. Kill a nigger, hire another.' They had to have a license to kill anything but a nigger. We was always in season."[6]

Around the turn of the century, existing traditions of racial segregation were increasingly codified into legal statutes as the social doctrines of white supremacy gained a new foothold in formal law. Across the South, pulpit-thumping preachers and campaigning politicians declared that just as man was created by God to have dominion over the beasts of the earth, so too was the white man placed upon the earth to have dominion over all other races. Many of the white folk sitting in the pews or crowded together in public meeting places fervently agreed. The federal government had not been able to force them to change their attitudes during Reconstruction, no matter how many blue-coated soldiers or Yankee carpetbaggers came south, and no social crusaders in the North would make them change now. This was how Jim Crow segregation was conceived and born, founded upon the false mythologies of a Lost Cause that existed only in romanticized memory. It was nurtured in the paranoia and hostility of a citizenry that feared the transformations of a new emerging social order. It was confirmed by the bastardization of Scripture invoked by those whose actions were the very antithesis of Christian charity.

In the years between 1895 and 1917, racial terrorism in Texas metastasized into its full malignancy. In 1919 the recently formed National Association for the Advancement of Colored People (NAACP) released a carefully researched report on lynching in a booklet titled *Thirty Years of Lynching 1889–1918*.* This study listed 3,395 verifiable lynchings committed in the United States during that thirty-year period. Of the lynchings tallied, 2,834 of those crimes occurred in the South. The North, the West, and separate territories such as Alaska combined to account for the remaining 561 cases. A vast majority of the victims, 2,650 men and women, were identified as persons of color. Texas ranked third in terms of total number of lynchings, with 335 (Georgia was first with 386; Mississippi came next with 373).[7] What set Texas apart on that ledger of murder, however, was the sheer savagery that characterized lynchings in the Lone Star State.

In the majority of lynchings between 1890 and 1918, the victim was accused of murder; if the victim was formally charged or convicted by a court, the lynching occurred when that person was forcibly taken from the custody of law enforcement and put to death by a mob. Sometimes local sheriffs or marshals resisted the mob and attempted to protect their

* In many of the sources from 1917–18, the NAACP is also commonly referred to as "the Association."

prisoners; too often they did not. Besides a charge of murder, other alleged crimes for which people were lynched included rape (alleged or proven), assault, larceny, arson, and murderous assault. In the western states during these years, the offenses usually cited in lynching cases were murder, the stealing of horses or cattle, or acts such as "train-wrecking," and people of all races were victims. In the southern states, however, the alleged offenses that provoked lynchings were often far more trivial, such as "enticing a servant away" from an employer (Georgia, 1894), "disobeying ferry regulations" (Louisiana, 1897), and "disorderly conduct" (Florida, 1896).[8]

Hundreds of other cases were undeniably racial in nature. A Black man named John Brown was lynched in Alabama in 1891 for "testifying against whites." J. M. Alexander was lynched for "protecting a Negro" (Alabama, 1895). An "unnamed Negro" was lynched for "bringing a lawsuit against a white man" (Louisiana, 1909), and Charles Shipman was lynched for "disagreement with a white man" (Texas, 1918). In the small town of Sale City, Georgia, in 1917, Collins Johnson and D. C. Johnson were lynched for "disputing the word of a white man."

All of these alleged offenses were what historian Leon Litwack was describing when he wrote in 1998, "The initial shocks of racial awareness laid the groundwork for learning the necessary rituals of subservience and subordination. Some of them were prescribed in law; most of them existed by habits and customs that were enforced no less ruthlessly than the law."[9]

Another thing that characterized lynch mob violence in the South was that it posed a very real danger not only to those accused of crimes but also to anyone else who happened to be associated with the offense, however remotely, or who simply happened to be Black and unfortunate enough to cross a lynch mob's path when it was out for blood. John Hayden was lynched in Alabama in 1898 because he was "mistaken for another" Black man. Reporting on a 1903 lynching in Georgia, a writer for the *New-York Tribune* wrote: "A mob, formed near Liberty County, pursued through seven counties a Negro supposed to be Ed Claus, who had assaulted Susie Johnson, a young white woman, and lynched him, hanging him and shooting him full of holes. After he was lynched it was found he was not Claus."[10] When lynch mobs failed to lay hands on the person they were hunting, they sometimes expended their violence on friends or family of the accused.

In Rome, Tennessee, in 1901, an African American woman named Bailie Crutchfield was lynched by a mob because her brother was accused of stealing a purse. "The mob took Crutchfield from the custody of the sheriff, and started with him for the place of execution, when he broke from them and escaped," the NAACP report stated. "This so enraged the mob," a contemporary newspaper account reported, "that they suspected Crutchfield's sister of being implicated in the theft and last night's work was the culmination of that suspicion."[11] The coroner's jury returned the usual verdict, that the woman came to her death at the hands of parties unknown.

All across the South in the first decades of the twentieth century, for Black people there was rarely any recourse to law or official authority that could be relied upon to protect them from the mob or to prosecute their murderers after they were hanged, shot, or burned alive. For most of that era, lynching was a national crisis, not a regional one, though it was always concentrated in the South. Through it all, the federal government chose not to involve itself in crimes committed in the individual states, at least not when the overwhelming majority of the victims of those crimes were Black.

When Woodrow Wilson was elected president in 1912, many African Americans initially hoped that with his reputation as a progressive academic he might finally exert the power of the U.S. government to protect them from the scourge of racist violence. In an open letter published in March 13, 1912, shortly after Wilson's inauguration, W. E. B. Du Bois, a founder of the NAACP and a leading African American activist, challenged the president to act against the injustices that Black Americans endured on a daily basis. "We want to be treated as men," Du Bois wrote to Wilson. "We want to vote. We want our children educated. We want lynching stopped. We want no longer to be herded as cattle on street cars and railroads. We want the right to earn a living, to own our own property and to spend our income unhindered and uncursed. Your power is limited? We know that, but the power of the American people is unlimited. Today you embody that power, you typify its ideals."[12] Du Bois was hopeful, but he would be disappointed.

Wilson was a southerner, born in Virginia and raised in Georgia. His earlier academic career had indicated his stance on racial issues. As president of Princeton University from 1902 to 1910, Wilson had enacted policies specifically designed to prevent Black students from enrollment. Within a few months after his inauguration, any early hopes that he would take a stand against the oppression of African American citizens increasingly gave way to frustration as it became clear he was not an ally in the struggle for civil rights.

Du Bois was never a man to back down from a fight. Six months after his first letter to Wilson, he published another. Confronting the president on his lack of action on the problem of racial violence, Du Bois declared, "It is no exaggeration to say that every enemy of the Negro race is greatly encouraged; that every man who dreams of making the Negro race a group of menials and pariahs is alert and hopeful . . . They and others are assuming this because not a single act and not a single word of yours since election has given anyone reason to infer that you have the slightest interest in the colored people or desire to elevate their intolerable position."[13] Wilson was unmoved by this criticism, just as he remained impervious to every other voice that implored him to do something to alleviate the suffering of African American citizens. Six more years passed before the president would even consent to publicly criticize the crime of lynching, and in that time 325 more people were lynched in the United States. Two hundred and sixty-four of those victims were Black.

The moral complicity of Wilson's stubborn silence became even more critical as the nation moved closer to involvement in the war then raging in Europe. James Weldon Johnson, the African American activist who was an important figure in the nascent NAACP, pointed this out in an article he wrote two years before the Houston Incident:

> It is worthwhile to think about the hypocrisy of this country. Here we are holding up our hands in horror at German "atrocities," at what is being done in Belgium and at what is being done on the high seas, while the wholesale murder of American citizens on American soil by bloodthirsty American mobs hardly brings forth a word of comment. We have a president who still continues to talk about humanity, about bringing peace and righteousness to all the nations of the earth, but who has yet to utter one word against this outraging of humanity within the territory over which he presides. Americans, in their smug hypocrisy, look upon the Turks for their treatment of the Armenians as cruel barbarians; but . . . the American lynching record makes the Turkish treatment of Armenians look like deeds of mercy. . . . It is our duty to ourselves and to those who come after us to cry out against lynching and every other form of wrong that is practiced against us.[14]

Lynchings increasingly became macabre spectator events and were often commemorated by the collecting of souvenirs and publication of photographs celebrating the incident. After a mass lynching of five African Americans on June 15, 1918, in Sabine County, Texas, the Harkrider Drug Company published a postcard photo of the murder. The photograph showed the five victims hanging from a tree, with a caption that read:

The Dogwood Tree
This is only the branch of a Dogwood tree;
    An emblem of WHITE SUPREMACY.
A lesson once taught in the Pioneer's school,
    That this is a land of WHITE MAN'S RULE.
The Red Man once in an early day,
    Was told by the Whites to mend his way.
The negro, now, by eternal grace,
    Must learn to stay in the negro's place.
In the Sunny South, the Land of the Free,
    Let the WHITE SUPREME forever be.
Let this warning to all negroes be,
    Or they'll suffer the fate of the DOGWOOD TREE.[15]

Lynching was a national plague, but in Texas it took on an especially brutal aspect. While lynching murders decreased in most southern states in 1915 and 1916, they increased in Texas as something already terrible transformed into an abomination of racist violence. It was as if some sort of communal malevolence existed in the cultural and societal makeup of the Lone Star State at that time, a malice that turned lynchings into scenes of unparalleled sadism.[16] The punishment of death was no longer enough to satisfy the crowds that gathered to watch these public murders. Increasingly, prolonged torture and unrestrained viciousness became the hallmarks of Texas lynchings.*

---

* All sources, including the 1918 NAACP report on lynching, agree that white people and persons of Latin ethnicity (usually referred to as "Mexican" in the parlance of the day) were also lynched in that era, but African Americans made up the overwhelming majority of lynching victims. And it is indisputably true that in the worst spectacle lynchings, involving torture, maiming, and burning of the victims, the victims were always Black.

The most infamous spectacle lynching in Texas occurred on May 15, 1916, when nearly fifteen thousand white citizens crowded into the city of Waco to watch the maiming, torture, and burning of sixteen-year-old Jesse Washington, accused of raping and murdering a white woman named Lucy Fryer. The perpetrators sold his teeth as souvenirs for five dollars each; the chain used to suspend him in the fire went for twenty-five cents a link. That murder quickly became known across the nation as "the Waco Horror." Seven years later, when the *Houston Informer*, an African American newspaper, referred to Waco as "Barbecueville," it did not need to explain to its readers what event inspired that name.

Within the state, Texas's own newspapers responded to lynchings in a variety of ways. When the *Waco Semi-Weekly Tribune* reported on the lynching of Jesse Washington, it stated, "Not all approved, but they looked on because they had never seen anything of the kind." In the next sentence, however, the writer underscored the moral responsibility of everyone who witnessed that murder, including those who may have privately disapproved of it. "No hand was raised to stop the movement," the reporter wrote, "no word spoken to halt the progress of those who carried the negro to his death."[17] By not speaking out against the crime, every spectator was morally complicit in the act. Two days after Washington's murder the *San Antonio Express* declared, "The Waco disgrace is the disgrace of Texas."[18] Even the *Houston Post*, which a year later would promulgate unsubstantiated rumors and call for racist reprisals after the violence involving the soldiers of the 24th Infantry in that city, said of the Waco lynching, "From no angle viewed, can there be the least excuse, much less justification."[19]

Ida B. Wells, the anti-lynching activist, was only one of many commentators who pointed out the hypocrisy of white American society when it came to the issue of racist violence. "American Christians," she wrote, "are too busy saving the souls of white Christians from burning in hell-fire to save the lives of black ones from present burning in fires kindled by white Christians."[20]

Not all white southerners condoned this savagery. One witness to the 1916 Waco lynching wrote, "I am a white man, but today is one day that I am certainly sorry that I am one. I am disgusted with my country."[21] The voices in white society that condemned racial violence, however, were never as numerous as those that cheered on the lynch mobs or condoned them by remaining silent about the crimes, and those who spoke out against the mobs after the fact seldom did anything to stop a lynching in progress. "Polite southern society was likely to pronounce lynching distasteful and to see lynching as the work of poor whites," Herbert Shapiro says in his study of racial violence, "but the leaders of society did nothing to put a stop to the practice and in actuality tended to see lynching as most regrettable but justifiable."[22]

T he other distinct form of racial violence that terrorized Black citizens in that era was mob violence targeting not just an individual but entire communities. In the fourteen years before the 1917 Houston Incident, race riots in four major cities struck at African American populations. Only one of these incidents occurred in a southern state.

In July 1903, a mob in Evansville, Indiana, attacked the city's Black community and burned it out. Twelve people were killed, more than forty were injured, and two thousand African American citizens were forced to flee their homes. Three years later another mob in Atlanta, Georgia, murdered twenty-five Black people, injured more than ninety others, and destroyed most of the city's African American–owned homes and businesses. In August 1908 a race mob in Springfield, Illinois, famous for its association with Abraham Lincoln, murdered at least nine Black citizens, burned out the largest African American neighborhood in the city, and turned more than two thousand Black residents into refugees. The Springfield mob was particularly mindless in its violence; at least seven of its own perpetrators, all white men, were themselves killed in the rioting by other mob members or the militia.

Those three incidents, terrible as they were, were minor in comparison to what happened in another Illinois city, East St. Louis, in 1917. On July 1–3, just seven weeks before events unfolded in Houston, as many as two hundred African American citizens were murdered and hundreds more injured when labor disputes and racial animosity erupted in a massive race riot. Eyewitnesses described the indiscriminate killing of Black people by mobs of white rioters, and a reporter from the *St. Louis Post-Dispatch* wrote an explicit account of what he saw during the riot:

> For an hour and a half last evening I saw the massacre of helpless negroes at Broadway and Fourth Street, in downtown East

St. Louis, where a black skin was a death warrant. I saw man
after man, with hands raised, pleading for his life, surrounded
by groups of men—men who had never seen him before and
knew nothing about him except that he was black—and saw
them administer the historic sentence of intolerance, death by
stoning. I saw one of these men, almost dead from a savage
shower of stones, hanged with a clothesline. Within a few paces
of the pole from which he was suspended, four other negroes
lay dead or dying, another having been removed, dead, a short
time before. . . . "Get a nigger" was the slogan, and it was varied
by the recurrent cry, "Get another!" . . . The sheds in the rear
of negroes' houses on Fourth Street had been ignited to drive
out the negro occupants of the houses. And the slayers were
waiting for them to come out. It was stay in and be roasted, or
come out and be slaughtered.[23]

The East St. Louis race riot would be the worst such crime in American
history until eclipsed by the violence that destroyed the Black community
of Greenwood in Tulsa, Oklahoma, in 1921.

At least three hundred buildings in East St. Louis, most of them
owned by African American residents, were destroyed. Property damage
was estimated to be nearly $8 million in today's dollars, a staggering blow
to an already economically disadvantaged community. Nearly six thousand
Black residents fled the city to escape the rampaging mobs, and later cen-
sus reports indicated that years passed before the city's African American
population returned to its pre-1917 levels.*

The violence in East St. Louis could not just be blamed on the actions
of racist mobs, however, because the institutions of law and order that
should have put down the riot were culpable either by omission or by
commission. The city police completely failed to protect Black neighborhoods, and in fact were ordered not to use force against the mobs. When

---

* The actual death toll of the East St. Louis race riot is hard to pin down. A congressional investigation into the violence a few weeks after the incident estimated the number
of deaths at thirty-nine, but the city's police chief said that at least one hundred Black
residents were murdered. Tallies from within the city's African American community put
the number much higher.

Governor Frank Lowden sent the Illinois National Guard into the city to restore order, the guardsmen either stood by as Black people were attacked or, in several instances, actually joined in as participants and perpetrators of the violence.[24] A local newspaper reported, "All the impartial witnesses agree that the police were either indifferent or encouraged the barbarities, and that the major part of the National Guard was indifferent or inactive. No organized effort was made to protect the Negroes or disperse the murdering groups. . . . Ten determined officers could have prevented most of the outrages. One hundred men acting with authority and vigor might have prevented any outrage."[25] This was not just the personal opinion of one journalist, as the federal government's official investigation later showed.

The congressional report concluded its condemnation of the East St. Louis police by saying, "Instead of being guardians of the peace they became a part of the mob by countenancing the assaulting and shooting down of defenseless negroes and adding to the terrifying scenes of rapine and slaughter."[26] In spite of this clear determination of both complicity and cooperation in a crime of horrific proportions, no meaningful legal action was ever taken against the East St. Louis police department or the members of the Illinois National Guard who abetted and participated in the massacre.

For the Black soldiers of the 24th Infantry posted to Houston in the summer of 1917, race riots such as these were not just remote newspaper accounts of shocking occurrences in distant places. Many of those men came from states where this mob violence occurred; some of them had grown up in those very cities. As the history of that era repeatedly showed, no African American community could be truly confident of its safety, no matter how far north of the Mason-Dixon line they lived. "The fact is," one Black educator wrote in 1915, "that lynching has gone on for so long in many parts of our country that it is somewhat difficult to draw at this time a sharp line marking off distinctly the point where the lynching spirit stops and the spirit of legal procedure commences. You cannot tell what the most peaceable community will do at any moment under certain circumstances."[27] To live under such a reality was to live under constant fear.

On top of this communal threat, Black soldiers serving in the South were acutely aware of the personal risks they faced from racism in states firmly in the grip of Jim Crow laws; in Texas alone, five serious incidents of violence against Black troops had occurred since 1900. Every report of a race riot or lynch mob anywhere in the country reinforced a truth that was an inescapable part of these soldiers' lives—their families, friends, and hometowns were never truly safe from the threat of racial violence, even while they themselves were serving in the military, defending a nation that refused to accept them as fully enfranchised citizens.

The racism the soldiers of the 24th Infantry encountered in Texas was not subtle, restrained, or concealed in any way. Nor was it mere intimidation. Recent history had made painfully clear what could happen to Black soldiers in Texas, and President Wilson's repeated refusal to condemn lynching, along with the War Department's refusal to use its economic power to insist that its soldiers be given the respect and decent treatment they deserved, made it all but certain that it was only a matter of time before another outburst of racial violence would claim more lives.

3. SEMPER PARATUS

Black men had fought for the United States during the Civil War, and at the nation's founding in the American Revolution, but the creation of six all-Black regiments in 1866 marked the first time African American soldiers were ever included in the peacetime establishment of the Regular Army. Those units were the 9th and 10th Cavalry and the 38th, 39th, 40th, and 41st Infantry, each designated as a "Colored" regiment in the parlance of the time. The soldiers in those regiments were all Black, under the command of white officers. But as Congress gave, it could also take away; in 1869 cuts to the military budget resulted in the consolidation of the four Black infantry regiments into just two, the 24th Infantry and 25th Infantry. Throughout the Indian Wars era, those units served with distinction at posts all over the frontier as well as in Cuba, the Philippines, and Mexico. Along the way they acquired their famous nickname of "Buffalo Soldiers," and the 24th Infantry Regiment earned the motto that still appears on its crest today—"*Semper Paratus*," or "Always Ready."*

The soldiers of 3-24 Infantry were a diverse group of men in a regiment sharply delineated by the racial segregation policies of that era. All the commissioned officers—the lieutenants, captains, and so on—were white men. All the enlisted men, including the noncommissioned officers—the corporals and sergeants—were Black. Considering a sample group of

---

* Different explanations are given for how the Buffalo Soldiers acquired the nickname, and what it originally meant. Most sources agree that the name was conferred on them by Native Americans during the frontier period because many of them had black curly hair. The Black regiments quickly embraced the nickname, making it part of their military identity. In homage to this nickname, the 9th Cavalry Regiment incorporated a buffalo into both its heraldic coat of arms and its regimental distinctive insignia, which it retained even after racial integration in the 1950s. Soldiers in that regiment still wear that insignia today.

110 of the enlisted men, they came from all parts of the country: sixty-seven of them were born in southern states; twenty came from border states such as Kentucky, Missouri, and Maryland; the other twenty-three were northerners. Their average age was twenty-four, which was normal in an army where the largest proportion of soldiers in any unit were always young men on their first or second enlistments. The NCOs among them were generally a bit older, usually men in their mid-twenties to late thirties. Almost all of them were unmarried, which was also normal in all Army units of that era regardless of their racial makeup, because junior enlisted soldiers needed their commanders' permission to marry and few men could support a wife on a private's pay.* According to their service records, only four men in that group were married at the time of the Houston Incident, though a few may have been secretly married. That, too, was common in many units. A few of these men were comparatively well educated, but most had only finished school up to the middle grades. Before enlisting in the Army, most of them worked as farmhands, porters, cooks, store clerks, waiters, or freight handlers, or in similar jobs.†

For African American communities in the early twentieth century, Black soldiers such as these men were the living embodiment of Black pride. Each of them, whether veteran or new recruit, was the direct heir of the famed Buffalo Soldiers of the frontier era. They were men who had managed to step at least a pace or two beyond the limitations placed on them by a racially biased society.

Their detractors, however, were never willing to consider them as individuals even before the Houston Incident, and those denigrations went back decades before most of those men were even born. Racist stereotypes had always littered segregationists' objections to African American men serving in the military. "It was a decidedly risky experiment to attempt making soldiers of such people," a man named W. Thornton Parker wrote in the *North American Review* in 1899. "Recruited from the most dangerous and shiftless of the freed negroes, they were naturally lazy, and disin-

---

* In military terminology, a "junior" soldier is one in the lower enlisted ranks below the rank of sergeant. The term does not mean that the soldier is younger in age.

† The 110 men referred to here are not a random sampling, as these were the men who were later convicted by the three courts-martial held after the Houston Incident. As a group, however, they are an accurate representative sampling of their battalion as a whole.

clined to do the work required of them. They spent all their leisure time in gambling, drinking and quarrelling."[1] The historical evidence shows, however, that the disciplinary records and desertion rates of Black units were better, proportionately, than those of contemporary white regiments. Black soldiers could get into trouble, especially if alcohol was involved, and their rosters always contained a few men whom their sergeants regarded as unrepentant troublemakers or loud-mouthed hotheads, the same as in any other Army unit. But Black regiments during the frontier period had far lower desertion rates than were reported in white regiments, and that trend still held in 1917. American society castigated Black soldiers much more severely than white soldiers for the same sorts of misbehavior and held them to an unfairly higher standard of conduct than was expected of other men, one more instance of the inequality of their situation.

Some white commentators who spoke up to support African American men's right to serve in the Army were apparently only willing to praise the Black regiments so long as they were posted somewhere else, preferably far away. The hypocrisy in this sort of thinking was apparent to anyone who cared to notice. "Whenever, by the routine of the War Department, a colored troop or a colored company was assigned for duty in a New England post," one Army officer wrote in 1907, "the Representatives in Congress of the threatened State have intervened and the unwelcome orders have been cancelled."[2] The senior senator from Vermont, Redfield Proctor, "admitted that the most arduous struggle of his whole career was the one during the Cleveland administration to keep negro troops out of Fort Ethan Allen."[3] This attitude of "let them serve, but not near me" was all too common in the decades between the Civil War and the First World War. "New Englanders have always peculiarly loved the negro," an Army officer named Matthew Steele wrote in an article published in 1906, "but they do not love him in their midst; they prefer him away in Georgia or Louisiana, whither they can send him their sympathy by mail."[4]

In addition to criticizing those attitudes, Steele also confronted the policy of racial segregation within the military. "Is it not time to do away with the 'color line' in the army of the United States?" Steele asked. He pointed out that the "Ninth and Tenth regiments of cavalry and the Twenty-fourth and Twenty-fifth of infantry are the four upon which the ban of color has been laid; by implication, colored men are, and always have been, excluded from the ranks of all other regiments." Such a policy might be the law, but Steele argued it was unjust. "This law is today the only one upon the statute-books of the national Government which treats the negro citizens as a class apart—which sets up a 'Jim Crow car' for them, as it were, and requires them to ride in it or none," he wrote. "No more exclusive law can be found in the codes of Alabama or Mississippi." Speaking as a combat veteran himself, Steele distilled his argument down to the only point that ultimately mattered to a soldier: "The soldiers of the regular army, white and black, have always given a good account of themselves in campaign and battle," he wrote. "In a fight, the color of a man's face cuts no figure, so long as it be not pale."[5]

When war with Spain broke out in 1898, patriotic spirit touched African American communities just as strongly as it did the rest of the nation, but for Black citizens it also carried with it a real dilemma: Should they volunteer to fight for a country that treated them so abysmally? As one writer for the *Colored American*, an African American newspaper in the nation's capital, wrote in March 1898, "While the air is filled with war clouds and sanguinary talk . . . the colored man is in a quandary. Why should he desire to take up arms against any foreign government, when the United States, his adopted country, offers him such little protection?"[6] It was a legitimate question, one for which there were no simple answers. In another editorial, the same newspaper declared:

> We want for ourselves every right and privilege accorded to any other American citizen, and will be satisfied with nothing short of it. We are not more anxious to be shot at or killed than any other class, but the principle of military and civilian recognition is at stake, and we wish to be called on equal[l]y with our fellow-countrymen to bear the nation's burdens as well as to share her joys. . . . We want colored troops with colored officers. . . . We have the brains, the courage, and the strength. Give us the opportunity. All we desire and all we can expect is an equal chance and fair play.[7]

That was no more than what Black soldiers themselves had asked for from the moment they first took their place in the Army's ranks. It was the very thing for which they were willing to risk their lives. They wanted to serve their nation, and they expected the nation to respect them for it.

Anyone who hoped that a war against a foreign enemy would ease domestic racial animosities and lead to new, enlightened feelings of patriotic brotherhood that transcended the color line was quickly disappointed. The military buildup of troops in southern states in preparation for the invasion of Cuba and Puerto Rico brought large concentrations of Black troops into close contact with hostile southerners to a greater degree than had happened since the end of the Reconstruction era. It was like applying a proverbial match to gunpowder. "It would seem," wrote an editor of the *Richmond Planet*, "that the war . . . would tend to allay race prejudice and bring closer together the races in the South. It has had an opposite tendency for the number of lynchings has been steadily on the increase."[8] As one historian notes, "The reason for the increased violence against African Americans was simple: white Americans resented the sight of Blacks with weapons—even (or perhaps especially) if the Blacks were in the uniform of the US Army. Also, Black Americans with guns and in uniform had a disquieting tendency to insist on their civil rights."[9]

This was especially true of the veteran soldiers in the Regular Army's four Black regiments. They had paid their dues in the tough service of the frontier garrisons, they had earned the right to be recognized as fighting men of proven ability, and they were not about to quietly submit to the prejudices of bigoted civilians who objected to their presence. As the editor of one newspaper wrote, "The members of the Twenty-Fifth Infantry were so long in Montana that when they came into contact with the laws of Tennessee compelling the whites and Afro-Americans to ride in separate cars they strenuously objected, declaring that their uniforms entitled them to sit in any car on a train."[10] That refusal to accept segregated seating in southern railway cars was a harbinger of what would happen nineteen years later in Houston.

Southern society was outraged by the idea that any Black men might behave as if they were the social equals of white people. In 1898 the *Commercial Appeal* in Memphis expressed the opinions of many southerners when it declared, "The colored soldier must not permit himself to be betrayed into the assumption that he has changed or benefited his social condition by wearing a blue coat and carrying a gun. If he forgets himself, he will soon be reminded of his delinquency in a convincing manner."[11] A writer for the *Tampa Morning Tribune* told his readers, "The colored infantrymen . . . have made themselves very offensive to the people of the city. The men insist upon being treated as white men are treated and the citizen will not make any distinction between the colored troops and the colored citizens." African American newspapers did not let that sort of insult stand without rebuttal. The editors of the *Colored American*, writing in August 1898, declared, "The trouble between the negroes and whites at Tampa, Chattanooga, New Orleans and other points is due almost without exception to the fact that narrow-minded cads and shortsighted shopkeepers insisted upon making a difference in the treatment of United States soldiers. . . . Fair play would have prevented all the turmoil that has disgraced Uncle Sam's army in the South since the war began." Fair play was precisely what many people absolutely refused to give Black soldiers. An 1898 editorial in the *Washington Post* stated, "This is a white man's country, and the whites are not willing and cannot be compelled to accept the negro on equal terms in any relation of life." Local officials made similar statements. When a Black soldier was put on trial in Macon, Georgia, the city prosecutor declared in his opening statement to the court, "I am going to show a nigger soldier that he is the same as any other nigger."[12]

The Spanish-American War thoroughly disenchanted Black citizens who hoped they might gain a measure of acceptance and equality through military service. A teenager during those years, Ned Cobb, never forgot what the experience taught him. He did not have much formal education, but he was a keen observer of the world around him. "I've had white people tell me, 'This is a white man's country, white man's country,'" he recalled. "They don't sing that to the colored man when it comes to war. Then it's all our country, go fight for the country. Go over there and risk his life for the country and come back, he aint a bit more thought of than he was before he left . . . [A]fter the battle is fought and the victory is won—I'm forced to say it—it all goes over to the whites." It was a bitter lesson, and Cobb saw it play out over and over. "The colored man goin' over there fightin', the white man goin' over there fightin', well, the white man holds his ground over here when he comes back, he's the same; nigger come back, he aint recognized more than a dog," he said.[13] As William Calvin Chase, the fiery, eloquent editor of the African American newspaper the *Washington Bee*, declared in an editorial, "There is no inducement for the negro to fight for the independence of Cuba . . . when his own brothers, fathers, mothers, and indeed his children are shot down as if they were dogs and cattle."[14]

For Black soldiers, at least one small change for the better occurred by the time of the Spanish-American War—the Army finally began to commission a few African American officers to serve in the Black regiments. It was a tentative movement toward recognition of their abilities not just as followers but also as leaders. Even that, however, was a hesitant step out of the darkness of a racially tainted system that kept African American soldiers separate, differentiated, and disadvantaged.

Captain Steele deplored the policy of military segregation, which he felt cost the army the services of well-qualified men. "Of a truth, the law which places the mark of color on four of our regiments is out of date now, if ever it was timely," he wrote. "It is contrary to the spirit of the fourteenth and fifteenth amendments to the Constitution, and to the good sense of the twentieth century. There is no reason why blacks or whites should be excluded by the law of the land from any troop, battery or company in the service. Recruiting officers should enlist the best men to be had, without distinction of color, and each man should be assigned to a regiment according to his choice and the best interests of the service."[15]

4. The Ghosts of Brownsville

Lieutenant Colonel William Newman was a worried man, worried enough that in July 1917 he lodged a formal protest against the orders he had just received from the War Department directing him to take 3-24 Infantry, the battalion of which he had assumed command just a day earlier, from Columbus, New Mexico, to Houston to guard the construction of a new military training facility named Camp Logan. Newman had more than twenty-five years' service in the Army by that point in his career and had been with the regiment for two years. He had experience as an officer of Black soldiers, and within a year of joining the regiment he learned just how dangerous Jim Crow Texas could be for those men.

In April 1916 Mexico was in the chaos of a revolution. Occasionally the violence spilled across to the U.S. side of the international border, and in March of that year Pancho Villa attacked Columbus, New Mexico, in a bloody raid, provoking the United States government to send General John Pershing into Mexico with some ten thousand troops with orders to capture Villa, or at least reduce his ability to mount further attacks on American territory. The Army garrisoned towns all along the border from Arizona to Texas with soldiers from the Regular Army and the National Guard, and as part of that tactical alignment Newman, who was then serving with 1-24 Infantry, took two companies of that battalion to Camp Del Rio, a temporary post just outside the small Texas border town of the same name. White Texans may have worried about what was happening south of the border, but apparently the idea of being protected by Black soldiers instead of white troops upset their narrow sensibilities even more than the thought of being raided by Mexican revolutionaries.

On the night of April 8, several soldiers tried to enter the Greentop, one of Del Rio's several brothels. They were refused entry, and racist insults were thrown at them along with a few punches from the establishment's bouncers. What happened next depends upon whose version of the story one believes, but an altercation ensued that brought law enforcement to the scene. At some point in the uproar, a soldier named John Wade was shot and killed by a Texas Ranger. The police report claimed he was shot "while resisting arrest." A separate military investigation, however, revealed that Private Wade was shot in the back multiple times, evidence that clearly contradicted the police version of events. Del Rio police officers claimed that soldiers initiated the violence and did all the shooting that night, but the Army insisted the police fired first, not the soldiers.

Wade's killing provoked some of his fellow soldiers to seek their own measure of revenge. When word spread through the unit that he was dead, two soldiers armed themselves from their company's rifle racks and headed back into town to get some payback of their own. They shot up the brothel where the trouble had started, and it was only through sheer luck that no one else was killed.

Lieutenant Alexander Chilton was the First Battalion's duty officer that night, and his quick, effective leadership was probably the one thing that prevented the kind of large-scale outbreak of violence that overtook its sister battalion, 3-24 Infantry, sixteen months later in Houston. As soon as Chilton realized some men had gone into town without authorization, he mustered the entire battalion and locked down the unit's weapons. Within a few minutes he knew exactly which soldiers were absent from camp. An ammunition count revealed twenty-four rounds unaccounted for, precisely the number the two soldiers later admitted to firing during their unsanctioned raid. Lieutenant Chilton then personally went into town and conducted a fast but efficient investigation of the scene.

Another crucial factor that kept the Del Rio incident from escalating into widespread violence was that Chilton could rely completely on the corporals and sergeants in his battalion. Professional noncommissioned officers who knew their business, they kept military discipline intact among their platoons and squads while their officers tried to keep the situation from blowing up around them. By dawn the two miscreant soldiers were apprehended and back in Army custody, and greater trouble was averted.

Depictions of this incident in some local newspapers were predictable, and predictably exaggerated. According to those accounts, the actions of two hotheaded privates were tantamount to a full mutiny by the entire garrison, and the soldiers were supposedly bent on murdering any white person they might encounter. The Army quickly transferred the two companies of Black soldiers away from Camp Del Rio at the demand of the local populace and the political machinations of the district's fiercely racist congressman, Representative John Nance Garner. The two soldiers who fired their weapons in town were court-martialed for their part in the incident, but the Army failed to demand federal prosecution of the civilian law enforcement officer who killed Private Wade.

Del Rio was only one in a series of incidents in Texas's history of violence against Black soldiers. The first serious, large-scale clash between Texans and Black soldiers had occurred sixteen years earlier, in 1900, in another border town. El Paso did not have a history of the sort of lynch mob violence that marred East Texas, and it had a long, mutually beneficial relationship with the Army. On the night of February 7, a small group of soldiers from 1-25 Infantry hatched an impulsive, ill-considered plan to storm the town jail in an attempt to free from custody one of their comrades who had earlier been arrested for public intoxication. Both the soldiers and local lawmen were armed, and in the short fight that followed, a policeman, Officer Newton Stewart, and a soldier, Corporal James Hull, were killed.

There was no question that the soldiers who attacked the city jail were guilty of violating both civil and military law. The Army's investigation declared that the indicted soldiers were guilty of unlawful violence that night, and six soldiers were convicted for their part in it, but it also determined that racist behavior toward African American soldiers had been on the rise in El Paso before the incident. Local law enforcement officers and customs officials who manned the border crossing points frequently targeted Black soldiers with both verbal and physical abuse, and the town itself was as rigidly segregated as other southern communities. The Army concluded that this unrelenting and increasing bigotry contributed to the soldiers' growing anger, a festering canker of resentment that culminated in an outbreak of violence that killed two men and sent six others to prison.

If anyone needed confirmation of that, it was only necessary to read the statements of local officials. El Paso's city attorney attributed the violence to the "inherent meanness" of African Americans and declared that a Black man was "not fit to be a soldier and should never be allowed to have a gun in his hands." "The negro is the same wherever you find him," the local Collector of Customs claimed. "Put him into a uniform and he thinks he can run things to suit himself."

The most infamous incident in the list of civilian-military violence in the state had occurred in August 1906, in southeastern Texas. In late July, the First Battalion of the 25th Infantry Regiment (minus its Alpha Company) arrived to garrison Fort Brown, a small military installation adjacent to the border town of Brownsville. The unit arrived from a previous assignment at Fort Niobrara, Nebraska, where they had enjoyed good relations with the local civilian community. Texas, as they quickly discovered, was an entirely different social landscape. "The obvious problem was that Brownsville was a Jim Crow town that rigidly enforced segregation etiquette and had no interest in welcoming the black troopers," one historian notes. "One black soldier recalled years later that the town park featured a sign announcing: 'No niggers and no dogs allowed.'"[1]

At around midnight on August 12, someone shot up the town, firing several hundred rounds at businesses and lighted areas. A white bartender, Frank Natus, was killed by a bullet that came through a window of a saloon, and a Latino policeman, Joe Dominguez, was wounded. No one could identify the perpetrators, nor even say how many men were firing in the darkness, but the citizens of Brownsville immediately insisted that soldiers from Fort Brown were involved. The officers of 1-25 Infantry vehemently denied this, with good reason. As soon as the battalion commander, Major Charles Penrose, heard the fusillade of gunfire in town that night, he ordered an immediate stand-to and mustered his entire battalion. His company officers and NCOs reported all their personnel accounted for—no soldiers were out of ranks, and just as importantly, no weapons were missing from the arms racks. Penrose then ordered an inspection of every rifle and determined that they were all clean and unfired.

Residents of Brownsville disregarded that evidence and insisted the unidentified shooters were soldiers from the garrison. Their primary evidence was a handful of .30-caliber shell casings allegedly found in the town's streets, but Major Penrose insisted that all his ordnance stocks appeared to be intact. While supposedly incriminating spent brass found in the streets were indeed cartridges of a type issued with the army's new M1903 Springfield rifles, that caliber and type of ammunition was also widely available for civilian purchase.

The War Department sent the Southwestern Division's Assistant Inspector General, Major Augustus Blockson, down to Brownsville as its primary investigator. His mind was apparently made up before he even got off the train. He accepted without question civilian accusations against the soldiers at almost every turn, claiming that nine to fifteen soldiers had raided the town, and he thought the racial climate in the town offered all the probable cause he needed to place the blame on the men of 1-25 Infantry. "Causes of disturbance are racial," Blockson wrote in his report. "People did not desire colored troops here, and showed they thought them inferior socially by certain slights and denial of privileges at public bars, etc. Soldiers resented this. . . . I consider it necessary to remove the colored troops—the sooner the better."[2]

Brownsville police arrested twelve soldiers on suspicion of shooting up the town, but even in a Texas court the evidence against them was insufficient to sustain the charges and they were released to the Army's custody. Blockson was convinced that someone in the battalion was guilty, so the dozen men were held in close confinement at Fort Sam Houston in San Antonio while the government proceeded in its investigation against them and every other soldier who was in Brownsville that night. President Theodore Roosevelt ordered the Army's Inspector General, Brigadier General Ernest Garlington, to "endeavor to secure information that will lead to the apprehension and punishment of the men of the Twenty-fifth Infantry." The wording of that statement made it very clear that Roosevelt, like Blockson, had already made up his mind about the situation.

Garlington quickly decided the Buffalo Soldiers were maintaining a "conspiracy of silence," and Roosevelt was all too ready to agree with him. If the individuals responsible for the Brownsville Incident could not be identified, the president wrote, "orders will be immediately issued from the War Department discharging every man in Companies B, C, and D, without honor." Determined to keep the African American vote firmly in the Republican pocket in that year's midterm elections, he issued his order the day after the congressional elections that November. There were no trials, no reviews, and no appeals. Even in an era of officially sanctioned racism, Roosevelt's action seemed an egregiously unfair judgment of men against whom an offense was alleged but never proven.

For Black Americans, Roosevelt's treatment of the soldiers of 1-25 Infantry was an outright betrayal of their previous support for him and the Republican Party. William Calvin Chase's editorial ferocity had not diminished since his condemnation of American racism during the Spanish-American War. Now, writing about Roosevelt's treatment of the men of 1-25 Infantry, he was absolutely incensed. "Negroes are not fools, at least not all of them," Chase wrote in the *Bee*, "and this after-election order is well understood by them."[3]

Black newspaper editors, community leaders, and clergyman used their various platforms to protest the government's treatment of 1-25 Infantry, but another crisis that same year quickly eclipsed the trouble in Texas, at least for several months. Six weeks after the shooting in Brownsville, a two-day rampage by race mobs in Atlanta killed more than thirty Black citizens, injured hundreds more, and destroyed property in the Black neighborhoods of the city. "This cataclysmic event," a midcentury article declared, "made Brownsville seem pale in comparison. The lives of the soldiers of the Twenty-Fifth were not in jeopardy and the dead in Atlanta were a more important issue."[4] By the time the activists could finally turn their attention back to Brownsville, Roosevelt and the Republican Party had used the intervening time to shift public perceptions on the matter.

It seems most likely that the attack on the town was staged by civilian perpetrators who were never identified. The officers of 1-25 Infantry certainly believed that was what happened. "The sentiment in Texas is so hostile against colored troops,"[5] one officer reported, "that there is always the danger of serious trouble between the citizens and soldiers whenever they are brought into contact." Most historians today accept the idea that the entire incident was concocted to discredit the 25th Infantry and force the Army to transfer them away from Brownsville and its hostile population. If there was indeed such a scheme, it succeeded.*

The 3rd Battalion of the 24th Infantry arrived in Houston that summer in 1917 because of a chain of events set in motion three years earlier, far away in the Balkans. On a Sunday morning in June 1914, a

---

* The injustice of the government's handling of the Brownsville Incident remained unredressed until the 1970s, when President Richard Nixon retroactively granted honorable discharges to the 153 men whom Roosevelt summarily dismissed from the Army. By that time, only one of the former soldiers was still alive to receive the government's apology.

Serbian nationalist named Gavril Princip assassinated Austrian archduke Franz Ferdinand and his wife, Sophie, setting in motion the train wreck of treaty alliances and irrational militarism that propelled Europe into the First World War in a precipitous rush to mutual mass destruction. The United States stayed out of the war for nearly three years while the nations of Europe fought each other to a bloody standstill, but American involvement was perhaps inevitable. Finally, after a German submarine sank yet another ship in a series of attacks on American-associated vessels, the U.S. Congress formally declared war on Germany on April 6, 1917.

At that time, the United States was simply not prepared to fight a modern war on the scale of the fighting then being waged in Europe. In 1916 the Regular U.S. Army had an end-strength of about a hundred thousand men on active duty, the largest peacetime army the United States had ever maintained. It was a small but professional military force, and it had gained valuable experience in recent low-intensity conflicts such as the Philippine-American War and the Punitive Expedition into Mexico. The massive, industrialized conflict then raging in Europe was an entirely different kind of challenge, though. In the campaigns of Ypres, the Somme, and Verdun on the Western Front, the British, French, and German armies had lost as many men in a matter of months as the U.S. Army's entire strength. In that meat grinder of a war, the diminutive U.S. Army would likely fight itself out of existence within six months. Before any American troop ships set sail for France, the nation needed to create a huge new force as quickly as possible.

Nineteen years earlier, the U.S. government had learned a hard lesson about how not to expand the Army in time of need. The declaration of war against Spain in April 1898 prompted a massive outpouring of public support and martial spirit that produced a wave of volunteers for military service in numbers the War Department was simply not equipped to handle. Thousands of National Guardsmen volunteered for active service; thousands more civilians who were not yet on the muster roll of any state's militia unit also rushed to join the ranks.*

---

* For a detailed discussion of this problem in the Spanish-American War, see John A. Haymond, *The American Soldier, 1866–1916: The Enlisted Man and the Transformation of the United States Army* (Jefferson, NC: McFarland, 2018).

Around 200,000 volunteers enlisted for that war, and at least 136,000 of them spent their entire time in uniform inside the United States. The combined factors of a war that was much shorter than anyone expected, a logistics and transportation system that was woefully inadequate for the task at hand, and a National Guard force whose average level of training and readiness for deployment was nothing less than abysmal created a situation that practically guaranteed most of the volunteers would spend the war in frustration and inactivity and never get near a battlefield.

The amended Militia Act of 1792 had originally provided for the existence of the National Guard in the form of state militias, but the outdated restrictions of that law completely obstructed the process of activating the Guard to augment the Regular Army when it was needed. By law, in time of national need the president could only *request* the service of the militia; the War Department then had to specify how many troops were to come from each individual state, and state governors would then call on their National Guard companies to step forward for federal service, on a strictly voluntary basis. There was no legal requirement for guardsmen to volunteer for overseas service, though, and consequentially many did not come forward to answer the call. As a result, rather than the ready legions of trained volunteers the War Department expected, what it actually got were thousands of eager volunteers straight from civilian life who had no more experience of military service than what their overly enthusiastic imaginations provided. Of those Guardsmen who did volunteer, it quickly became apparent that their training "in all aspects of military operations was, for the most part, grossly inadequate to the demands of active duty and extended field operations."[6]

The debacle of 1898 would not be repeated in 1917. This time, the Army was not going to depend on reluctant state militias or poorly trained National Guard units to round out its manpower; it would create and train a professional force from the boots up, and those troops would not embark for France before they were trained to at least the basic standards of military proficiency.

Six weeks after the declaration of war against Germany, the groundswell of patriotic fervor had not yet gathered its full momentum and only about seventy thousand men had volunteered for enlistment, not nearly enough for the immediate need. Conscription was the only other option by which to fill the ranks. President Wilson, somewhat reluctantly, ordered the Selective Service Act into effect on May 8, 1917. This initially required all men fit for military service, aged twenty-one to thirty, to register for the draft. By the time the war ended eighteen months later, conscription had brought some 2.8 million men into the military. For the first time in the nation's history, African American men were included in nationwide conscription, but the cloud of segregation still hung over them. The registration forms of Black men were marked by having a corner torn off, so their race was clearly indicated. The vast majority of African Americans thus inducted were assigned to noncombat roles such as labor battalions or stevedore units, relegated to rear-echelon drudgery rather than front-line combat battalions.

Just as during the Spanish-American War, the prospect of fighting for a country with such an abysmal record of racial injustice presented African American citizens with a serious dilemma. Patriotism ran high in Black communities, but so did criticism of their nation's social flaws. A Presbyterian minister named Francis J. Grimké expressed the feelings of many Black citizens when he said, "A government that is so blinded by prejudice, so lacking in sense of justice . . . is not worth serving. . . . Let them fight their own battles and go to the devil."[7] The month the Selective Service Act took effect, the NAACP hosted a conference at Howard University to debate the matter. After stating their concerns and reluctance, the delegates decided their duty as citizens was to support the nation in the war, even as they acknowledged the problem of racial segregation in the military. They promised the government the loyalty and patriotism of its Black citizens, but pledged to continue their struggle for racial justice once the national crisis was past.[8] Black Americans were ready to do their part for their nation, but they expected the nation to honor its obligations to them in turn, as it never had in times past.

This was clearly expressed in the resolutions published after the Washington Conference that year. The delegates declared, "We . . . earnestly urge our colored fellow citizens to join heartily in this fight for eventual world liberty; we urge them to enlist in the army. . . . Let us, however, never forget that this country belongs to us even more than to those who lynch, disfranchise, and segregate. As our country it rightly demands our whole-hearted defense. . . . Absolute loyalty in arms and in civil duties need not for a moment lead us to abate our just complaints and just demands."

———

It was one thing to conscript an army; it was another thing altogether to train it to a standard of combat readiness. Regular Army posts such as Fort Sill in Oklahoma and Fort Riley in Kansas could only handle training cohorts of several thousand men each year, nowhere near the numbers that conscription was bringing in. The quickest solution was to construct temporary military training camps around the country, situated near cities served by the major railroad lines necessary for the movement of regular troop trains. Military training camps promised an infusion of millions of dollars of federal funds into the coffers of any city lucky enough to host one. And if that temporary camp should eventually be designated a permanent military installation, with the coveted designation of "fort" instead of "camp," then the money would just keep coming.

In Texas, the cities of El Paso and San Antonio had long enjoyed the economic benefits of their relationships with the major Army posts of Fort Bliss and Fort Sam Houston, respectively, and other cities looked at that economic security with envy. A scramble for a place at the federal trough ensued as more than a dozen towns across the state nominated themselves as locations for new military camps and waited to see if fortune and the War Department would favor their applications. Fort Worth, Waco, and Houston were big winners of the military lottery when the War Department chose them in June as the sites for the construction of Camp Bowie, Camp MacArthur, and Camp Logan, respectively. San Antonio's good luck continued when open acreage next to Fort Sam Houston was designated as the location for an enlarged training cantonment to be called Camp Travis.

The news thrilled Houston's city government, but their enthusiasm dimmed when they learned the Army was sending Black soldiers to the city to guard government property during the camp's construction. That did not sit well with white Houstonians committed to maintaining the strictures of Jim Crow segregation, and the Chamber of Commerce inquired about the availability of other troops for the guard force. The War Department tersely replied that the only Regular Army units available to undertake the duty were the Black infantrymen of the 24th Infantry Regiment. The regiment's First Battalion would go to Waco to guard Camp MacArthur; Third Battalion would entrain for Houston.* The guard force would only be posted in the city until construction of Camp Logan was completed, about seven weeks at the most. Unstated in the War Department's telegram, but clearly implied, was a warning—Houston should stop complaining and count its blessings. If not, the Army could very easily look for another city to host the training camp.

That this was the message both implied and inferred was made very clear after Third Battalion arrived in the city. A member of the Chamber of Commerce told Lieutenant Colonel Newman he thought Black soldiers should never have been sent to Houston.

"Well, why didn't you tell the Department Commander so?" Newman demanded.

"Well, we couldn't make any other reply," was the answer.[9]

Newman said he gathered from that statement that the city government "feared it would lose Camp Logan" if it complained or protested any further.

Joseph Cullinan, president of the Houston Chamber of Commerce, assured the government that, "in a spirit of patriotism, the colored soldiers would be treated all right." Another member of the chamber told Major General James Parker, commander of the Southwestern Department, headquartered at Fort Sam Houston, "The negro soldiers will be properly received and their comfort will be given due consideration. You need anticipate no trouble as long as they comport themselves as soldiers should." What he meant was that Houston expected the soldiers of 3-24 Infantry to submit to the restrictions of Jim Crow segregation.[10] Thus, blithe assurances were made and empty promises rendered, all so that Houston might not lose the cash cow represented by Camp Logan.

Complicating matters, the city was in the middle of political upheaval that summer. The popular chief of police, Ben Davidson, had just been fired by Mayor Ben Campbell. In his place, the head of the city parks department, Clarence Brock, was appointed to the office of chief of police, though he

---

* The regiment's Second Battalion was sent to Deming, New Mexico, at the same time the other two battalions went to Texas.

had no law enforcement experience. Perhaps worse, Brock did not have much support within the police department, and many of the officers on the force still thought of Davidson as their boss. The mayor then died of a heart attack in July, leaving a city official named Dan Moody to act as mayor pro tem until a mayoral election could be held later that year. All of these facts were to have a direct impact on the Army's ability to engage with the local government that summer.

On August 13, C. F. Richardson, the editor of the *Houston Observer*, sent a letter to the Secretary of War asking that the 8th Illinois Infantry, a National Guard regiment that included a battalion of Black soldiers, be sent to Camp Logan for their training. To make the case for this request, Richardson wrote, "We possess one of the best white communities in this country, regardless of section and in view of the cordial spirit that is existing between the 3rd Battalion of the 24th Infantry now in our midst and the white citizens, we do not anticipate any trouble between the garrison and the citizens." Events would reveal the error in that statement, either deliberately or unintentionally ironic.

5. A Nest of Prejudice

Early on the morning of July 26, 1917, the troop train carrying 654 men of the 24th Infantry Regiment's 3rd Battalion pulled into Houston. The soldiers on the train that morning had widely differing expectations of what the assignment might mean for them.

Some of the long-service veterans in the battalion, the men who knew Texas's reputation for racial violence, were quietly apprehensive. Other soldiers looking out the train windows that morning, however, were excited at the new posting. They were coming off hard service in remote, dusty border encampments along the Mexican border, and many of them had endured the rigors of the tough campaign into Mexico as part of the Punitive Expedition against Pancho Villa that concluded five months earlier. They were eager to experience a bit of city life, with its attractions of female companionship, dance halls, and restaurants that offered better fare than Army rations. Their anticipation was also heightened by the fact that Houston was home to a sizeable and dynamic African American community nearly thirty thousand strong, concentrated in the city's Fourth Ward, which encompassed the historic freemen's neighborhoods of the San Felipe District.

Houston had a reputation as an island of relative calm in the storm of Texas's racial violence and the city proudly represented itself as a shining example of the New South. Its public face was that of a growing metropolis free of the violent extremism that infected other southern cities. Beneath that carefully maintained veneer, however, the truth of Houston's race relations was more complicated and less pleasant. White Houstonians frequently pointed out that their city had not seen a lynching since the end of the Civil War, but that fact alone did not tell the full story of what it meant to be a Black citizen in the City on the Bayou.

A correspondent for the NAACP, Martha Gruening, described Houston as "a hustling and progressive southern city . . . and, as southern cities go, a fairly liberal one." She followed that positive note with a caveat: "It is, however, a southern city, and the presence of the Negro troops inevitably stirred its Negrophobe element to protest."[1]*

Racial harmony in the city was a scale that tilted only one way, with a system in which white citizens held all the power, influence, and control. One midcentury historian described it as a tenuous situation that required "the patience of blacks to accept the hundred forms of insult and humiliation which most of them were daily required to endure, and upon the discretion of whites not to push the Negroes too far." Official policies and long-standing customs were used to keep Black citizens firmly in their prescribed place. Many white Houstonians agreed with Benjamin Riley, a prominent Texas temperance campaigner, who declared in 1906, "The dominant characteristic of the negro is that of submission and tractableness."[2] For Black citizens, their ability to live unmolested in a society dominated by white supremacists often came down to how convincingly and consistently they could conform to that denigrating image.

Just how widely this view permeated white society in that era was demonstrated in 1909 by a survey of southern university students who were asked by a professor to write essays describing their personal views on African Americans in their respective states. One student wrote, "The negro of today is insolent, ungrateful and even brutish in his attitude toward the white people." One of his classmates declared, "No man with a drop of Southern blood in his veins will stoop so low as to associate with the black man, no matter how highly educated he may be." Another respondent wrote, "The negro is more like a mule than anything I can think of. . . . It is said of a mule that he will carry you ninety-nine times to kill you the hundredth. So it is with the negro: he will prove faithful for many years and at the last kill you and all your family. You cannot get the brute out of the negro; therefore he must be kept under subjection."[3]

For Black Houstonians in 1917, that attitude was already the reality of their daily lives. Houston might have been free of mob violence and

---

* Gruening, as a white woman, was able to move through southern society without attracting the dangerous animosity that activists such as Ida B. Wells incurred just by the fact that they were Black.

lynchings, but its African American residents were required to defer to white people in nearly every public space and personal interaction. Black men were expected to remove their hats when speaking to white people; any Black pedestrian who failed to yield the sidewalk to a white person would be lucky if he was just shoved off into the gutter; the usual outcome was that he might be assaulted and arrested. Most white-owned businesses were off-limits to African Americans. If Black citizens were allowed in at all, white shop clerks addressed them as "boy," "Sambo," or "Sal," rather than "mister" or "ma'am," and they had to wait until any white customers were served first. "Local white newspapers championed this practice by consistently applying insulting labels to blacks," one history of Houston's race relations noted. "They referred to black women as 'negresses' and to blacks in general as 'darkies' and 'coons.'"⁴ Often the poorest, least-educated strata of white southerners were most aggressive in demanding the greatest deference from their Black neighbors.

Lorenzo Greene, who later made his mark as a prominent African American historian, visited Houston when he was in his late teens and kept a detailed diary of his observations on what life was like for Black residents of the city at that time. In a conversation with a local African American physician, Dr. B. J. Covington, Greene expressed his opinion that Houston seemed better for Black people than any other southern city he had visited in his travels. Dr. Covington agreed, but added that "there were many things which nullified, to some extent, their advantages." "Racist attitudes especially toward Negro women here," Greene wrote, "are such that, if he [Dr. Covington] can help it, [he] does not ride with Mrs. Covington on the street cars, because his wife, like any Negro woman, is prone to be insulted by any person with a white skin. Worse, it is impossible for him or any Negro to be a man in the presence of his woman. For any Negro to resent such an insult whether he be husband, father, brother, or sweetheart, would be tantamount to suicide." Greene, who at that time was a bachelor, came away from the conversation deeply disturbed by "the racial dilemma faced daily by Southern Negro men who loved their women yet who feared to protect them against the insulting advances of the most ignorant white man."⁵

Even in relatively peaceful communities such as Houston, Black citizens were never allowed to forget they lived a precarious existence under the shadow of a very real threat within boundaries defined entirely by white society. "Fear of violating those boundaries—unintentionally or as perceived by whites—haunted black men and women in their daily routines, compelling them to act with extreme caution in the presence of whites," one historian says. "That included avoiding any words, gestures, or facial expression that might be misinterpreted and staying away from whites altogether if possible."[6]

This unwritten code of social survival was not a new development brought on by the turn of the century. Frederick Douglass, when he wrote about the dark days of slavery as it existed eighty years earlier, had described southern customs that were nearly identical to what Black Houstonians faced in the first decades of the twentieth century. "Does a slave look dissatisfied? It is said that he has the devil in him," Douglass wrote in 1849. "Does he speak loudly when spoken to by the master? Then he is getting high-minded, and should be taken down a button lower. Does he forget to pull off his hat at the approach of a white person? Then he is wanting in reverence . . . Does he venture to vindicate his conduct, when censured for it? Then he is guilty of impudence, one of the greatest crimes a slave can commit."[7] The institution of legal slavery might have been abolished with the end of the Civil War, but the passage of time had not in any meaningful way changed the racial attitudes of many white southerners.

All across the South, resistance to any suggestion of social equality for African Americans intensified as the calendar turned over to the new century. "The death of slavery is recognized," one southerner told a reporter from a northern newspaper. "But we don't believe that because the nigger is free he ought to be saucy; and we don't mean to have any such nonsense as letting him vote."[8] This attitude was just as common in Texas as it was in Mississippi, Georgia, or Alabama, and all across the South local governments took steps to protect the white monopoly on political power.

In 1900 an election in Bryan, the seat of Brazos County, about a hundred miles from Houston, was disrupted when segregationists "made a show of force and permitted no Negroes to vote." The Negro Baptist State Sunday School Conference declared that Brazos County was unsafe for Black residents. Local newspapers fiercely denied that charge, but in the following five months two prominent local Black political activists were murdered in the county. In September of that year, neighboring Grimes

County hosted a rally by the White Man's Union in which the following poem was read during the opening ceremony:

> Twas nature's laws that drew the lines
> Between the Anglo-Saxon and the African race,
> And we, the Anglo-Saxons of Grand Old Grimes,
> Must force the African to keep his place.[9]

In a 1914 book entitled *Race Orthodoxy in the South*, Thomas P. Bailey declared, "Is not the South being *encouraged* to treat the negroes *as aliens* by the growing discrimination against the negro in the North, a discrimination that is social as well as economic? Does not the South perceive that all the fire has gone out of the Northern philanthropic fight for the rights of man? *The North has surrendered!*"[10] It was simply a continuation of the abandonment of Black southerners that had begun with the inauguration of the Hayes presidency thirty-eight years earlier, the political betrayal that paved the way for decades of oppression under Jim Crow segregation.

Bailey held nothing back in his polemic of white supremacy. "Here is the racial creed of the Southern people as expressed by a group of representative Southerners during the past few months," he wrote, then listed fifteen points that he described as "the leadings of Providence." He left no doubt as to his stance on racial equality—as far as he was concerned, it did not and could not exist. "This is a white man's country," he declared; "the negro is inferior and will remain so. . . . Only Southerners understand the negro question. . . . Let the South settle the negro question."[11]

Bailey's racist screed found ready acceptance with many white southerners who agreed that they alone knew best how to deal with Black Americans. The language used in their arguments differed depending on the speaker, but the message was always the same—to keep an entire race of people "as near the state of bondage as possible." Some apologists of segregation disingenuously tried to cast racial violence as something that was not only justified but also perhaps even necessary for the greater good. In 1905 a mob in Waco, Texas, lynched a man named Sank Majors after he was accused of assaulting a white woman. The *Waco Times-Herald* praised the lynching as an example of southern justice. "The negro's best friend is the Southern white man," the paper insisted, declaring that white men only meted out such severe punishment when it was merited, thereby providing a cautionary example that would warn other Black people of the dangers of stepping over Jim Crow's rigid lines.[12] A northern journalist took a more realistic view. "The Negro who makes his appeal on the basis of this old relationship [enslaver-enslaved] finds no more indulgent or generous friend that the Southern white man," he wrote, "but the moment he assumes or demands any other relationship or stands up as an independent citizen, the white men—at least some white men—turn upon him with the fiercest hostility."[13]

Behind Houston's façade of civic tranquility, Black residents found little real tolerance and almost never any opportunities to improve their situation. Among themselves they described the city as "a nest of prejudice." Segregation was an indelible reality of their lives, both as a matter of legal ordinance and social custom, just as much as it was for other Black communities all across the South. Beginning in 1910, "Southern cities with large black populations—such as New Orleans, Baltimore, Richmond, Louisville, and Atlanta—passed residential segregation ordinances to ensure that African American housing would be legally confined to specific parts of the cities."[14] The same process occurred in Houston. During this period of civic development Houston created numerous municipal parks and public spaces, and Black residents were banned from all but one of them. Segregated waiting rooms in railway stations and whites-only drinking fountains came into existence at the same time. When the city expanded its electric grid and installed streetlights in residential neighborhoods, no lights went up in the parts of town inhabited by Black citizens, and the paved sidewalks literally stopped where white neighborhoods ended. The only reason the Black neighborhood in the San Felipe District had been able to get its sidewalks paved was that a Black-owned brick company donated the materials. Segregation also extended to opportunities for employment, limiting African Americans to mostly menial and unskilled work. "Black professionals," as one history of Texas says, "were restricted to being teachers and ministers, and black business owners were restricted to special operations, such as barber shops, deemed acceptable to the white population."[15] Black entrepreneurs faced systemic challenges in raising the necessary capital to start businesses, as well as restrictions deliberately designed to keep them from competing with white-owned businesses.

Just as Houston's Black community could only live in their designated neighborhoods, drink in their own bars, and eat in their own restaurants, after death they were also denied equality. Black Houstonians could only be buried in separate cemeteries, as if the pine trees and spreading live oaks with their garlands of Spanish moss could not bear to shade the dead of all races together. Separate housing, separate schools, and separate facilities and services were designated for Black residents, and in every instance, separate also meant of inferior quality.

These acts of disenfranchisement were repressive enough by themselves, but Black Houstonians also lived under a constant danger of violence from the local police. When 3-24 Infantry arrived in Houston that summer, the city's police department had 159 officers in its ranks. Just two of those officers were African American, and they were only permitted to work in the city's African American neighborhoods. In communities such as the San Felipe District, some officers of the Houston police department were notorious for racial brutality, and this was particularly true of the "Special Officers" who conducted horse-mounted patrols. Harassment, arbitrary arrests, and beatings for petty infractions were commonplace. As one African American researcher wrote in a 1913 study of law enforcement in Houston, "No black, regardless of status or standing in the community, was immune from such treatment."[16] A Black physician who left Houston because of his fear of the local police told NAACP correspondent Martha Gruening in August 1917 that 'having a home is all right but not when you never know when you leave in the morning if you will really be able to get back to it that night."[17] Reverend Elijah C. Branch, the pastor of an African American congregation, agreed with that assessment. "Law-abiding [Black] citizens," he said, "feared the police in getting over the city at night more than they feared the highwaymen."[18] Black Texans all over the state understood that fear. Just eight days before the Houston Incident, the African American newspaper *Houston Daily Post* reported, "Willie Shears, an Independence negro, was shot to death at Caldwell Sunday night while resisting a deputy sheriff who attempted to arrest him. The coroner's verdict says it was a clear case of suicide."[19]

A photograph of the "Special Officers" of the Houston police, taken a few years before the 24th Infantry arrived, shows the horse-mounted section of the department. In the foreground, two policemen hold six hounds on leashes. The mounted police were especially feared by the city's Black residents, but a frisson of something even worse is in that photograph. In an era when the dark days of slavery were still within the living memory of many elderly African Americans, that image must have conjured up scenes of Black men and women fleeing through night-shrouded forests and swamps with baying dogs and slave-catchers hot on their trail.

Houston's culture of racially oppressive law enforcement is a historical fact, but it is important to note that not all of the city's police officers were of a single type, any more than the soldiers of 3-24 Infantry were all of one type. There is no denying that some officers on the force were ardent racists and outright bullies, and most of them seem to have supported and enforced the segregation laws without any moral qualms. There were a few exceptions, though. Ira Raney was a police officer who worked the Fourth Ward, which included the Black neighborhoods of the San Felipe District. Raney was a family man with a wife and eight children at home. He had a better reputation among African American residents than many of his fellow officers did, and on one occasion he took a Black child to his own home for his wife to look after until the child's family could be located. But the more benign attitudes of a few policemen like Raney were never enough to offset the rampant racism that marked the department's daily interactions with the Black community.

In June 1917, Houston's city council began cracking down on prostitution within the city limits and focused their efforts on the established brothels then concentrated in one disreputable area of town. Vice had always been a part of the city's social landscape in both the white and Black communities, and prostitution, liquor, and gambling headed the list of popular sins for both groups. The city's anti-prostitution program, however, was stated in language that expressed familiar racist stereotypes: Black men were depicted as gamblers, larcenists, and drunks, and all Black women were immoral. A white South Carolinian expressed the views of many segregationists when he said of African Americans, "All the men are thieves, and all the women are prostitutes. It's their natur' to be that way, and they'll never be no other way."[20] Parallel stereotypes were hardly ever applied when the offenders were white people, even though the same types of criminal behavior were to be found in both communities and often in the same proportions.

Rather than keeping prostitution quietly contained behind closed doors, the new policy simply pushed the working girls out into public view. Most of the white prostitutes moved to other towns to continue their vocation, but many of the Black prostitutes had no choice but to ply their trade on the streets, which put them in view of the police. The police aggressively arrested Black prostitutes, but rarely detained the white men who were some of their most frequent customers. As the anti-prostitution campaign gained momentum, the city's local Anti-Saloon League mounted a simultaneous effort to ban the sale of alcohol within city limits. Predictably, these efforts to prohibit legal alcohol produced an immediate surge in the production of unlicensed booze, and "with few exceptions, the bootleggers arrested for violating the liquor laws were Negroes, even though whites were the greater offenders."[21]

Another area where segregation brought the two sides into frequent conflict was Houston's public transportation system of railroads and street-cars. Residents of all races rode the streetcars, but African American passengers were required to sit in the sections marked off by signs carrying the designation "Colored." "In their homes and in ordinary employment," one contemporary commentator said, "they meet as master and servant; but in the street cars they touch as free citizens, each paying for the right to ride, the white not in a place of command, the Negro without an obligation of servitude. Streetcar relationships are, therefore, symbolic of the new conditions."[22] For segregationists, those conditions threatened the status quo of white supremacy.

Black Houstonians could not directly challenge the segregated street-car seating without risking violence from angry white citizens and arrest by the police, but this did not mean they passively acquiesced to the situation. In 1903, the community undertook a two-year boycott of the transit company in protest of the segregation policy. That effort was unsuccessful, just as the early attempts at bus boycotts during the civil rights movement in the 1950s did not achieve their goals the first time around.[23]

Those two elements—the Houston police department's long history of racist brutality and the policy of segregated seating on streetcars—became the point of intersection where simmering anger spilled over into outright violence when 3-24 Infantry entered that volatile mix.

6. Breaking Point

Third Battalion arrived in Texas while they were still adjusting to the sort of internal problems that would challenge any military unit. A few weeks before boarding the train for Houston, they received a large cohort of replacement personnel. Nearly fifty new soldiers, recruits fresh from the replacement depots, joined the battalion.

Army units are insular social organizations. This is even more the case in combat arms formations such as infantry or cavalry, sometimes to the point where soldiers identify so closely with their platoons and companies that they regard other soldiers, even those in the same battalion, as outsiders. Newcomers, whether they be new recruits or older veterans who transfer in from other units, are not automatically accepted into the fraternity—they must first prove themselves, and acceptance is not guaranteed. Assimilation and cohesion take time, but Third Battalion had no time. The new recruits of 3-24 Infantry were still untested, unassimilated, and not completely accepted, when the battalion set out for its Texas assignment.

Besides the disruption caused by taking in that many new troops all at once, at the same time the battalion experienced an even more destabilizing change when it lost many of its most important veterans. Twenty-five of its best and most experienced NCOs were selected for the new Colored Officers Training Camp the War Department created at Des Moines, Iowa. While this was a splendid professional opportunity for the men who had the chance to earn officers' commissions as second lieutenants, it seriously impacted the battalion's social structure, internal discipline, and combat readiness.

Noncommissioned officers are the institutional memory of the Army, and experienced sergeants form the professional core of any well-ordered military unit. They are the primary trainers of junior soldiers and the bulwark of discipline in the ranks, to the point where an infantry battalion that lacks a strong core of competent NCOs might not even be considered combat-effective. "A good first sergeant is indispensable to the making of a good company," one officer of the Indian Wars era wrote, "for without him the best efforts of the captain would be rendered abortive."[1] That crucial foundation was what 3-24 Infantry lost when its senior Black leaders—the sergeant major, three of the four company first sergeants, and twenty-one sergeants and corporals—were sent to Des Moines just three weeks before the unit went to Houston. Their departure left a gaping hole in the battalion's internal leadership. Many of the junior men promoted to fill those vacancies were not of the same professional caliber as the long-service veterans who went to the officer training course.

While Third Battalion's roster called for sixteen commissioned officers (all of whom were white), most of those essential positions were vacant and the battalion entrained for Houston with only seven officers. In the battalion's three rifle companies, only India Company had more than one officer, and not a single second lieutenant was on the roster even though each company should have had at least one.* In practical terms, if the company officers were ever absent (as they inevitably would be in the normal course of military duties), authority would automatically devolve to the NCOs, and most of the soldiers newly promoted to those critical roles lacked experience and reliability.

The battalion commander would usually be considered the most important officer in the chain of command, but Lieutenant Colonel William Newman assumed command of 3-24 Infantry just one day before the battalion set out for Houston. He had not yet had time to get to know his men, and they did not know him. Newman would be reassigned to another position on August 20, just three days before the trouble erupted, and in those intervening thirty-four days he barely had enough time to make a real impact on the temper of the unit, though orders he issued during those weeks were examined in detail in the aftermath of the August

---

* Captain James Reisinger of Kilo Company fell ill in early August and was replaced by Lieutenant Charles Snider, so Reisinger had no role in the events of August 23. Second Lieutenants Edward Hudson and John Jack were assigned to the battalion on August 13, so they were still very new to the unit when trouble broke out.

incident. On the official Table of Organization and Equipment, the battalion's second-in-command, or executive officer, should have been another field-grade officer with the rank of major, but 3-24 Infantry at that time had no majors and Newman had no executive officer upon whom he could rely. Each of the battalion's four rifle companies—India, Kilo, Lima, and Mike Companies—should have had an experienced captain in command, but here again the personnel shortages cut deep.

Captain Kneeland Snow was India Company's commanding officer. At thirty-eight years of age, Snow was the oldest company-grade officer in the battalion as well as being the seniormost of its four captains by dint of his time in service. He began his military career as an enlisted man in the Hospital Corps just after the Spanish-American War, then received a commission as a second lieutenant in 1901. His rise through the ranks was hardly meteoric—in sixteen years he had only been promoted twice—but even so, he was the next senior officer in the battalion's chain of command after Newman. Nothing in his service record suggests he possessed the personal or professional qualities needed to deal with the challenges the battalion encountered in Houston.

Snow was also inclined to put his personal amusements ahead of his military duties. After the troubles, Newman was asked if he had ever needed to discipline any of the battalion officers while they were in Houston. Newman said no, but added that when they first arrived in the city he thought "the officers were inclined to leave camp too much."

"Was Captain Snow the cause for your giving the instructions about officers remaining more in camp?" the investigator asked.

"Well, he was to some extent," Newman said. "He seemed inclined to go out right often to play golf."[2] That was not an exaggeration. Snow himself admitted, "I am very fond of golf. I used to play golf very often when I could get away," and he made sure he got away several days a week.

Lima Company was commanded by Captain Bartlett James, a Virginian from a family with a long history of military service. A West Point graduate, James was the goat of the Class of 1916, meaning that he graduated at the absolute bottom of the academic rankings of his year group. His poor academic record apparently was not an accurate measure of his ability as a leader, because he proved himself to be a talented and conscientious officer. Among Third Battalion's three captains, James was the most junior in terms of time in service, but even in such a short time with the battalion he had made a positive impression in his company and was very popular with his soldiers.

The position of sergeant major is critically important to a well-functioning infantry battalion, because the sergeant major is both the senior noncommissioned officer in the unit as well as the battalion commander's closest advisor. An effective sergeant major should embody the military ethos and enforce the professional standards for the battalion's NCOs. A company sergeant named William Washington was promoted to fill that vital position just before the Houston posting, and at the battalion's moment of crisis on August 23, he was most conspicuous by his utter ineffectiveness.

Down in the rifle companies, the senior noncommissioned officer in each company was its first sergeant. The departure of the best men for officer training meant that only one of those crucial positions was still held by an experienced NCO when the battalion arrived in Houston. In India Company, a sergeant named Vida Henry was frocked up to fill the first sergeant slot.* Henry was a thirty-five-year-old veteran of thirteen years' service with the regiment, but he lacked many of the qualifications normally required of a senior noncommissioned officer. Colonel Newman described Henry as "inoffensive, and not forceful enough, nor well educated enough to be a 1st Sergeant of a company," yet he was promoted out of sheer necessity. The battalion simply did not have enough depth in the critical NCO ranks.

On the morning Third Battalion arrived in Houston the officers formed their men up by companies and they marched to the site the Army had contracted for the battalion encampment. Crowds of Houstonians, Black and white citizens alike, gathered to watch as the soldiers marched through the streets with their NCOs calling cadence.

Their temporary home was a ten-acre plot of land leased from a local family named Moys. It was surrounded by residential neighborhoods, but

---

* Frocking is a military practice, less common now than in times past, of raising a soldier to fill a position for which the next-higher rank is usually required. A frocked soldier is allowed to wear the higher-rank insignia commensurate with the new position, though not yet formally promoted to that rank.

not within the city proper. Situated on the western edge of Houston's city limits, this ground lay about a mile from the location where Camp Logan was being constructed, hardly any distance at all for infantrymen accustomed to regular route marches. The temporary camp was laid out in the orderly geometric pattern so dear to the military mind, in a large square delineated on three sides by a barbed wire fence with a drainage ditch marking its frontage along Reinerman Street. The rear of the encampment butted up against a forested patch of scrub oak and pine trees. The camp itself was laid out in five sections: the officers' tents formed the front rank, with the tents of each of the four companies laid out in lines behind them in sequential order: India, Kilo, Lima, and Mike. An open area, designated as a "street," marked each company's turf, bracketed by the company supply tents closest to officers' row at the upper end and the communal latrines at the opposite end. The supply tents were the domain of the company supply sergeants, who were responsible for the security of weapons and ammunition when those were not issued out to men assigned to guard duty. The picket line for the horses and the battalion guardhouse were situated along the western side of the camp. The company streets were used for each company's morning roll call and the retreat formations each afternoon.

For the city's Black citizens, Third Battalion's arrival and the sight of Black men in military uniform were a source of immense pride, and they were eager to meet the soldiers. Thelma Bryant, who was a twelve-year-old girl in 1917, remembered, "The soldiers took the black community by storm. My teachers were dating soldiers, and two of them married soldiers from the camp." The infantrymen were just as enthusiastic to mingle, and to enjoy the company of a vibrant, urban Black community.[3]

Newman was very concerned about how interactions between his soldiers and Houston's white residents would play out in the city's racially striven environment. His veterans had served in the Philippines, Mexico, California, and the western territories. In cities such as San Francisco, Cheyenne, and Manila, they had mingled with white civilians on public transportation, in movie theaters, and in restaurants. At their previous military posts, they had played on baseball and football teams with white soldiers from other regiments. After those experiences, they were not inclined to meekly accept the racial oppressions of Houston's Jim Crow segregation. In his statement after the troubles, Newman said, "When I took my battalion to Houston I knew that the Texans' idea of how a colored man should be treated was just the opposite of what these Twenty-Fourth Infantrymen had been used to."[4]

Among white citizens, reactions to the soldiers' arrival ranged from the simply curious to the overtly hostile, amid the sort of casually patronizing racism that marked many of their attitudes toward African Americans. A Houston housewife named Belle Costello, who seems to have aspired to be a writer, penned an article for the local newspaper *The Houstonian* in which she regaled readers with her impressions of scenes in the battalion's new camp. "Brown tents for brown soldiers loom up on one side together with sundry and many 'refreshment stands,'" she wrote, and went on to describe "the unruffled colored soldier enjoying with the philosophy of his race the good of the present moment with a watermelon under one arm and the hand of his dusky inamorata tucked under the other."

Beneath the veneer of amiability on the battalion's first day in the city, tensions and hostility were already present and gathering force. The soldiers arrived still outraged over the race massacre that had nearly destroyed the Black community in East St. Louis just a few weeks earlier. They also brought their determination to stand up against Jim Crow segregation. They were met by a considerable portion of Houston's white population who were already predisposed to resent Black men in uniform and a police force with a reputation for using brute force to uphold the racial status quo.

In an effort to stave off trouble between his soldiers and white Houstonians, Newman implemented policies to make the battalion camp as welcoming as possible to Houston's Black residents. Bringing the best parts of that community to his soldiers, he reasoned, would help keep his men safely close to camp, rather than out in the potentially hostile spaces of the city. He opened the camp to civilian visitors between the hours of 1:00 and 10:45 p.m. and allowed soldiers who were not on duty to freely socialize with the visitors. Soldiers were allowed to go into town, but passes were awarded based on each soldier's good-conduct record and reputation for reliability, and every soldier had to be back in camp by 11:00 p.m.

"I felt that anything I could do to hold the men in camp would lessen the chances for a clash between them and white people of Houston," Newman said later. "It is the practice in the Army to let soldiers leave post or camp during certain hours. I had no reason for with-holding this privilege from men of my command. Nearly all of them were rated by their Company Commanders as first conduct grade men, and therefore presumed to be men who would conduct themselves in an orderly manner when out of camp. I couldn't put a string of sentinels around the camp and pen them up as if they couldn't be trusted," he said. "That would have made them ill-tempered and caused them to feel that they were being discriminated against because they were colored soldiers." Rather than make it so that his soldiers had to go into Houston for recreation and to socialize, he tried to bring the best parts of the civilian community to them.[5]

Shortly after the battalion's arrival a white Houstonian named Roy Owens came to Newman with a suggestion. Owens owned a large pavilion close by the battalion camp, and he wondered if Newman would allow his soldiers to use it as a dance hall. Owens figured to turn his unused property into a profitable enterprise, if he could get soldiers and civilian women to use it as a nightspot. Newman agreed, but "only on condition that he would run an orderly place and allow no bootlegging." That condition was apparently met, because Newman later said he only knew of a single case where a soldier was reported for being drunk and disorderly at the dance hall.

On one level Newman's policies worked—Black families flocked to the camp to meet the new arrivals, and leading members of the African American community were regular visitors each day. Local clergymen conducted religious services for them, civic groups brought books and home-cooked food for them, one local woman from the Carnegie Library set up a small lending library for the soldiers in the camp, and Black businesses conducted a thriving trade with the battalion. Many of those civilian visitors, not surprisingly, were young women eager to meet the young men of Third Battalion, and it was their presence in particular that quickly attracted the negative attention of some white Houstonians. After the trouble on August 23, critics alleged that the battalion encampment had been a disreputable den of iniquity and vice almost from the day 3-24 Infantry arrived in the city. That charge was recycled in numerous publications over the following decades, but never on the basis of any reputable evidence.

The racist animosity that Newman feared made its appearance very quickly. One of the company officers overheard some soldiers who were working in the officers' mess talking about interactions they had had with white civilians in town. They described a day when some of their comrades were walking down a Houston street and encountered a group of young white men on a corner. As the soldiers passed by, the civilians said, loudly enough to be heard, that "the United States did not care what they put a uniform on, anymore." Other incidents were much more aggressive, and deliberately provocative in the use of racial slurs.[6]

White Houstonians on the alert for evidence that the military new-comers might disrupt the city's racial status quo quickly found it in the fact that the soldiers refused to comply with segregated seating on the street-cars. In an attempt to avoid conflict in the city, Newman had issued orders requiring his men to obey the Jim Crow statutes no matter how offensive they were, telling his soldiers "that when enlisted men rode on street cars, they must ride in that portion of the car set aside for colored people as required by the law of the State of Texas; and that no enlisted man must enter a hotel, restaurant or picture show usually patronized by white people."[7] Not surprisingly, that order did not go over well with the men of 3-24 Infantry.

The seating in the streetcars was divided by small signs that said "Colored." These could be moved forward or backward in the car depend-ing on whether more white or Black passengers were aboard. What infu-riated many soldiers was the conductors' practice of moving the signs backward into the "Colored" section if additional white people got on, thereby reducing the number of seats available to Black passengers, and in some cases African Americans were required to get off the car to make room for more white people. The infantrymen usually refused to give up their seats. More outrageously, in the minds of Houston's white citi-zens, the soldiers frequently sat wherever they pleased, and on a couple of occasions actually took the signs down and dared the conductors to do anything about it.

In at least one case this defiance brought matters to a head, violently. One evening two Black soldiers riding the streetcar refused to comply with the Jim Crow ordinance, as they often did, but at that moment the tram happened to be passing by two policemen sitting in a parked car. The motorman stopped the streetcar and the conductor got off to tell the police officers that he was "having trouble on the car with some nigger soldiers." The policemen boarded the tram and savagely beat the soldiers with their sidearms, then dragged them off onto the sidewalk, battered and bloodied. They then got back into their vehicle and drove away with-out bothering to make an arrest. As usually happened in such cases, the battalion adjutant went to the police station to lodge a formal complaint against both the excessive force used against the men and the use of the racist slur against soldiers of the U.S. Army. Also as usual, the complaint went nowhere and changed nothing.[8]

Captain Haig Shekerjian held the post of battalion adjutant, the unit's personnel officer. He was born in Turkey to an Armenian family who immigrated to the United States when he was a child. Shekerjian was the first person of Armenian descent to graduate from the U.S. Military Academy at West Point, a point of great pride among the Armenian community in America at that time. Among the 3-24 Infantry officers who received their commissions from West Point, Shekerjian was the only one who had graduated in the upper half of his class. He also had sixteen years' service in the Army, including two years leading Black soldiers in the Twenty-Fourth Infantry, but he transferred over to Third Battalion only a few days before it went to Houston. By most contemporary accounts he was a conscientious and capable officer.

One obvious solution to the problem with the racial conflict on the streetcars was to ban the soldiers from riding. Newman did not bother to even consider that option—as far as he was concerned, his men had just as much right as anyone to use the city's public transportation—so he suggested another idea. In a July 30 meeting with David Daly, manager of the firm that operated the trams, Newman asked about the possibility of adding extra cars for the soldiers' exclusive use during the hours when most of them were off duty. Daly rejected that suggestion but said the company would consider putting additional trams on the line to handle the larger numbers of passengers. Conductors would also be told to move the segregation dividers forward into the "whites only" sections to accommodate more Black passengers when groups of soldiers boarded the cars.

In order to get even that inadequate concession, Newman had to commit to reminding his battalion about the requirement to obey local laws, even when those laws were Jim Crow ordinances. Not only did this halfhearted compromise do nothing to resolve the problem, but it also left the soldiers increasingly resentful of the continuing insult of Houston's racial repression.[9]

On another occasion, trouble broke out on one of the streetcars when a policeman used the word "nigger" in front of a group of soldiers who were riding the tram. Only the efforts of their own NCOs kept the matter from escalating into a brawl. The incident was reported to Newman, who then lodged a formal complaint with the chief of police, but if he expected some redress, he was disappointed. "I don't remember that he ever told me of any action taken," he said, which was the way the Army's conversations with local officials generally went.[10]

Concerned that altercations between his soldiers and the local police were occurring with increasing frequency, Newman suggested to the chief of police, Clarence Brock, that Third Battalion could put Black military policemen, also known as provosts, in the African American neighborhoods where off-duty soldiers spent much of their time. That way, if a soldier got drunk and disorderly, he could be dealt with by men from his own battalion, rather than by Houston policemen, who had a tendency to beat a man bloody while taking him into custody just because he was Black.

Brock accepted the idea of provosts to work in concert with the city police, at least ostensibly. This detachment of provosts would consist of sixteen of the best soldiers in the battalion—eight NCOs and eight privates—who would work in teams of two to patrol the San Felipe District and lower Milam Street, which the police believed were the most troublesome spots.

This attempted policing compromise failed in some critical points. Newman made one concession that undermined the arrangement from the beginning and planted the fatal flaw that would bring the hostility between civilian police and the battalion's provosts to a final point of conflict. Military police were always armed in the performance of their duties, but Chief Brock objected to the idea of armed Black soldiers exercising a law enforcement role in his city, even if they were restricted to the African American neighborhoods and only had policing powers over other soldiers. Newman apparently did not resist this demand, and so his provosts went out armed only with billy clubs. The brassards they wore on their arms that identified them as military police did not engender any professional respect from civilian police officers, and their lack of weapons meant that Houston's police felt no inclination to treat them any differently than they did Black civilians, and with no more respect. If Brock ever actually instructed his officers to cooperate with the military provosts, as he assured Newman he would, he never enforced that requirement. Newman, for his part, ordered his men "to conduct themselves so as to win the commendation of the citizens of Houston," but the civilian policemen treated the Black soldiers however their personal inclinations or prejudices led them, and the violent bigots on the force continued to behave as they had always done.[11]

Of the battalion officers, Captain Shekerjian had the most frequent contact with the police, because in his role as adjutant it was his duty to collect soldiers from the police station whenever they were arrested. Every time he did so, he brought up the issue of the police officers' incendiary language. In a later conversation with one of the Army's investigators, Shekerjian said that "a great many of the soldiers did take offense at the fact that almost everybody insulted them, in their opinion, by calling them niggers, sons of bitches, and other vile names. One man made a statement to me that someone had said that it only cost $5.00 to kill a nigger."[12]

Nothing that Shekerjian or Newman said to police officials seemed to make a difference. The situation grew more volatile with each passing day as verbal insults were increasingly accompanied by outright violence at the hands of the police.

———

The most frequent confrontations occurred at Camp Logan itself, where Third Battalion carried out its mission of securing government equipment and materials used in the construction of the training installation. A roster of guard duty was established, with each of the battalion's four rifle companies providing 148 soldiers for the guard mount each day on twenty-four-hour shifts.* Soldiers were posted to control the entry points to the camp, checking the identifications of contracted civilian laborers of all races, monitoring the delivery of construction materials, and ensuring that no pilfered items went out the gates when the workday ended. Other soldiers were assigned to guard the government warehouses, particularly at night. Each soldier on duty was armed with his service rifle and five rounds of ammunition, but they were only to carry their weapons loaded without having a round chambered. On its face, these duties were straightforward enough, but they proved to be one more area of increasing clashes between soldiers and white civilians.

Two areas of conflict arose almost immediately. The first, ironically, was because of how conscientious Third Battalion infantrymen were

---

* The company responsible for the guard mount at Camp Logan each day was also required to provide the sentinels at the battalion encampment, which usually consisted of a dozen soldiers on fixed posts or roving guard, with one NCO as sergeant of the guard.

in carrying out their duties. Their orders were to require every person passing through the gate to show identification, and they did so scrupulously. Many of the white workers passing through the gate objected to having to show their passes when required to do so. It was not the requirement itself that irritated them, but that it came from Black soldiers. The guards strictly enforced the policy of having all persons show their passes until the city engineer, E. E. Sands, complained that he "was not in the habit of showing his pass to negroes." On this point, as on too many others, the military authorities bowed to civilian prejudices, and the requirement to show passes at Camp Logan's gate was relaxed.

A more serious problem was that the white laborers and contractors working at the camp brought their racial animosities to work with them, and that resulted in a continually escalating round of confrontations between them and the soldiers. The Third Battalion men resented any use of the word "nigger" by the white workers, whether directed at them or not, and many of those workers made a deliberate point of using that slur often and loudly.

The civilian paymaster at the camp, W. T. Patterson, recounted later that one day he told another white man, within earshot of one of the soldiers, that an African American worker had accidentally injured another Black man with a pick, but he used the racist slur when describing the two men. The soldier took exception to that word. "Look here, I want you to understand that we ain't no niggers," he told Patterson. "I am no nigger!" Patterson said that the soldier "went on to tell where he came from and that they were all on equal footing there . . . He went on to explain that he was on equal rights with white folks." The paymaster, a lifelong resident of Texas, seemed shocked that a Black man would challenge him on his language, and so forcefully.[13]

Houston civilians were not the only ones to report the use of racial slurs as a common occurrence at the camp. The Army engineer overseeing the construction project, Captain W. P. Rothrock, later told a military investigator, "At one time a negro employee was bitten by a snake. White employees were standing around and one remarked that he should be given some whiskey for the snakebite and another remarked that whiskey was no good for a nigger snakebite. The guard whose post is nearby heard the remark and walked up and wanted to know what the white employee meant by saying 'nigger.'" Rothrock tried to put a stop to the continuing problem of racist language by telling the construction contractors that he would fire any of their employees whom he found talking to military personnel. To his credit, he followed through on that threat. Newman also ordered the soldiers not to interact with the civilian workers other than in the course of their duties. Rothrock felt that Third Battalion's soldiers were consistently professional in their conduct. "The guards' work as guard was very effective at all times," he said, "and they were very necessary as the contractors had over 3000 men in the vicinity of the camp."[14] The soldiers, for their part, returned the racial slurs with equal vehemence. They took to referring to the white contract employees as "white bastards" and "goddamn sons of bitches."

White Houstonians took a dim view of Black men responding to insult with insults of their own. One civilian contractor, who happened to be moonlighting from his day job as a deputy in the county sheriff's department, thought the soldiers were "very impertinent." Another civilian said that the Black infantrymen "never lost a chance to act ugly with the white man." John Hulen, a Houstonian who was also a brigadier general in the Texas National Guard, spoke for many of Houston's elite when he said Third Battalion soldiers "seemed to think they had greater privileges than other negroes in the community."[15]

Occasionally the animosity at Camp Logan threatened to break out in actual violence, particularly when the men involved let their tempers get the better of them. On August 20, a contractor backing up his automobile accidentally bumped an African American boy. The boy was not injured in any way, but the contact had not gone unnoticed. Of all the men in Third Battalion who could have witnessed the incident, Private Pat McWhorter was perhaps the last person one would have wanted to do so. He had a reputation in the unit as a hothead, a soldier who repeatedly showed a tendency to react first and think about it much later, if ever. McWhorter ran over to the car, working the bolt of his rifle to chamber a round as he did so, and pointed his weapon at the driver. He demanded to know what the driver meant by trying to run over the kid. When the contractor told him it was none of his affair and called him "a vile name," McWhorter grew even angrier, until eventually other soldiers intervened and the car full of civilians left the camp. One of the men in the vehicle, however, was Houston city commissioner David Fitzgerald, and he lost no time reporting the altercation to McWhorter's company commander. McWhorter received a battalion-level punishment, but the admonition did nothing to ameliorate his impulsive temper. Three days later he was one of the most vocal participants in the trouble that broke out in the battalion camp.

Recalling the conflicts that occurred between soldiers and white laborers at Camp Logan, Captain Rothrock later said that he reported every one of those incidents to Newman, who confirmed his statement and said, "Either I or one of my officers investigated every case of friction that occurred in Camp Logan, and where the soldier was found to be at fault he was disciplined for it." When the investigator asked if any white worker was ever punished for insulting a soldier, Newman said that Rothrock had indeed carried through on his threat to fire any workman who used a racial slur when speaking to a soldier.

Even so, that did not put a stop to the provocations. Sergeant William Nesbit was on duty as sergeant of the guard one day at Camp Logan and overheard some white workmen who were installing plumbing pipes say of the soldiers on the guard detail, "Those niggers would look good with coils around their necks." A rumor was already going around that some Houstonians had been heard saying that one of the Black infantrymen would be lynched before the battalion left the city, just to make a point.[16]

Nesbit was regarded as one of the most reliable NCOs in the battalion. He came from a Massachusetts family with a long history of social activism and a proud legacy of military service. Thirteen members of his extended family had fought for the Union during the Civil War, including his grandfather, who later served as president of the Pennsylvania State Equal Rights League. In contemporary accounts, Nesbit was often described as a "mulatto" because his mother was a white woman. He was well educated, erudite, and highly regarded by his fellow soldiers even though he was one of the youngest sergeants in the battalion. He was a veteran of the Mexican campaign and had six years' time in service in 1917. Nesbit took the workmen's remark as a serious threat and had his soldiers walk their guard posts in pairs from that point on, for their mutual protection.

———

While the men of Third Battalion were dealing with the hostility that confronted them every day in Houston, they were also thinking and talking about one of the most savage examples of racist violence to occur during their lifetimes. The East St. Louis race riot had erupted just two weeks before they arrived in Texas, and ever since then the newspapers had been filled with terrible stories of African American neighborhoods in that city attacked by rampaging, homicidal mobs of armed men, of innocent people lynched in the streets or burned in their homes for no reason other than that they were Black, of hundreds dead and thousands of African American citizens driven from the city as refugees. Those reports also carried the news that the policemen and National Guardsmen who should have protected people from the mobs had either stood by and watched the killing or in some cases actually joined in the massacre.

A group of battalion NCOs that included Sergeant Vida Henry formed a relief committee and took up a collection to support the displaced refugees of East St. Louis. They raised $146.60, a not inconsiderable sum pooled from soldiers who, at the bottom end of the rank structure, only made about $30 a month in pay. In the letter to the NAACP's *The Crisis* magazine that accompanied these funds, Corporal George Singleton, filling the role of battalion chaplain, told the NAACP the contributions would have been greater but for the expenses of living in a major city. The soldiers expressed their "deep and heartfelt sympathy" for the victims of East St. Louis and pledged their ongoing support. The soldiers' activism also extended to an interest in forming a military chapter of the NAACP in India Company, or perhaps the entire battalion.

In the midst of these pressures, with each passing week the police in Houston seemed more reactive and more prone to use violence against any soldier who "got out of line." The night of August 18, Privates Grant Mems and Richard Brown were arrested and brought to the police station. They had refused to comply with the Jim Crow ordinances on the streetcars, which was bad enough in the eyes of the law, but then they took offense when the police officers called them "niggers." Both soldiers were badly knocked about, with blood all over their uniforms, and when they were hauled up in front of the desk sergeant at the station, they attempted to file a formal complaint against the arresting officers for excessive force and racist language. The police sergeant, W. C. Wilson, refused to accept their grievance. "The word 'niggers' is all we ever called them," he later told an Army investigator. "I have always known them as 'niggers.'"[17]

Once again Captain Shekerjian made the trek over to the station to obtain the soldiers' release and to remonstrate with the police department about its officers' incessant use of racist slurs. He talked to Chief Brock personally and tried as forcefully as he could to convince him that such language was unacceptable, especially when directed against uniformed soldiers of the U.S. Army. Brock insisted that his officers meant nothing by it—that sort of language was just how people talked in the South, he said.

Shekerjian thought that was a feeble excuse. "No man would use a word at which others took offense unless they meant to insult them," he replied.[18]

Brock repeatedly assured the Army officers that he had instructed his policemen to refer to the soldiers as "colored" rather than the racial slur, but no change in the frequency of racist language was ever noticeable. After the troubles, a Houston newspaper referred to the problem of police using the slur in an article that disparaged Brock's efforts to curtail the insults, limited and ineffectual as they were, as just "silly." "This decision," the writer smugly informed the paper's readers, "was undoubtedly intended to help in preserving order and to smooth the ruffled feelings of the blacks and near blacks, who ignorantly thought 'negro' meaning black, was more a reflection than 'colored,' meaning anything from the deepest jet, or darkest brown, to the yellowest mulatto."[19]

For the soldiers of 3-24 Infantry, the increasing frequency of verbal insults and physical abuse exacted a toll. Even more frustrating, many of them felt that their officers did not really understand what they, as Black men, were dealing with in Houston, and that the officers' efforts to fix the problem were completely ineffective. No matter how many official complaints were lodged, nothing changed. No matter what promises or assurances city officials made, the harassment, insults, and brutality continued.

In every army there is always something of a divide between officers and the rank-and-file soldiers, but that separation between leaders and the led can exacerbate problems in any unit that does not have clear communication and understanding both up and down the chain of command. In 3-24 Infantry, where all the enlisted men and NCOs were Black and all the officers were white, a perpetual division existed that involved more than just the privileges of military rank. As the days passed in Houston and the racial problems continued, the disconnection between the soldiers and their officers widened. Some officers seemed annoyed by the endless litany of complaints about racial insults and police harassment. Frustrated by the fact that nothing was getting better, many soldiers simply stopped reporting the problems. That might have led the battalion leadership to assume that morale was improving, but what it really meant was that feelings among the men were turning dangerously in the opposite direction. Frustration was turning into desperation, and some soldiers reached what was perhaps an inevitable conclusion. Private E. E. Fields said that many of his comrades "claimed that when they came in [after being arrested] they would be put in the guard house whether right or wrong, so they might as well fight it out" with the policemen. If they were going to be insulted and beaten by the police, they might as well give as good as they got and deal out a few punches of their own, and at least get the satisfaction of fighting back.[20]

In this increasingly volatile situation, Camp Logan neared its completion, and the War Department began sending troops there for pre-deployment training. The training support units—logistics, supply, and cook and baking companies, all of them white soldiers—were already on site ready to operate the camp. The first training units would be not raw recruits but state National Guard units that needed to be brought up to Regular Army standards before they shipped out for France. Incredibly, the first units the War Department chose to send to Camp Logan in mid-August were elements of the Illinois Infantry, a National Guard command that included three companies from Chicago and Carbondale, respectively—the very same National Guard units that had been present and participated in the massacre of Black citizens in the East St. Louis race riot not two months earlier.

The soldiers of 3-24 Infantry knew very well who those National Guardsmen were and what they were accused of doing in East St. Louis. They had hated those Guardsmen at a distance when they read of the massacre in the newspapers, and now they were here in front of them in Houston. One newspaper later claimed that the Black infantrymen publicly declared they would "fix that bunch from the Chicago slums" before they left their assignment in Houston.[21] Whether that claim was true or not, there was no denying that the arrival of the Illinois National Guard ratcheted up the strain in Houston by several degrees.

On Monday afternoon, August 20, Lieutenant Colonel Newman left Houston and 3-24 Infantry. He was reassigned to the officers' training course in Des Moines, Iowa, a posting that came with promotion to full colonel. With his departure, Third Battalion lost a commander who was sincerely well-intentioned, if not always effective in his efforts to deal with their grievances. What they got as his replacement was an officer who was utterly inadequate for the responsibilities and challenges of that role in the current situation. Captain Kneeland Snow was promoted to major and assumed command of the battalion.

Thursday morning, August 23, started off much the same as every other day since Third Battalion had arrived in the city. India Company was on guard duty at Camp Logan that morning, and at 1:00 p.m. 148 men of Kilo Company marched over to relieve them. That was the same hour at which soldiers who were not on duty were free to socialize with visitors to the camp, or to head into town if they had a pass. A recreational event was planned for the soldiers later that evening—the Houston Chamber of Commerce had organized a "watermelon feast" in Emancipation Park, the only park Black citizens were permitted to use in the city.

At about 1:30 that afternoon two police officers, Lee Sparks and Rufus Daniels, were riding their regular patrol route through the Black neighborhood in the San Felipe section of town. The two men were part of the horse-mounted division of the Houston Police Department. Sparks, in particular, was "known to the colored people as a brutal bully" and one of the meanest men on the force, a reputation of which he seems to have been rather proud.

As the two policemen came down the street, they saw three young Black men throwing dice in an alley. If it really was a craps game in progress, that was a violation of city ordinances against gambling. As soon as the young men saw the police officers, they scattered. One fellow jumped a fence and ran into a yard. Sparks drew his pistol, fired a shot in his direction, and gave chase. He lost track of the young man in the closely grouped houses, and so simply barged into the house he thought his quarry had run into.[22]

It was the home of a woman named Sara Travers, a mother of five who at that moment was ironing clothes. Mrs. Travers was barely dressed when Sparks entered her house.*

---

* All quotations in the interaction between Sara Travers and Lee Sparks come from statements both parties made to separate investigators in the weeks after the incident. Mrs. Travers gave her most complete statement to the NAACP's investigator, Martha Gruening, while Sparks gave his to Chief Brock, the city of Houston's Citizens' Commission, and the two Army inspectors general, Colonel George Cress and Brigadier General John Chamberlain.

"Did you see a nigger jumping over that yard?" he demanded of her.

"No, sir," she replied, but Sparks ignored her and searched the house anyway. While he was doing that Mrs. Travers went out in her yard, holding her baby, and called over to a neighbor across the street if she knew what the commotion was all about. The other woman answered, "I don't know; I think they were shooting at crap-shooters."

Sparks happened to be coming out of her house at that moment and he heard that comment. "You're a God damn liar," he allegedly shouted. "I shot down into the ground. You all God damn nigger bitches. Since these God damn sons of bitches of nigger soldiers come here you are trying to take the town."

Sparks forced his way back into Mrs. Travers's house. "He came into the bedroom then and into the kitchen and I ask him what he want," Mrs. Travers recalled. "He replied to me, 'Don't you ask an officer what he want in your house. I'm from Fort Ben and we don't allow niggers to talk back to us. We generally whip them down there.' Then he hauled off and slapped me. I hollered and the big one—this Daniels—he ran in, and then Sparks said to him, 'I slapped her and what shall we do about it?'"

"Take and give her ninety days on the Pea Farm 'cause she's one of these biggety nigger women," Daniels replied.* The two policemen grabbed her by the arms and dragged her out of the house.

"I asked them to let me put some clothes on," Mrs. Travers said, "and Sparks says, 'No, we'll take you just as you are. If you was naked we'd take you . . .' Took me with my arms behind my back and Daniels, he says, if I didn't come he'd break them." Daniels was a big, imposing man, standing well over six foot two and weighing nearly two hundred pounds. The police officers marched her down the street to the nearest police call box and telephoned for a paddy wagon to come take her to the police station.

The gunshot, all the shouting, and Mrs. Travers's cries had attracted a crowd, and a neighbor woman came out with shoes, a bonnet, and an apron for her. At about the same time Private Alonzo Edwards of Lima Company walked up on the scene. According to Mrs. Travers's telling, Sparks "went

---

* The Pea Farm was the county work farm, where people convicted of misdemeanor offenses could be sentenced to periods of forced labor. Not surprisingly, most prisoners put to work on the county farm were people of color.

over, and before the soldier could say a word he said, 'What you got to do with this?' and he raised his six-shooter and he beat him—beat him *good*." Edwards, she said, "didn't do a thing but just raise his hand to ward them off. Didn't even tell them to quit, nor nothing."

One witness said that Edwards approached the policemen and offered to pay whatever fine Mrs. Travers might have incurred, if they would release her. Another said that he only asked them to allow her to get dressed before they took her in. Regardless of what the soldier did or did not say, Sparks reacted violently. He hit Edwards "about four or five times" over the head with the barrel of his heavy revolver and beat the young soldier down to his knees. "That's the way we do things in the South," Sparks supposedly said as he stood over him. "We're running things, not the damned niggers." All sources agree that Edwards made no offensive or aggressive movements, and hardly even attempted to defend himself against the blows.

Another soldier from Third Battalion, an unidentified sergeant, saw Edwards go down under Sparks's assault. Edwards called out to him, and one of the policemen squared up on the sergeant and said, "If you come over here, we'll give you the same." The sergeant kept his distance, and Edwards asked him, "Must I go with them?".

"Yes," the NCO said, "go with them and we'll come along after you." That was the normal routine every time a soldier was arrested—the soldier would be hauled in, word of his arrest would get back to the battalion, and an officer would go over to the police station to collect him. A short time later the paddy wagon arrived and Private Edwards and Mrs. Travers were taken in, where she was charged with using "abusive language" against the arresting officers. Edwards was badly cut up by the blows to his head but was simply put in a cell without any medical attention. Mrs. Travers was eventually allowed to return home that evening, and the charge against her was later dropped.

A short time later, at about 2:00 p.m., Corporal Charles Baltimore got off a streetcar on San Felipe Street. He was in uniform and was wearing the arm brassard that identified him as one of Third Battalion's military policemen, and he was at that moment on duty as such. Another soldier, perhaps the same NCO who had seen Sparks and Daniels beat Private Edwards, stopped the corporal and told him what had happened. It was a brutal beatdown, he said, and Edwards looked to be badly hurt when he was taken away. The arresting officers were still on the scene.*

"It being my duty to investigate such matters," Baltimore said in the statement he gave later that afternoon, "I approached the two policemen standing on Wilson and San Felipe streets, and asked them, in what I thought a respectful tone of voice, what had been the trouble with the soldier whom they had just arrested."

That infuriated Sparks. He replied that Edwards "had been in trouble with some woman," and drew his pistol. "Don't you like it?" he said.

Baltimore's physical actions in that moment depend upon whose version of events one accepts. Sparks later claimed that the corporal literally got in his face, almost belly to belly, and pushed up against him in a threatening manner. A Black witness, who was driving a butcher's delivery wagon down the street at that moment and saw the confrontation, said Baltimore never came into physical contact with either police officer. "I didn't hear what he said," the driver reported, "but whatever was said between [Baltimore] and the police officers made him stop about half a block away and fold his arms."

"I tried to explain that it was my duty to investigate such matters," Baltimore said in his statement, "but before I had a chance to finish my explanation, he struck me over the head with the barrel of his gun." Baltimore made no attempt to fight back, though he was a tall, athletically built young man, a couple of inches taller than Sparks, but neither did he just stand there and let Sparks hit him. He turned and ran down the street. Sparks fired at least three shots at him, even though Baltimore was unarmed. One source asserted that Daniels also fired his weapon, at least once.

Sparks later claimed he fired into the ground behind Baltimore, warning shots to make him stop running. According to every African American observer at the scene, that was a lie. "They shot right straight at him and into a street full of women and children," one witness said. "They haven't found any bullet holes in the sidewalk either, and it wasn't there that they

---

* All quotations in the following description of the confrontation between Baltimore and Sparks are taken verbatim from statements made by both individuals to Captain Shekerjian, Colonel Cress, and the Houston Citizens' Commission. Statements of civilian witnesses appear in Martha Gruening's report to the NAACP.

fired. It was at Baltimore, and no mistake." The driver of the butcher's wagon corroborated that and said, "One of the officers took out his revolver and commenced firing at him, right at him."

Baltimore ran down the block and went into a house on the right side of San Felipe Street and tried to hide. Sparks chased after him, pistol in hand, ordered him outside, and said he would kill him.

"I again tried to explain, that I was doing my duty in asking why the soldier had been arrested," Baltimore said, "and without saying anything further, he struck me over the head, two more times with his gun."

Sparks later boasted, "When I run him down and caught him he talked polite then, and he didn't seem like the same nigger he was when he first came up to me." He justified his decision to draw his gun by saying, "I didn't feel like wrestling with that big nigger," even though Baltimore had shown no inclination to fight, nor even to argue.

The two policemen arrested Baltimore and took him down to the police station. With all the shooting, and the sight of Baltimore bleeding badly from head injuries, some of the witnesses on the street thought he had been shot. Within moments that was the story that began to spread, and the rumor that reached the Third Battalion camp a short time later was that the well-liked young corporal had been killed.

Charles Baltimore was one of India Company's junior NCOs and one of the most popular men in the battalion. He was twenty-four years old that summer and came from a close family in Pennsylvania, though his father, Armistead, and mother, Annie, had died a few years before. Like Sergeant William Nesbit, Baltimore was highly regarded by the officers and senior NCOs in his unit. His military personnel records evaluated his character rating as "excellent." In June that year, his company commander recommended him for the new officer candidate training school for African American soldiers at Des Moines, Iowa. Fewer than 5 percent of enlisted men of any race ever qualified for commissioning as officers; the fact that Baltimore was one of them indicates that he was an intelligent, mature, and responsible young man whose leadership potential was recognized by the Army.

Captain Shekerjian was in his tent when a soldier, accompanied by a civilian who had just come in from town, came to tell him that "a military police [*sic*] had just been shot through the head by a civil police officer." The adjutant immediately drove over to the police station.

He found Corporal Baltimore not dead but "sitting in the chief of police's office with a gash over his right forehead," his uniform shirt stained with his blood. Shekerjian asked him if he had been shot. Baltimore said no, "but that he had been shot at."

Shekerjian had a four-way conversation with Chief Brock and two of his detectives about what had happened and what should be done about it. "After we had finished," he said, "all four of us were firmly of the conclusion that officer Sparks had been at fault and that his assault upon Corporal Baltimore was caused by the fact that he doubtless had lost his temper in previous arrests that he had made."[23]

When Sparks was called into the office to give his version of the incident, he claimed that Baltimore "had used profanity towards him." A Houston magazine later claimed that "Corporal Baltimore approached Sparks that afternoon in a blustery, offensive manner and demanded, with a string of abusive profanity, why Sparks had arrested Edwards," and tried to excuse Sparks's reaction by saying, "Policemen the country over do not like to have their actions offensively questioned by anyone of any color."[24] The other policeman, Rufus Daniels, said he never heard any profanity from the corporal and did not corroborate Sparks's claim that the soldier had pushed up against him in a threatening manner.

Brock told Sparks that he was suspended without pay pending a full investigation into his actions. That enraged Sparks. As Detective E. F. Dougherty later described the exchange, "Sparks told [Brock] that he did not think he was getting a square deal. He says, 'It looks like you are sticking up for a nigger and any man that sticks up for a nigger is no better than a nigger.'" As if that was not provocative enough, Sparks compounded his racism with insubordination. "If Chief Davidson was here he would have told these Army officers to take their damned niggers and get back to camp as quick as they could," Sparks said, and stormed out of the office.[25]*

---

* Sparks was supposed to be suspended from duty, but he was brought back on duty that night when the trouble broke out. When one of the Army inspectors general, Colonel Cress, asked Chief Brock whether Sparks was back on duty, Brock said he was. "Every day?" Cress asked. "Every day, with pay," the chief told him.

The evidence of Sparks's own actions, then and later, makes a lie of his claim that he was not shooting to kill when he fired at Baltimore. Just an hour earlier he had shot at a young man guilty of nothing more than playing dice, a petty misdemeanor that did not justify the use of lethal force. A willingness—perhaps even an eagerness—to use his gun in his interactions with Black citizens was a verified part of Sparks's record, a record that would soon get even worse. Just a few days after firing his weapon at Baltimore and the other young man, Sparks shot and killed an unarmed Black man named Wallace "Snow" Williams, who apparently had been playing craps in his own yard. Just as in the two shootings on August 23, Sparks shot at an unarmed man whose back was turned to him—the coroner's report showed that Williams was killed by bullets in the back of the neck and the back of his shoulder. A witness to the shooting, William Johnson, claimed that Sparks "pulled this negro out and kicked him in the head before he died." The stark emotion of Johnson's testimony was far more effective than good grammar could ever convey. "We are not in Russia," he said. "We are in the Land of the Brave and the home of the Free where Mr. Wilson our great president has on his shoulders the Burden of all, black and white, and if its to keep a black man from the Laws of Justice and Give the white man all the doubt like this Lee Sparks has did why we have not got no law here in the South, or Law just for one race that for Lee Sparks and his kind of murderers?"[26]

In killing Wallace Williams, Sparks graduated from being simply a racist bully to being a murderer. The only reason he did not kill Corporal Baltimore that afternoon when he shot at him was because he missed when he fired. A few weeks later, he did not miss when he shot at Williams. Sparks was indicted for the assault on Baltimore and for killing Williams. The all-white jury deliberated for less than one minute before acquitting him on all charges.

———

Within an hour of Baltimore's arrest soldiers were repeating the rumor that he had been killed, and their anger grew with each retelling. Some men began muttering that they had taken as much abuse as they were going to take, and that it was time to get some payback against the police. The groundswell of misinformation reached the guard detail at Camp Logan just as quickly.

One of the contract watchmen at Camp Logan was at the front gate when the hourly relief of the military guard took place. "At 3:30 Thursday afternoon they brought Albert Wright, Company I, and placed him on guard at the gate," the watchman recalled. "As soon as the sergeant placed him on duty and turned away he went to swearing, and I stopped him and asked him what was the matter and what he was cursing about, that we did not allow any such language around the gate. He made the remark that 'one of the damn policemen has shot up one of our men and we are not going to stand for it.' I told him they would have to comply with the law just the same as we do, and he said, 'I'll be damned if I do.'"[27] The watchman called Major Snow at Third Battalion's headquarters to report this outburst, but Snow attributed no more importance to it than he did to the other murmurings he was hearing in the battalion area. The soldier was just shooting off his mouth, he said, and was a new recruit, so the outburst should simply be ignored.

After about an hour, when Shekerjian had still not returned from the police station, Snow went over there himself to see about the two soldiers the police had assaulted and arrested. Rumors that the patrolmen had killed Baltimore were only growing, and he wanted to get the corporal back to the battalion as quickly as possible. Shekerjian agreed that Baltimore should go but thought it would be wise to leave Private Edwards at the police station overnight. "Edwards was so badly beaten up, and there was so much blood on his clothes," he said, "that I decided it would be bad policy to take him to camp before morning when I could get clean clothing for him." Shekerjian was worried about how his fellow soldiers would react if they saw how severely the police had injured him.

Snow was still at the station after 4:00 p.m. when W. F. Kessler, the police department's captain of detectives, came in. He told Brock and the two Army officers that he had heard in town there might be trouble that night. Soldiers out on pass in the civilian neighborhoods were openly expressing their outrage over what many of them still believed was Baltimore's murder. Kessler took the possibility of unrest seriously, but Snow did not. He "thought this impossible" and assured the policemen that Third Battalion was in no danger of disorder.

When Snow and Shekerjian brought Baltimore back to the battalion camp, Snow called the company first sergeants to the headquarters tent and showed them that the corporal was alive, although somewhat bruised and battered. He assured the assembled NCOs that Sparks would be punished for the assault on the two soldiers and told them to pass the word among their companies that Baltimore was alive. What he should have done was to form up the entire battalion and show the men that Baltimore survived, and addressed their outrage directly, but he never did. Rumors that the corporal was dead had flashed through the battalion like summer heat lightning; the message that he was alive was not communicated nearly as quickly, nor as clearly.

Over the next couple of hours, various people came to the camp with warnings that some kind of trouble might be brewing, though few had any concrete details to offer. Roy Owens, who ran the dance hall just outside camp, told Snow he had heard some soldiers making threatening comments. Snow thought he was "feebleminded" and ignored the warning. Other people said they had overheard soldiers warning friends to stay away from camp that night because there might be some form of trouble. Snow dismissed their concerns, also.

Just before the 6:00 p.m. retreat formation that evening, Snow finally took some active steps to get control of a rapidly deteriorating situation that he still did not fully understand. He assembled the senior NCOs and told them he was canceling the watermelon party at Emancipation Park. All passes were revoked and the entire battalion, except for the guard detail, was restricted to camp for the night. He stressed to the NCOs that this was not in any way a punitive action against the soldiers, but was only intended to keep them out of trouble that night, and he told them to convey that message to their companies. He promised, again, that the policemen responsible for mistreating their fellow soldiers would be punished in due time. What he did not understand was that he was already out of time.

An Army investigator later asked Captain Shekerjian what effect Snow's explanation had on the men.

"As far as I could see they received it all right, sir," the adjutant said. "I questioned several reliable men in the company as to how the men felt about it, after the first sergeant and officers' explanation, and they said that the feeling had gone down in their belief." Shekerjian may have believed that, but he was not close enough to the soldiers in the squads and platoons to know for sure if the earlier feelings had subsided. Some soldiers themselves later said that much of the anger had cooled by sunset that evening. But the battalion was still disturbed, and the resentment at their treatment by the police was now dangerously close to a breaking point. Along with that resentment, their fear and feeling of being under threat in a dangerous environment where they were hated and persecuted had reached a point where a single point of ignition would touch off a cataclysmic eruption.

7. THE CATACLYSM

With everything that had happened earlier that Thursday after-noon, one might have expected Third Battalion's commander to be uneasy. Two of his soldiers, one of them a popular noncommissioned officer performing his official duty, had been brutally beaten and arrested by the civilian police. One man was so bloodied that the adjutant had thought it best to leave him in the police station overnight out of concern that the sight of his battered face would further upset his fellow soldiers. As the sun began to set, several NCOs reported signs of unrest among their platoons and squads. There was muttering in the ranks and groups of soldiers were overheard telling each other they had had about all the abuse they were going to take from those "Jim Crow peckerwoods" in the police department. And now vague but persistent rumors were spreading through the battalion that white Houstonians might be contemplating some kind of violent mob action against them. A competent officer certainly would have recognized the volatility of the situation; a prudent officer would have immediately moved to get control of it.

Kneeland Snow was neither prudent nor competent.

Snow was planning to go into town that evening with a civilian friend named B. A. Calhoun, and he did not want to miss out on his recreation. He convinced himself that whatever unrest was reported was mostly just talk, soldiers shooting off their mouths as soldiers always did. He was sure he had effectively dealt with that by restricting the entire battalion to camp for the night. But at about eight o'clock, as he and Calhoun were preparing to leave camp, Vida Henry, the acting first sergeant of India Company, approached him.

"Major, I think we are going to have trouble tonight," Henry said.*
Snow asked what reason he had for thinking that.

"I don't know," Henry replied. "I just feel that way."

It was not a compelling argument, but Snow at least decided to walk over to India Company with Henry to see for himself. As they walked through Kilo Company's section of the camp, they came upon several soldiers pilfering five-round clips of ammunition out of the back of the company supply tent, and Snow realized for the first time that the threat of trouble was real.

Snow ordered the camp guards to detain the soldiers, and he hurried over to his headquarters tent and told the company buglers to sound "Officers' Call." Only four of the battalion officers were in camp at that time—Captains Shekerjian and James, and Lieutenants Snider and Jack—and Snow ordered them to fall their companies in at the upper end of the company streets, without arms. They were then to conduct a roll call to account for all their soldiers, and have their NCOs conduct a sight inspection for any unauthorized ammunition.

This check was underway when Snow realized that, as dark as it was, they could easily miss any loose ammunition purloined from the supply tents. He ordered the officers to have their soldiers return to their squad tents to get their rifles, which were normally kept under each man's cot, and return to formation to turn in all weapons to the supply sergeants. His logic was sound enough—without rifles, as he later explained, "if I did not get all the ammunition, they would not be able to use what they had"—but his earlier lack of clear communication with his soldiers turned that decision into disaster.

The company officers were just beginning to supervise the collection of weapons when Snow received a phone call from Ben Davison, the former chief of the Houston police. Davison told him that he had heard, from the only African American detective on the force, that earlier that afternoon

---

* All quotations in the following two chapters are taken verbatim from sworn statements given to two Army investigators, Colonel George Cress and/or Brigadier General John Chamberlain, or in testimony before the Houston Citizens' Commission. The citations for these sources are listed in the notes.

a Black soldier had been overheard in town saying Third Battalion was going to "shoot up the town" that night.

That information surprised Snow enough to make him think that maybe some men really had been planning personal payback, but he assured Davison the crisis was past. He had the battalion under control, he said. He was disarming the unit, and there was no longer any cause for concern. Several enlisted men were on duty in the headquarters tent at the time and they overheard what Snow said in that phone call, and it alarmed them. Word quickly spread through the battalion that their commander had let it be known to Houston's civilians that the battalion was being disarmed, leaving them vulnerable to anyone who might decide to move against them. That was never Snow's intent, but he did nothing to correct that misapprehension. He never understood how it was interpreted by his soldiers.

When Snow hung up the phone with Davison, he went to tell his friend Calhoun he would just be a few more minutes and then they could leave for their evening's diversions.

Calhoun asked him if it was still a good idea to leave the camp, with all that was happening right then.

"No, it has been settled," Snow assured him; "we caught it in time."

Down in the four rifle companies, the weapons turn-in was not proceeding as smoothly as Snow thought. Most of Kilo Company's men were on guard duty at Camp Logan that night, so there were fewer rifles to account for and not as many soldiers to check for illicit ammunition. Captain James had ordered Lima Company's nine squad leaders to collect all the rifles from their men's tents, and then he personally went around with a lantern and checked each tent to be sure nothing had been overlooked. But over in Mike and India Companies the weapons collection was far from complete, and it was in those ranks that trouble was brewing.

Snow had been India Company's commander until just three days earlier, when he was promoted to the battalion command slot after Colonel Newman's departure. He now decided to speak to his former company directly, confident he could reason with them. He gathered the soldiers around and told them he knew some men had pilfered ammunition from Kilo Company's supply tent. He warned them against attempting any ill-considered acts of personal vengeance. He told them it "was utterly foolish [and] foolhardy for them to think of taking the law into their own hands" and promised them that the policeman who assaulted Edwards and Baltimore would be punished by the civil authorities.

The soldiers were unconvinced by Snow's assurances. "Well, Major, what are we going to do when a policeman beats us up like this?" one soldier in the ranks asked.

"Report it to me," Snow said, but that satisfied no one. They had reported previous incidents of abuse from the police every time they occurred, and yet that mistreatment kept happening.

Corporal James Mitchell told Snow that they were all "tired of the State of Texas." Was there any way, he asked, "to get the battalion moved from Houston?"

Snow thought that Mitchell was being insolent by asking the question, but he tried for a placating response. "No, Corporal," he said, "it is not in my power to do it."

"We are treated like dogs here," Mitchell insisted, and a mutter of agreement among the assembled soldiers indicated the sentiment was held by more than a few of them.[1]

Things were not going well in Mike Company, either. The company commander, Captain Lindsay Silvester, had left camp about an hour earlier because he had dinner plans in town. Even after Baltimore's trouble earlier that afternoon, and even though he knew of the rising anger and deepening unrest in the battalion, Silvester decided his social plans took priority over military matters. When he left camp at 7:15, he told his company supply sergeant, "You had better stay around your tent tonight," to keep a close eye on the ammunition stocks. That suggests he was fully aware of the potential for trouble that night, yet he still left his company and went out to enjoy himself in town. In his absence, Lieutenant John Jack was left trying to exert control over a unit he had joined just ten days earlier. He had to rely on his first sergeant to verify the roll call since he did not know the soldiers well enough to recognize them by sight. First Sergeant Parker sent the men to their tents to collect their rifles, told the squad leaders to check for unauthorized ammunition, then ordered the company to line up at the supply tent to turn in their rifles.

No one moved. As Parker later said, when he gave the order, "didn't a soul moved . . . didn't one come out." Some men later claimed to have not heard him, but most of them were of the same mind as Private Pat McWhorter, who muttered loud enough to be heard by several men, "Don't a man budge." Apparently, no one wanted to be the first to comply with the order to disarm, not when the hotheads in the company were so set against it. As Private Frank Draper later explained his own failure to obey the order, he did not respond "for the simple reason that I didn't want to take a chance of turning in my rifle among 180 other men standing fast; I imagined it was the same as committing suicide." Many men, as it turned out, were afraid of giving up their weapons amid rumors that a racist mob might be assembling against them. Others, feeling the peer pressure, feared what their more belligerent comrades might do if they complied with the order to disarm.

Lieutenant Jack took out his watch and said, "I'll give you two minutes to get those rifles up there."

The entire company remained silent. No one moved.

Sergeant Parker asked the soldiers if they were "bucking," meaning "disobeying a direct order." Someone in the formation said defiantly, "Yes, we are bucking." Parker called the company forward by alphabetical order, and still no one moved in the ranks. He was an experienced NCO, however, and he then did the smartest thing he could have done, which was to order the sergeants and corporals in the company to turn in their weapons first. Those NCOs, of whom greater discipline could usually be expected, had more to lose by any act of disobedience, and their example might break the impasse among the junior enlisted men.

There was one more moment of continued hesitation, and then the NCOs began to come forward as Parker called out their names, but they did it with obvious reluctance. Several minutes into it, only about two dozen rifles had been turned in, and then Sergeant Joseph Anderson stepped up beside his first sergeant.

"Parker," he whispered, "you better take those rifles any way you can get them."

Anderson, from his position at the rear of the company formation, had seen a group of soldiers dropping back from their platoons. Those men had apparently decided they were not going to turn in their weapons, and as they moved away into the darkness, they were heard muttering that the men complying with the disarm order were "cowards." At this point in the disarming, many of Mike Company's men were still holding their rifles. Almost all of India Company's soldiers were also still armed, and that was to have tragic consequences.

As the battalion adjutant, Captain Shekerjian did not have a company to supervise, so he was trying to keep an eye on the entire battalion. With the four rifle companies formed up under their respective officers and NCOs and the weapons turn-in apparently underway, he headed over to his personal tent at the head of the India Company street. The sun had fully set by that time and the camp was dark.*

Just as he reached his tent Shekerjian heard what he later described as "a muffled roar." He turned and could see just far enough up the street to realize that a crowd of men was rushing the India Company supply tent. To Shekerjian it looked as if nearly the entire company was "struggling to get into the supply tent; men were yelling and acting like lunatics." The soldiers were going for the ammunition boxes.[2]

India Company's supply sergeant, Sergeant Fox, was standing nearby with a rifle, but he was doing nothing to halt the melee at the supply tent. Shekerjian ran up to him and demanded, "What are you doing with that rifle?"

"Everybody is getting them," Fox said.

"Do your duty and get these men in order!" Shekerjian shouted. Then he shoved his way into the crowd and tried to pull the men away from the mad scramble at the entrance of the tent.

Someone yelled at him, "They are coming!"

"Who is coming?"

"The mob is coming to the camp!"

Shekerjian apparently had not heard it, but one single shout precipitated the pandemonium. A soldier, whom most witnesses later identified as Private Frank Johnson from India Company, ran down the street yelling, "Get your guns, boys, here comes the mob!" Whether that was a prearranged signal or a spontaneous response to a perceived threat, it was enough to set off a battalion-wide panic.†

* The sun sets early in the southern states. According to the almanac for 1917, sunset on August 23 was at 6:54 p.m. Early Evening Nautical Twilight (EENT) would have ended within thirty minutes after that, so by 8:00 p.m. the camp would have been in conditions of darkness approaching full night.

† Various witnesses later testified they saw and heard Private Frank Johnson run down the company street, yelling that a mob was coming. Johnson, whose nickname was "Big Frank," was distinctive enough in his appearance that most men familiar with him would have recognized him even in poor light. Private James R. Hawkins, who wrote the only

Shekerjian tried to shove men out of the tent and shouted at them to stop, but they ignored him in the frenzy of grabbing clips of ammunition and seizing rifles at random from the weapons racks. "Ammunition boxes were being tossed out of the supply tent," the adjutant later said. "I grabbed at least two of them as they were thrown out and did keep men from taking ammunition from those boxes until someone came up and knocked me down. I had a flashlight and as I got up, flashed this light towards those ammunition boxes. Someone said, 'Drop that light or I will put a bullet through you.' I put out the light but didn't drop the flashlight. I recognized the man and found him later to be Private Ira Davis of Co. 'I'."

At about that moment, toward the upper end of India Company, someone fired a single shot, and an instant later two more rounds were fired near the supply tent itself. That triggered an absolute fusillade of uncontrolled fire as almost every soldier who had a rifle started blasting away into the darkness. "Immediately every man threw himself on the ground and commenced to fire away apparently in all directions," Shekerjian later said. "I could judge only from the flashes and from the direction in which the men were firing. I continued to dash from one man to another, calling out to cease firing and shaking them to make them understand that there was no danger except by themselves. No one paid any attention to the commands."

As Shekerjian tried to stop the shooting, a soldier crawled up to him, staying low to avoid the crossfire of wild firing.

"For God's sake, Captain, help me hold the ammunition," the man shouted over the noise of gunfire. "That is all that can save us now!" Shekerjian told him to guard the ammunition remaining in the supply tent, then he ran back out into the street just as another volley of wild, uncontrolled firing broke out.

Behind him, Corporal Robert Tillman, Sergeant Rhoden Bond, and Sergeant William Fox were trying to hold the ammunition, but the damage was already done. In the initial rush on the supply tent the NCOs lost control of most of the company's ammunition stocks, and thousands of rounds were grabbed in the chaos. Fox blew his whistle to signal a halt to the shooting, to no avail. The company bugler began blowing the call for

---

soldier-view account of that night, specifically named Johnson as the man who first shouted that a mob was coming. Hawkins wrote his account seventeen years after the event, but at least ten different witnesses told the same story.

"Cease Fire," but he stopped when someone shot a hole through the tent wall beside him.

Private Wiley Strong, a thirty-one-year-old soldier in Mike Company, had just turned in his rifle to his first sergeant when he heard someone shout, "Here they come!" Strong thought that the first shots he heard were fired by soldiers in India Company. "Everybody who could, grabbed ammunition and rifles from the storeroom," Strong said. "The men of Company M had guns. The men of Company K had guns. Company I was the first Company to commence shooting." In that first volley of gunfire, Strong was struck by a bullet in the abdomen.[3]

Shekerjian said that he "could see that there was considerable firing in every company. Co. 'K' least because that seemed to be deserted. 'I' Co., however, seemed to be shooting, almost en masse, and as rapidly as possible, rifles pointed in every direction. The firing practically ceased and I was trying to fall the men in together into shape, apparently with no assistance whatever from any noncommissioned officer. I saw Sergeant Henry and rushed to him and said, 'For God's sake make these men realize what they are doing and be fast about it.' I didn't think at that time of any possible disloyalty of Sergeant Henry." As Shekerjian worked his way along India Company's street he saw Corporal Larnon Brown gathering men together, calling out, "Let's go,—Let's go." It seemed to Shekerjian that Brown was the most active leader at that part of the camp. He heard other soldiers shouting, "Let's go to town and get to work," "Clean up the goddamn city," "Stick by your own race," and "To hell with going to France; get to work right here."

India Company was no longer under the control of any officers.

Someone shouted, "M Company has gone," and Shekerjian thought he was losing the entire battalion. He ran to the rear of the camp, where Lima Company was located. He knew almost all of Lima Company should be in the cantonment because they had no men on guard duty that night. As he passed between the tents in Kilo Company's section he ran into the company's senior noncommissioned officer, First Sergeant Thurman.

"Where is 'K' Co., Sergeant?" Shekerjian demanded.

Thurman was distraught. "I don't know, sir," he replied, "They are gone."[4] Fortunately, Thurman was wrong about that—most of Kilo Company was on the guard mount at Camp Logan, Mike Company was pulling itself together, and Lima Company was standing fast—but in the darkness and confusion no one was yet sure who was where. Almost all of India Company, however, had formed up under Sergeant Vida Henry and at that very moment was preparing to follow him out of camp.

Over in Lima Company, most of the rifles had been collected when the shout of "They are coming, they are coming!" was heard. First Sergeant Samuel Venters remembered that in an instant his entire company transformed itself into a shoving crowd of men shouting, "Give me my rifle, give me my ammunition!" Venters was knocked down in the stampede and dropped his lantern; after that he was not sure who among his soldiers went where or did what.

An Army investigator later asked Corporal Sherman Foster of Lima Company if he had had trouble preventing soldiers from grabbing ammunition in the chaos. "Yes sir, I had some trouble," Foster said. "As they got the rifles all turned in somebody ran through the camp and hollered 'the gang is coming.' I then rushed right to the supply tent to the rifles." He found his company commander, Captain James, there overseeing the serial number tally of the company's rifles. James asked what the matter was. Someone shouted, "The gang is coming to shoot up the camp!" At that moment a shot was fired, Foster recalled, but he thought it came from *outside* the camp perimeter, from somewhere out near a store on Washington Avenue. As in the other companies, the shout that a mob was coming triggered a mad rush on the supply tent by men desperate to arm themselves against the perceived threat.

Foster said that James drew his .45 pistol and shouted to him, "Are you a man?"—meaning, was he man enough to stand his ground and do his duty?

"Yes—yes, I am a man," Foster replied.

"Take charge here and guard this ammunition," James ordered. He stepped in front of the crowd of frenzied soldiers and blocked the entrance to the tent. "The first man who comes up I will blow a hole through him!" he warned.*

---

* Military regulations, then as now, not only allow an officer or NCO to use force in the performance of their duty but in some cases actually *require* it. Securing weapons and ammunition from unauthorized possession is one such circumstance where the use of lethal force is authorized and appropriate.

As James recalled it, he was in the supply tent counting the company's rifles to ensure they were all accounted for when he heard "yells in camp that the civilians were coming into camp and that there was a large mob just outside the camp. About six men of my company came to the door of the ammunition tent and seemed very frightened and said there was a mob right outside the camp and asked for their rifles." James ordered them back into formation, but the shouting and confused noise in the entire cantonment were growing louder. The enlisted men on duty in the supply tent had already grabbed their rifles and loaded them. They did not know what was happening, but they knew the sound of trouble when they heard it.

James said he then asked "if there was any man there who would help me guard the ammunition." Corporal Foster stepped forward, and as James turned to give him orders "the first shot was fired in camp, followed immediately by a burst of firing which seemed to come from I Company." At that, Lima Company stampeded in panic. James tried to hold them back, but his entire company rushed the tent. Even the threat of his drawn pistol did not keep them back, and in the crush he was knocked down and the lamp went out. "They grabbed their arms, tore open the ammunition boxes, and some of the men began firing out between the boxes in the tent," he recalled. It was sheer bedlam, and his company had lost all semblance of military order in the overwhelming panic—"There must have been thirty or more men in that little space of ten feet square and more trying to get in every moment." When James finally managed to get outside, he found soldiers firing wildly into the darkness. "They were firing in every direction and from the flashes of the guns of the ones I was closest to, most of them were firing up in the air, some as much as an angle of 45 degrees." It took him nearly another half hour to get his panic-stricken men to calm down enough to stop shooting.[5]

Sergeant Rhoden Bond also described a wild melee of confusion and terrified men. It seemed to him that his company lost all semblance of military order in one maddened instant. "It was impossible to stay them," he later testified. "Captain Shekerjian and others did their best, but no one could do anything with them. I have been in a lot of night attacks and skirmishes, and things like that, but never a thing like that before. These men were just raging. It all happened just like a big rush of wind. I was sitting down writing a letter and Sergeant Scott was taking up rifles. I had my guard in there and the mechanics. The first thing I knew the tent went over. Some men came up through the tent and turned the boxes over and got me down and threw boxes of ammunition on me and nearly broke my leg. After we got up Captain Shekerjian came in and tried to help us."[6]

As Shekerjian was moving from man to man in India Company's area, trying to get them to stop firing, Sergeant Nesbit shouted to him, "Lie down, Captain! They are shooting all over." Nesbit himself was trying to organize a hasty perimeter defense, exactly what an experienced NCO would do if he believed the battalion was facing a real, external threat. Several witnesses testified that Nesbit never fired his own weapon, but repeatedly ordered "cease fire" and tried to get the men around him back under control.

Shekerjian was in the thick of it, and so was Captain James, and the new lieutenants, John Jack and Charles Snider, were doing their ineffectual best, but the officer who should have been putting himself in the middle of the confusion, getting the battalion back under control, making his presence known to the men under his command, was nowhere to be seen.

When the shout went up that a mob was advancing on the camp, and men rushed for their weapons, Major Snow was at that moment over in India Company's area. He started to try to intervene, and then someone shouted at him to put out his light. A few seconds later the first shot rang out from somewhere at the upper end of India Company's area, and then the entire camp erupted in a roar of wild, unaimed rifle fire, with men shooting in all directions.

Snow turned and ran from the camp, leaving his battalion to tear itself apart and his junior officers and sergeants to fend for themselves.

———

The deaths and injuries of that night began in that first panicked outburst of gunfire. Third Battalion's camp might have been on the outskirts of Houston's 1917 urban footprint, but it was still surrounded by residential neighborhoods on three sides of its perimeter. The military-issue M1903 Springfield rifle had a maximum range of more than a mile, and its muzzle velocity of 2,800 feet per second meant that when its metal-jacketed .30-06 caliber bullet struck a wood-framed house that was less than a hundred yards away, the bullet could penetrate an outer pine board wall, punch a hole through a person inside the house, and carry on through at least one more interior wall before stopping. Any houses close to the camp, and anybody in those structures, were vulnerable if they were unlucky enough to be in the line of fire. Tragically, several people were.

A Mexican laborer named Manuel Garedo was killed by a bullet that struck him as he was sleeping in a garden shed at the home of Petra Sanchez, where he was a boarder. Another bullet hit A. R. Carstens as he was walking toward his house. It killed him on the spot. His body was found in a ditch in the morning. Carstens left a widow and four children. A man named E. A. Thompson was wounded by another stray bullet. He died the next day. Three other Houstonians—a man named G. W. Butcher, a girl named Alma Reichert, and a young woman named Medora Miller— were wounded in the wild firing from Third Battalion's camp, but they at least survived their injuries.*

Alma Reichert was standing in her father's small grocery store when the shooting broke out. As one of her friends remembered, "The bullet that hit Alma in the stomach first went through two walls of an icehouse, then through two more walls of another building, then through one wall of the grocery store. This slowed the bullet down and probably saved her life. Alma was inside bleeding for hours, but her family was too terrified to go for help."[7]

Other families in the area were just as terrified in the chaos, because no one really knew what was happening with all the gunfire in the night. Glidden O'Connor was a ten-year-old boy at the time and remembered that his family barricaded themselves in their house. "My mother and two younger brothers were already in the bathtub, covered with a feather bed. My father had a pistol and told me to load my rifle with 'longs' [.22-caliber long rifle cartridges]. Then we stood watch." A short time later, O'Connor "saw several black soldiers walk up to the intersection, shooting out the streetlight, and then walk down my street."[8]

A woman named Mrs. Kniggs, whose house was very close to Third Battalion's camp, was home with her two children, aged three and six. Eight or nine rifle bullets came through the wall of her house, two shots barely missing her and the children. She later said she was "so scared that she did not know what to do."[9]

---

* Alma Reichert is also identified as "Alma Reichard" in some sources. The Harris County district attorney, John Crooker, identified her as "little Thelma Reichert" in his official statement, implying that she was a small child, and gave her the wrong first name.

No one knew whether it was safer to stay in their houses or try to flee to another part of the city. The next morning the *Houston Chronicle* claimed, "Houston has a night of terror as Negro troops stationed here mutiny and rove the city, shooting and killing and invading homes and business establishments," but that was an outright exaggeration of what really happened. Even in all the chaos that night, the soldiers who marched out of camp never attempted to enter any home or business. There was no looting and no pillaging, though during those terrifying hours many feared it would happen. But it was true there was shooting and killing, and innocent people died that night. Any attempt to explain the soldiers' actions, and any effort to offer mitigation for it, must begin by acknowledging that grim truth and recognizing the lives lost. .

It is hard to say exactly how long that first outburst of uncontrolled firing lasted. No one was checking their watches in the midst of all the gunfire in the dark, but most witnesses recalled it lasting for about thirty minutes, swelling and abating in varying levels of intensity. There is a peculiar, almost predictable rhythm to the sort of shooting that happens when soldiers are caught up in a panic, especially when effective command and control are not present to get them quickly back under control. Individual pauses occurred as each man fired his weapon empty and reloaded. Other pauses occurred as men repositioned themselves. Officers and NCOs moved from man to man to try to make them stop shooting, and most men eventually stopped pulling the trigger when a sergeant was physically pushing their weapons down and yelling in their ears. But those individual cease-fires only held as long as the calming presence of a leader was present, because as soon as the NCO moved on down the line the soldiers were once again left alone with their fears. Fear is extremely contagious, especially in a unit with a large number of untrained, inexperienced soldiers, and darkness exacerbates fear. Several times that night, the shooting slackened and started to diminish, and then someone somewhere along the perimeter would fire a shot at something imagined in the darkness, and instantly everyone would begin blasting away again without really knowing why or at what they were shooting.

After Major Snow fled the camp, there were no more officers in India Company's area. Acting First Sergeant Vida Henry was the senior

NCO present, and when the shooting slackened, he assumed control of the company. When the first protracted bout of firing finally stopped, Henry ordered India Company to form up and told the men to make sure they had full canteens and plenty of ammunition. He was going to lead the company out in a sortie and meet the threat of the advancing mob head-on, in an offensive action.

Several junior NCOs thought that was a bad idea. Sergeant Nesbit argued the better tactic was to stay in the camp, where the massed firepower of three rifle companies could defend the camp from a strong static position. At least three other NCOs made the same argument, but Henry was adamant. When Corporal James Wheatley tried to persuade him to stay and defend the camp, Henry replied, "There will be no camp to return to," and he ordered India Company into a column of fours with an advance guard, a main body, and a rear guard composed of Corporals Wheatley, Jesse Moore, Larnon Brown, and Charles Baltimore.

One question later asked repeatedly was why more than a hundred soldiers fell in and followed Henry out of camp that night. Major Snow's earlier order was that all soldiers were to remain in camp, so Henry's decision to march out could be (and later was) interpreted as deliberate disobedience of that order. However, that after-action analysis never considered a crucial question of military law and operational necessity—namely, what happens when the tactical situation changes after an order is given, particularly when the person who gave the original order is no longer in control of a rapidly changing situation?

Shouts that an armed mob was advancing on the camp precipitated the panic, and if such a mob was real, that posed an actual military threat. Sergeant Henry chose the military option of taking a rifle company out to meet it head-on—and subsequent events would prove the mistake of that choice. But he was the senior military authority present in India Company at that moment, with Major Snow somewhere out in the civilian streets and every other battalion officer busy trying to regain control of the other companies. As far as the enlisted men knew, when their first sergeant ordered them to form up and march out, it was a legitimate order. Some men were eager to go, others wanted to stay with the battalion, but most of the soldiers in the area obeyed and fell in with the rest of their company. Henry's personal motivations in giving that order have been the subject of intense debate ever since, but the individual soldiers were caught in a dilemma. It is probable that none of them really knew what was happening in that moment, so they followed the only operational authority they could see and hear. At least one soldier later testified that he would have remained in camp if only he had heard his officer's voice countermanding Henry's order, but there were no officers there to exert that essential leadership.

India Company moved out of the camp, armed and ready for a fight. As they passed through the gate, a Kilo Company soldier on guard there, Private Bryant Watson, left his post and fell in with them. That was an outright violation of military regulations. Watson was on guard duty, and nothing excused his choice to abandon his post and join another unit in their sortie.

———

As Third Battalion disintegrated into chaos, a farmer named R. R. McDaniel happened to be driving by the camp's front gate with several Black field hands who worked for him. Suddenly a soldier ran up out of the darkness and jumped onto the running board of his car. A volley of rifle fire broke out from inside the camp just as the car drew abreast of the camp perimeter, and the unknown soldier jumped off and disappeared into the night.*

McDaniel accelerated to get out of the area, and as he did, Major Snow appeared from the direction of the camp, running like a man pursued by his nightmares. He jumped into the car, tumbling in on top of the men in the backseat.

"Oh, lord, save me!" Snow cried. "Oh, God, take me away from here; they are going to kill me!"[10]

McDaniel told him to keep quiet, and jerked the steering wheel around, trying to make a hard three-point turn in the middle of the narrow road. The car's turning radius was not tight enough and he ran the vehicle into a ditch. McDaniel and the field hands piled out to manhandle the car back onto the road, at which point Snow also jumped out, but not to help. He sprinted off down the road, leaving the other men behind.

McDaniel and the others quickly wrestled the car back onto the road, and they soon caught up with Snow, who was still running hard down the road. McDaniel managed to get him back into the car.

---

* McDaniel did not know who this man was and never identified him.

A few minutes later, they encountered a policeman named L. E. Gentry and his partner, A. F. Butler, who were driving toward 3-24 Infantry's camp to investigate the gunfire. Snow was still panic-stricken. "Go back or you'll be killed," he shouted to the police officers. "They're killing everyone back there!"

A few blocks farther on, McDaniel stopped the car at a drugstore. The field hands took off to make their own way back home while McDaniel helped Snow inside and asked the pharmacist to give the major something to calm him down, as he was still so hysterical as to be "practically useless." Snow tried to use the store's telephone to contact the Illinois National Guard camp but couldn't get through. The pharmacist asked him what the trouble was, and Snow sat down and put his handkerchief over his face. "It is terrible," he gasped. "They shot at me fifteen times and I don't see why they didn't kill me." He was so agitated that the pharmacist finally gave him a dose of ammonia spirits to settle him down.[11]*

After about thirty minutes McDaniel put Snow back in his car and drove off to find someone of military authority. He later said that Snow "huddled in the rear of the car and would not get on the front seat with him."[12]

Back in the Third Battalion camp, the company officers were struggling to regain control of their panic-stricken troops. In Major Snow's absence, Captain Shekerjian was the next senior officer in the chain of command. That left him responsible for trying to salvage everything that Snow had abandoned.

Shekerjian ran out toward the camp perimeter and found most of the soldiers there lying prone, oriented outward, sporadically firing out into the darkness beyond the fence line. The men of Lima Company were deployed in a line of skirmishers, indicating that some degree of command and control was in effect. To Shekerjian's eye, "the non-commissioned

---

* Snow later claimed that McDaniel was drunk and that he had to persuade him to cooperate with his military mission. He may have been trying to discredit McDaniel's testimony, which described Snow as being panic-stricken and nearly hysterical. However, when an Army investigator later asked the pharmacist, F. B. Dwyer, if McDaniel was "perfectly sober" that night, Dwyer replied, "Judging from what I could see of him he was."

officers seemed to hold them pretty well," so he moved on to check Mike Company's status. "M Co. seemed to be deserted, but I saw one man and asked him where M Co. was." For a moment, Shekerjian thought his fears that Mike Company had left camp with Sergeant Henry were confirmed, but the soldier told him no, Mike Company was holding firm under the only officer it still had present, Lieutenant John Jack. "I saw Lt. Jack and heard his voice speaking," Shekerjian remembered. "I felt from the general attitude that M Co. was in fair shape. I therefore hurried back to L Co. to help out my utmost there."[13]

Over in Lima Company, Shekerjian asked the men where their company commander was. A soldier told him Captain James was "talking to the company." Shekerjian asked him "if everything was all right in L Co." The man replied, "We are staying with our captain."

James was moving up and down the skirmish line of his soldiers, reassuring them that he was with them, urging them to hold fast and not break. The young officer's efforts appeared to be working; when Shekerjian got there Lima Company seemed to be holding firm. "I asked Captain James if his men would stay together," he said. "The men around him answered, yes, they would." Shekerjian put the question to the soldiers directly, shouting to make himself heard over the gunfire still blasting out from different parts of the camp. Would Lima Company stand their ground?

"We are staying with our captain," the men shouted back.

The junior officers and NCOs were slowly managing to restore order to Lima and Mike Companies. The moment of greatest crisis seemed over, and at that moment a group of India Company men led by Corporal Larnon Brown came back into camp. They were trying to convince the remainder of the battalion to join the men Sergeant Henry was leading out of camp.

"They were yelling, 'Let's get L and M Companies," Shekerjian said, "and as they came down, called out 'Come on L Co."

Captain James put himself physically between his company and the men from India Company and shouted, loud enough for his own soldiers to hear him, "L Company stays with their Captain!" All up and down the skirmish line, his men took up the call and echoed it back: "L Company stands by its Captain!" Many of these men shared the opinion held by their first sergeant, Samuel Venters, about their company commander. "Captain James is every inch a soldier, an officer, and a gentleman," Venters said later, "and all of the men like him and would be willing to go down with him, to die with him. I think all the men in the company thought the same."[14]

It was hard to tell in the dark, but Shekerjian thought that about thirty or forty men of India Company were in the group that returned to camp to try to convince soldiers of the other companies to join their sortie into the city. The adjutant got face-to-face with Brown and tried to persuade him not to march out with Sergeant Henry's column.

"Wait a minute, Corporal," he said. "Let me talk to you."

As Shekerjian recalled it later, Brown was deeply emotional in that moment. When he responded, he spoke quietly but intensely, and the adjutant saw tears on his face. "Captain Shekerjian, we ain't going to be mistreated," he said.

Shekerjian tried one more time to persuade the soldiers to remain in camp. "I called out to halt and listen to me," he said, "and then every way conceivable I tried to hold these men back. I asked them to stay with me." Some of the men wavered and seemed swayed by his appeal, but others shouted, "Let's go, we have work to do." Shekerjian claimed that at least one man whom he could not identify in the darkness yelled, "Put a bullet into him and shut his goddamn talk." No one acted on that murderous suggestion, but most of the men turned around and headed back out of camp to rejoin Henry's column. A few of them remained behind with Shekerjian. He had been standing more or less in the middle of this group as he tried to reason with them, and he recalled that all the men behind him stayed put, but the others whom he was not physically blocking followed Corporal Brown out into the night. It was a stark example of how critical an officer's personal presence was to reasserting military order and discipline in a chaotic situation.

One question asked over and over during the initial uproar and panicked firing, when the officers and NCOs of Lima, Kilo, and Mike Companies were desperately trying to regain control of their men, was "Where is Major Snow?" Everyone was looking for the battalion commander, but no one could find him. Shekerjian was asked several times where Snow was during those critical moments, and he remembered that the last he had seen of his commanding officer was just before the cry of an approaching mob went up and everyone started shooting. He did not see Snow again for almost four hours.

When Snow finally, briefly, returned to the camp, he told Shekerjian he had been busy sending a telegram to the department commander at Fort Sam Houston and "he had been delayed coming back helping to establish the Militia lines across the street." Since those National Guard troops who cordoned off the streets were under the command of their own officers, all of whom knew the layout of the city quite as well as Snow, and since several of those officers were actually senior to him in rank, there was absolutely no tactical necessity for Snow to have delayed his return to his own battalion.

Captain James, who had managed to hold Lima Company together by the sheer effort of his personal presence, had also lost track of his battalion commander when he most needed him. "I looked all around for Major Snow," James later said in his official statement; "I had not seen him since he gave orders to make the check" for rifles and ammunition. James said he did not see Snow again until sometime around 10:45 that night.[15] Lima Company's supply sergeant, Rhoden Bond, had a similar recollection when he was asked what his battalion commander was doing at that time. "I [had] not seen [Major] Snow from just after the shooting started until after it was all over," he said in his testimony.[16]

Kilo Company was under the tenuous leadership of Second Lieutenant Charles Snider. Snider was a newly commissioned officer two ranks junior than was usual for a company commander, and he had joined the battalion only nine days earlier. He barely knew any of the men in his company well enough to recognize their faces, and they did not yet know him. When the panic erupted, he "went to look for Major Snow and couldn't find him." Not knowing what else to do, Snider returned to his company. "Captain Shekerjian told me to stay with I & K Co's. and I remained with them until 2 a.m.," Snider testified, and he claimed that at no point earlier that afternoon had Major Snow ever told him any of the details about the trouble involving Corporal Baltimore downtown. The battalion commander's order to restrict the men to camp that night was never conveyed to Snider as it should have been—rather than hearing it directly from his battalion commander, he only learned of it from his company first sergeant when the word went out to collect the rifles at about 8:05 that evening. Snider's only advantage that night was that Kilo Company had the guard mount at Camp Logan, so most of his soldiers were on duty over there and not present in the battalion cantonment.

In contrast with Snow's decision to absent himself from camp, not only did his junior officers stand their ground and try to keep the battalion together, but at least one officer who had prior permission to be away from camp that night endeavored to get back to the unit when the trouble broke out. Second Lieutenant Edward Hudson was one of the two newest officers in the battalion, having joined the unit just nine days earlier along with Lieutenant John Jack. Hudson had barely had time to introduce himself to his company, but if he was new to the 24th Infantry, he was certainly not new to the Army. He had ten years' prior service as an NCO and earlier that summer had been promoted from sergeant when he accepted a lieutenant's commission in the expanding Regular Army. He knew soldiers, and he knew where he was supposed to be when his unit was in trouble.

Hudson was downtown in Houston on a pass when he heard the distant sound of heavy, sustained rifle fire coming from the direction of Third Battalion's cantonment. He immediately realized something was very wrong—no large training exercise was scheduled for that night, and even at that distance he could tell the difference between the high-velocity crack of live ball ammunition and the sound of lower-powered blank cartridges. The gunfire he was hearing was live fire. Something was very wrong, and Hudson immediately set out to rejoin his unit.

When he reached the fire station on the edge of the San Felipe District, he found Major Snow there with a group of National Guard officers. Snow was still highly agitated and busying himself with minor tasks. "He ordered me to go back to camp and watch I Company," Hudson recalled, "and that in case any trouble came up for me to pick men I could depend on." It was a ridiculous order. Not only did Snow still make no effort to return to the battalion himself, but he also now directed one of the most junior officers in the unit to assume control of the company that was at the heart of the whole trouble, the company that Snow himself would be expected to know best. When Hudson recalled his conversation with his commander that night, he said, "I had been with the company about ten days." In such a short span of time, how was he to know who among the rank-and-file soldiers was dependable and who was not? Nonetheless, Hudson did not argue about it but continued on into the night to find out what was happening to his battalion.[17]

Among the group of National Guard officers at the fire station, a hasty plan emerged for a response to the crisis. Captain L. A. Tuggle would take a couple of truckloads of soldiers from 5th Illinois Infantry and go to

3-24 Infantry's camp. What he would do when he got there would depend entirely on what sort of situation he found—no one yet knew if the men who remained in camp were under the control of their officers, nor even if any officers were still alive. At the same time, Captain Joseph Mattes, the commander of Alpha Battery, 2nd Field Artillery of the Illinois National Guard, would try to determine exactly where were the Third Battalion soldiers who had left camp. The first confused (and wildly exaggerated) reports claimed that mutinous bands of Black soldiers were rampaging through the streets shooting at every white face they saw, but the military authorities did not yet know exactly how many men were involved, who was leading them, or where they were going. Houston police officer E. J. Meineke and a Texas National Guardsman named Corporal M. D. Everton joined Mattes as guides, since they were familiar with the city, and two other Guardsmen, Corporal Zimmie Foreman and Private Alphens Jones, made up the rest of the group. Mattes and the other men climbed into an open-top touring car, with Foreman driving, and they headed in the direction of the sporadic gunfire they could hear occasionally reverberating from the San Felipe District.

In the meantime, a new threat was developing. A crowd of angry Houstonians, all of them white men armed with rifles, shotguns, and pistols, had begun gathering at the fire station. They had some idea of marching down to Third Battalion's camp. The military officers immediately put a stop to that, because they understood that if an armed mob of civilians approached the camp, which finally seemed to have quieted down, it would precipitate a new round of gunfire, and this time there would be targets for the soldiers to shoot at. The loss of life would be catastrophic if that were allowed to happen. Captain William Rothrock, the Camp Logan engineer officer, positioned a car across the street to block it off, then climbed up on the hood where he could be seen and ordered the crowd to not advance any closer to the camp. He and the other military officers would use force, if necessary, to keep any civilians from advancing on Third Battalion's cantonment. National Guard troops were placed to cordon off the approaches to the camp, covering the streets with machine guns, and the civilian would-be vigilantes were kept at bay.

A mile away at Camp Logan, the sound of heavy gunfire from Third Battalion's camp had carried clearly through the night. Civilians living near the camp thought it was some sort of tactical training, or "mock battle," though they wondered why the Army was doing so much shooting on a night exercise. Soldiers who were on the guard detail at Camp Logan, however, recognized it as live fire, not blank ammunition, and thought their battalion encampment was under attack.

Sergeant Arthur Taylor was on duty that night as sergeant of the guard at one of the Camp Logan warehouses. At about 8:30 the soldiers of the guard detail heard the shooting break out in the direction of Third Battalion's cantonment. A short while later a panic-stricken soldier from the battalion camp, Private Blaine Adams, arrived, bringing a wild story of the battalion being fired on by civilians and overrun by an armed mob. That mob was now coming to Camp Logan to attack the Black soldiers there, he claimed.

"We had only five rounds of ammunition [each] and we didn't have enough to protect ourselves against a mob," Taylor recalled. "Five rounds was nothing to protect ourselves. If the men are falling back here for protection we can't do anything after five rounds is gone. I said the only thing we can do is go to the 27th Illinois for protection. I had 21 privates there and 2 corporals." Taylor and the soldiers of his detail headed for the nearby camp of the Illinois National Guard, where he reported to Captain George Allen, the commanding officer of one of the Illinois rifle companies.

In the investigation after the incident, Taylor was asked, "What made you think it was necessary, with a guard of about 30 men and five rounds of ammunition, that you couldn't protect yourself against anything that might come up?"

"Well," Taylor said, "from the report we got from Private Adams he told me that the mob was coming that way and driving his soldiers back on me and I have read in the papers that there are often 1000 men in a mob and we only had five rounds of ammunition." Thinking of the tactical situation from the perspective of an infantryman, Taylor's logic was correct—he had neither men nor ammunition enough to hold off an attack by a large mob, assuming that mob was determined to make a fight of it, and Camp Logan was not a defensible position. Taking shelter with a larger military unit, even one as distrusted as the Illinois National Guard, was a tactically sensible decision. Taylor's statement also showed the degree to which the specter of a southern race mob was a very real fear among the men of 3-24 Infantry.[18] When an officer of the Illinois battalion told Taylor later that night to have his men hand over their weapons, the sergeant flatly refused. "No sir, not on your life," he said. "We want some protection and we are not going to give up our only protection."[19]

Another group of Third Battalion men on guard duty at Camp Logan that night made different decisions. They had been on guard since 1:00 that afternoon, but they had all heard about the police beating up Private Edwards and Corporal Baltimore earlier that afternoon. The rumor that first flashed around the guard posts was that Baltimore was dead. By 6:00 p.m. they heard the correct version of the story when the chow wagons brought their supper, and they learned that Baltimore had returned to the battalion battered but alive. The soldiers on the chow detail also told them the mood back at camp was growing more resentful and angrier. Two hours later they heard the fusillade of gunfire break out at their battalion cantonment.

The military warehouses situated along the railroad tracks at the edge of Camp Logan were designated as the Lower A Division guard post. When the shooting began, just before 8:30 p.m., an argument quickly developed over what might be happening back at the battalion. One of the soldiers, Private Babe Collier, said he was sure someone was "shooting up the camp"; another soldier thought that a white mob must be "killing our men over at the camp." Several men insisted they should immediately head to the battalion camp to aid their comrades. The corporal of the guard at Lower A Division was Corporal John Washington, and he thought the suggestion of going to Third Battalion's camp was tactically unfeasible. "What's the use to go to camp?" he said. "You will get killed trying to get in." It was a real concern, for a couple of reasons. On the one hand, they might have to fight their way through untold numbers of armed civilian attackers, if such existed; on the other, they might find themselves trying to enter their own camp in the face of heavy fire from soldiers who probably would confuse them with an attacking force. Washington apparently did not point out to his men that abandoning a guard post or absenting oneself from one's appointed place of duty were both extremely serious violations of military regulation. Nonetheless, within a few minutes fifteen soldiers of the Lower A Division left their guard post without authorization and moved out of the Camp Logan perimeter into the surrounding neighborhoods.

8. THE KILLING

The Third Battalion men of the guard detail were not the only Regular Army soldiers at Camp Logan that night. Most of the others were white troops in support units, and none of them were armed. Captain Warren M. Morgan of the Army Quartermaster Corps commanded Bakery Company No. 34. In the statement he later gave to military investigators, he remembered, "The shooting began about 8:25 by my time and about 30 minutes later an automobile passed me on the road." This automobile was a jitney driven by E. M. Jones. Several passengers of the vehicle were soldiers dressed in the same olive drab uniforms worn by Houston's police, which may have been a factor in what happened next.

About half a block from where Morgan was standing, he noticed a small group of soldiers moving along the darkened street—the men who had left their post at the Lower A Division guard detail. These men shouted, "Halt!" and then suddenly opened fire on the passing jitney, probably because they mistook the military passengers' olive drab uniforms for police. "Almost instantly within three to five seconds they commenced firing and I should judge about 20 shots were fired," Morgan said. "I lay down for safety, being in the line of fire. As soon as they had ceased I went up near the car and called to the sentries and no one answered. . . . Not knowing what the cause of the battle was or who it was carrying it on I didn't stop and talk to those people but came on to camp and warned the Truck Company of the fact that I saw a company of armed 'nigger' soldiers within about 150 yards of their camp, then came on to my own company, got them out of camp and scattered, we being unarmed. In coming to my own camp between

Warehouse Nos 1 and 2 I saw about a company of 'nigger' soldiers coming through there."[1]*

Jones, the driver of the jitney, was severely wounded in the shooting. One of his passengers, a man named Charles T. Clayton, was hit high in the left arm by a bullet that shattered the bone. The wounded men were transported to the nearest medical facility, the Illinois National Guard's aid station. Jones arrived first, shortly after nine o'clock, but there was nothing the battalion surgeon could do for him. He died of his wounds about ten minutes after arriving. He left a wife and six children and his widowed mother, who lived with his family. Clayton survived, but the damage inflicted by the high-velocity bullet was so severe that his arm had to be amputated and he was never able to return to his work as a lineman.

Other casualties were inflicted as Sergeant Henry's column of infantrymen moved through the civilian neighborhoods. The soldiers used the cover of darkness to mask their movements, especially for the first part of their route. Many people saw and heard them as they passed along their streets, but most kept their heads down and tried not to attract their notice. Armed men in the night were dangerous, especially when no one really knew what they were about or what was going on. A few civilians, however, were less cautious.

As the column of soldiers passed a house at 4910 Lillian Street, several teenagers came out onto the porch. One of the boys, Willie Drucks, asked his half sister Mary Winkler to turn on the porch light so he could see who was passing by in the street. When the light came on it illuminated several soldiers at the rear of the column. One of the rear-guard NCOs, later said to be Corporal Jesse Moore, gave the order "shoot that light out." In response, two soldiers knelt and fired. If they were supposed to aim for the porch light, it seems clear that they ignored the order and instead aimed at the three young people on the porch. Mary's brother Fred Winkler was killed instantly, and Willie was hit in the arm, a terrible wound that later required the amputation of the limb. Mary snapped off the light and the soldiers vanished into the darkness.[2] As they passed another house a short

---

* It is unclear why the transcriptionist of Morgan's statement put those racial slurs in quotation marks, but they appear that way in the original typewritten transcript of his interview with Colonel Cress, the Southern Department inspector general. Those quotation marks do not appear in almost any other witness statement that used the racial slur.

way down the same street, the soldiers saw a twelve-year-old girl named Jeanette Thiel and two of her family members watching them from a window. There was no shooting in that instance; instead, soldiers shouted at them to get away from the window and moved on down the street.[3]*

A Houstonian named Charles W. Wright, who lived a few blocks away from Third Battalion's camp, ran out into the streets to see what the shooting was all about. He suddenly found himself surrounded by Black soldiers. Wright stopped and raised his hands, and an instant later he was shot through both arms. The wounds caused catastrophic tissue damage and loss of blood. Wright died of his wounds a short time later, but not before relating to his brother the story of what had happened to him.[4]

When the soldiers reached the intersection of Lillian and Bethje Streets, they split into two separate groups and began moving parallel to each other, about a block apart. That division of the force made it even more difficult for later investigation to pinpoint which men were where during the chaos that night, or who did what. It was a critical issue, because people were killed in different locations *after* that separation.

A few moments after the main body split up, the soldiers who continued moving down Lillian Street came upon a group of four uniformed policemen—T. A. Binford, L. G. Bryson, Tom Goodson, and Charles McPhail—along with a civilian named W. A. Wise, all of them grouped under a bright streetlight. The policemen were in the process of loading an injured man into McPhail's car. The wounded man was G. W. Butcher, who had been struck by a random bullet during the first uncontrolled firing from the battalion camp.

When the soldiers saw the police uniforms they opened fire, prompting McPhail to speed away, leaving the other four men to drop Butcher on the road and take cover. The policemen returned fire, but revolvers against military rifles made for a one-sided firefight. Both Binford and Wise were wounded and Butcher took a bullet in the groin before the soldiers broke contact and moved on in the darkness. Incredibly, after suffering multiple gunshot wounds, Butcher survived.

---

* The Harris County district attorney, John Crooker, claimed that the soldiers fired at the Thiel family but missed; he also claimed that the soldiers deliberately fired into almost every residence they passed with the specific intent of killing or injuring the occupants. No other source supports his allegations.

At the corner of San Felipe and Wilson Streets, the soldiers encountered two mounted policemen, Ross Patten and W. H. Long. The mounted officers of the Houston Police Department had incurred a particular enmity among the Black soldiers because of their reputation for aggressiveness in their dealings with both African American civilians and military personnel. The infantrymen at the head of the column opened fire. Patten was wounded in the arm and leg, and his horse was killed; Long galloped off down Timpson Street and escaped.*

———

In at least six separate incidents that night, soldiers encountered automobiles that approached them in the darkness. Their actions in those moments ranged from disciplined restraint to ambush and outright murder.

In one of the first of these incidents, a car driven by a civilian named J. D. Dixon came up the street from behind Henry's column and unexpectedly met the soldiers at the rear of the formation. When the shooting broke out in Third Battalion's camp, a cry had gone up in Dixon's neighborhood: "You had better run for your lives, the colored soldiers are on a riot." Dixon quickly loaded his wife, two children, and his brother into the car, and only realized that Henry's column of soldiers had already passed his house when he drove up behind them.

Two soldiers in the rear guard leveled their weapons at the car and ordered Dixon to stop. He explained to them ("very politely," as he said later) that he was just trying to get his family to safety and asked them what was going on. "The men told me a lot of damn white people had it in for them, and they wasn't going to stand for it," Dixon recalled, but once the soldiers realized the car contained a woman and children, they did not detain them any further. One unidentified soldier who seemed to be in charge, later described as "a large yellow negro," told him to take his family home and stay off the streets, and he did.[5†]

———

* Patten's name also appears with the spelling "Patton" in some records. Patten died of his wounds on September 8, 1917.

† Though not certain, it is highly possible that this unidentified soldier was Sergeant William Nesbit. Being of mixed race, Nesbit was described in other contemporaneous sources as "yellow" or "mulatto," he was in the column of soldiers that night, and the restraint

Near the 1600 block of Washington Avenue, a car occupied by an Army Quartermaster Corps officer named Captain F. S. Haines, along with another Army officer, was traveling toward the battalion camp. The car rounded a corner, and the officers found themselves in the midst of armed soldiers in the street. As Haines later described it, "A bunch of negro soldiers came swarming out through the buildings and they came up to the car to see if we were armed and took our guns away from us." His impression of the soldiers was that some of them seemed keyed up and ready for a fight, while others were rather unenthusiastic about what they were doing—he thought some of them were "lukewarm and ready to quit." In the darkness Haines could not see any of the men well enough to be able to identify them later. "Lt. Perkins and I were in uniform," Haines said, "and they asked who we were and what we were doing there and I told them we were on our way to camp and they looked at Lt. Perkins' shirt collar and there was no doubt but they knew we were officers. I should judge there were sixty or seventy in the crowd and when I was there, there was about 30 or 40 rounds of shots fired," but he was certain that none of those shots were fired at him and his companion. He described the soldiers as "a grim lot of men."[6] One thing he clearly recalled was that one of the NCOs in the group, later identified as Corporal James Wheatley, spoke up to argue that they should allow Haines and Perkins to pass unmolested. "Don't you see," he reported Wheatley saying, "these men are officers in uniform."[7]

In another incident on a street just outside the battalion camp, an unidentified group of soldiers stopped a civilian ambulance by shooting out the front tire. The soldiers did not shoot at the three men in the ambulance but ordered them to dismount from the vehicle. The ambulance driver later reported that a soldier told him, "Get out you God damn white son-of-a-bitch, and run." The three men ran, sped on their way by a few shots fired over their heads.

The first lethal encounter with a moving car in the darkness occurred on San Felipe Street just after the incident where the horse-mounted police officers Patten and Long were fired on. A car containing police officers Rufus Daniels, W. C. Wilson, Horace Moody, and C. E. Carter, driven by a

shown in the interaction with the Dixon family was in keeping with Nesbit's personal reputation and previous conduct.

civilian named Charles W. Hahl, came down the street toward the soldiers. The infantrymen opened fire, Hahl stopped in the middle of the street, and the occupants scrambled out of the vehicle. At the sight of the police uniforms, a soldier allegedly shouted, "Here comes some more police; let's get them!" Daniels, the patrol officer who was usually partnered with Lee Sparks and who had been present when Private Edwards and Corporal Baltimore were assaulted and arrested earlier that day, ran toward the soldiers, firing a pistol. It was a foolhardy maneuver. Daniels was a big man coming straight on at very close range, and the soldiers shot him down. The other policemen took cover. Moody fired two rounds and drew an instantaneous volley of return fire. He went down under the barrage, shouting, "I am shot! My leg is shot off!" Carter and Wilson put a tourniquet on his leg, but the wound was fatal. Moody died the next day.[8]

The soldiers did not pursue the survivors but instead gathered around Daniels's body. Many of them were familiar with Daniels's reputation as a heavy-handed enforcer of the hated Jim Crow ordinances, and they recognized him when they looked at him lying dead in the street. "There is the white trash we got," a soldier said. Several men used the butts of their rifles to club his face before they moved on. One soldier, Private Harrison Capers, picked up the pearl-handled revolver Daniels had carried and stuck it in his belt.[9]

At about the same time this incident occurred, soldiers at the rear of the column saw Streetcar Number 317 turning onto San Felipe Street. Several soldiers opened fire on it and wounded the driver, W. H. Burkett. The streetcar represented no threat to them whatsoever, and there was no justification for shooting at it. Perhaps the soldiers fired on it simply because of their long-simmering resentment over the city's hated Jim Crow laws, of which the streetcar was a rolling embodiment.

A short time later, another civilian car came down the street and encountered the lead elements of the column. This vehicle contained two policemen and three eighteen-year-old civilians—James Lyon, Asa Bland, and Eli Smith. The three teenagers had decided to head toward the sound of gunfire to get involved in whatever was happening, and they were armed. As they drove toward San Felipe they encountered police officers Ira Raney and John Richardson and offered to give them a ride into the district. The policemen knew something serious was happening, but the teenagers acted like it was just an exciting lark.

The soldiers called out for the car to halt, but Lyon, who was driving, either did not hear or ignored the command, and the infantrymen opened fire. The car skidded to a stop and the men bailed out into the street. Accounts differ as to exactly what happened, but Raney was shot and killed. Smith was killed, too, but the others were still alive. Lyon was hit in the arm and tried to run but was shot down. He survived his wounds, as did Officer Richardson, who was also wounded, but not by bullets. Private Henry Peacock clubbed Richardson over the head so hard that he broke the wooden stock of his rifle. Other soldiers beat Bland down into the street with their rifle butts, but he also survived. The soldiers regrouped and moved on down the street, leaving the dead and wounded behind them.

Lyon, Smith, and Bland did not have to be there at that bloody intersection. They went looking for trouble with all the impetuosity of the young men they were and found more trouble than they probably ever imagined. Police officers Raney and Richardson *did* have to be there on that street, because they were law enforcement officers, and they went forward into harm's way because it was their duty. "It is one of the pathetic things of the after happenings," one of the city's newspapers later declared, "for the Houston public to know that Officer Raney is survived by a wife and eight children, and that the family has nothing whatever in the way of an income or savings." Raney's youngest daughter was only fourteen months old when her father was killed, and the long shadow of his death loomed over his family for decades after.*

At about 9:30 that night, an hour after the trouble began and about the time that Sergeant Henry's column of soldiers was moving into the San Felipe District, Captain L. A. Tuggle arrived outside Third Battalion's camp with several truckloads of the 5th Illinois Infantry's National Guardsmen. This was the first organized military response after the wild outbreak of gunfire. The camp was now dark and quiet. Whatever

---

* This quotation comes from a newspaper clipping that does not show the name or date of the publication. The original clipping is in the personal collection of Sandi Hajtman, Ira Raney's great-granddaughter.

the cause of the disturbance, it seemed to have ended, at least within the camp itself.

Tuggle decided to leave his troops at a distance from the camp and venture in by himself on foot, which in retrospect was probably the most sensible thing he could have done—the appearance of the hated Illinois National Guardsmen might easily have precipitated another outburst of violence among 3-24 Infantry.

Once inside the camp, Tuggle tried to find the battalion commander. He eventually located an enlisted orderly, who took him to the battalion headquarters tent, but Major Snow was nowhere to be found. "We walked down the street inquiring and found an officer," Tuggle recalled, "and he told me that Snow was not in camp and as I went along the street the various men would use the military courtesy and everything was quiet and the men all appeared to be under good discipline ordinary camp routine. Then finding out that I couldn't get to talk to [Major] Snow, I told the captain [Shekerjian] I would take my men and go down the street. He told me that some troopers had left and gone down Washington Avenue. He didn't tell me how many." This was the first confirmation Tuggle had that the trouble had moved into Houston itself and that the rumors he had heard of multiple shootings in the civilian neighborhoods were true and involved soldiers of 3-24 Infantry.[10]

With the battalion cantonment finally quieting down and the remaining companies back under control of their officers, Shekerjian finally had time to deal with his wounded. Incredibly, in all the uncontrolled shooting that had started in the center of the camp, with hundreds of rounds fired through and across the camp's interior lines, only Private Wiley Strong had been hit.* But Strong was badly hurt, gut-shot by a rifle bullet that ripped open his abdomen. The battalion medical officer, First Lieutenant W. S. Chaffin, treated him as best he could at the scene but told Shekerjian that Private Strong had to be evacuated immediately. Unfortunately, there was no ambulance.

Major Snow's civilian friend Calhoun was still in the camp, serving no purpose and being of no help to anyone, so Shekerjian found a use for him. He told Calhoun to drive into the city and send back an ambulance to

---

* Captain James later estimated that at least a thousand rounds had been fired, "judging by the cartridges I saw lying on the ground."

carry the wounded soldier to a hospital. He also gave Calhoun an explicit warning to convey to the police: "The men in camp were under his control and that he would meet any body of men sent out there, and under no circumstances would he allow any citizens to start firing in the neighborhood of the camp." Shekerjian knew all too well Texans' propensity for violent reaction, and he made it very clear that Third Battalion was able to meet force with force if any angry civilians decided to resort to vigilantism, or if the Houston police department attempted to disarm the battalion.[11]

At this point, with soldiers off the military reservation and the sound of occasional rifle shots still reverberating through the civilian neighborhoods, Third Battalion's officers tried to get a positive count of who was still in the camp. Several things kept this from being a straightforward or accurate process. The camp was in near-total darkness, and the head count had to be done in each company by lantern or flashlight. Forming up the battalion and calling the roster would have been simplest, but it was utterly impractical—the men were still on edge and unsettled, and no one wanted to leave the assumed safety of the hasty skirmish lines along the camp perimeter. The new officers—Lieutenants Jack, Snider, and Hudson—did not know the men in their units well enough to recognize them by face, so they had to rely on their NCOs to conduct the head counts and could not verify their accuracy themselves. In addition, some men were missing from the company areas for reasons that had nothing to do with Henry's march into town. In the chaos and fear that swept the camp, some men had hidden in their tents or in the ditches that bounded the camp. A few had run into the scrub brush behind the camp and remained there even after the shooting stopped. One soldier actually lowered himself into the cesspit of the camp latrine and hid there until the shooting stopped. Several soldiers left the battalion camp and sought shelter at the homes of Houstonians they knew. None of the head counts ever managed to get a full tally of the men who remained in camp, and 151 soldiers never got their names on any of the head counts.

Thus, no one could later be sure of all the men in Henry's column of soldiers, the men who were doing most of the shooting in town. This would become critically important in the investigations that followed and in the resulting courts-martial, because it was assumed that any man who did not get his name on one of the several head counts conducted that night must have been an active participant in the violence and was therefore complicit in the deaths and injuries that occurred. That legal fallacy—the requirement that soldiers had to prove they had never joined Henry's column, rather than the government being required to prove that they did—would have far-reaching effect on the judicial process that followed.

Private Isaac Deyo was one of the men directly impacted by the incomplete head counts. According to Deyo's own account, he was in his tent when the trouble erupted in camp. "At the first sign of disorder," he said, "I left camp, taking with me my rifle and belt. The belt was filled to capacity with ammunition pursuant to orders then existing on the 'Border.' [This meant that he had the standard five rounds of ammunition authorized to each soldier on duty.] I went immediately to Camp Logan." Two other soldiers were with him—Privates Warsaw Lindsey and William Burnette. When they got to Camp Logan, Deyo went to the headquarters building and asked for the officer of the day (OD). The OD for that night was Captain James, who of course was back at the Third Battalion camp at that time, so Deyo instead reported to the sergeant of the guard, Sergeant Brownson. "The sergeant advised us to stay in the guardhouse at that camp, during that night for protection," Deyo recalled, "saying that we could report back to our company commanders on the following day." The next morning, the three soldiers reported to their own officers. The point that Deyo repeatedly insisted on was that they turned themselves in to the sergeant of the guard *before* Henry's column of soldiers ever started shooting up the city streets that night.[12]

Among all the individual stories in Third Battalion, Deyo's was perhaps one of the most unique. Born in the Virgin Islands in 1879 when that was still Danish territory, Deyo was a Danish citizen when his family immigrated to New York when he was ten years old. At thirty-eight years of age, he was one of the most experienced soldiers in the battalion, with campaign credits from three different conflicts—the Spanish-American War, the Philippine-American War, and the Punitive Expedition into Mexico. In rank he was still only a private, but his lack of promotion seems to have been a matter of his personal preference, because his personnel records reveal that the battalion officers regarded him as one of the steadiest, most reliable soldiers in the unit. After his first enlistment ended, he remained in the Philippines with the U.S. Army Quartermaster Corps until 1909, then reenlisted with 3-24 Infantry. By the summer of 1917 he had nineteen years' combined service with the Army, either as a soldier or as a civilian contract employee. He expected that his impeccable service record would be taken into account when his actions that night were later questioned, but the faulty head counts took precedence in the Army's eyes.

———

By this point about an hour and a half had elapsed since Third Battalion lost its collective head when the shout went up that a mob was coming. Two separate groups of soldiers had gone off the military sites and moved out along the streets of the San Felipe District—one from the battalion cantonment and another, smaller group from the guard force at Camp Logan. Ten people had been shot and killed, eight of them civilians and two police officers. Two other police officers and two civilians had been mortally wounded and would later die of their injuries. Twelve other people were seriously wounded.

The shooting that killed police officer Ira Raney and teenager Eli Smith and wounded the three men with them had barely ended when the headlights of another approaching car came into view down San Felipe Street. Though no one among Henry's detachment knew it, this was the automobile carrying Captain Mattes, the artillery officer from the Illinois National Guard, along with Patrolman Meineke and three National Guardsmen. A soldier in the column shouted "Reload!" and soldiers scrambled to take up firing positions along the intersecting street as the car drew nearer.

Henry Pratt, an African American resident of the neighborhood, had a room at the rear of a nearby saloon. Pratt knew Vida Henry personally, and he later testified that he heard Henry's voice shouting at the vehicle to halt. A few seconds later, he said, Henry ordered the soldiers to open fire. Apparently, at the same time as that command was given, Mattes stood up in the open car, raised his hands and said, "Wait—"[13]

It was his last word. A volley of rifle fire at close range killed him instantly and also killed Meineke, who was sitting in the front passenger seat in front of him. Both Corporal Zimmie Foreman, the driver, and Corporal M. D. Everton were wounded, Everton mortally. Private Alphens Jones escaped injury only because Mattes and Everton fell back on top of him, pushing him down to the car's floorboard.[14]

As the smoke from the rifles dissipated in the night air, the first of Henry's soldiers to approach the car discovered that the dead and dying occupants were not all policemen, as they had assumed on sight of the olive-drab uniforms. They were fellow soldiers. This was not what even the most outspoken men in the detachment had planned when they set out to exact some personal vengeance against Houston's police; for the majority of the soldiers, who had initially believed they were marching out of camp to meet an approaching armed mob, it was the worst thing that could have happened. It marked the end of Henry's sortie into the city. None of the Third Battalion men had set out to murder other soldiers, especially not uniformed Army officers. The bullet-riddled, blood-splattered Ford sitting in the middle of San Felipe Street would bring down the harshest of military punishments on the men responsible, and every soldier knew it. All thoughts of further movement were abandoned. The remaining members of the detachment, now probably numbering no more than forty or fifty men, followed Henry down Heiner Street to the West End Ball Park to regroup and figure out what to do next.

Back in the shot-out ruin of the Ford, Corporal Foreman thought he was the only man still alive, and then he heard a moan coming from the backseat. It was Private Jones. Jones was not wounded, but he thought at first that he was—he was covered in Mattes's and Everton's blood. Captain Mattes had taken at least one round in the head when he was shot down, and the top of his skull was blown off. Jones was in shock and told Foreman he could not tell if he was wounded or not.

"Well, if you are not dead for Christ's sake go get help," Foreman told him. "I am all shot to pieces."[15]

A short time later, Henry and his soldiers stopped near the tracks of the Houston and Central Texas Railroad and took up a concealed position in a railway cut. Dozens of the less enthusiastic men had slipped away at various points in the march through town, and no one now knew what to do. One soldier in the original group, Private Bryant Watson, was dead, apparently killed during one of the confused firefights that night in the vicinity of San Felipe and Wilson Streets. Henry himself was wounded by a bullet through the shoulder.

Everyone now knew for certain that the reason given for their sortie, the belief that Third Battalion's camp was under threat of attack by a race mob, was untrue. They had found no crowd of armed civilians moving against the cantonment. The killing of Captain Mattes and Corporal Everton had completely taken the wind out of most of the men.

That was not what they had bargained for when they obeyed Henry's order to fall in with weapons and march out of camp, and they wanted no more part of it. It was too late for second thoughts, though—people were dead, no one knew how many, but they all knew there was going to be a reckoning.

Sergeant William Nesbit and at least two of the corporals, Jesse Moore and James Wheatley, had tried several times that night to persuade Henry of the mistake he was making and had urged him to return to camp. Corporal Charles Baltimore also argued for marching back to the battalion. Henry had refused that advice every time it was offered, and he refused it again.

"You all can go in," he said. "I ain't going in, I ain't going to camp no more."

A few soldiers thought the best course of action was a sort of "every man for himself." They would scatter and try to find shelter in the woods or in Black neighborhoods, if they could find anyone willing to hide them, but they were not willing to go back to camp to throw themselves on the Army's dubious mercy.

Sergeant Nesbit saw it differently. A serious mistake had been made, he believed, and now there was nothing for it but to face up to the reality of their situation and deal with whatever came of it. Most of the soldiers agreed with him, so Nesbit prepared to lead them back to the battalion.

Henry no longer had command of those men. Now, seeing them preparing to leave, he made a startling request. He asked several soldiers to shoot him. He thought death was the only option left to him, but he seemed unwilling to kill himself. Each man he asked refused to do it, and several of them tried to convince him not to shoot himself. Finally, Henry asked each of the men there to shake his hand before they departed with Nesbit. He handed his pocket watch to one soldier as he passed. Private Ernest Phifer begged Henry to at least "not shoot himself until we got away." A few moments later, as the soldiers moved off into the night, they heard a single gunshot in the darkness behind them.[16]

By 2:30 that morning, Vida Henry was dead and his ill-conceived foray into the city had collapsed, though the only people who knew that yet were the soldiers who had followed him out of camp.

At about the same time, Major Snow, still grasping at any excuse to remain absent from his command, sent a telegram to the commanding general of the Army's Southern Department, headquartered at Fort Sam Houston in San Antonio. "Serious clash has occurred between approximate one hundred 24th Infantry men and civilian population," Snow wrote. He claimed to "have situation in hand at present 24th Infantry camp quiet," and concluded, "Approximately 150 men still out have 400 Illinois troops after them will keep you advised of situation from 9 to 12 casualties so far." If Snow had returned to his battalion, he would have known that by that hour, most of the men who had followed Henry out of camp were already returning to the battalion.[17]

Over in the bivouac area of the National Guard's 5th Texas Infantry, the officers and NCOs had mustered their companies and ordered them to stand to, not knowing the cause of the heavy, sustained rifle fire in the night. Lieutenant Louis Sauter's family was lodged in rented rooms near 3-24 Infantry's camp, and he was worried about their safety. Shortly before dawn his company commander gave him permission to go and check on them, and to his great relief he found his wife and children safe. The entire city was in an uproar, however, and he described a confused scene of streets "full of white civilians excited and armed with various kinds of guns."[18]

Sauter started back toward his unit and was walking along Washington Avenue when he was accosted by an excited civilian who said he knew where a Black soldier was hiding. Sauter took it upon himself to lead a search to hunt the soldier down, though he had no idea who the soldier was or if the man was even involved in the night's uproar. The unknown soldier was a Black man, and that was all the justification most Texans needed for a manhunt that morning. "In a few moments I had gathered about a half a dozen armed men around me and under my direction we began search for the man," Sauter later told an Army investigator. "After fifteen minutes' search one of my posse, Allen Wells, saw the soldier run under a house and as he ran shot him in the leg with a shotgun. He shot him . . . but at first we could not find him. He had managed to crawl on and got over a fence into the next yard and under the house No. 10 Vida. Here we found him and dragged him out."

The wounded soldier was Private George Bivens of India Company. He was hit in the leg by a full load of double-ought 12-gauge buckshot at relatively close range, a terrible wound that nearly shredded his leg. He faced a more immediate danger than the gunshot wound, however, because an angry mob quickly formed around him and his captors. "As soon as we got him out," Sauter said, "a crowd of civilians gathered around and tried to shoot him and threatened to shoot me and three Medical Corps men that came to my assistance. I stood over the wounded negro with his rifle which I had picked up [and] stood the crowd off. Some of them were very violent and made some ugly threats and aimed their guns at me but I managed to get the wounded man to a Ford car and the Medical Corps men and some civilian driver took him to the Saint Joseph Infirmary."

Sauter then inspected the weapon he had confiscated from Bivens, a standard-issue Springfield M1903 rifle. It showed signs of having been fired, still smelled of cordite, and was loaded with four rounds remaining in its five-round magazine. He then resumed his walk back to the 5th Texas Infantry's camp. On the way, he came upon the car in which Captain Mattes and Corporal Everton had been killed. Sauter remembered that the bullet-riddled car was "sitting on the sidewalk at the junction of Seguin St. all shot up and covered with blood and [I] learned that several men had been killed."[19]

Houston's night of violence was over, though no one was yet completely sure of that. Fifteen people were dead—three police officers, eight civilians, two National Guardsmen, and two soldiers from 3-24 Infantry—and seventeen people were wounded. Within the next two weeks, four of the wounded would die of their injuries, bringing the total death toll to nineteen.

The shooting of the civilian jitney described earlier, when E. M. Jones was killed and Charles Clayton was wounded, was a distinctly separate act from all the other incidents where soldiers encountered moving automobiles that night. For one thing, the jitney shooting was perpetrated not by the men who marched out of the battalion bivouac under Sergeant Henry's leadership but by the fifteen soldiers who deserted their guard duty at Camp Logan's Lower A Division. The Camp Logan men could never claim that they followed the orders of a senior NCO that night, and they could not argue that they were responding to the belief that a mob was advancing to attack them, as so many of their comrades back in the battalion cantonment did. The soldiers who left Camp Logan had not experienced the panic brought on by the shout of an approaching mob. They moved out on their own initiative, without any orders from any authority figure to do so, and the only shots they fired that night were specifically directed at a civilian vehicle that posed no threat and did not even have a peripheral association with the hated police upon whom some soldiers may have sworn to avenge themselves. The jitney shooting was a deliberate ambush, plain and simple, and the death and injuries that resulted from it were clear cases of murder and attempted murder.

Early that Friday morning, a fast train arrived from San Antonio carrying Colonel Millard Waltz and several companies of white troops of the 19th Infantry Regiment. General James Parker had dispatched Waltz to Houston immediately after receiving telegrams alerting him to the trouble in the city. Waltz dismounted his men at the city's main train station and linked up with two batteries of a Coast Artillery unit just arrived from Galveston on the same mission. His orders were simple: He was to get Third Battalion back under military control, immediately. He did not yet know all the details of the situation in Houston—almost no one did at that moment—and he did not know if the men of Third Battalion were inclined to follow orders, so he took no chances. "I was going to disarm this battalion of the 24th Infantry and while I did not anticipate any trouble in doing so I wished to be prepared for it," he later said.

It was fortunate that Regular Army troops were close enough to Houston to reach the city quickly when the Army set about regaining control of the situation. The men of Third Battalion were far more inclined to allow themselves to be disarmed by other professional soldiers than they ever would have been if units of the Texas or Illinois National Guard had attempted to carry out that task. If a unit composed entirely of white Texans, or a battalion of the same Illinois Guardsmen who just seven weeks earlier had aided and abetted the massacre of Black civilians in East St. Louis, had attempted to disarm Third Battalion, it would almost certainly have provoked a firefight between two equally armed infantry units, and the loss of life would have been terrible. It was a matter of perceived safety. Third Battalion's soldiers believed they could rely on their fellow Regulars to protect them against any violent backlash from the groups of armed Houstonians who were that morning roaming around the city vowing vengeance. That was a very real threat, because numerous witnesses testified to seeing carloads of armed men driving around the city looking for any Black soldier, and angry mobs of armed civilians had already been turned back from the camp by the quick thinking of Captain Rothrock and other officers.

Houston policemen, armed civilians, and Guardsmen from several Texas and Illinois National Guard units had converged on the fire station during the night with the intention of marching on Third Battalion's camp. "Angry cries of 'lynch them' and 'come, let's go kill 'em,' were heard on all sides," one source reported. Captain Rothrock ordered armed soldiers to cordon off Washington Avenue with instructions to use lethal force to stop anyone who tried to pass. He warned the mob that it would be suicide for them to move against a camp of armed infantrymen who were already on edge—they would be shot to pieces if they attempted any act of vigilantism against Third Battalion. Rothrock's warning and quick action prevented the civilian mob from carrying out their threats, but tensions were still running high.

Waltz commandeered trucks from the National Guard and drove out to Third Battalion's camp. He deployed his men outside three sides of the camp perimeter and positioned several machine guns with sweeping fields of fire along the angles. He, by himself, would go into the camp to personally order the battalion to stack their arms and stand by under the command of their own officers. If they showed any signs of resistance or made any move to seize their weapons, his soldiers surrounding the perimeter were to "open fire on the camp and annihilate it." It was a grim threat, because Waltz himself would have been in the crossfire if anyone started shooting, and he knew it.

Waltz walked into the camp, found Captain Shekerjian and Major Snow (who had by then finally returned to his battalion), and waited while the officers assembled their men. He then climbed up on an ammunition crate so all the soldiers could see him.

"For the time being you are all confined to your camp," Waltz told them. "The 19th Infantry will surround your camp with a heavy guard and is interposed between you and the civilian community, both for your protection from any acts of aggression on the part of the civilians and to protect civilians from any acts of aggression on the part of any of you. . . . There will be no further disorders in or about this camp. The guard will shoot outwards against unauthorized persons attacking the dignity of this United States camp just as quickly as it will fire inward on you if you attempt any further disorder."[20]

In his subsequent statements to Army investigators, Waltz recalled that he was very much aware "that the 24th Infantry men's minds were full of the idea that they were going to be attacked by a mass of civilians." He refuted the newspaper stories that described truculent, angry Black soldiers who sullenly submitted to military authority that morning. "I studied the faces of the men as I addressed them and there was no signs, as stated in the public press, of resentment towards being disarmed or clenching of teeth," Waltz said. "I saw no indications of any sort of rebellion or resentment against having the arms taken away."

Even more importantly, he said, "I had in mind at that time that I would not have hesitated, alone, to have gone in and ordered these companies to fall in without arms and I believe they would have done so." Waltz was an experienced infantry officer who knew how to read soldiers—that Friday morning, he was confident that 3-24 Infantry was once again a battalion in good order and that they would follow commands. He was right about that, but there was one caveat. "I also formed the opinion," he said, "that if an attempt had been made to disarm them by other than regular troops there might have been some disorders."[21] Waltz took Third Battalion's worries about the threat of a civilian mob just as seriously as they did, and he also seems to have understood their mistrust of the two National Guard units in the city.

Other commentators did not take that view, but they were not in Houston that Friday morning, they did not have the troop leadership experience that Waltz had, and they did not see what he saw.

9. WHITEWASH

That morning after the violence, Houston was on edge and bracing for more trouble. Few people knew exactly what had happened during the night and no one knew if the trouble had really ended. Rumors flew nearly as fast as the telegrams tapped out to the state capitol in Austin and the War Department in Washington. Houston was locked down under martial law. The front page of that day's edition of the *Houston Chronicle* was totally given over to the previous night's events. A boldface headline declared, "17 Killed; 21 Are Injured in Wild Night." The following story claimed, "Houston has a night of terror as Negro troops stationed here mutiny and rove the city, shooting and killing and invading homes and business establishments." At the bottom of the page appeared a small piece under the heading "Murderous Riot Replaces Negro Watermelon Party."

The finger-pointing and blame began immediately. Military spokesmen, for the most part, were hesitant to draw any conclusions too quickly. "General Hulen said he had been unable to clearly establish the cause of the trouble," the *Houston Post* reported, "but intimated it may have resulted from the strained relations between the military police and the city police in Houston.* The Southern Department's headquarters would give no statement on the Houston trouble except to say that a thorough investigation would be made. Until that time and for lack of full information on the cause of the clash no statement would be issued." Major General George Bell Jr., the senior Regular Army officer who arrived in the city that Friday, was not as careful in his response to questions from the press. "Gen. Bell said it would be impossible for him to discuss plans for the court-martial," the

---

* Brigadier General John A. Hulen was at that time commander of Texas National Guard units in Houston.

Washington, D.C., *Sunday Star* reported. That much was acceptable for a representative of the Army to say, if Bell would have stopped with that, but he continued, "Mutiny in time of war is punishable by death. Murder at all times involves the death penalty." Those two sentences were potentially prejudicial to any subsequent legal proceedings. The reporters asked his opinion on what caused the outbreak of violence. Bell said he did not wish to speak to that. "It is to be assumed, though," he said, "that the negroes thought that someone had slighted them in some way."[1]

Civilian commentators were less circumspect in their opinions, whether they actually knew what they were talking about or not. Almost every civilian authority figure who spoke to the press over the next two days tried to absolve the City of Houston, its police force, and its Jim Crow laws of any responsibility for what had happened. Dan M. Moody, Houston's acting mayor, said, "The trouble, as I see it, was just an outcropping of bad negroes that have been itching to start something. They merely used the clash with the police earlier in the day as an excuse."[2] Texas officials at higher levels also seemed to have their minds made up, and even objected to the military's decision to wait on the facts before drawing a conclusion. The state's senators and congressmen were "much wrought up over the reports of the rioting and bloodshed in Houston as the result of the outbreak of the negro soldiers," the *Post* reported, "but they fear that there will be a disposition on the part of the War Department to await a full investigation into the trouble before action is finally taken."[3]

Chief Brock insisted that the actions of police officers Sparks and Daniels against Corporal Baltimore were in no way a catalyst for the violence. He characterized the incident on Thursday afternoon in very different terms than eyewitnesses did, and more importantly, very differently from how Sparks and Baltimore themselves described it in their own sworn statements. "A negro soldier tried to interfere with Officers Daniels and Sparks when they were arresting a negress," Brock told the newspapers. "The soldier was brought to the station and later another negro soldier, Sergeant [*sic*] Baltimore, interfered with them and they had some trouble with him." As far as he was concerned, the police were not at fault.

Brock concluded by telling reporters that the order he had issued before the trouble, "calling the attention of the [police] officers to the use of the word negro or colored in the place of the term 'niggers[,]' had been removed from the department records," thereby dispensing with any pretense that he had ever been serious about curtailing the police department's institutional culture of racism and its use of racist slurs.[4]

The public recriminations and calls for retribution dominated newspaper coverage of the trouble, but buried in the interior pages were other, more poignant details. In a short piece headed "Another Home in Sore Distress Result of Riot," the *Houston Chronicle* wrote, "In a little home in Cottage Grove, a home that has not even been paid for, is a woman and four small boys. They are living victims of the black madness of Thursday night." This was the family of A. C. Carsten, who was "shot down by the mutineers and in the fraction of a second wreck and ruin brought upon a defenseless home." The article went on to say that neighbors reported the family were left "destitute" and facing ruin because of the loss of their sole wage-earner.

The *Chronicle* was not entirely accurate in its assertion that Carsten was killed by the soldiers accused of mutiny and riot, because he was one of the people killed by random bullets in the wild, unaimed firing that broke out in Third Battalion's camp well before Sergeant Henry led his column of soldiers out into the city, but it was absolutely correct in its main point. A man who had nothing to do with the soldiers' grievances, who did not present any sort of armed threat, was killed just because he stepped into the path of a stray bullet fired in a moment of military panic and indiscipline, and his family truly was left destitute. That fact, and the lasting impact of the other innocent lives lost that night, must be taken into account in any balanced examination of this tragedy.

———

Texas newspapers were histrionic in their descriptions of the events of August 23, but journalists far from Houston were every bit as shrill and just as quick to level unproven allegations larded with racist stereotypes. In a feature article describing "the horror of the Thursday night affair," the *Fort Wayne Sentinel* in Indiana declared, "The colored soldiers were wholly unamenable to discipline. . . . [T]hese negroes armed themselves with the weapons furnished by the government and literally ran amuck in the city, shooting white people without discrimination. They refused to heed the words of counsel from their officers and finally rode them down in mad rebellion against authority and discipline." The paper might be considered correct to describe the violence that night as soldiers running amuck, but it was inaccurate to claim that the soldiers shot "white people without discrimination" because there were numerous incidences of white civilians being allowed to pass unmolested and unharmed when they encountered the Black soldiers in the streets. A woman named Maude Potts, a jitney operator, told the Houston Citizens' Commission that during the confusion that night she had suddenly found herself in the midst of the soldiers on San Felipe Street. "I heard a negro soldier tell me, 'Get away from here, white lady, we don't want to kill you, but we are after the white policemen who have called us names and have been beating our men up.'"[5] The *Sentinel*'s writer went on to describe the violence in Houston as an act of unjustifiable Black retaliation for the recent East St. Louis race riot. "Hotheaded leaders among negroes have had considerable latitude in preaching to masses of colored people in many places that they should be prepared to take reprisals for what occurred in East St. Louis," he claimed, and implied that similar uprisings among other Black units in the army were likely to occur. "In any event," he concluded, "the uprising among the colored soldiers at Houston is a grave warning that too many negro soldiers should not be concentrated in the south, or elsewhere, for the matter of that. If an entire company of negroes can lash themselves into a frenzy to rise against white men an entire regiment or brigade might just as easily incite itself to a turbulent and bloody revolt."[6]

African American newspapers took a very different view. A week after the trouble, an editorial in the *Cleveland Gazette* declared, "Thoughtful people were not surprised when they read of the tragedy in Houston. . . . Colored soldiers have suffered many insults and injustices at the hands of brutal civil officers and white civilians in the South. It is apparent that the time for our people to remain in the South has passed. Not that Negroes are more lawless, but they have determined to put an end to white brutality imposed upon them by lawless civil officers." The writer went on to praise Private Edwards for having stepped forward in Sara Travers's defense when she was dragged out of her house by Sparks and Daniels that afternoon. "In interfering, he was doing an act of justice toward a helpless woman," the *Gazette*'s writer stated. The op-ed concluded with a call to Black readers across the nation: "Whatever punishment is meted out to the boys of the 24th they will have the satisfaction that they suffered to end an almost intolerable condition facing the colored women of the South. Those of us, not in the army, should forever take our stand to protect our women against the insults and cruelties of white brutes whether in officers' or citizens' garb.[7]

Some African American newspapers were occasionally just as quick to print unsubstantiated speculations riddled with inaccuracies as were their counterparts in white journalism. The *Broad Ax*, in Chicago, published a story on September 1 that focused on the death of Captain Joseph Mattes. That was not surprising, since Mattes was a native of Chicago and the city was fixated on news of his death and the presence of Illinois National Guard battalions in Houston during the violence. The *Broad Ax*'s reporting, however, contained more fiction than good journalism should allow.

Under the headline "The Police and the Unregenerated and the Unreconstructed Red Necked Rebels of That City Were Responsible for the Members of the Twenty Fourth Regiment in Shooting Up the Town and Killing Fifteen or Twenty White Citizens," the newspaper claimed Captain Mattes was killed because of an unfortunate association. "His life was ended because he permitted himself to ride around in an automobile with one of the policemen who had been exceedingly brutal in his treatment of the colored soldiers," the writer declared. "That same policeman slapped the face of the colored woman before he attempted to arrest her and with his revolver he beat in the face the colored soldier who remonstrated with him for slapping the woman he was walking with." That was wildly inaccurate, because E. J. Meineke, the policeman who died in the same shooting that killed Mattes and Corporal M. D. Everton, was not in any way involved in the incident with Sara Travers, Private Edwards, and Corporal Baltimore earlier that day. Rufus Daniels and Lee Sparks were the two policemen responsible for that abusive interaction. The *Broad Ax* went on to claim that Meineke had believed he was entitled to "beat up or club up Colored soldiers wearing the blue uniform of Uncle Sam, and a colored woman who had not been charged with committing any crime other than walking with a Colored soldier who was at that time five miles away from the city limits of Houston." Everything was wrong with that depiction of events—American soldiers had not worn blue as their utility uniform since the Spanish-American War, Sara Travers was not walking out with either Edwards or Baltimore, the incident occurred in the San Felipe District, well within Houston's boundaries, and Meineke's reputation was impugned without any evidence of his actual conduct. But the emotions expressed in the *Broad Ax*'s article echoed the same feelings many other people were feeling across the country. "It is very hard to tell what will be the fate of those members of that famous regiment," the writer concluded, and the worry in that sentence touched every Black reader who heard the news from Texas.[8]

Tensions remained high in Houston, and rumors that further outbreaks of violence were imminent were rampant. Two days after the violence, the U.S. attorney, John E. Green Jr., was so concerned about the situation that he wrote a grim warning that appeared prominently in the Saturday edition of the *Houston Post*. "It is a crime to incite a race riot—a crime punishable under the statutes," Green declared. "Anyone who would do it is a traitor." He had heard "that some man had gone about the city in an auto telling white citizens that the negroes were forming to attack the whites; that a man answering the same description had told the negroes that the whites proposed to raid, burn and murder them." Green called for the public's help in identifying and arresting this unnamed provocateur. "At this time there should be studied effort to calm our people; to restore calm so that there may be an avoidance of any further trouble—certainly if trouble is incited then it will be much more serious than anyone can now foretell," he declared. "I repeat: It is a crime to incite trouble between the races."[9]

Green's warning was not frivolous, because some Houstonians were already acting on the assumption that anyone with a dark skin was a threat. That Friday afternoon a Black man named Jerry Johnson was shot down in the street by a National Guardsman, apparently because he did not immediately respond to an order to stop walking. According to the *Houston Post*'s report of the incident, "The soldiers were given orders to stop and investigate any negro in this section and he was regarded as a suspicious character." What made Johnson an object of suspicion was that he was a Black man of military age. After he was shot and taken to St. Joseph's Infirmary, Johnson insisted that he was not a soldier but a resident of the city with a wife and family. The bullet shattered his pelvis, an excruciating wound that proved fatal. "His recovery is doubtful," the newspaper concluded, without offering any comment on the utter lack of justification for the shooting. No official investigation into the killing was ever undertaken.

Explanations for the cause of the violence ranged from rumors loosely based on recognizable facts, to wildly exaggerated conspiracy theories. Newspapers across the country, in a rush to get something into print in the days after the incident, published outrageously hyperbolic editorials that drew more on imagination than evidence. The *Bellville Times*, a Texas paper, correctly described the Thursday afternoon altercation between the two Houston police officers and Private Edwards and Corporal Baltimore, but then veered off into freewheeling conjecture. "This, however, as later facts brought out disclose," the writer claimed, "was merely the match that started the fire—as the soldiers had been behaving improperly in other ways, having gotten beer to drink, and were in a surly mood, looking for trouble." He described the Third Battalion soldiers as "a bad lot, with an officer who could not control them," and concluded, "Outrages committed by negro troops in Waco and more recently in Houston are not convincing that the negroes from the north make soldiers in the south."[10]

The morning after the incident, Texas congressman Joe Eagle fired off a telegram to the Secretary of War. "Without stating who is to blame it is clearly a race riot and is a tragedy sufficient to compel the statement that it is a tragic blunder to send negro troops to Southern camps. I protest vigorously against the Illinois negro soldiers ordered to Houston being sent[;] by all means order them to Northern training camps and promptly order the negro troops who are already here sent elsewhere." Eagle may have hoped to gain some political traction among his white constituents from this demand, but the War Department did not agree to his request.[11]

Theories of mutinous plots and "Negro conspiracies" of riot and murder made for titillating copy, and many editors were eager to print it all, the more salacious the better. A newspaper in Fremont, Indiana, declared, "The mob, composed of members of the various companies of the Twenty-Fourth United States Infantry (negro), started its hunt for blood shortly after eight o'clock at night. It is apparent that the attack on the town was premeditated. There was no intoxication, and from all signs it was a carefully thought-out plan."[12]

In Houston, the condemnation was even more direct, and aimed at more than just the soldiers of the 24th Infantry. "The negro military units must not be quartered in Southern communities," the *Houston Post* declared in an editorial that ran that Saturday. "The Southern cities are not going to change their laws to suit the demands of negro soldiers, nor are they going to submit to insolence, mutiny, riot and murder. The negro soldiers resent our separate coach laws, our customs which prohibit mixed socializing . . . but this measure of separation is absolute and will be maintained." Houston, the *Post* stated, "is not going to have men, women and children ruthlessly murdered with United States army rifles in the hands of frenzied blacks, is not going to revolutionize her customs in order to conform to the views of any outside element whatever."[13]

The threat enclosed in that diatribe was hardly subtle. In saying that the well-being of Houston's Black residents "depends upon cordial relations with the white people," the writer was stating what every Texan understood as an immutable truth: The only fragile social safety African Americans could hope for was based on submission to the existing racial power dynamic.

The *Post* expanded its vitriol to include Black residents of the city who had had nothing to do with the violence. Under the headline "Round Up Negro Vagrants at Once," the paper proclaimed the existence of a conspiracy never proven: "Since the arrival of the negro troops at Camp Logan, an element of rebellious and disorderly negroes of the local population has freely mingled with them, the result being that their imaginations have become considerably inflamed. They have looked forward to such an outbreak as happened Thursday night." The only solution to prevent further outbreaks of racial violence, the paper claimed, was "to round up every idle negro and vagrant in this city and county and place him under duress, and there is a class of negro females who are quite as dangerous to the peace of the community as their vicious male consorts."[14]

Meanwhile, a jurisdictional dispute was developing in the midst of all the heated rhetoric. The Harris County district attorney, John Crooker, was determined to keep any prosecution of the alleged mutineers firmly in Houston, and by extension in his own hands. Some of his reasoning was almost certainly in reaction to the fact that the crimes committed that night impacted his city and his fellow citizens, but Crooker's public statements also suggest he was a man of considerable ambition. To say that it was a high-profile case did not even begin to describe the importance of the matter, and Crooker was very much aware that prosecuting the case would almost certainly be a stepping-stone to more important political office, as well as probably being the capstone of his legal career.

Thirty-four soldiers were by that point in the custody of the Houston police. Most of them were members of Henry's column who had dropped out of the sortie individually or in small groups and were arrested in the early hours of Friday morning. When it began to look as if the Army might send the entire battalion back to the 24th Infantry's regimental quarters in New Mexico to face military prosecution, Crooker quickly filed a charge of murder against all thirty-four men. His rationale, as he told a reporter for the *Houston Post*, was to justify their continued detention under his jurisdiction. "I can frankly say that I would not like to see those negroes taken to New Mexico," he declared. "If the government is going to try them before a court-martial, they should do it here." Crooker told the *Post*'s readers he would only be amenable to the soldiers being tried by court-martial if the Army would guarantee that it "could try and kill them any quicker than the courts of this county." As far as he was concerned, their guilt and condemnation were already assumed before any investigation of individual culpability had even begun.[15] Texas wanted blood, and Crooker was keen to have his name associated with that vengeance. The Army, however, was not in the habit of allowing civilians to choose the venues for its courts-martial, and the decision was not up to Crooker.

He was not the only elected official making outright threats of bloody-minded vengeance. Two days after Congressman Eagle's telegram to the War Department, the *Houston Post* printed a story in which it quoted Eagle as saying that because Third Battalion had "committed their diabolical crimes in Houston, slaughtering our men, women, and children unprovoked . . . these red-handed murderers would be shot right here where they killed their victims as an act of simple justice, as an example of discipline and as a warning." Since the congressman had no authority in either the criminal courts or the system of military law, his statement was little more than hyperbolic bluster pandering to Harris County's voters, but it still came dangerously close to inciting further racial violence.[16]

African American observers quickly pushed back against that. "At this writing Texas is clamoring for the right to try this number of colored soldiers in a court of murderous rednecks whose verdict is rendered before the trial begins," the *Cleveland Gazette* declared. "Poor Texas is not worthy of passing an impartial judgment upon anything concerning a Negro." The *Gazette* did not try to argue that the soldiers of 3-24 Infantry were blameless but felt whatever penalty must be paid was worth it. "Some of the men may be court-martialed and shot, but that matters not," the editorial declared; "they have struck a fatal blow at southern mob violence and official brutality."[17]

The stories appearing in the national press, and the published comments attributed to some Army officers, sounded to some readers too much like the language that southern newspapers often used in describing lynchings. Even more alarming, it sounded like the language used to *justify* lynchings.

Two days after the troubles, an African American attorney named James Waters Jr., in Hyattsville, Maryland, wrote a letter to General Franklin Bell. Waters sent his letter to the wrong man—Franklin Bell was in a military department completely unassociated with the Houston Incident, whereas George Bell was the senior Regular Army officer at Houston—but the error was minor because Waters was taking the Army itself to task, as an entire institution.

"Press advices published in this vicinity tell of a very regrettable clash between men of the 24th U.S. Infantry and policemen and civilians in Houston," he wrote. The newspapers, he said, reported "that the civil authorities at Houston have demanded an absolutely free hand to deal with the colored troopers as they see fit. That means that the Negro troops will be burned at the stake, with the utmost fiendishness, such as marked the work of the mob at Waco." Even worse, in Waters's view, was a quote in that day's edition of the *Washington Times*, which stated, "Army officers today predicted that the military, instead of the civil authorities, would win the right of trial, and that the verdict would be death before a firing squad." As an attorney, Waters knew that sort of statement was dangerous and highly prejudicial against men whose guilt was assumed but not proven.

"The foregoing prediction of the army officers quoted shows that so far as the officers quoted are concerned the colored troopers have already been tried and condemned to death even before a single word has been uttered before any constituted authority," he wrote, and requested that the general send him "some word as to the probable mob-murder of the colored troopers, and also concerning what, if any, action can be taken to see to it that the army officers, if they cannot defend their men, will at least keep silent and say nothing against them."[18]

Waters was not the only civilian to take such pronouncements by Army officers seriously. The week after the violence, Major Snow received a telegram from San Antonio. The writer, a Catholic priest at the Santa Rosa Infirmary, asked for "information whether any Catholic priest for negroes 24th Infantry held at Fort Bliss re case of execution so as they may get death consolation." Based on newspaper reporting, many people believed that inevitable and summary death sentences would quickly follow the troubles.[19]

Had the trouble in Houston occurred four months earlier, Crooker probably would have managed to keep the prosecution firmly in his personal grasp. Normally, crimes committed by soldiers in the civilian sector fall completely within civilian jurisdiction, and the Army can only prosecute offenses committed by its personnel on military reservations or in the course of military operations. But in August 1917 the United States was in a state of declared war against Germany, and that gave the Army prosecutorial authority over its soldiers in all jurisdictions. Crooker could posture and blow all he liked, but the case was going to be tried in a military court-martial, not a Harris County courtroom.

The Army was not inclined to engage in a lengthy debate about jurisdiction, particularly not while the soldiers in question were still in Houston and thus within reach of vengeful-minded Texans. At 4:30 a.m. on Saturday morning, the men of Third Battalion, unarmed, boarded a train bound for their regimental home station in Columbus, New Mexico, accompanied by two companies of Colonel Waltz's 19th Infantry as guards.

Waltz, as the tactical commander on the scene, was fully aware of the threat of civilian violence against the accused rioters if Houstonians realized they were being moved beyond their reach, and he took every precaution he could. The fear of vigilante violence was thought to be so real that the commanding general of the Southern Department sent a telegram to Brigadier General Hulen, commander of Texas National Guard troops in Houston. He ordered Hulen to talk to local railroad officials "and request them to insure by every means in their power that a successful attempt is not made to destroy train by [explosives]. To insure this a pilot locomotive pushing some flat cars should precede the troop train and right of way should be watched by section hands." To make sure this request was understood to have military force behind it, Hulen was further instructed to "inform the railroad authorities that I will hold them responsible for the safety of the troops."[20]

The Army's concerns about vigilante violence were so great that some men were put on the train who in other circumstances would have been considered unable to travel. The soldiers in the city jail were taken from police custody and reunited with their unit, over the protests of local officials. Five other soldiers who had been injured during the violence, or in the morning after, were in the hospital at St. Andrew's Infirmary in the city—Privates Bivens and Strong were the most seriously wounded. Waltz conferred with Third Battalion's medical officer, Lieutenant Chaffin, about their status.

"Are they able to go?" Waltz asked.

"Three of them are perfectly well and able to go," Chaffin said. "I took them down with me the day before yesterday, and after the disorder I was afraid to take them back to camp as I feared they would be fired on by citizens in the town. The other two are wounded."

"Can they be moved?"

Chaffin said they could not—in his medical opinion, Bivens and Strong were too badly wounded to travel.[21]

There were no trucks available for transport, so Waltz took a staff car and went to the hospital himself to retrieve the three ambulatory men and saw to it that they were placed on the train bound for Columbus, New Mexico, along with all the rest of Third Battalion and his two guard companies. "Just as I was about to board the train for Fort Sam Houston with the other two companies of my regiment," he stated later, "I received instructions from General Bell to take these two wounded men with me to Fort Sam Houston, that they would be sent to me at the train. I reminded the officer delivering the message what the surgeon of the 24th Infantry had said as to their condition and that I had no medical attendants or litters and no way of taking care of them on the train except in the baggage car."

Any discussion on the question stopped when General Bell himself arrived at the train station and issued a direct order—"they had better be taken to Fort Sam Houston even if they died, than to have them lynched," Waltz recalled. "He was afraid of a lynching."

Half an hour later Private George Bivens was brought to the station in an ambulance. The officer who accompanied him said that the other wounded man, Private Wiley Strong, who had been gut-shot, "was certainly dying (and he did die) and the infirmary authorities would not consent to his being removed from the infirmary." Bivens was loaded onto Waltz's train, and it moved out of the station. "I brought this one wounded man to Fort Sam Houston with me," Waltz reported. "One of the officers' rolls was opened and he lay on the roll until we arrived here and he died next day following an operation for amputation of his leg which our surgeon here had found necessary on account of his condition."[22]

Bivens was already dying when he began the train journey, which must have been an excruciating ordeal for him. In that era before effective means of treating infection, Bivens's leg wound had begun to fester. Upon arrival in San Antonio, he was immediately transferred to Base Hospital No. 1 at Fort Sam Houston. There, he was examined by an Army doctor, Major A. L. Blesh, but nothing could be done for him. "The patient was fired upon inflicting wounds as follows: four puncture wounds of inner surface of right leg; six on outer surface, four of them grouped below the knee. Apparently made by buckshot fired from a shotgun, which patient says was the weapon used," Blesh wrote in his report. By that point, Bivens had contracted gas gangrene, and there was only one treatment possible— "amputation of right leg, upper third of femur." Before he died, Bivens made a brief statement about what happened to him in Houston. "Patient was in a condition of profound shock and toxemia," Blesh wrote in his report. "This was *not* a dying statement on the part of the patient." That last was an important detail, for legal reasons. A dying declaration could be used in court as a posthumous witness statement, but Bivens's statement was not given that degree of veracity, apparently because he was in such a fevered state that the medical officer was not sure that he was truly lucid.[23]

On the troop train carrying the other men of Third Battalion away from Houston, a group of regimental officers on the train began conducting official interviews with soldiers, inquiring about who had been where on the night of August 23, who had done what, and who knew what others had done. The Army had begun the process of gathering information for courts-martial, and right from the start it was clear that due process of military law would fall by the wayside. It seems likely that none of the soldiers interviewed in that first round of questioning were advised of their legal rights against self-incrimination, because as of yet, no evidence that such warning was ever given has been found in the records.*

* In military law circa 1917, there was nothing like the Miranda rights warning that Americans are familiar with today. However, whenever officers questioned soldiers on matters that might open them to legal jeopardy, they were required to inform them they did not have to answer questions and that anything they said could be used in court-martial. The requirement that law enforcement officers must advise a person of their rights when being arrested did not enter American law until the Supreme Court case *Miranda v. Arizona* in 1966.

As the train rumbled through the East Texas town of Schulenberg, a soldier threw a note out the window. "Take Tex. and go to hell," it read. "I don't want to go there any more in my life. Let's go East and be treated as people." It was signed "24th Inf."

News that the accused rioters had been snatched from Texas's grasp outraged many people in the state. "The secret removal early this morning of 34 negro soldiers held in the county jail in connection with the Thursday night riot has plunged the city into a ferment," the *Escanaba Morning Press* brayed. "Military authorities responsible for the action are bitterly criticized in a statement by hundreds of people in which it is asserted pledges were made that the men would be executed immediately." No such pledges had been made, of course, because even in that highly charged moment the U.S. military was not in the practice of ordering summary executions without trial.[24]

Texas congressman Atkins Jefferson McLemore, who sat on the House of Representatives Committee on Military Affairs, tried to outmaneuver the Army by introducing House Resolution 131 on August 30. The resolution demanded that the Secretary of War "return for criminal trial the soldiers participating in the recent riots at Houston, Texas," and protested "against the sending of negro soldiers to the South." The War Department took the most expedient route in its reply by simply ignoring McLemore for as long as possible. The accused rioters would face military justice, not a Texas court.

Two days after the Army moved the men of Third Battalion out of Crooker's reach, Houston convened an investigative body to gather evidence about the violence of Thursday night. Variously referred to as the Houston Board of Inquiry or the Citizens' Commission, it quickly became apparent that this body had only one agenda—to absolve the city and its white residents of any responsibility for the conditions that had led to an outbreak of violence. John Crooker himself had a prominent role as the commission's primary questioner of witnesses, which gave him some of the public exposure he sought and certainly suited his political ambitions.

At the same time this board convened, the Army sent the first of two inspectors general (IGs) to conduct an official military inquiry into the incident. Colonel George Cress was the IG of the Southern Department, the major command headquartered at Fort Sam Houston that had operational authority over the 24th Infantry Regiment. In addition to conducting personal interviews with soldiers and civilian witnesses, Cress attended most of the commission's sessions as an official observer. He was immediately struck by its lack of impartiality.

"While the committee in its investigation was thorough," Cress later reported, "it was evident that their object was to show that this trouble was essentially a race trouble, that the members of the 24th Infantry were the sole aggressors, that they were entirely to blame for the trouble and that no blame rested upon Houston or the Houston police, and that the Corporal Baltimore affair on the afternoon of the 23d was a mere circumstance." He disagreed with that interpretation of events. "Everyone concerned appeared to lose sight of the one fact upon which I endeavored to hold attention," he said; "namely that Corporal Baltimore at the time of this arrest was a United States soldier on duty as a guard under the orders of his officers and that he was on duty under specific arrangements between the city authorities and the military authorities; in other words, that this assault was one upon the United States uniform while on duty."

Cress told the commission members that he believed a major share of responsibility for the troubles lay with the Houston Police Department. When he raised that point, the commission suggested he should provide them with the names of witnesses and conduct his interviews as part of their sessions.

Cress refused to do so. He recognized that he had a better chance of eliciting statements from witnesses, particularly Black Houstonians, in one-on-one interviews. If he attempted to get their testimony in a formal setting in a room filled with the authority figures of Houston's white-dominated judiciary and police force, those witnesses would likely be intimidated into making guarded statements, if they were willing to talk at all. Instead, he told the commission that they only needed to examine their own chief of police to find out how undisciplined and poorly led their police department was.

Testimony the commission obtained from members of the police clearly supported Cress's argument about "discord and lack of discipline" in the force. It also demonstrated beyond any doubt that a rampant, unrepentant culture of verbal abuse had existed and that policemen deliberately used racial insults against the soldiers almost habitually. This was borne out by the testimony of policemen such as Ed Stoermer, who was called to tell the commission about an altercation he had had with a Black soldier the week before the troubles.

Stoermer said that on Sunday, August 19, he was approached by a streetcar conductor who told him, "I have got a nigger on that car and he won't get out of the white section." Even though Stoermer was not on duty at the time—he described himself as being at home, and in his "short sleeves," so not in uniform—he took his revolver and boarded the tram. "I seen the nigger sitting up there in front, and I asked some white people to get off who were in the car, because I didn't know but what I would have to kill him," he told the commission, and then described how he accosted the soldier, "knocked him in the head" with his pistol, and arrested him. "He was a pretty good nigger when I got him to jail," he concluded. In written transcripts of testimony where racist language appears over and over, Stoermer's account is noteworthy because he used the racial slur at least once in every single sentence he spoke.[25]

Perhaps the most important witness to the incident that actually sparked the violence was Lee Sparks, the police officer who assaulted Private Edwards and Corporal Baltimore. If one man could be said to be personally responsible for setting the whole tragic course of events in motion, it was Sparks. There was no ambiguity to Sparks's racism—Captain Shekerjian had already told one of the Army's investigators that on the afternoon of the incident, he heard Sparks say that "a nigger was a nigger to him without regard to his uniform," a sentiment completely in keeping with the policeman's reputation as an unrepentant bigot.[26]

Sparks first appeared before the Citizens' Commission on August 30, and under oath said that he had "told the negro Edwards three different times to get back, but that when he kept coming in he struck him four times with his revolver. He then made him sit down and wait for the patrol wagon, and he and the negro woman were put in it together and sent to the police station." He claimed Edwards was drunk at the time.

When Sparks was recalled to the stand the next day, however, he enlarged on his previous testimony. "I arrested the negro woman for abusive language," he told the commission. "While I was waiting for the wagon Edwards came up with about 20 negroes following him and said he wanted the woman. I said he couldn't have her. He said he was going to have her and reached over. I hit him over the head three or four times till his heart got right and he sat down." The only "abusive language" Sara Travers ever apparently used was to ask Sparks why he had barged into her house, but as far as Sparks was concerned the fact that a Black woman had the temerity to question him was excuse enough to arrest her.

As an observer, Cress paid close attention to Sparks's testimony, and he came away with no doubts about the policeman's racist attitudes as well as his propensity for excessive use of force. "He told with apparent satisfaction of the beating up of these soldiers," Cress wrote in his report. "He said that whenever he arrested a 'nigger' it was usual for him to 'make his heart right' by beating him up." Sparks admitted that Corporal Baltimore had not resisted arrest, had not tried to fight with him, and had not been violent in any way, but none of that mattered to him because "he never recognized Baltimore as an officer with any authority, that he recognized him as a 'nigger soldier.'"

As an Army officer, Cress was incensed by that. "During his testimony Officer Sparks exhibited the attitude of a Texas outlaw rather than that of an officer of the law," he wrote, and noted that Houston newspapers largely ignored this testimony and "made light of the whole affair." They also paid little attention to other testimony that portrayed the city police as racist and quick to use lethal violence against people of color.

When Third Battalion's medical officer, Lieutenant Chaffin, was interviewed by one of the Army investigators, he told of a conversation he had with a police officer shortly after the battalion arrived in Houston. The policeman said he would be "damn glad when the negro soldiers left town." When Chaffin asked why, he was told the soldiers were causing trouble in the city and had allegedly beaten up a streetcar conductor so severely the man was not expected to live, something that had never actually happened. "A man whom I rode into town with one day said that in Texas it cost 25 dollars to kill a buzzard and five dollars to kill a nigger," Chaffin said. Another Houstonian told him that if the War Department sent the Black battalion of the Illinois National Guard to Camp Logan, "we will kill some of the sons of bitches, if they don't behave."[27]

For its part, the commission pursued its predetermined conclusion and continued to interpret all the testimony it produced as exonerating the city of any responsibility. One of its methods in this process was to gather testimony from white Houstonians eager to portray 3-24 Infantry's camp as a seething den of iniquity and its soldiers as an undisciplined rabble of moral delinquents given to public indulgence of all sorts of depraved vices. Chief Brock in his testimony claimed, "Colonel Newman told me, when I spoke to him about [the soldiers] shooting craps and having negro women, that he let them shoot craps and let the women in camp because it kept the men satisfied. I heard through reports by officers that many negroes were drunk at the camp." Brock did not actually name any of these officers, however, and the commission did not press him to provide evidence for his claims.

When a Houston resident named Kyle Paulus appeared before the commission, Crooker asked him, "Tell us just what you observed in passing with reference to whether or not negro women had access to the soldier camp, how long they stayed there, and what were the regulations, if any, or the lack of them." Why a civilian who was not associated with the Army in any capacity would be expected to have any knowledge of military regulations on a particular installation is not clear, but the commission frequently asked such questions.

"I have seen them there ever since the camp has been there, and particularly since Colonel Newman has left, but there was some of them there before," Paulus said. "When they first went out there, there wasn't so many of them, but lately since this dance hall has been there, why they have been there in bunches. I have seen them laying down on the ground with niggers, all laying there together, talking." Paulus never said that these civilian women were having sex in public with soldiers, but that was the implication, and the commission interpreted it as that.

"Do you know whether or not the women had anything with them, or whether they were searched?" Crooker asked, still fishing for testimony to support his claim that civilian visitors had smuggled alcohol into the camp.

"I have seen them go in there—you take where this dance hall is, and the women walked in there just like you would walk down Main Street; nobody stopped them or anything," Paulus said. "I have seen them walk through there time and time again, and those niggers living out there would do the same thing."[28]

For all of the racist language in Paulus's statements, he was almost a social progressive when compared to other white citizens who testified before the commission. Crooker asked another man, "Now, you said you noticed some conditions in the camp in the camp on the occasions when Colonel Newman was there and after he left. Now, how do you get at that?"

"On this day that I went in there, the day of the trouble," the witness answered, "why you could catch that nigger smell—I don't know, it is like a rattlesnake. I said there was some agitation in there; you could feel it."[29]

These stories of drunkenness and lasciviousness grew more lurid with each repetition, always rendered through the lens of racist tropes. Several witnesses enlarged upon their stories in each subsequent telling, as if trying to outdo the sensationalism of their earlier testimony. Other people interjected themselves into the discussion and claimed to have insight into the matter but never offered any evidence for their claims. Many of these commentators repeated versions of the salacious stories that were filling the newspapers, but each claimed some personal knowledge.

One of the most verbose of these was J. W. Link, the president of a Houston land development company. Six days after the violence, Link wrote a long, rambling diatribe of a letter to Texas oilman Joseph Cullinan in which he claimed to know for certain how things had been in Third Battalion's camp. He declared that "negro women by the hundreds were admitted to the camp day and night, and permitted to stay and remain there . . . and bring all kinds of intoxicating drinks. Hundreds of people saw these negroes drinking whiskey openly in the camp." He never named any of these witnesses and did not actually say he had observed it himself, but that did not stop him from assuring Cullinan, "This whiskey was largely carried to the camp by a perfect horde of negro women," and insisting that "their camp was like a heathen community."

Link did not limit his polemic to just the 654 men of 3-24 Infantry. He condemned all Black soldiers, whatever their regiment. "They have never been anything but an obligation and disgrace to the American Army. . . . In my judgment, there must be a distinction between the negro soldiers and the white soldiers," he wrote. "When armed, the negro wants to be lawless, and has but little knowledge of his obligations to the Government, and possesses practically no national patriotism. . . . The minute you give them a gun and authority, they become overbearing and dangerous." He concluded his rant by declaring, "The negro is happiest, and most contented, when he is under the dominion and control of the white man."

Reading through Link's entire letter, one is struck by the fact he never used a single racial slur in his diatribe. His brand of racism, however, was nonetheless blatant and obvious, and it was expressed in the clear, articulate language of an educated man who was an unapologetic white supremacist.

In one sense, that made his polemic even more dangerous and unsettling than the barely literate scribblings of some white people who littered their testimony with slurs and profanities.[30]

In the face of all the lurid allegations made against the men of 3-24 Infantry in the weeks that followed the troubles, the truth of the matter was something far less nefarious than what these stories claimed.

The Third Battalion had a reputation for very good order and discipline, but its soldiers were just as human as those of any other regiment. Some of them were apt to get in a bit of trouble if trouble was available, but they were no threat to the civic peace. They were just young men in a tough, exclusively male occupation, and when they had a chance to let loose a little, some of them did. For the majority of them, when they had a pass to leave camp, they were eager to socialize with local girls, go dancing, and enjoy themselves. Many of them were also content to remain at camp and enjoy the company of people who came to visit in accordance with Colonel Newman's policy.

The soldiers of 3-24 Infantry were very aware of the high regard in which they were held by the local African American community and just as aware of the hostile scrutiny of white Houstonians, and most soldiers in the battalion conducted themselves with blameless professionalism when they were off duty. By and large, it is clear they were proud of who and what they were, and largely abstained from the stereotypical military sins of drunkenness, brawling, and frequenting prostitutes.

The battalion's officers and NCOs all stated under oath that their soldiers were so well disciplined that even the common sort of "leadership challenges" were rare in the unit. What disciplinary issues did arise were minor and were limited to offenses such as coming back to camp late after a pass. In many regiments, payday usually brought with it the possibility of trouble because of some soldiers' propensity for blowing their pay on alcohol. That sort of strife was almost unheard of in 3-24 Infantry. One India Company NCO, Corporal Leonard Watkins, remembered the August 14 payday that month precisely because, he said, "in all of my service which is eight years and over I never witnessed a more quiet payment, the men seemed as though they were ashamed to be seen drunk or drinking, and during our stay in Houston I took special notice of the good conduct of the battalion as a whole." Captain Bartlett James, commander of Lima Company, found the same to be true of his soldiers. "There were fewer men who showed signs of intoxication after payday than has been usual," he reported.[31]

As soon as 3-24 Infantry arrived in Houston, purveyors of vice began to appear almost as a natural element of military life, but they found little business for their wares. Lieutenant Colonel Newman's decision to open the camp to the city's African American community made positive sorts of social diversions available to his men, and that helped dull the appeal of the illicit ones. The prohibition against alcohol in the camp was absolute and strictly enforced, and no unbiased witness ever claimed otherwise. Prostitutes were strictly barred from plying their trade in the cantonment, and on the few occasions when a woman was even suspected of being a working girl, she was immediately escorted out of camp, usually at the request of the enlisted men themselves. Newman issued no orders banning soldiers from playing cards or throwing dice when they were off duty, and that was seized on by some Houstonians as a flagrant violation of the city's laws against gambling, but no concerned citizens voiced any such complaint until after the trouble on August 23.

Another measure of the high level of military discipline in Third Battalion was the frequency with which summary courts-martial were convened to deal with minor infractions.* The standards of conduct in the battalion were clearly defined, and any violation of those standards was dealt with quickly and firmly. Samuel Venters, the acting first sergeant of Lima Company, stated that "all violations of discipline were reported promptly to the commissioned officers of the camp, and immediately dealt with, the summary court being active and fixing unusually severe penalties." Sergeant Rhoden Bond of India Company believed the battalion "was in discipline the best in the regiment." Captain James recalled that when a large number of soldiers came back to camp late for the 11:00 curfew after being out on their first pass in town that July, Colonel Newman "issued

---

* To a reader familiar with modern military justice in the form of the Uniform Code of Military Justice (UCMJ), any use of the term "court-martial" sounds very serious. It is important to note, however, that in 1917 the UCMJ did not yet exist, and the U.S. Army was still governed under the Articles of War. There were no Article 15 proceedings to deal with minor offenses at the company or battalion level, so the equivalent was a battalion-level summary court-martial, which could impose the same sorts of punishments awarded by a company or field-grade Article 15 proceeding today: a demotion in rank, extra duty, loss of several weeks' pay, or restriction to quarters.

strict orders that all absentees be tried by summary court." That apparently fixed the problem quickly, because "the absentees at the 11:00 p.m. check fell off to a negligible number."[32]

Colonel Cress produced compelling evidence from other white Houstonians to counter the Citizens' Commission claims that the men of Third Battalion were degenerate and undisciplined. A woman identified as Mrs. Miller, whose house was close to the battalion camp, told him, "We ladies when we first heard negro soldiers were going to be stationed here were very much alarmed but they behaved so well that we soon forgot entirely there were any soldiers about. We never heard them except when the bugles blew."[33]

Mrs. Moy, whose family had leased to the Army the acreage that Third Battalion used as its camp, had a similar experience with the infantrymen. When Cress asked her how things were with the soldiers before August 23, she said, "They came over here quite frequently and they came and used my telephone quite frequently. I didn't have any trouble. They didn't disturb me in any way. They were always good-natured. They were very nice in every way."

"Did you notice any signs of intoxication among the men?" Cress asked.

"No sir, I didn't," she replied.

Testimonials also came from farther afield. The Chamber of Commerce in Columbus, New Mexico, where the entire 24th Infantry Regiment had been stationed before the posting to Texas, sent a telegram to the Army's Southern Department a few days after the trouble in Houston. "During the five or six months the Twenty Fourth Infantry was stationed here we learned to trust and believe in them," the telegram read; "we believe them to be one of the best disciplined regiments in the army. We would be glad to have the Twenty Fourth returned and other colored troops sent here for training."[34]

As the Army's lead investigator, Cress was particularly concerned by the incessant accusations that military discipline was lax in Third Battalion. Almost every white witness he interviewed repeated that accusation, and their stories grew more lurid and salacious with every telling. Dan Moody, Houston's interim mayor, told Cress, "I believed that something was going to happen. . . . That is what we had to contend with. There were colored people who resented things that had been done to them, or their friends, and they would go out and talk to [soldiers], and it helped to bring this about. I heard that there were certain negro women who did this and smuggled things in the camp which were not allowed."[35]

This idea that Black women had corrupted the military camp, either by smuggling things into the cantonment or by their own immoral presence, was repeated over and over.* Cress had his doubts about it. "The Houston City Board of Inquiry apparently made a special effort to show conditions in and about the 24th Infantry camp, in the matter of women and liquor, in their worst possible light," he wrote in his report, but he did not accept such stories unchallenged. He pointed out that in their testimony, military officers "agree there was very little trouble in the matter of intoxication among these soldiers." He was not inclined to take Houston's version of things at face value. "In weighing the evidence due consideration should be given to two important points," he wrote in his report: "First, that the citizens desirous of maintaining troops at Houston, etc., would find it of great advantage to them if they could prove to the satisfaction of the Federal Government that responsibility for the riot lay with the military forces; Second, that there was a political fight on, and the Committee in order to secure the relief of Chief Brock and other officials would find their best argument in the proof of laxity and inefficiency against these officials."[36]

When Cress asked Captain Shekerjian about these allegations that Third Battalion's camp was a veritable den of iniquity, Shekerjian indignantly insisted that he and the other officers had maintained a well-ordered camp in full compliance with military discipline.

When asked if he ever told Colonel Newman that he thought allowing Black women in camp, Shekerjian said he had not, because he did not think there was anything wrong with the policy.

"Did you think the effect of allowing women in camp conducive to improved discipline or not?"

---

* Even Martha Gruening, the NAACP's investigating correspondent who interviewed witnesses after the August incident, seems to have accepted as factual these stories of lewd women in camp and rampant drinking. Gruening was only in Houston for a few days, however, and it does not seem that she spent much of her time testing the truthfulness of these particular allegations.

"It seemed to me that it kept the men more contented and kept them around camp," the adjutant replied. "The women, to all appearances, were good women."

Cress pressed him on that point, asking how the officers ensured that no women remained in camp or were in the soldiers' tents after 9:00 p.m. "Didn't you suspect that women did frequently remain in camp through the night?" he asked.

"No sir, I did not suspect it because the non-commissioned officers would not permit them to remain in camp," Shekerjian said. "I remember on occasions thinking that perhaps men were taking women under trees that were near camp and that were actually in the camp grounds and after Taps I walked down through those to see if there were any men and women and on no occasion did I find any." He was certain that the battalion NCOs had enforced the commander's rules exactly as they should have.

Cress tried another tack and asked if he had ever seen women leaving camp in the morning. Shekerjian said he never did, and he had a solid explanation for why he was so confident that women were not in camp when they were not supposed to be.[37] In the summer heat, the sides of the soldiers' tents were always rolled up to allow air to flow through, so anyone passing by in the company street would have easily seen if anything untoward was going on. At night, the NCOs on duty regularly conducted checks of the company areas, so it was not as if the camp was ever unsupervised or unobserved.

Cress put the same sort of questions to Major Snow when he interviewed him a second time a month after the incident, but those questions were much more consequential than when they were asked of the battalion's junior officers. Snow was the battalion commander, and ultimately responsible for the unit's character and performance. The battalion's permissive visitation policy might have originated with Lieutenant Colonel Newman, but from the moment Snow allowed that policy to continue unchanged after he assumed command, he became the only man responsible for it.

Cress asked him to explain his reasons for allowing civilian visits to continue, and Snow described the sorts of people who came to camp. "The people coming in there were [a] very respectable class," he said. "There were as many men as women and as many children as men and women together. . . . The Colonel [Newman] thought it would give them a chance to meet the better class of colored civilians of the city; once a preacher came out called the Colored Billy Sunday and they arranged meetings for the men in camp."[38]*

Furthermore, Snow insisted, this positive characterization of the Black civilians who visited the battalion camp was shared by the soldiers themselves. "I spoke to Sergeant Henry only a day or two before this occurrence about the civilians in camp," Snow said, "and to [Corporal] Singleton who was acting as Chaplain and also the officers and they all spoke about the appearance of the negro visitors we were having that they appeared to be a very high class of civilians. Don't remember any women who looked like lewd women. One man asked permission to get married and he brought his girl over to my tent. She was working for a family down in Houston and she was a very respectable sort of girl." This detail was important, because Army regulations of that era required that any enlisted man who wished to marry had to first obtain his commanding officer's permission, and he had to show that his intended wife was a reputable woman of good character.[39]

Most of the soldiers in Third Battalion were bachelors, but there were a few married men among them, mostly NCOs like Sergeant Samuel Venters, a native Texan, originally from Galveston down on the Gulf Coast with relatives in Houston. Third Battalion's posting to Camp Logan was a rare opportunity for Venters to catch up with his extended family, and his wife and relatives visited him at the battalion cantonment during those weeks. He, too, told Cress that the women he saw at the camp were "first class people."[40]

Captain James refuted allegations of lax discipline and immoral conduct in the camp. "I know of only one case where there was trouble in camp caused by a woman," he said. "That was in my own company where the men of my company went to the sergeant of the guard and asked that the woman be removed from the camp. The first sergeant told me about it later in the afternoon and told me that the men did not want that kind of women in camp; that their wives and friends came out there and they didn't want that kind of women in camp, and that the privates in the company had asked that this woman be put out of camp. I know as a fact that my sergeants who are married had their wives in camp. I have seen negro girls

---

* Billy Sunday was a nationally famous revival preacher and evangelist in the first decades of the twentieth century, known for the energy and showmanship of his sermons.

and negro men in the camp but they were always perfectly well behaved so far as I saw. I never saw any signs of anything wrong."

James had a personal perspective on this question that he shared with his former battalion commander, Colonel Newman. James's younger sister Harriet had joined him in Houston, and she often spent time in the battalion camp and dined with him in the officers' mess. A Virginian of traditional, genteel upbringing, James never would have permitted his sister to remain in camp if doing so would have brought her into contact with prostitutes, smuggled liquor, or public indecencies of the sort that many white Houstonians claimed were a regular feature of Third Battalion's camp. "If the class of people coming into camp, especially the women, had not, to all appearance, been respectable," James said in a sworn statement on September 22, "or if there had been any likelihood of unpleasantries taking place, I would not have had my sister in camp." According to him, there was no laxity in the camp, and discipline was strictly maintained.[41]

Colonel Newman specifically referred to Harriet James's presence in the camp as one of the proofs that the battalion maintained very high standards, and he doubled down on that by pointing out that his own family members were also regularly in camp with him. "My wife and little boy frequently sat with me near my tent late in the afternoon and after supper until nine or ten o'clock," Newman said. "If conditions had been such as stated by witnesses before the citizens' committee, I would not have permitted them to come to the camp."[42]

———

Colonel Cress, in his role as the Southern Department's inspector general, seems to have come to his inquiries with a relatively open mind. He was trying to find out what had happened in Houston, and why, and who was responsible for the criminal violence and the breakdown in military discipline. From language in his official report, it is clear that Cress subscribed to some of the racist stereotypes prevalent in that era, but at least he did not come to the process with his mind already made up about the details of the case. He did not ask the sort of leading questions that would elicit answers that fit his predetermined conclusions. In that, at least, he was a good investigator. The same could not be said for the Army Inspector General.

Brigadier General John Chamberlain arrived from Washington a few days after the August incident. His orders were to carry out an investigation parallel to but separate from the one Cress was conducting. He was not to interfere with Cress, though he was his superior both by rank and position. But whereas Cress approached his task with an open mind, Chamberlain, within the first couple of days, accepted a narrative that he completely bought into, and from that point on he seems to have conducted his interviews and phrased his questions in ways that permitted only one possible interpretation of the event. In particular, Chamberlain seems to have wholeheartedly accepted the Citizens' Commission's allegations that 3-24 Infantry's camp was a squalid morass of indiscipline, overrun with vice.

In his written report he left no doubt as to whose version of events he accepted. "The testimony before the Citizens' Committee is, to my mind, conclusive to the effect that the camp was frequented by women of bad repute," Chamberlain wrote, "many of them well known to the police as prostitutes; that these women visited the men's tents and that their profession was at times plied in the tents. Mr. Davidson, Ex-Chief of Police of Houston, testified that he had frequently visited the camp and that conditions in this respect he regarded as scandalous." Having said that, Chamberlain then placed a slight caveat on the testimony upon which he was basing his conclusions. "Other civilians gave damaging testimony along these lines, but like all testimony given under circumstances such as existed at this time, it is exaggerated and to a great extent unreliable," he wrote, but then he completely nullified whatever moderating effect such a qualification might have provided by concluding, "However, no doubt exists in my mind that conditions were scandalous."[43]

Colonel Newman gave his official statement on September 20, well after the allegations made by the Citizens' Committee had made their rounds, and he categorically refuted those claims of lax discipline and rampant immorality in the camp. "The point is made that I allowed *women* to come in and out of camp freely," he said. "This assumption is in error. I allowed *civilians*, both white and black, to come in and out of camp anytime they wished to do so between reveille and 10:45 p.m. Naturally there were women among them. From a reading of the testimony of the witnesses that appeared before the citizens' committee of Houston, one would infer that only women came to the camp and that I encouraged lewd women to come to the camp. That is entirely untrue. . . . [A]ll the people who visited the camp were respectable people. I judge of this by their general appearance and conduct. . . . [N]ot one action was observed by me to indicate that a lewd woman was in the camp." Newman pointed out that he was in the habit of inspecting the camp regularly, "day and night," and that he observed the camp guards performing their duty of making sure that all visitors departed the camp by 10:45.[44]

When Chamberlain interviewed Captain Shekerjian, he phrased most of his questions in ways that suggested he had already accepted the salacious stories as true. "There is a great deal of convincing testimony to the effect that it was not unusual for a few of these women at least to spend the night in these tents in camp," he said; "to make a long story short, that the red-light district of San Felipe Street was practically moved out to the 24th Infantry camp. These women were there in the evening, many of them in the men's tents, on their bunks, and they were living a perfectly free and easy life there in camp. What do you know about that?"

"I don't believe these reports to be so," Shekerjian said. He might have been tempted to call those allegations "outright lies," but he was speaking to a general officer and probably thought it prudent to moderate his language.

"It is not a question of reports," Chamberlain insisted. "I am speaking now of the sworn testimony of people who have seen these things going on around camp and of women friends of these men, some of them who acknowledge that they had stayed there overnight and many of them until ten or eleven o'clock and that they frequented the men's tents. When a negro wench from the red-light district frequents a man's tent you know what it means."

"I know women have been in the tents but I do not think that anything was wrong," Shekerjian said, which certainly was true of the civilians' daytime visits under the supervision of the battalion NCOs. "It was the endeavor to bring the men into contact with the better class of the negro population. The orders were that any woman who was a prostitute was to be put out of camp."

"Who was to find out who were prostitutes?"

"The noncommissioned officers."

"How would they know?" Chamberlain pressed. He may have thought it was a clever question, but it would have prompted incredulous laughter from any experienced infantry NCO. The sergeants in the battalion, wise in the ways of sin and familiar with all the ways in which soldiers could get themselves into trouble, could probably have recognized a working girl at fifty yards, guessed within ten cents how much she charged for a roll in the hay, and calculated to a fair degree of certainty the odds of catching a dose of the clap from her.

"They would be more likely to know than anyone else," Shekerjian said, which was a simple fact of Army life.[45]

Newman's testimony was a convincing rebuttal of the Citizens' Committee's allegations, though Chamberlain was never willing to take it into account. "The only conclusion that can be reached about the testimony to the effect that I allowed lewd women in the camp and bootlegging," Newman said, "is that it is an afterthought, and is a result of the prejudice that these witnesses have against negro people in general. . . . In judging of this testimony," he concluded, "consideration must be given also to the fact that the prevailing opinion among white people in the south is that *all* colored women are immoral."[46]

It was an important observation, and an accurate one, but Chamberlain chose to ignore it.

———

The weekend following the violence, funerals were conducted for people killed in Thursday night's violence. Captain Joseph Mattes's flag-draped coffin was escorted to the train station by an honor guard of soldiers from his unit, the 2nd Field Artillery of the Illinois National Guard, for transport home to Chicago. When it arrived there, hundreds of spectators turned out to watch the procession as his coffin was carried through the city to the church on an artillery caisson.

The funerals for Houston police officers Ira Raney and Rufus Daniels were held at their respective homes. Fellow officers served as pallbearers, and both men were buried in the city's Evergreen Cemetery. E. M. Jones, the driver of the civilian jitney that was fired on by soldiers from the Camp Logan guard detail, was buried with his widow and five of his six children in attendance at the graveside. His family, the newspaper reported, "express their gratitude to the Illinois troops who were kind enough to take charge of Mr. Jones's body Thursday night following his death" until his body could be taken to an undertaker.

Two of the people killed in the violence that night went to their graves without eulogies or mourners. The bodies of Sergeant Vida Henry and

Private Bryant Watson were handled by a Jewish mortuary firm owned by Sid Westheimer, because the city's African American funeral homes were afraid to be associated with the man believed to be the ringleader of a mutiny that had cost so many white lives.

Henry's death was initially believed to be a suicide, and the first reports from soldiers in his column said they believed he killed himself with a single rifle shot after they left him at the railroad tracks. No one actually saw him shoot himself, however. The first newspaper accounts described something different. The *Press* declared, "His head was shot off with a shotgun," which was a bit of an exaggeration. All three city newspapers assumed that Henry was killed sometime later that night, perhaps by a civilian, as he walked along the tracks. One reporter suspected the police killed him but put his time of death too early to fit the timeline that later developed from multiple witnesses.

The coroner's inquest into Henry's death included statements from the mortuary staff who examined his corpse. Joseph Cooper reported that the body was "dressed in a service uniform, wearing socks, underwear, and an identification plate. The pockets held 'a couple handful of cartridges . . . of a caliber used in a Springfield rifle,'" but no cartridge belt was on the body. The embalmer, H. D. Goldstein, stated that Henry's "head was badly crushed with a blunt instrument, and he had a knife or bayonet wound about five inches deep ranging from the clavicle to the heart; either wound would have caused death." Justice J. M. Ray, who presided over the inquest, personally inspected Henry's corpse as part of his inquiry. "After viewing the body of the above deceased and hearing the foregoing testimony, and in view of the surrounding," he wrote in his official report, "I am of the opinion that the said deceased came to death on the 23d day of August A.D. 1917, as a result of having his skull crushed and a knife or bayonet wound at the hands of persons unknown."

Henry and Watson were buried in the city's African American burial ground at College Park Memorial Cemetery, quietly and without ceremony. The location of their graves was noted but no markers were placed. Not until a century later, in 2017, were headstones placed to show where they were buried.[47]

The fear that kept Black mortuaries from handling the final disposition of Henry's remains was shared by most African American residents in the aftermath of the violence. A small piece titled "Advice to Houston

Negroes" appeared in the *Chronicle* a few days after the troubles. "Stay off the streets, except when going to and from your work or places of business," it read. "Remain at home, except when it is absolutely necessary for you to go out. Don't assemble on the streets. Talk as little as possible about this regrettable and horrible happening. Don't become alarmed and leave the city." The writer promised that authorities would "see that the responsibility is properly placed where it belongs and that the severest punishment (as it should be) is meted out to the guilty parties." The author of the article was J. J. Hardeway, secretary of the Houston Negro Business League, but his assurance did not assuage the worry of many Black residents that they might be blamed for what happened. Police and the National Guard had begun going door-to-door in the Black neighborhoods, confiscating all firearms. If any sort of mob violence developed, Houston's Black citizens were now completely defenseless. Hundreds of them left the city in the following days, and they did not return until it seemed certain that it was safe for them to do so.[48]

W hile the Citizens' Commission was busy absolving Houston of any responsibility for the tragedy, Colonel Cress carried on with trying to find out what had actually happened on August 23, and why, and who was to bear the ultimate blame. He quickly recognized at least two distinct sets of answers to those questions—the officially scripted version of events coming from city officials and white citizens who were testifying before the commission, and the version he got from the testimony of military witnesses and those of Houston's Black citizens, at least the ones who were willing to speak to him.

He soon found the obvious holes in Houston's official claims of racial harmony and wise governance. In his initial report to Major General John W. Ruckman, the newly appointed commander of the Southern Department, Cress wrote, "It was evident, when this investigation was first undertaken, that politics was a strong factor in the administration of city affairs; that there was no coordination between the sheriff's office and police department and no effort or desire on the part of the citizens generally to change their attitude toward the negro soldier." That internal schism and lack of meaningful effort in race relations struck Cress as a major cause of the troubles. "The Houston City Police officers," he wrote, "appear to have had, prior to this trouble of August 23rd, a reputation for treating negroes badly and the attitude among them and among the white citizens generally, is, in substance, that a nigger is a nigger, and that his status is not affected by the uniform he wears."[49]

Cress believed that the only commentators who could truly speak to the state of military discipline in 3-24 Infantry, or the alleged lack of it, were other Army officers. They, after all, were members of the military themselves, and they knew what correct discipline looked like when they saw it. If they were officers not associated with Third Battalion, that added even more veracity to their testimony.

Captain David VanNatta, a company commander in the 2nd Illinois Infantry, told him, "At different times since Aug 17, 1917, the date of my arrival at Camp Logan with my command, I have heard various people talking about the colored troops being here. The sentiment was very strongly against them being here or any more colored troops being sent here for any purpose. At various times I have had occasion to observe members of the 24th U.S. Infantry doing guard duty and they were apparently well instructed and performed their duty in a soldierly manner and apparently, were well disciplined." He described the night of the violence, when two of Third Battalion's soldiers who were then on guard duty at Camp Logan came to him for help. "I believe from what I have observed that the members of the 24th U.S. Inf. stationed here were ordinarily an efficient and well-disciplined body and that local conditions have had a tendency to cause them to be under great mental stress since they have been here."[50]

Captain Ralph C. Woodward of the 3rd Illinois Infantry told much the same story. "My personal observation of the men who have been stationed throughout this camp convinces me that the men were well disciplined and thoroughly instructed in regard to the method of guard duty," he said. "The detail stationed at the warehouses were constantly on the alert and on several occasions I noted that these men were watching the various soldiers and civilians in the vicinity of the warehouses and cautioned them in regard to smoking in or about these buildings, also that men coming into the camp after dark were invariably halted when passing near the post of those sentries who were stationed along the rows of mess-halls." He found no fault with their military bearing, their conduct, or the way in which they carried out their assigned duties, and he had no complaints about their behavior off duty, either.[51]

Not many Black Houstonians were willing to go on record about the racial situation in the city. They knew all about it—after all, it was the oppressive reality of their daily lives, and they faced a real threat of retaliation if they spoke out. As one man told NAACP investigator Martha Gruening, "It's like this, lady—I could talk all right, but I'm afeard. I know a lot, but I live here, and my family lives here, and all I got is here . . . and there's prejudice here—and you see how 'tis." He said he saw Wallace Williams after Lee Sparks shot him in the back and killed him on August 26, and added, "And what's more, I've seen three more colored men beat up without any cause by the police since the riot. There's a lot more I *could* say, only I'm afeard."[52]

Many people were afraid, and only a few were willing to take the risk of speaking out to refute the commission's version of events. Henry Pratt, the headwaiter at the Houston Club, was one of them. Cress asked if he had overheard any complaints from the soldiers about the way they were treated in Houston.

"Yes sir, I heard some complaints," Pratt said. "They often called them 'niggers' and they got sore about it, and they had a scrap with some white fellows the other evening and then they would always arrest the colored soldiers and let the other people go. I think they were sore at the city police. I don't think the city police treated them right." Pratt also reported that Houston's Black citizens had long been on the receiving end of bad treatment at the hands of both policemen and white civilians. "They are frequently beaten up and nothing done about it," he said.

Ernest Smith, principal of an African American school, was also willing to go on record. Cress asked him, "In your opinion was this trouble on the 23rd the culmination of what was brewing or was it just a spontaneous result of the arrest of the two soldiers on the afternoon of the 23rd?"

"I think it was just a spontaneous disturbance, and came about from that one act, that the man thought the woman was being imposed upon, and the officer beating him up," Smith said. "That kind of thing has happened here more than once. The class of men we have had here for [police] officers have not always respected our men's rights. The better class of white men have had no trouble with the negro citizens or colored soldiers."

Major Snow, for his part, believed the unrelenting racist harassment from the police lay behind all the problems. "Tonight's trouble is the culmination of the general dissatisfaction that has existed in the Battalion on

account of the way some of the police officers have treated them," he said
in his statement to General Hulen. "I received many reports from men
of the Battalion of mistreatment on the part of the officers of the Police
Department of Houston. A good deal of the trouble was caused by the use
on the part of the police officer[s] of the word 'nigger' which the men of
the battalion considered an insult to their race." That much was accurate,
but he then opined that the soldiers "do not have a kindly feeling toward
it that possibly most of the Southern negroes do have." Snow seems to
have believed that Houston's African American residents did not object
to being called racist slurs.[53]

The chief of police, Clarence Brock, talked with Cress several times
and used the opportunity to try to shift responsibility for the incident
directly onto the soldiers. "It seems that the boys at the negro camp resented
anybody calling them niggers," Brock said, "but as this is a southern place
it is hard to keep people from calling them niggers instead of negroes and
that caused a little friction."[54]

The fact that soldiers had expressed their anger over the segregated
streetcar seating by sitting wherever they pleased in defiance of the Jim
Crow regulations, and even going so far as throwing the "Colored" signs
out the windows, came up frequently in Cress's interviews. "On two or
three occasions in the last two weeks," General Hulen of the Texas National
Guard told him, "responsible citizens stated to me that they feared there
would be some trouble with the negro soldiers. . . . They seemed to think
that they had greater privileges than other negroes in the community
and that they were disrespectful and sometime abusive to the citizens."[55]

One of Hulen's regimental officers, Colonel John Hoover, had a
slightly different perspective on the matter. Hoover was a southerner and
a Texan, but he was also a career Army officer, and he considered the problem more from a military perspective than from the conventional southern
view. "There has always been trouble between the police of Houston and
the negroes," he told Cress; "from conversations with citizens of Houston it
has been worse in the last three or four months than heretofore and in my
opinion it is due to lack of discipline and leadership in the police department." Hoover believed the fault ultimately lay with the police. "From what
I can learn from indirect sources," he concluded, "there was no teamwork
between the police of the City of Houston. In fact, I do not think the Chief
of Police of Houston knows the duties of the military police."[56]

Several of the 3-24 Infantry soldiers Cress interviewed agreed with that assessment. "Yes sir, there was talk among the men that Texas had kind of a reputation for treating colored people badly," Sergeant Cecil Green of M Company told him. "The men seemed to think they would be subjected to that kind of treatment. . . . [A]s provost sergeant, I would stop on my beat every now and then by some colored people who would talk about, for instance, 'I notice the white people won't bother you colored soldiers; that you won't take what we have to.'" Since Green was one of the NCOs detailed to the military police detachment who were supposed to establish a liaison with the civilian police officers in the San Felipe District, he had direct knowledge of how Houston's police force had interacted with the battalion's provosts in the city.[57] If Cress needed corroboration from the other side, he got it from Houston policeman J. E. Richardson, who told the IG that he "knew no arrangements to work with the military police." Chief Brock had apparently never carried through on the promises he made to Colonel Newman or Captain Shekerjian that he would instruct his officers to cooperate with the soldiers serving as military provosts.

On September 17, while the Army continued its investigations, a rather strange letter arrived at the War Department in Washington, D.C. Addressed to Secretary of War Newton Baker, this letter claimed that the truth of what had happened in Houston, and the identities of the persons who were really involved, was being concealed from the government.

The anonymous writer appeared to not be very well educated, and the handwriting was poor, but the allegations in the letter were startling. "There are persons who can give a detailed account of what happened and the causes therefore but they will never divulge the facts in Houston," he said, but suggested that "if the trial is held elsewhere they may talk freely." The letter-writer warned Secretary Baker that he was not being given the true story and he should not trust the account coming out of Houston. "Quite a deal of the Evidence before the City investigating Council is manufactured. . . . [T]hey have a new information here but the Negroes and some of the whites is afraid to be interviewed by him [Cress] because the local inquiry Board will summon them before their Board and they fear intimidation." A list of seven names followed, supposedly all people who could provide the government with a true account of the incident and of information that was being covered up in an attempt to absolve Houston of any responsibility for the violence. From the addresses given with those names, it appears they were all Black residents of the city. The anonymous writer signed the letter, "Yours for law and Justice." It does not appear that any official investigator ever made an effort to follow up on the allegations in this letter or sought to establish the veracity of these claims, and the letter was simply filed away in the War Department's archives, where it remained for nearly fifty years.[58]

10. FAILURE OF COMMAND

Major Snow had certainly not distinguished himself by his conduct the night of the troubles, and the more he talked the more obvious that became. At 5:00 a.m. that Friday morning, while the blood was literally still wet in the streets, he made his first official statement on the matter to Brigadier General Hulen, the senior National Guard commander in the city (and the senior military officer on the scene until Major General George Bell arrived from Fort Sam Houston later that morning). Hulen's aide, Lieutenant William M. Nathan, served as recorder during the interview and wrote down Snow's report in shorthand. Nathan was thoroughly unimpressed by 3-24 Infantry's commanding officer. "I remember distinctly Major Snow's inability to direct his thought with clearness," Nathan wrote in the margin of his typed transcription of his shorthand notes. "At any rate, he was a weak and rotten disciplinarian . . . he wavered when he needed firmness."[1]

According to Snow's version of events, he had diligently tried to intervene when soldiers began pilfering ammunition and weapons, and he said that when the panic broke out in the camp, he "got down in the line with the men and shoved their rifles to the ground and told them not to do it. But they paid no attention to me whatsoever." When the shooting started, Snow claimed, "a considerable amount of it seemed to be directed at me."

Captain Bartlett James, who stayed with his soldiers that night and was in the midst of the uncontrolled firing as long as it lasted, contradicted the several statements Snow made claiming that he was deliberately fired at, or that mutinous soldiers had tried to kill him. James thought none of the shooting was aimed fire, and he was certain that it was not aimed at the officers in particular. If anyone had truly wanted to kill the battalion officers that night, it would have been easy enough to do so.

"Did you consider that during the firing in camp you were in imminent personal danger?" one of the Army investigators asked him.

"No, except by accident," James said. "I am surprised that fifty or seventy-five men were not killed in camp. They were firing in all directions up and down the company streets, but the idea that I would get shot never entered my head." As James recognized, the only danger when all bullets were stray bullets, and it was a very real danger, was that a man might get hit by an unaimed round. Even so, that risk never kept him, Shekerjian, and the other two officers from functioning and doing their jobs. Snow was the only officer in the battalion who claimed to have been deliberately shot at, or to have narrowly escaped attempted murder.

In his statement to General Hulen, Snow glossed over his panic-stricken, headlong flight from the camp with a single anemic sentence: "I endeavored to get to Camp Logan but was unable to do so." After he abandoned his battalion, nothing prevented Snow from going to Camp Logan. Several soldiers did so that night. Snow claimed the shooting in the battalion camp stopped at about 8:15 that night, by which time a "considerable number of armed 24th Infantry men were marching in the direction of San Felipe Street." That was information he could only have gained after the fact, because when Sergeant Henry led most of India Company out of camp, Snow was no longer there to see them leave. He had already fled.

Over the next two days, Snow made several public statements in which he attempted to shift any blame for the incident off himself. A serious reckoning was coming, everyone knew that, and Snow knew it, too. What only remained to be seen was whether the prosecution would be in a civilian or military court, and exactly who would find themselves facing charges. Several of the pronouncements Snow made to the press were not only self-serving but also highly prejudicial to future legal proceedings. Two days after the incident, the *Waco Morning News* reported that "Capt. L. F. Snow, commanding the battalion, said late tonight that the action of the negroes 'was practically mutiny.'" The reporter got Snow's rank and first name wrong but otherwise quoted him accurately enough. Snow said "there was repeated disobedience of commands" among the soldiers and insisted he had done everything in his power to control men who were determined to throw off military authority. He told the reporter, "After leaving camp the negroes committed murder," a statement that any defense counsel worthy of the title would later have protested vehemently. Snow barely knew more than anyone else about what actually happened that night after he abandoned his post, or who had done what, but he was never one to wait on the evidence. He was now scrambling to avoid the consequences of his personal failures as the commanding officer of a battalion that seemed to have mutinied and disintegrated into lawless violence.[2]

Snow was questioned several times in different settings by people with varying levels of authority. Two days after the incident he managed to sidestep a summons to testify before the Citizens' Commission. Snow attended the commission's session just long enough to say, "I am here in answer to your summons, but I am under instructions from the War Department that I cannot testify. I came here to tell you that."[3] The civilian board could not compel his testimony, but official Army investigators could.

As IG of the Southern Department, Colonel Cress ordered Snow to give a statement under oath. Lying in a sworn statement would be an act of perjury, and Snow seems to have been mindful of not telling a completely fabricated story. Instead, he gave Cress the most anemic version possible of his actions, leaving out almost every damning or critical detail about his panicked flight from the camp that night.

When the shooting started in camp, Snow said, he suddenly found himself alone and completely unsupported by his company officers and NCOs. "I was unable to connect myself with anyone at all," he told Cress. "I did not see any non-commissioned officers around there. I concluded that the situation was getting to be a general mix-up and that I had better push out from camp." "Push out" was a decidedly understated description of his headlong flight from camp when he abandoned his post, but Snow was not yet finished smoothing over the truth of his actions. "I went to a telephone somewhere down on Washington Street in the direction of town," he went on, "and called up the police and just as I was starting to talk the wire was cut or disabled so that the conversation was interrupted. The firing at that time was dying a little. Not quite so much going on . . . I tried to call up Camp Logan to get the Illinois troops over but could not get Camp Logan." The closest Snow got to accurately describing his loss of composure and panicked state of mind was when he told Cress, "I was about all in at that time."

Resuming his narrative, Snow said, "As quick as I could I got back to camp, but the firing had subsided by the time I reached there. The firing lasted from about 8:00 to 8:30 or a little later. Then the men were quiet when I got back to camp." Thus, Snow admitted he left his battalion to fend for itself and took off on his own without attempting to help the company officers deal with a volatile, dangerous situation. When he finally got himself back to camp "as quick" as he could, which was actually several hours later than he claimed, all was quiet and some semblance of order had been restored, all without any orders or direct action on his part.[4]

In his statement to another Army investigator, Snow gave an even less accurate version of his departure from the camp. "I went out to the Officers' line to Washington Street," he said, "and I found a Ford machine down the street some place between Fire Engine House No. 11 and the camp, and I asked the driver if he would take me to a telephone and he said yes." This was his only description of his panicked interactions with R. R. McDaniel, the civilian who drove him to the drugstore and then on to the fire station. "At the Fire Engine House I had some policeman turn in an alarm to Police Headquarters and went further down the street and attempted to get Camp Logan on the phone," Snow concluded.[5]

Cress asked him why he had not sent another officer or one of the NCOs to get help, rather than going himself. "I didn't see a single officer or man whom I recognized during the time of the firing," Snow replied. "I hadn't seen any of the other officers and was afraid they were killed. I didn't have anyone I could send that I could trust. I considered that I should get help as quick as I could."

Snow then described how when he finally returned to his battalion he found Kilo, Lima, and Mike Companies all positioned in a defensive perimeter around the camp, with most of the men oriented along the western edge of the camp.

"What was the object in placing them on the west side of camp?" he was asked.

"They could do less harm there than anywhere else should any get nervous and start to fire as there were less houses on that side," Snow said, "and I believe that, with the exception of 'I' Company, the reason why the rest of the men joined in as much as they did was because they were stampeded and feared a white demonstration against them."

"What orders did you give to the men in forming a skirmish line on the west side of camp?"

"I myself gave no orders," Snow said, "Captain Shekerjian did that before I got back to camp." That was perhaps an inadvertent admission that he had left it to his junior officers to hold the battalion together in his absence. It was a critical point, and Cress did not let it pass unremarked.

"How long were you absent from camp?"

"I should think about thirty minutes," Snow replied, "possibly not that long but it seemed a long time to me." In fact, he had absented himself from his command for nearly four hours.

The investigator then asked about the altercation between Corporal Baltimore and the two Houston policemen that precipitated the whole incident.

"The man who was beaten up was one of the best men in the company," Snow told him. "He was a man who was very much respected and liked in the company and it was a great shock to them all to hear of him being treated that way and they seemed very anxious that he get justice out of it. They had the idea that every time a negro soldier would be arrested he would be knocked over the head with a gun."

"How did Corporal Baltimore feel with regard to his trouble?"

"The Superintendent of Police told me that he didn't seem resentful at the police, but when I was talking to the company I wasn't exactly pleased with the way he did seem," Snow said. "He made the remark that he thought it was a pretty dirty deal. I think he tried to rouse the men himself. The men say, I was told by Alexander who was quite willing to tell me anything he knew, Baltimore and Corporal Moore were placed at the rear of the column with orders to shoot any man who fell out, which would indicate that Corporal Baltimore was one of Henry's chief assistants." Not only was that hearsay, it was also a very dangerous allegation for Snow to make, because by doing so he was claiming that Charles Baltimore and Jesse Moore were leaders of a mutinous conspiracy that no one had yet proven.

In fact, the U.S. Army's infantry field tactics manual called for NCOs to be assigned to the rear of any column in order to control stragglers and prevent men from falling out of the unit formation. If Sergeant Henry genuinely believed he was leading his column of troops out to meet an advancing threat, it stood to reason that he would position reliable NCOs at the rear of the element. Either Snow was unaware of that or he chose to put a different interpretation on the fact.

Army investigators were not dependent only on Snow's version of his actions that night, because they had testimony from other witnesses who offered very different impressions. Colonel John Hoover of the 5th Texas

Infantry National Guard encountered Snow during the troubles and had a vivid recollection of his appearance and behavior that night. Cress asked if Snow had presented himself as calm and collected when he reported to General Hulen, nearly eight hours after his battalion erupted into chaos and six hours after his junior officers had restored order without him. "Major Snow was considerably agitated," Hoover recalled, "and said he was suffering pains in the stomach. He also said that he had been shot at several times by unknown members of the 24th Infantry." Snow's claim to have been deliberately fired on by mutinous soldiers was something no other witness corroborated.[6]

At one point during the chaos that night, while sporadic gunfire was still sounding in the streets, Captain F. S. Haines found Snow in conversation with the officers of the Illinois National Guard at the San Felipe District fire station. Haines, along with another Army officer, had inadvertently driven into the middle of Sergeant Henry's column a short time earlier. The soldiers had not fired on them but made them dismount from their vehicle. Haines said he knew where the errant Third Battalion soldiers were inside the San Felipe District and offered to lead a detachment to intercept them.

Referring to this, Cress asked Snow, "Did you go with them?" It was a pertinent question, since those were Snow's soldiers, many of whom he knew personally (they certainly all knew who he was), and if any officer should have been expected to be able to talk them down, it would have been their own commanding officer.

Once again, Snow dodged his responsibilities. "I believe I had in mind to go by the police station first to get what reports they had been getting from the San Felipe District," he said. He told Cress he did not accompany Captain Haines and the National Guard troops who went into the San Felipe District because he thought it more important that he send a telegram to Southern Department headquarters in San Antonio alerting them to the crisis, a task that any one of the dozens of officers of various units could just as easily have done. After completing that chore, he gave General Hulen a full report of the event, which occupied most of the rest of the night. By the time that was done, the sun was up, the outbreak of violence was ended, and order restored. Only then did Snow return to his battalion and stay there. "I reached camp before reveille and the camp was quiet," he told Cress. "No trouble of any kind was reported."[7]

Despite Snow's efforts to portray his actions in the best light possible, so many witnesses contradicted him that Cress had to give serious credence to the possibility that Third Battalion's commander had completely lost his composure and his military bearing. When Cress interviewed A. F. Butler, one of the two policemen whom Snow encountered on the road that night when he was fleeing the camp in McDaniel's car, Butler put the time of the encounter at about five or ten minutes past eight o'clock. Cress asked if Snow was alone when they saw him.

"No sir, he was in the back seat of an automobile with a gentleman who was driving."

"Did you noticed anything about the condition of the man who was driving?" Cress asked.

"The driver appeared to be just a little excited but he did not appear intoxicated," the policeman said, contradicting Snow's claim that McDaniels was drunk.

"Was Captain Snow very much excited?"

"I never saw a man so excited before in my life, I think," Butler said. "My partner asked him if he had been shot and he said, 'I don't know whether I am or not.'"[8]

Testimony such as this was bad enough for Snow's reputation, but it was potentially even more damaging when the witnesses to his dereliction were fellow Army officers.

Captain W. P. Rothrock was the U.S. Army engineer officer in overall charge of Camp Logan's construction. He also had encountered Snow at the San Felipe fire station the night of the troubles and had a vivid recollection of his bearing at that time. "He told me that the negro troops were rioting and were beyond control of the officers," Rothrock told investigators. "I asked him if we could not help the officers by going out to the camp. He thought not as either the officers would have been killed or would have the troops in hand by that time." If Snow actually said that, it was an indefensible statement. By his own admission he was willing to either abandon his junior officers to death at the hands of mutinous troops or, assuming that they were still alive, leave them to handle things without him. Either way, it was clear that he had no intention of returning to the battalion for which he was responsible. "He said that he anticipated that there was going to be trouble earlier in the evening," Rothrock said. "I asked him why he did not get in touch with [the junior officers]. He said he had thought they would be able to hold the troops in hand."

The Army investigator asked, "Was he very much excited or rattled at the time he was talking to you?"

"Well, he could not take command at Washington Street," Rothrock said. "He was not in physical shape or mental shape to take command or I would not have assumed command." In the Army's culture and practice of command and control that was a critical point, and it spoke volumes about Snow's apparent inability to function that night. No Army officer would presume to usurp command of another peer officer's unit, particularly not a unit of a different tactical formation, unless the necessity was dire and obvious. Likewise, no officer would voluntarily relinquish command of his own unit if he was still able to lead it. In the professional evaluation of his fellow Army officers, Snow was in such a state of mind that night that he was no longer able to function as Third Battalion's commander.[9]

As Cress worked his way through a long list of witnesses, he spoke with many of Third Battalion's NCOs. Most of the sergeants and corporals said they had tried to keep control of weapons and ammunition and told of being overwhelmed in the chaotic scramble in the dark when their soldiers panicked at the shout that a mob was coming. For the most part, they had tried to do whatever they could to reassert military control in the emergency.

Several of Cress's interviews, however, revealed that failures of leadership were not limited to just the battalion commander. Cress was particularly critical of the acting battalion sergeant major, William Washington. In his official report, he wrote that Washington "had retired [gone to bed] when shooting commenced; that he remained in tent until it was over and then with Corporal Baxter reported for assistance to a Lieutenant of the Illinois N.G."

Washington's own statement was an admission of dereliction of duty from start to finish. "I was in my bunk at the time the shooting commenced," he told Cress. "When they commenced to fire I rolled out of my bunk and laid on the floor until the shooting was over."

"Don't you think it was the duty of a non-commissioned officer to help quell a disturbance in camp?" Cress asked him. The idea that the sergeant major would just flatten himself on the floor and never venture out to where his battalion was tearing itself apart and losing all discipline was inconceivable. To make matters worse, Washington said that after the shooting stopped he left the camp with a corporal and sought shelter with another unit, without even informing any of the battalion officers that he was leaving.

"I gave them all the assistance I could by getting out and if I saw any disturbances, or anything of the kind, I would quell it as best I could," Washington insisted, referring to the days leading up to August 23. "That night when the disturbance commenced it was beyond anyone's power to do anything. The shooting was going on at that time."

Cress asked him if he ever discussed the agitation in the unit with the battalion commander before things disintegrated that evening. "No sir, I had no talk with Captain Snow prior to then," Washington said. "I heard they were disarming the men as they had been taking ammunition and that Captain Snow had been out there and that the noncommissioned officers should help. I said, 'Captain, I have helped all I can. I have quelled all the disturbance I have seen brewing and I think the treatment of the police has driven them into this.'"*

"You didn't go around the men and try to keep them from getting their ammunition and try to quiet them?"

Washington all but shrugged. "I didn't see anything I could do, sir. Captain Snow had his non-commissioned officers assisting him and I had been working hard all day, and sometimes I had to work to the middle of the night, I was tired."

Cress was incredulous. "Do you consider that sufficient for not helping in an emergency?"

"I am not giving that as an excuse, but am just stating the circumstances," Washington said. "While I saw conditions were bad, I was quite sure the officers had the upper hand of the thing. I couldn't do more than they did."[10]

The idea that the battalion's sergeant major simply went to bed when his unit was in a state of alarm, chose to hide when trouble broke out, and never made any effort to help the officers and other NCOs in

* It is unclear why Washington persisted in referring to Snow by the wrong rank, even though he was well aware of Snow's recent promotion.

their struggle to restore order was the absolute antithesis of everything expected of a senior noncommissioned officer. Cress asked him no more questions, perhaps because he concluded there was nothing more to say about Washington's bald-faced dereliction of duty, but he wrote a scathing assessment of Washington's conduct in his report. In his professional assessment, Washington was guilty of outright cowardice.

———

There was absolutely no question that India Company's first sergeant, Vida Henry, led the soldiers who marched out from Third Battalion's camp that night. Almost every witness agreed that Henry ordered India Company to fall in with weapons and ammunition, and that he personally led the sortie. His death at the railroad tracks certainly proved he had gone into town that night. What his motivations were for doing so and what his actual intentions were, however, remain controversial and still largely conjectural today. Two theories have been put forward: Either Henry believed the camp faced an impending attack by an advancing armed mob, and he made a deliberate tactical choice to lead a company of infantry out to meet force with force, taking the offensive against the threat, or he led the soldiers into town in an act of outright mutiny to enact a violent retribution against the Houston police department for their continued racist abuse, which had culminated in the beating and arrest of Corporal Baltimore earlier that afternoon. The first option can be seen as a legitimate, if hasty, military response to a perceived threat; the second can only be interpreted as a criminal act for which there is no excuse or exculpation. Determining which of those was actually behind his action remains a challenge for historians. It was not much easier for investigators in 1917 to come to the truth of the matter, but they seem to have quickly settled on the second interpretation of his actions.

Many of the eyewitnesses had different understandings of why Henry did what he did. When Cress interviewed Sergeant Rhoden Bond, India Company's supply sergeant, he asked him, "Did Sergeant Henry go out himself?"

"Yes sir, he went out himself."

"How many men did he have with him?"

"I don't know," Bond said. "I went to persuade him not to go but I saw he was in such a mood that I was afraid of him and jumped over behind some planks. From rough judgment he took 125 or 130 men with him."

"What kind of man was Sergeant Henry?"

"Sergeant Henry is a good soldier, in my estimation, beyond up until this time. I have known him since 1905."

"Had he been drinking?" Cress asked.

"No sir," Bond said. "I don't believe the man had a drink." He concluded, "Sergeant Henry had just lost his mind at the time and did not have any control over himself; for Henry was always obedient [to the military] and when we tried to talk to him he ran right over us."[11]

Sergeant William Fox agreed that Henry had led the men who marched out that night. "Do you know Sergeant Henry pretty well?" Cress asked him.

"Yes sir."

"What do you think was the reason for him taking the men out?"

"I think he thought that he was going to get killed anyway, from what he said," Fox said.

"Why would he be killed?" Cress said.

"I don't know about that, that is what he thought."

"Do you think Sergeant Henry organized this trouble?" Cress asked.

"I don't think there was any organized trouble," Fox said. "I think there was just a big scare and a stampede." He, at least, did not believe that a preconceived conspiracy to mutiny existed in the camp that night.

"Did you see him try to stop the excitement?"

"No sir, not after it started," Fox said. "When I saw him after the firing started in the company street he said, 'Fall in.' He had on a rifle and ammunition[.] [I]t was dark. . . . He said, 'Fill your canteens and get your rifles!' He said, 'We are in it now and have got to go.' I said, 'Where are you going?' And he said, 'To the hills.'"

Fox was a combat veteran and an experienced NCO, and he thought that was a bad tactical choice. He and other NCOs argued the better option was to stay and defend the camp, using the massed firepower of the battalion's rifle companies to hold a strong position against any approaching mob. "I suggested that we form a skirmish line around the camp," he told Cress. "Sergeant Barnes and I and others tried to talk to him, but he would not listen."

"Where was Major Snow?" was Cress's last question, and Fox replied, "I don't know," which was everyone's answer to the question so many people had asked that night.[12]

The question of whether Sergeant Henry was the primary instigator in a mutinous conspiracy or simply took charge of the chaotic situation and led the men out of camp because he sincerely thought it was the best tactical option is hard to answer with certainty. Several sources immediately after the incident depicted him as the ringleader of such a conspiracy, and those interpretations are still widely accepted today. That assumption, however, leaves some important questions unanswered. One possible explanation, rejected outright in the later courts-martial, was that Henry truly believed the camp was under attack and took it upon himself to lead a proactive defense that turned out to be a fatal mistake. A more frequently repeated theory was that he had planned a mutiny all along, orchestrated its outbreak under cover of darkness, and used the manufactured threat of a race mob to cover his movements. Perhaps, some suggested, he might have sympathized with a group of angry soldiers who were already planning criminal vengeance, and then stepped forward to lead them once he was sure they were actually willing to not just talk but act.

One soldier, Private Leroy Pinkett, said that at about 6:00 p.m. that evening a group of soldiers were talking, with several men saying it was time for them to get their own retribution against the police, when Sergeant Henry walked up. Instead of putting a stop to that kind of talk or reporting them to the officers, Pinkett claimed that Henry said, "Well, don't stand around like that. If you are going to do anything, go ahead and do it." The implication was clear: that Henry basically told the troublemakers to put up or shut up. When they committed themselves to actually making good on their threat, he not only joined them but led them.

Occasionally, the investigators' interviews turned up bits of information on Henry that were probably unexpected. During one of Cress's conversations with Captain Shekerjian, the adjutant told him, "I noticed during the night that Private Fields, the orderly at the telephone was gone. Everyone had full confidence in Fields and his absence was a shock. At reveille [the next morning] he returned and asked me if he did right; that he had run up to the Illinois camp for help as soon as the outbreak started; that, as the men started to town, Sergeant Henry came to him at the telephone and said, 'Take a knife and cut that wire,'—that he broke and ran. This wire was cut." If Fields was to be believed, then Henry's actions were a deliberate attempt to subvert lawful military authority, and that was the interpretation the Army took as the investigations continued.

Shekerjian believed that Sergeant Henry was at the center of the whole affair, but he was less certain as to why he had done it. Cress asked him, "What do you think might have been Sergeant Henry's object when he reported to Captain Snow there was going to be trouble?"

"I don't know," Shekerjian said. "Some officer[s] seemed to think that he was trying to double-cross Major Snow. Inside of me, I believe that Sergeant Henry up to this time didn't intend to go himself but was trying to protect himself with Major Snow. I think he was anxious for this to be pulled off himself for revenge. When he saw how things were going, he took charge to get quick action."

"Did you regard Sergeant Henry as a leader?"

"Sergeant Henry was the chief leader," the adjutant said, leaving no doubt as to his position on that question.

A s the investigators gathered more statements and conducted multiple interviews with Third Battalion's officers, a troubling theme began to emerge in the statements. The Army expected its soldiers not just to be obedient to lawful orders from their officers but also to be loyal to their officers and support them in the mission. Loyalty goes both ways, however, and in several instances some of those officers made statements that suggested they were not loyal to the men under their command.

When Colonel Newman gave a statement at Southern Department headquarters in October, he was asked, "Have you formed any opinion as to what brought on the riot of August 23?"

"I believe it was due to the brutality of Policeman Sparks that got these men all worked up," Newman said, but then added, "I have found the colored soldier a very impulsive man. He acts on the spur of the moment, and I don't believe he reasons very much about anything. I think he acts entirely on impulse."[13]

Captain Lindsay Silvester was already the target of official criticism for his decision to leave camp that night to keep a social engagement in town. Even though he knew how unsettled the battalion was at the time, and even though he thought it necessary to warn his supply sergeant to keep a close watch on the ammunition stocks, he still did not stay with his company. When General Chamberlain took his statement, it quickly became clear that Silvester had no sense of loyalty to the men in his charge.

"You had perfect confidence in your company and felt that you could depend on them?" Chamberlain asked.

"I have never had confidence in them since I have been assigned to this regiment," Silvester said.

"How long have you been with the regiment?"

"Since October, 1915."

"You have never had any confidence in them, but still that fact did not keep you in camp that night?"

"No, sir. I have kidded myself into believing that I was loyal."

Chamberlain seemed taken aback by that. "I do not understand that remark."

"I was assigned to them and have made the best of it," Silvester said, and added that he resented being assigned to a Black regiment.

"Is that the spirit in which you have gone through your duties thus far in your military career, that you have 'kidded' yourself into thinking things?"

Silvester tried to walk his statement back a bit. "No sir. I have taken them very seriously."

Chamberlain pressed him on it. "I don't understand what you mean when you say you 'kidded' yourself into believing that you were loyal."

"I thought I was loyal," Silvester said, "but I am convinced now that there was no question of knowing that the colored soldiers will not stand up." In his opinion, the problem was not his failure of leadership but that he could not rely on his soldiers because they were Black men.[14]

Captain Shekerjian had acquitted himself well that night, but in the days that followed he also made statements that put a disturbing racial cast on his views of the men in Third Battalion. Chamberlain asked him, "What rumors had you heard, if any, or had you heard anything which caused you to fear that there was going to be trouble that night?"

"We always feared trouble, sir," Shekerjian replied.

"Why?"

"Just because of the negro nature combined with actual or fancied wrongs."

Chamberlain focused on the second part of that statement. "What actual or fancied wrongs had they received outside of the Baltimore affair?"

"They continually complained about men in town calling them niggers. There were several cases of fighting because they had been called niggers," the adjutant told him.[15]

The fact that Chamberlain never reacted to the phrase "just because of the negro nature" suggests that he knew exactly what Shekerjian meant by it, and that he accepted it without comment. Even Colonel Cress, who at least tried to keep more of an open mind than Chamberlain in his investigation and who concluded that Houston's racism lay at the heart of the troubles, expressed that same troubling attitude at least once in a racist generalization that impugned every soldier in 3-24 Infantry simply because they were Black.

In the official report he filed on September 13, Cress listed the issues he believed had the most bearing on the outbreak of violence the night of August 23. The first items he pointed to were the lingering effects of the East St. Louis race riot on the soldiers' state of mind, the "general treatment and attitude of the Citizens of Houston to the negro race," and the disrespect those citizens showed to African American soldiers of the U.S. Army. Hundreds of pages of testimony from a variety of sources supported those three conclusions. Farther down his list, however, he stated: "The tendency of the negro soldier, with firearms in his possession, unless he is properly handled by officers who know his racial characteristics, is to become arrogant, overbearing, and abusive, and a menace to the community in which he happens to be stationed." By the time the first court-martial convened on November 1, nearly every official comment on the Houston troubles was being rendered in that sort of language, leaving no doubt that the Army was not just taking the racial element into account as a factor in the incident but also interpreting everything about the soldiers themselves through a lens of racist tropes and stereotypes.

11. INVESTIGATIONS

When the Army took 3-24 Infantry out of Houston by train on the morning of August 25, it also ordered its sister battalion, 1-24 Infantry, back to New Mexico from its assignment guarding Camp MacArthur in Waco. The entire regiment was being consolidated in one place far away from Houston while the Army gathered evidence for the court-martial that everyone knew was coming. Texas's congressional representatives had protested to the War Department over the decision to remove Third Battalion from the state and were now demanding harsh and immediate punishments for all the men suspected of the violence. With pressure coming down from his superiors in Washington, D.C., Major General Parker telegrammed the commander of Fort Bliss to say, "In view of the gravity of offenses charged against rioters it is believed best to take no chance of any of them escaping or of any collusion through sympathy on the part of other members of that regiment hence instructions to have all guard duty done for the present by white soldiers."[1]

The next day Parker received a reply. "Report arrival two companies Nineteenth Infantry with Third Battalion Twenty-Fourth Infantry from Houston," the message read, in the stilted language characteristic of telegrams. "All suspects approximately one hundred in stockade under Twelfth Cav and Nineteenth Inf guard. Remainder battalion disarmed in old machine shops corrugated iron quadrangle." Soldiers of the regiment who were not associated with the trouble in Houston were bivouacked on their old campground on the post. The telegram then recommended that the men suspected of involvement in the violence should be transferred to more secure confinement at Fort Bliss. If there was any further uprising in the Black battalions, authorities worried the "first objective would be release [of] these men." The Mexican border was only three miles to the south and the Army feared an international escape. In the event of a breakout, units at Fort Bliss were authorized to pursue the escapees into Mexico on the conditions that they did not get into firefights with elements of the Mexican army and that their pursuit did not require establishing lines of communication or resupply. Another recommendation urged that "on arrival Waco and Deming battalions [the regiment's First and Second Battalions, respectively] be authorized take up all rifle ammunition, bolts, or firing pins of all rifles and all bayonets leaving pistols with sergeants [for] moral effect as well as reasonable precaution." The entire regiment would be disarmed, even those troops who had had no part in the troubles. The telegram concluded by saying that officers reported "Houston battalion men [in] ugly mood," which was hardly surprising.[2]

An internal investigation by a regimental board began at this point, building on the questioning that had begun on the train as the battalion traveled west across Texas. Each soldier of 3-24 Infantry who was thought to have participated in the violence of August 23, or who might have knowledge about the incident, was questioned by a board of three officers headed by Captain Homer Preston, an officer from the Second Battalion.

By the time Preston finished his work about six weeks later, 380 soldiers of Third Battalion had faced his board under what can only be described as hostile conditions. Formal charges had not yet been preferred against any of those soldiers, but the word "mutiny" was already widely being used to describe the incident in Houston, and under military law there is no more serious offense than mutiny, at least in terms of how soldiers perceive it. Any man charged with mutiny faced the threat of the death penalty. The seriousness of the situation would normally have mandated that legal protections would be in place during the questioning, but the board seems to have quickly taken on the characteristics of an inquisition.

Preston was soon sending enthusiastic, self-congratulatory reports back to Southern Department headquarters at Fort Sam Houston telling of his success in obtaining evidence against the accused soldiers. Each week he added more names to the list of likely defendants. In one message to Colonel Cress, he said he had employed "various and devious methods" during his interrogations of soldiers, then hastened to assure the IG that his tactics were "all proper however."

The methods Preston described as devious but proper included threatening men with heavy prison sentences if they refused to talk or telling them they would be executed if they continued to stubbornly maintain their innocence. One accused soldier later said, "When I told them what I did, they told me I was lying, and said I was going to get hung," and he was threatened that he might not leave the interrogation room alive unless he told the truth. Private Douglas Bolden said that Preston and the other two officers "bulldozed you down there at the investigation"; under such a barrage of shouting and threats, "you hardly knew what you had to say or what you said." Another soldier from India Company said, "They cussed me out because I said I didn't know anything about it, and they said they were going to see that I had a rope around my neck." Other soldiers reported the same sort of threats and intimidation.[3]

One of the officers on the board later admitted that whenever he thought soldiers were insolent or insubordinate during his questioning, he would tell them he would ensure they wound up with "a noose around their necks" unless they cooperated and answered his questions. This type of language was an outright violation of the 1917 Manual for Courts-Martial, which in its Military Rules of Evidence stated, "Voluntary confessions are those not induced or materially influenced by hope of release, fear of punishment or injury, or influenced by words or acts such as promises, threats of harsh treatment or the like, made by someone competent to effectuate the promise." The nature of the questioning conducted by Preston's board quickly became more of an interrogation than an interview. Military law recognized that even if a soldier was warned that a confession might be used against him, any coercive acts by investigators could still produce an involuntary, and therefore inadmissible, confession. That was the underlying problem with how Preston's board conducted its business. The government had a legal obligation to prove that any confessions used in prosecution were entirely voluntary, but that would be one more point where the courts-martial failed to meet the Army's own regulations and customary practice.

While Preston was using his "devious methods" to extract information from the soldiers in the Fort Bliss stockade, Colonel Cress and Brigadier General Chamberlain traveled to Columbus to continue their separate investigations. They spoke with Third Battalion's officers, NCOs, and enlisted men in a markedly different tone than that Preston was using, but the objective was the same—to determine who had done what, who had been where that night, and why it had all happened in the first place.

The effort to answer that last question repeatedly came back to the panic that overtook the battalion that night.

The question would be critical to the accused mutineers' defense in the later court-martial. Did the men of 3-24 Infantry really believe that a civilian mob was coming to attack their camp? If such a fear really existed, then it might explain the degree of overwhelming panic and why that panic swept across the entire battalion, as well as the wild, uncontrolled firing that broke out in camp. It could not have excused soldiers' loss of military discipline and any unlawful acts that followed, but it certainly could have been applied in their favor when the court considered possible sentencing. It might also have had a bearing on each defendant's relative degree of responsibility.

From the outset some investigators believed the cry that a mob was coming was just a carefully prearranged signal for mutinous soldiers to seize their weapons and start shooting, all part of an elaborate plan in which a large group of men would march into Houston to shoot up the town. Almost every military witness who was in any position of authority that night, however, whether officer or NCO, disagreed and insisted most of the men in the battalion sincerely believed that attack by a race mob was imminent in those chaotic moments.

Sergeant William Fox was assigned to India Company, the unit most directly involved in the violence in town that night, but he had remained in camp after Sergeant Henry led most of the company out. When he was asked if Henry's action was all part of a preexisting plot, Fox said, "I don't think there was any organized trouble. I think there was just a big scare and a stampede."[4]

Colonel Cress asked Lieutenant Snider, commander of Kilo Company, how he would characterize the panic in camp that night. "From all accounts that I could get it was because they were frightened and fired for protection," Snider said.

"Do you think your men were afraid of a mob from town?"

"Yes, sir," Snider said. "I think that was the cause of their excitement, and when that report came 'here they come, boys, get your rifles,' this was repeated throughout the different company streets."

Cress then asked him the most important question, that of individual motivation among his soldiers. "In your opinion did your company enter into the trouble Thursday night with a view to joining the rioters who left camp or with the single purpose of protecting themselves?"

Snider thought carefully before he answered. "I think there was a few of them that entered into it," he said. "There were three of them who were arrested in town and one of them, Corporal Edmonds, lived downtown. He [stayed] at his house, he tells me, until the next day." Snider believed the men of his company who joined Henry's march into town were a distinct minority among his soldiers. "I think it was just to protect themselves," he said of the shooting in camp that night. "There was no intention to go to town. If there had been they could have done so—that is, before I got them collected together. After they were collected everything was quieted down. They thought they were being attacked and their desire to get their guns was for self-protection."[5]

Captain James, who had managed to hold Lima Company together in the midst of the chaos, agreed with Snider. "I would say that they were crazed with fright. I could see their faces as they came in," he said. "Most of them thought a mob of civilians was coming into the camp."[6]

Shekerjian also saw it that way. When Cress asked him, "What were the men afraid of?" he replied, "It was the alarm that came in—'Here they come, get your guns,' and the rush came on from camp."

Both Cress and Chamberlain asked similar questions of the enlisted men in the battalion, and their answers were much the same. Private Blaine Adams said that he was in the process of turning in his rifle when "some man came running yelling, 'Here they come! Get your rifles! Get your rifles!' . . . I was under the impression it was a big mob of citizens," Adams said. "I didn't have any rifle and ran, sir."

Unarmed, Adams left the camp and ran to Camp Logan, where he found Sergeant Taylor and twenty-three men of Kilo Company's guard detail.* "I went by the warehouse and told them I thought the citizens of Texas were attacking the camp," Adams recalled. It was this excited and erroneous report, coupled with the sounds of heavy rifle fire from the battalion cantonment, that made Sergeant Taylor believe he was facing an oncoming superior force, and that was what caused him to decide to leave his post and fall back on the Illinois battalions for protection with the

---

* It bears remembering, at this point, that Major Snow claimed he tried to get to Camp Logan that night but was unable to do so. At least a dozen enlisted men ran or walked the mile distance to Camp Logan around the same time he left the battalion, and all of them reached it with no difficulty.

men of his detail. Colonel Cress accepted that statement as truthful; in his official report, Cress wrote, "Sergt. Taylor with guard at warehouse total 24 men, left post on hearing firing at 24th Infantry camp and reported to Captain Noble—later to Captain Allen; he was afraid the mob was coming his way. Private Adams, Co. M, reported to Captain Allen that night and said [a] mob was coming."[7]

Several details of what happened in the camp that night strongly support the idea that many soldiers genuinely believed they faced an external threat. When the panic broke out, there was no effort to eliminate the lawful military authority represented by the battalion's officers and NCOs. Likewise, there was no concerted movement among most of the companies to group up and head out of camp, as one might expect if there actually had been a plot to riot in the city or attack the nearest police station. Most men did one of two different things in all the chaos—either they dropped to the ground and started shooting out into the darkness or they moved to the perimeter of the camp and set up a hasty skirmish line with their own companies. A few others, a smaller number that no one has yet managed to tally with any certainty, either fled the camp as individuals or tried to hide themselves until the panic subsided.

Chamberlain was sure that 3-24 Infantry was holding to a conspiracy of silence. In a conversation with Shekerjian, the IG made his opinion very clear. He asked if the soldiers were willing "to help out and get hold of the men at the head of it."

"Not the majority of the men" was Shekerjian's answer.

"Even the better class of noncommissioned officers are not going to tell what they know about it," Chamberlain said. As far as he was concerned, the NCOs would withhold information simply because they were Black men, like the accused.

"They say they do not know," Shekerjian protested.

"But of course they know," Chamberlain insisted. His mind was made up—as far as he was concerned, every man in the battalion was either guilty or knew who was. Either way, they were all complicit.[8]

As the official questioning by the regimental board and the two inspectors general continued, Cress interviewed Corporal Baltimore at the Fort Bliss stockade. Baltimore had given his initial statement to Captain

Shekerjian the afternoon of his altercation with Sparks, but this was the first time either of the IG officers spoke with him personally.

Baltimore told the same story as in his first statement, expressing himself in a calm, intelligent manner. He fully appreciated the seriousness of the situation. When Cress asked him if he wanted to say anything about where he was during the shooting (by which he clearly meant the shooting in town that night), the young corporal demurred. "No, sir, I don't want to make any more statements, I made one on the train coming up." He had told the same story over and over; there was no question that he had left camp with the men of India Company when Sergeant Henry ordered them to march out, and he may have felt there was no point in repeating himself.

He did, however, offer an additional comment on his interactions with the Houston police before August 23. Cress asked him, "Prior to that time had you had any trouble with the city police?"

"No, sir, nothing to amount to anything."

"Had any of the men that you know of?"

"The city police—not the mounted police—seemed to be all right," Baltimore said. "I never had any trouble at all. Those mounted police were different. I didn't come in contact with them much. You would just see them now and then." Baltimore concluded his statement by saying, "The policeman who arrested me remarked about another colored soldier, 'There goes another one of those northern sons of bitches we should get.'"[9]

Cress was still compiling his full report, but on September 1 he sent a long memorandum to Southern Department headquarters at Fort Sam Houston. He recommended "that certain members of the 3rd Battalion, 24th Infantry, who left camp and went into town murdering and rioting, should be tried for mutiny, murder, and riot; that the men who remained in camp firing their rifles and who got beyond control of their officers, were not guilty of mutiny, but that their conduct was the result of panic that rose from fear of attack, first by mobs from Houston and later fear that those men who left camp would return and shoot them up." All the evidence he was gathering increasingly pointed to the fact that the battalion had experienced a genuine belief that they were confronted by an armed race mob.

Cress went on to describe the continuing efforts of Captain Preston and his regimental board to identify the men who had participated in the violence in Houston but advised that it was a difficult undertaking. "The night of August 23rd, due to rain, was very dark and great difficulty will

be experienced in getting names of individuals. While each company commander claims to have checks of absentees, their accuracy is doubtful and
in the confusion, it is quite possible some men hid away in camp to keep out
of trouble, and were as [a] result not seen and not checked." He concluded,
"The officer who is to act as Judge Advocate should also begin working on
the case."[10]* The government was solidifying its case against the accused,
and still none of those men were represented by legal counsel.

———

When Cress referred to the extreme difficulty of getting an accurate
check of which men were in camp that night, it was because in
every interview he conducted with those who had attempted a head count
it was apparent that none of the company officers or NCOs had been able
to account for all their soldiers amid the chaos.

Captain James told him, "I had a check made of the men on the skirmish line, had every tent in the company gone through and each man's
name written down that could be found in camp, around L company or in
the skirmish line." As thorough as that effort was, it was hampered by the
fact that he could not be everywhere at once. At one point that night James
and Shekerjian had walked a short distance outside the camp perimeter,
and when they returned a few minutes later, he said, "I was told by Private
Good of L Company that Corporal Pecoe of [India] Company had come
into camp from the direction of the railroad and brought about 40 men
with him."

* In the Army, when one says "JAG" they mean the Judge Advocate General's Corps, the
legal branch of the service to which the Army's attorneys and judges belong. The judge
advocate general, colloquially referred to as the "TJAG," is the senior officer of the branch;
today that position is held by a three-star, or lieutenant, general. When Cress referred to
the "Judge Advocate" he meant the officer who would serve as the trial judge advocate.
The trial judge advocate is the military attorney appointed to serve as prosecutor, representing the government's case against the accused. The title does *not* mean that he or
she is the judge in the trial. JAG officers must be qualified, bar-certified lawyers. In 1917
court-martial panels were not headed by military judges, but the senior officer appointed
to the panel served as its president. If questions of military law arose during trial, the panel
would refer them to the trial judge advocate, because he was usually the only legal expert
in the courtroom. It was up to the members of the panel, however, to make the final legal
determination based on that advice.

"Did they get the names of those men?" Cress said.

"No, sir, they did not."

When General Chamberlain questioned Lieutenant Snider about the head count, he asked, "The first time you took check how many men were absent?"

"Three men only and they had gotten their passes in the afternoon," Snider said, having granted those men prior authorization to be out of camp.

"How about the second check?" That was the check made after the shooting erupted and was finally quieted.

"About 28 men absent on the second check."

"Did you take any more checks?"

"No, sir," Snider said, "not that night because the company was split up then."

"How split up?"

Snider explained that some of his soldiers had mixed in with Lima Company's skirmish line, which both he and Captain James were aware of at the time. Kilo Company's men, with most of their unit on guard duty over at Camp Logan that night, had wanted the security of the greater numbers offered by Lima Company.

"Were all those men absent on the second check confined?" Chamberlain asked, referring to the accused soldiers who were now confined in the Fort Bliss stockade.

"No, sir. Some of them came in without rifles between the second check and before the firing started in Houston."

"What has that got to do with it?" Chamberlain demanded, once again demonstrating the limited range of thought he brought to his role as an investigator.

"They went out of camp when the firing started and they came in without rifles," Snider explained. These were men who had fled, unarmed, in the initial panic, but who returned to camp before Sergeant Henry's column of soldiers started shooting in the town's streets. This would have been a space of time lasting approximately forty-five minutes to an hour.

"How many of those men were there?"

"About fifteen of them," Snider said, but it was not clear if those fifteen men were on any of the different head counts taken that night.[11]

The issue of head counts was also put to Major Snow, though of all the officers in camp he would have known the least about which checks were made at what time that night since he was not there.

Chamberlain asked him if an accurate check was taken in camp that night. Snow assured him that it was and claimed, "Every man in camp, we have his name," but that was not at all truthful.

"Did you take any precautions or attempt any precautions" Chamberlain asked, "to pick up and get hold of any men who should come into camp to see whether they were armed or whether they had fired their rifles?" It was a very salient question.

"No, sir," Snow said. "I was there only a very little time during the entire night because I was down with General Hulen under his orders." That was not entirely true, since Snow had in fact only reported to General Hulen sometime after 4:00 a.m., hours after the situation at Third Battalion's camp had quieted.

"Do you know whether or not any effort was made or precautions taken to pick up men who should come in or out of camp after that time?"

"No, sir, I don't know of any. Personally I thought of it." Snow then clarified that he only thought of it much later, the next morning, long after such action should have been taken. The conversation then turned to the matter of what warnings or intimations of trouble Third Battalion's commander received before the trouble broke out that night. Snow insisted he had had no warnings, or at least none that needed to be taken seriously.

"Now, think pretty hard about that, Major Snow, because your testimony is at variance with other testimony," Chamberlain warned him. "Did you receive any word from the police department or have any communication from them at all in regard to the probabilities of trouble that night? The chief of police testifies, and other members of the force testify, that the question of danger or probability of trouble that night was discussed with you; that they anticipated or feared trouble but that you assured them that you could handle the situation and that you would take every precaution and that there was absolutely no possibility of trouble. Do you recall that?"

"No, sir, I do not," Snow said. In fact, he had received at least six such warnings from people who might be expected to be reliable sources.[12]

Despite what Snow claimed, the battalion never did get a total head count that night, and no one was certain which soldiers stayed in camp, which ones went out with Henry, and which of them fled or hid during the panic but never participated in the violence in the city. This problem was identified from the very beginning of the official investigations. In his final report, Chamberlain pointed out that "no steps were taken to identify or to check individuals returning to camp. A good many men came into camp with rifles or ammunition without the fact being noted." He also noted that the morning after the trouble, Snow's actions were nothing short of incompetent. When Snow went to collect his soldiers who had taken shelter with the Illinois National Guard, Chamberlain said, he "failed to take names or to examine rifles, an oversight which cannot be understood and which is believed to be inexcusable."[13]

Out of eleven separate head counts taken that night, no single list accounted for more than forty-six men; one listed only eighteen names. That confusion and incomplete tallying was to be the specter that hung over many of those men when they faced a court-martial a few weeks later.

The violence of August 23 made headlines across the country and continued to be widely reported in the weeks that followed as the Army carried out its investigations. Unfortunately, few facts were released for public dissemination because the Army had locked down the release of any information. As a result, most civilian commentators made statements on the case that were filled with conjecture and error. This was just as true in some of the nation's African American newspapers, which were writing for Black readers desperately concerned over the welfare of the soldiers now accused of mutiny and murder.

The Chicago *Broad Ax* got most of the details of the altercation between Corporal Baltimore and Lee Sparks correct and left no doubt as to what it believed led to the violence that night. "So much has been said in connection with the race riots at Fort [*sic*] Logan, Houston, Texas, in which well onto twenty White and Colored people lost their lives, mostly White, that it is almost useless to enter into all of the details or causes leading up to the riot," the paper declared, and referred to "the unregenerated and the unreconstructed red-necked rebels residing in Houston, including its police officers who were solely responsible for the riot and for the shedding of so much human blood."

The paper deplored the killing of Captain Mattes but said that he would not have died had he not been in a car with "the same policeman who had been so horribly brutal in his treatment of the Colored soldiers." That was not correct, since Officer Meineke was not implicated in the confrontations between Third Battalion soldiers and city policemen. Turning its attention to the uncertain future of the soldiers now in custody at Fort Bliss, the paper said, "It is very hard to tell just what will be the fate of those members of that famous regiment." Houston, the article concluded, was a "40th rate town" of people "full of the most bitter race prejudice—that all White gentlemen have been created for the sole purpose of ruling over Colored people."[14]

W. E. B. Du Bois expressed the feelings of many Black citizens in a moving article he wrote for *The Crisis* a few weeks after the troubles. He summarized the details of the matter to the best that he knew and said, "It is hard for one of Negro blood to write of Houston. Is not the ink within the very wells crimsoned with the blood of Black martyrs? Do they not cry unavenged, saying—'Always WE pay; always WE die; always whether right or wrong.'" Houston was a catastrophe born out of an entrenched, societal injustice, Du Bois said, but it was very different from anything that had ever happened before. "This, at least, remember, you who jump to judgment," he wrote, "Houston was not an ordinary outburst." Du Bois did not try to excuse the killing of policemen and civilians that night, which he recognized as criminal, but he could still see the provocations, the insults, and the ultimately unbearable abuses that had ignited the whole bloody affair. "We ask no mitigation of their punishment," he wrote of the soldiers. "They broke the law. They must suffer. But before Almighty God, if those guiltless of their black brothers' blood shot the punishing shot, there would be no dead men in that regiment."* White Southern society, he believed, needed to consider its own responsibility for creating the intolerable situation that brought about this tragedy.[15]

---

* What Du Bois meant by that last sentence was apparently the same idea expressed in the Gospel of John, chapter 8, verse 7: "He that is without sin among you, let him be the first to cast a stone." All of white American society, Du Bois believed, was guilty of the blood of their Black neighbors, either actively or passively, as long as racist segregation, lynching, and mob violence were permitted to exist anywhere in the nation.

Some African American observers were deeply conflicted over what had happened in Houston. They condemned the southern racism that had brought matters to such a bloody clash, but they also worried about the damage the incident might do, not just to the reputation of the 24th Infantry Regiment but also to that of Black soldiers in general. "The shooting up of the town in Texas by Negro troops of the regular army is one of the most serious of misfortunes," a Black educator named Dr. Charles Purvis wrote to a friend the week after news of the incident appeared in the newspapers. "No matter how badly treated the soldiers have been they should know that any overt act on their part increases the prejudice that exists against the colored citizen. I do not believe there is moral courage or enough of a sense of justice to secure for the black soldiers an unbiased investigation. Ignorance, and rum, I fear are at the bottom of the trouble." The charge that many of the men of Third Battalion were drinking that night was being frequently repeated in white newspapers, and fervently claimed by the Houston Citizens' Commission, but it was a lie. Unfortunately, the lie had quickly gained traction as fact in public opinion, and Dr. Purvis seems to have accepted it as true, even if reluctantly.[16]

One group of individuals had a very personal and professional reaction to Third Battalion's trouble in Houston—the NCOs who had left the battalion just before it went to Texas for the Colored Officers Training Camp in Iowa. Toward the end of September, Chamberlain informed the Secretary of War that he had received a surprising request—those men were "willing to give up their prospects for commissions so as to return to the regiment and redeem its reputation."

"Regimental Sergeant Major Walter B. Williams came to me as spokesman for the members of the 24th Infantry," Chamberlain wrote. "They felt that if they had been present with the regiment the trouble could not have occurred; that many of the noncommissioned officers and many of the men left with the regiment were new men." They understood all too well the damage done to the battalion's internal structure when it lost so many of its experienced NCOs. The IG described these men as "the very best material among the noncommissioned officers of the regiment and includes the Regimental Sergeant Major, the Battalion Sergeant Major Third Battalion, the First Sergeant and three other Sergeants from Company I, the company in which the mutiny started." It was an offer that would have had great professional cost to those soldiers, but in the end nothing came of it. The Army denied their request to return to the 24th Infantry in their former ranks as NCOs to help rebuild and restore the honor of the regiment to which they felt such a deep loyalty.[17]

For the families and friends of the soldiers of 3-24 Infantry, the lack of reliable information was distressing. They knew their men were with the battalion in Houston when the violence broke out, and then the mail service and telegraph lines suddenly went silent as far as their soldiers were concerned. No further letters came from their men, and letters sent to them went unanswered. The only soldiers anyone knew the condition of in those weeks were Sergeant Henry and Private Watson, who were killed in the city that night, and Privates Strong and Bivens, who died of their wounds in the following days, because their deaths were reported in the papers.

No one would find out which men were in peril of their lives at the hands of military justice until the first court-martial convened on November 1 and the list of defendants was finally published.

In the first week of September, a change of command took place at Fort Sam Houston that was to have far-reaching consequences for the coming courts-martial, and for the men who would shortly be on trial for their lives. Major General James Parker was posted to a new assignment, and Major General John Ruckman took over the position of commanding general, Southern Department.*

John Wilson Ruckman was fifty-nine years old, originally from Sidney, Illinois, and a West Point graduate in the Class of 1883. Ruckman's

---

* Biographical information on MG Ruckman is largely based on information compiled by his great-grandson Peter S. Ruckman, who was an associate professor of political science at Rock Valley College in Rockford, Illinois. Professor Ruckman presented a paper titled "John Wilson Ruckman: Scholar, Soldier, and Public Figure" at the Conference on Illinois History in October 2007. He also maintained an online biography of MG Ruckman until he died in 2018, shortly after he was interviewed by the author of this book. Other biographical information comes from *Historical Register and Dictionary of the United States Army from Its Organization, September 29, 1789 to March 2, 1903.*

West Point tenure was less than stellar. In his second year at the academy, he was suspended after he accumulated 143 demerits and had to restart with the next year's second-year cadets. His troubles apparently were not academic in nature but stemmed from behavior and conduct issues.[18] As a result of this interruption in his West Point education, he graduated a year later than expected.

An artillery officer by branch who spent most of his service years in Coast Artillery assignments, Ruckman's career was marked by two distinct characteristics—he demonstrated a considerable talent for the science, theory, and doctrinal applications of artillery, and he was extremely ambitious. He was the only serving Army officer in that era to graduate from both the Army War College and the Naval War College, which was a testament to his academic inclinations. As for his ambition, as a colonel in 1915 he solicited letters of recommendation from every senior officer he had ever served with to support his bid for promotion to general officer rank. His campaign proved effective, because on August 21, 1916, he was promoted to brigadier general and got his first star.

What his service record conspicuously lacked was any meaningful troop leadership time beyond the relatively quiet environment of Coast Artillery installations, which were exclusively limited to white soldiers. Ruckman had never served with Black soldiers at any level. He was a skilled logistician and an impressive academic, but he had no combat experience. He had served in Cuba with the U.S. occupation forces in 1898, but only after the fighting there had ended. The nature of coastal artillery was strictly defensive, and the United States had not faced a seaborne threat against its coastal installations since the War of 1812. That lack of time at the sharp end of the spear, however, did not stop him from delivering his personal views on the subject. In his Naval War College thesis, which argued that a system of national conscription was a societal benefit, he wrote, "Abundance of experience exists to prove that Americans are not afraid to face death, particularly when they are disciplined and know the nature of the danger. We know that however bravely they face death that they shun discipline and obedience. . . . Untrained, [the American] lacks the qualities of subordination and fortitude to fight successfully for the country. Being ignorant of the nature and necessity of discipline and with exaggerated ideas of his own ability and independence, he regards discipline as a disagreeable expression of tyrannical power of his officers and does not yield gracefully." It seems that Ruckman believed that rigid discipline was the most essential prerequisite to combat efficacy. If he ever understood that real, effective discipline might take different forms in combat arms units in different tactical environments, he never said so.

On August 21, just two days before the trouble in Texas, Ruckman was promoted to major general. He arrived in Fort Sam Houston two weeks later as the new commanding general of the Southern Department and found himself thrust into a situation of extreme political pressure and public notoriety, the likes of which few officers ever encountered in their careers. In the aftermath of the violence in Houston, no one in the government seemed to be interested in a long, drawn-out judicial process, and the chorus of voices in Texas demanding swift vengeance against the accused soldiers only grew louder with each passing week. Ruckman was under immediate pressure to move the process along quickly, and that process was expected to arrive at the "proper" conclusion.

That there was going to be a court-martial was certain, but the question of where it should be held was not a simple one. Ruckman thought it should be at Fort Bliss, where the soldiers were already in confinement and the investigations were well into their process. The Secretary of War, Newton Baker, argued for a trial in Houston itself. Whether or not that was to placate the more strident voices in Texas's congressional delegation is not clear, but it certainly would have pleased them. Even Baker, however, could not ignore the potential for witness intimidation if the trial was held in Houston, especially if those witnesses were Black citizens. Finally, a compromise decision was reached—Fort Sam Houston would be the trial venue. There were several reasons that was a reasonable choice. As an active military installation, the post could be secured during the court-martial and the thousands of troops on hand could maintain order if that became necessary. Also, San Antonio was only several hours by train from Houston—close enough to allow witnesses, journalists, and observers to attend, but far enough away to keep attendance manageable.

On September 13, Ruckman met with Colonel John Hull and Major Dudley Sutphin, the two JAG officers appointed to prosecute the case against the accused mutineers. Hull would be the trial judge advocate for the court-martial and Sutphin would serve as his assistant. Hull and Sutphin lost no time in taking the train out to Columbus, where they began conducting interviews of their own with soldiers of 3-24 Infantry. From that point on, Preston's regimental board basically functioned as the prosecutorial team's dedicated investigators, a role they continued to fill during the first court-martial. And even as the government continued gathering evidence against the accused men, still no one had been appointed to act as their defense counsel.

Colonel Cress and Brigadier General Chamberlain finished their separate investigations and filed their reports—Cress to Major General Ruckman at the Southern Department, and Chamberlain to the War Department—on the same day, September 13.

Cress for the most part firmly blamed the incident on the city of Houston's hostility to Black soldiers, its racially abusive police department, and the harassment directed against the soldiers from the day they got off the train. There never would have been an outbreak of violence, he argued, had those factors not existed. "The white labor [at Camp Logan] apparently lost no opportunity to refer to these guards from the 24th Infantry as 'niggers,'" he wrote; "the city police and people generally did the same; the negro soldier in uniform, whether on duty or not, was treated the same as any other individual of his race, and no efforts appear to have been made in any respect to discourage the use of this appellation." He emphasized this conclusion, saying, "This word 'nigger' appears in practically every case of disorder reported, and with the same result; a display of anger on the part of the soldier."

Cress dismissed the charge that soldiers' drunkenness played a part in the troubles as completely fabricated. He believed that racism, not whiskey, was behind it all. "Due to the weakness and inefficiency of their city administration and to the attitude of the white citizens towards the negro, these colored soldiers were not always treated right," he stated.

Cress was less willing to officially acknowledge Jim Crow segregation as an issue of provocation. He believed the racism of Houston's citizens and police was a problem, but he did not address the racist law itself as a factor. The soldiers, he felt, had a duty to obey existing laws even when those laws were unjust. "That in the removal of segregation signs and other similar incidents demonstrate that these men of the 24th Infantry, sworn to uphold the law, were not willing to comply with laws repugnant to them," he wrote, "and an overbearing spirit was shown in several cases, where, on apparently slight provocation, they threatened bodily harm to the supposed offender; these conditions, while indicative of a certain lack of discipline, are mainly the result of racial antipathies, which appear to be growing constantly worse and which neither Colonel Newman nor his officers, nor the Army as a whole can remedy without the adoption of a national policy towards the negro and the assistance and cooperation of all good citizens, white and negro, in support thereof." The men of Third Battalion, he declared, "showed a spirit of insubordination and lack of proper discipline in that they failed to observe the segregation laws of the State of Texas."[19]*

Chamberlain took much the same view in his report, and he also faulted the soldiers for not submitting to Jim Crow laws. "The ultimate causes of the trouble were racial," he wrote. "Certain men of the 24th Infantry apparently resolved to assert what they believed to be their rights as American citizens and United States soldiers. They failed, and in some instances refused to obey local laws and regulations affecting their race, they resented the use of the word 'nigger.'" Both IG officers at least pointed out the fact that the catalyst to the violence was a police officer's unwarranted assault on a uniformed United States soldier who was engaged in the performance of his duty.

Cress gave no credence to the testimonies produced by Houston's Citizens' Commission, but Chamberlain did. Even though he admitted that some stories told by the commission's witnesses were "exaggerated and to a great extent unreliable," he still insisted "no doubt exists in my mind that conditions were scandalous" in Third Battalion's camp. He remained fixated on the idea that the camp had been a veritable den of prostitution and bootlegging. Cress never accepted this as fact, but Chamberlain all but shouted it from the rooftops.

---

* On a point of technicality, Cress overstated the matter when he wrote that the soldiers were "sworn to uphold the law." The oath of enlistment taken by American soldiers in 1917 was essentially the same in its wording as the modern oath: "I, [name], do solemnly swear that I will support and defend the Constitution of the United States against all enemies, foreign and domestic; that I will bear true faith and allegiance to the same," etc. This oath is one of the things that makes the US military unique in the world, in that it binds its members not to a person (monarch, president, or any other individual), nor to a flag, and not even to the nation itself, but instead to a concept of political theory—the U.S. Constitution.

Both IG officers agreed the panic that swept over the battalion that night was real, and that soldiers sincerely believed an armed mob was moving on them. However, each also accepted the idea that a preexisting conspiracy to mutiny must have been behind Sergeant Henry's sortie into the city. Cress wrote, "There was a prearranged plan for revenge, in all probability conceived in 'I' Company, and assisted by a few men from each of the other companies, and that the alarm was part of the plan, made with a view to involve the entire command."

On the question of which men in Third Battalion were guilty of mutiny and murder, Chamberlain threw the net very wide. "There are doubtless several not at present in the stockade who are guilty, and against some of whom convincing testimony will be discovered," he wrote in his report. "As to just how many will be discovered against whom guilt can be fastened, cannot at this time be stated. Up to the time that I left Columbus, the attitude of the men of this battalion generally was to know nothing, to say nothing, and to protect the guilty ones." Chamberlain was still convinced Third Battalion was maintaining a conspiracy of silence. "I called together about 25 of what was believed to be the most reliable noncommissioned officers of the battalion," he wrote, "and endeavored to make them understand that not only the 24th Infantry, but the entire colored race was on trial, that if the innocent men of the battalion persisted in protecting the men who had deliberately mutinied against the authority of the United States and indulged in riot and murder, that it would tend to destroy faith in the colored man as a soldier . . . Whether or not this talk had any effect, I do not know; I have little hope that it did."[20]

Both IG officers thought Captains Shekerjian and James conducted themselves well that night. Cress called their actions "very commendable," and Chamberlain said they were "beyond criticism," and he included Lieutenants Snider and Jack in that praise. Major Snow and Captain Silvester, however, were an entirely different matter.

"While the testimony given before the Citizens' Commission evinces cowardice on the part of Major Snow," Chamberlain wrote, "other and more reliable testimony to my mind entirely repudiates such charge . . . that he lost his head, I believe, but that he showed cowardice I do not believe." Several pages later, however, he wrote that Snow "exhibited inefficiency and criminal negligence of a character which, in my judgment, demonstrates his unfitness to command." Cress believed that Snow "showed gross neglect and inefficiency in not interpreting conditions within his command and in not taking more effective steps to prevent trouble and effect the arrest and identification of the rioters."

In Chamberlain's opinion Silvester was guilty of "inefficiency and criminal negligence," while Cress described Silvester as "neglectful of his duties." Both IG officers agreed that Snow and Silvester's failings were so egregious that they should face courts-martial of their own. "When the cases of the mutinous soldiers have been disposed of," Chamberlain wrote, "Major Snow and Captain Silvester should be brought to trial." He believed that General Ruckman "fully concurs and action will, at the proper time, I believe be taken by him."[21]

12. A Mystery Within
a Tragedy

Lima Company's commander, Captain Bartlett James, was only twenty-four years old when he was caught up in the troubles in Houston that August. Despite his youth and his lackluster academic record at West Point, he was clearly a talented officer with real leadership ability. His soldiers rallied around him that night in a greater show of solidarity and loyalty than any of the other companies did with their officers. That was entirely because of his personal leadership, not just in that moment of crisis but over a period of months before the battalion ever went to Houston. He had served with those men during the Mexican campaign the year before, a combat experience that forged a strong bond between Lima Company's infantrymen and their young commander.

James came from a military family in Danville, Virginia, and the fact that his family had fought for the Confederacy during the Civil War (and that his grandfather was a zealous member of the Ku Klux Klan) did not seem to hinder his relationship with his soldiers in the moment of crisis. They trusted him, and he did his best for them.*

He was the third of four brothers to serve in the U.S. military in his generation. His oldest brother, Fred James, was killed in action in 1906 while serving with the 8th Infantry in the Philippines. Another brother, Jules James, was a graduate of the Naval Academy and in 1917 was serving

---

* All personal and family information on Captain Bartlett James that appears in this text is based on an interview the author conducted with Mr. Jules James, Captain James's great-nephew, in 2021, and a short biographical sketch of Bartlett James and his brothers that Mr. James wrote in 2017.

aboard the USS *Oklahoma* as a lieutenant. His other brother, Russell James, was also an Army officer and was posted to Eagle Pass, Texas, as a captain with the 3rd Infantry. On February 28, 1917, Russell was found dead of a single gunshot wound to the head. Bartlett James was still in Columbus with 3-24 Infantry when he learned of his brother's death. The Army's official investigation into the death quickly concluded that Russell died by suicide. That family tragedy was still hanging over Bartlett when the violence broke out in Houston six months later.

In September, while the Army was still investigating the Houston Incident, the Navy granted Lieutenant Jules Bartlett a short leave of absence, which he used to travel from San Diego to Eagle Pass, apparently with the intent of conducting a personal investigation into his brother's death. His parents were unwilling to accept the verdict that Russell had killed himself. Rumors in Russell's unit suggested that he was murdered after uncovering a horse-stealing enterprise that was selling U.S. Army cavalry mounts across the border into Mexico, or that he was caught up in a love triangle with a married Mexican woman and he had fallen afoul of an angry husband. Jules considered all those theories as well as the Army's official version of events. Before he left Eagle Pass to begin the long train journey back to San Diego, he wrote home and told his mother, "I am more firmly convinced than ever that he was murdered." Whether that was what he truly believed or he was only trying to spare his parents' feelings is uncertain.

In that same letter, Jules mentioned that he had tried to arrange a meeting with Bartlett, his last remaining brother, in Columbus on Friday, September 14, but had not heard back from him in time to keep the train schedule. What is certain is that Bartlett knew of the rumors surrounding Russell's death, and from his correspondence with his parents it is clear he knew of their grief over having lost another son and of the lingering, unanswered questions caused by that supposed suicide.

On September 11 the correspondence log for Southern Department headquarters recorded a letter from H. T. Werner, the editor of the *Houston Post*, Werner inquiring "whether or not court-martial of members 24th Infantry will be open to the public and proceeding of court will be permitted to be published." It was shaping up to be the most sensational court case in Texas history, and the *Post* was keen to have its reporter in the courtroom. The Southern Department's chief of staff wrote the next day, "The court-martial which will be convened for the trial of certain members of the 24th Infantry will unquestionably be open to visitors which will include members of the press, almost without exception the proceedings of courts-martial are open to the public. So far as I can see at present there is no reason why the meetings of the court in question should not be open." When that court would convene was still to be determined, but everyone knew it was coming on fast.[1]

Other inquiries the Army received on the matter were more sympathetic and altruistic than Werner's. Since the trouble in August the NAACP had tried to get any information it could on the men of Third Battalion. Throughout the month of September, the general public knew almost nothing of those soldiers' situation beyond the fact that they had been returned to New Mexico and that the Army was in the process of gathering evidence to be used in the upcoming court-martial. African American community leaders, academics, clergymen, and private citizens from all over the country wrote to the NAACP asking for information and urging a concerted effort to help the men of 3-24 Infantry.

In the midst of that effort, the NAACP continued its business on the national level, advocating not just for the men of 3-24 Infantry but also for all "members of the race" throughout the nation. A particular concern in those weeks was the welfare of African American men affected by the ongoing nationwide military mobilization as the summer turned into fall. On October 1 the association submitted to Secretary of War Newton Baker a memorandum calling his attention to some of their immediate concerns, including:

1. The unfortunate arrangement of the draft registration circular with its "tear off a corner if of African descent."
2. The fact that colored men were not allowed to volunteer in the regular army even up to their proportion in the population.
3. The fact that various branches of the service—the artillery, the aviation corps, and the like, not to mention the Navy, are closed to them.
4. The failure to allay the growing suspicion that the Government is going to attempt to draft Negroes for labor and menial service, and not as soldiers.

Another item on the list was the forced retirement of Colonel Charles Young, the highest-ranking Black officer in the Army, in June that year.*

The NAACP memo concluded, "It must be remembered that Negroes are human beings, that they have deep seated and long continued grievances against this country; that while the great mass of them are loyal and willing to fight for their country despite this, it certainly will not increase their loyalty or the spirit in which they enter this war if they continue to meet discrimination which borders upon insult and wrong." In response to this appeal, Secretary Baker promised "his determination to have Negroes treated justly and as soldiers," but the NAACP had heard such assurances before. Time would tell if words would be matched by actions.[2]

Chamberlain's official report on the Houston Incident was released to the public shortly after he filed it with the War Department, and from the NAACP's perspective it contained both good and bad news. The association agreed with Chamberlain's conclusion that Houston's Jim Crow culture and its abusive police department were largely responsible for the troubles, but they were alarmed by his description of the soldiers' actions that night as mutiny and murder. From a legal standpoint, it was imperative to move as quickly as possible to secure some legal representation for the men of Third Battalion who were accused of those crimes. What they needed was a civilian attorney with a formidable reputation, and so much the better if he was not only a southerner but a Texan. When a man named Andrew Jackson Houston offered his services, he seemed exactly what they needed.

---

* Charles Young was one of the most extraordinary Army officers of his era. Born into slavery in Kentucky in 1864, he was only the third Black man to graduate from the U.S. Military Academy at West Point, Class of 1889, and he made a twenty-eight-year career of the U.S. Army. By 1917 he was the first African American officer ever to hold the ranks of lieutenant colonel and colonel. When the United States entered the First World War, however, it became increasingly apparent that if Young continued to serve, he would likely be promoted to brigadier general, which would make it inevitable that he would command not only Black troops but also white soldiers and, more to the point, white field-grade officers. The War Department removed him from active duty in May 1917, claiming that he was no longer physically fit for duty. Young traveled 497 miles by horseback from Wilberforce, Ohio, to Washington, D.C., to disprove that claim, but his request to be reinstated to military service was denied. He was posted to Liberia as a military attaché in 1919 and died on a reconnaissance in Nigeria in 1921 at the age of fifty-seven. In 2022, Young was posthumously promoted to brigadier general in a ceremony at West Point.

Houston's surname was not a coincidence. He was a son of Sam Houston, one of the founders of the Texas Republic, who twice served as president during its short existence as an independent country, the man for whom the city of Houston was named. In Texas, that name was as legendary as Bowie or Travis. A. J. Houston, as he was often known, was much more than just his father's mythic reputation, however. He was appointed to West Point as a military cadet but dropped out of the academy to pursue a career in law, and by 1917 he had accrued almost forty years' experience as an attorney and had served as a U.S. marshal for eastern Texas. He also had some limited experience as a soldier, holding the rank of colonel in the Texas National Guard. In the Spanish-American War he used the cachet of his name to raise a troop of volunteer cavalry that served in Cuba with the famous Rough Riders, though he did not deploy with the unit.

One detail in A. J. Houston's career might have given the NAACP pause when they considered his offer of legal help. Twenty-five years earlier he had been associated with the "lily-white Republicans," the faction within the Republican Party that sought to turn back the limited gains African Americans had managed in the political sphere during the era of Reconstruction. The degree to which he believed in that agenda is debatable, or something important had changed in his personal stance in the intervening years, because in 1917 he proved himself willing to stand with the soldiers who were accused of murder and mayhem in the city that bore his family name.

On August 30, one week after the violence, he reached out to a friend named John Milholland, a former treasurer of the NAACP, to offer the association his legal services. Unfortunately, precious weeks would pass before his offer finally reached the people who could decide whether to accept it.

By the latter half of September, the Army's process was accelerating toward a court-martial, and as far as the two inspectors general were concerned, trials were warranted for more than just the rank-and-file soldiers of Third Battalion. On September 17, Brigadier General Chamberlain, who by then was back in Washington, D.C., wrote to Colonel Cress saying, "Yesterday I mailed you, special delivery, copy of all recorded testimony taken by me in connection with the 24th Infantry mutiny. Some of this testimony may be of assistance in working up the case, especially when it comes to the trial of the officers." Chamberlain had more officers than just Major Snow and Captain Silvester in his sights. "This testimony is also enlightening as to the state of discipline and as to Colonel Newman's responsibility," he concluded. "I feel that he should not escape without at least a severe reprimand." Cress did not agree on Newman's culpability, but Chamberlain remained convinced that 3-24 Infantry's former commander's permissive visitation policies in Houston had created a culture of immorality in the battalion that contributed to the troubles.[3]

The Army's senior echelons saw it differently. Taking the two IG reports in comparison, most military observers seemed to agree with Cress's position on the question of command responsibility, and a few weeks later the Adjutant General (AG) of the Army informed Chamberlain that "no further action will be taken in the case of Colonel William Newman. . . . By order of the Secretary of War."[4]

Snow and Silvester, though, were another matter. The day after Chamberlain mentioned Newman in his letter to Cress, the AG wrote bluntly to General Ruckman: "In connection with the mutiny in the 3rd Battalion, 24th United States Infantry, at Houston, Texas, on the night of August 24 [sic], 1917, the Secretary of War directs that you report what action you propose to take in the cases of Major Snow and Captain Silvester."

Either Ruckman ignored that directive or his staff lost track of it in the midst of everything else that was going on, because two weeks later, on October 2, the AG sent another letter to the Southern Department. It called Ruckman's attention to the earlier letter, and then the tone sharpened. "As it does not appear that a reply has been received in this office, information is requested as to the status of the matter. By order of the Secretary of War." That last sentence demanded an immediate response.

"The cases of Major Snow and Captain Silvester have been investigated conjointly with that governing the conduct of men of the 3rd Battalion, 24th Infantry," Ruckman wrote in reply. "It seems highly probable that both of these officers will be tried by court-martial. It is believed that their trial should be deferred until the trial of enlisted men has been completed as more complete evidence will then be available from which to judge as to the culpability of these officers."[5] One can attach different interpretations to Ruckman's choice of words in that telegram. He did not say that Snow and Silvester would be court-martialed; he said it was "highly probable."

Apparently, Ruckman was more ambiguous than the two IG officers on the question of officers' responsibility in the Houston affair. He was focused on the enlisted men.

———

B ack in the city of Houston, interest in the upcoming court-martial of the accused rioters remained intense. Most civilian observers were determined to see that the Army did not let those men escape retribution and punishment, and the fact that no one yet could be sure who among Third Battalion's 654 soldiers would even be charged in the case did not stop local newspapers from calling for their blood. Meanwhile, another trial related to the troubles attracted attention in the city.

In the archived files of the Army Inspector General there is a small, yellowed newspaper clipping from the *Houston Chronicle*, stamped "Rec'd Off. Insp. Gen. Oct 15 1917." The clipping reported the indictment of police officer Lee Sparks for two incidents—his assault on Corporal Baltimore the afternoon of the troubles, and his killing of Wallace "Snow" Williams a few days later. The clipping reads, "Indictment by the Harris County grand jury of Lee Sparks, member of the Houston police department, for aggravated assault on Sergeant [*sic*] Baltimore, is an echo of the mutiny by negro troops in Houston on the night of August 23." There is absolutely no neutrality in the *Chronicle*'s reporting. From start to finish the article touted Houston's moral superiority and defended the city's Jim Crow segregation. "Action by the grand jury typifies complete accord by the people of Houston to law and order," the article declared. "Not only did this community refuse to be guided by the mob spirit in dealing with the most outrageous situation that ever arose in the community life of the nation, but it has also set in motion the machinery of its own laws to punish its own official, if convicted of having in any manner transcended his authority or been guilty of conduct unbecoming an officer and a gentleman.

"In what other American community can there be found a parallel case representing the forbearance of red-blooded Americans in the fact of a murderous assault by savages wearing the uniform of their common country?" the writer declared, which may have been one of the few times in that era that the *Chronicle* ever in print acknowledged Black men as fellow American citizens. "Those who seem to favor the reestablishing of

This view of Camp Logan shows the wood-frame buildings used as administrative offices and mess halls that the soldiers of 3-24 Infantry were responsible for guarding during the camp's construction starting in July 1917. The white canvas tents are troop tents similar to those of 3-24 Infantry, whose camp also fronted on the street. *Photo courtesy of the Memorial Park Conservancy.*

Interior of a Houston streetcar, showing the hated "For Colored" sign that imposed racially segregated seating. *Photo courtesy of Houston Metropolitan Research Center.*

The "Special Officers," or horse-mounted section, of the Houston Police Department, with tracking dogs. The Special Officers had a particularly brutal reputation among the city's African American residents. *Photo courtesy of Houston Metropolitan Research Center.*

Front page of the *Houston Chronicle* on August 24, 1917. The morning after the violence, the papers were full of wild exaggerations and speculation. The story at the bottom of the page refers to the "Negro Watermelon Party" that was supposed to have occurred the previous evening.

Corporal Charles Baltimore in uniform, some time before the troubles in Houston. He was sentenced to death in the first court-martial, *US v. Nesbit*. *Photo courtesy of the Veterans Administration and National Cemetery Administration.*

Corporal Jesse Moore. Based on his youthfulness in this image, this photo was probably taken during his first enlistment, when he served as a private under his real name, Jesse Ball. He was sentenced to death in the first court-martial, *US v. Nesbit*. *Photo courtesy of Angela Holder.*

Private First Class Thomas C. Hawkins served with the 24th Infantry in the Philippines before he was posted to Houston in the summer of 1917. He was sentenced to death in the first court-martial, *US v. Nesbit*. *Image courtesy of Jason Holt, Esq.*

Sergeant William Nesbit was the ranking non-commissioned officer and lead defendant among the sixty-three soldiers tried in the court-martial. He was sentenced to death in that trial. *Image courtesy of Charles Anderson.*

Major Kneeland Snow was Battalion Commander of 3-24 Infantry in Houston during the troubles. His dereliction of duty was criticized by two Inspectors General, but he was never held accountable for that failure of command.

Haig Shekerjian was 3-24 Infantry's Battalion Adjutant in 1917. In this photo six years after the Houston troubles, he is shown as a major. Shekerjian transferred from the infantry to the chemical corps in the intervening years. *Photo courtesy of Carlisle Barracks archives.*

Ira Raney, a police officer in the Houston Police Department. was killed in the violence of August 23, 1917. In this photo from a few years before the incident he is shown with his wife and children. Raney left a widow and eight children. *Image courtesy of Sandi Hajtman.*

Major General John W. Ruckman was the convening authority of all three courts-martial related to the Houston incident. His decision to execute thirteen men in secret without the opportunity for appeal or outside review of their sentences outraged many people, including his superiors in the War Department. This photo shows him as a Brigadier General, shortly before he took command of the Southern Department. *Image courtesy of P. S. Ruckman, Jr.*

Colonel John A. Hull was the judge advocate, or prosecutor, in the first two courts-martial, *US v. Nesbit* and *US v. Washington.* This photo circa 1927 shows him as a major general, when he was The Judge Advocate General of the Army. *Image courtesy Library of Congress.*

In 1917 and 1918, Major Harry S. Grier served as the sole defense counsel for all 118 accused soldiers of 3-24 Infantry during the three courts-martial, though he was not a qualified attorney and had limited experience in serious legal cases. *Photo courtesy of Carlisle Barracks archives.*

US v. Nesbit court-martial, November 1917. Only two photos of the largest murder trial in US history are known to exist. In this photo, the sixty-three soldier defendants sit behind the rope line at the left in the ad hoc courtroom of Gift Chapel. *Photo courtesy of National Archives and Records Administration (NARA).*

In this enlarged image of the *Nesbit* court-martial, Major Harry Grier sits by himself in the row of tables closest to the raised dais. To his right are the prosecution team of Captain Tom Fox, Harris County District Attorney John Crooker (in civilian clothes), Major Dudley Sutphin, and Colonel John Hull. The man seated on the dais in front of them, facing to the left, is Major Kneeland Snow, with the court-martial panel beyond him. *Photo courtesy of NARA.*

Soldiers of 3-24 Infantry in Houston the morning after the violence of August 23, under guard by troops of the 19th Infantry. *Photo courtesy of the Fort Sam Houston Museum.*

Private Abner Davis was sentenced to life imprisonment in the first court-martial, even though the prosecutor, Colonel Hull, later admitted he probably never left camp the night of the troubles. Even after a JAG review of his case pointed out the numerous legal deficiencies of the evidence used to convict him, Davis remained imprisoned for years. *Image courtesy of NARA.*

Front page of the *San Antonio Express*, December 11, 1917. The thirteen men condemned by the first court-martial were hanged at dawn that morning in secret. The executions were not officially announced until later that day.

All nineteen men executed by the courts-martial that followed the Houston trouble were originally buried by Salado Creek, close to the execution site. During the 1920s the burial plot was fenced and marked by this sign. The numbers on the left of the image show the graves of James Wheatley (No. 8), Pat McWhorter (No. 9), William Nesbit (No. 10), Thomas C. Hawkins (No. 11), Risley Young, (No. 12), and Frank Johnson (No. 13). *Photo courtesy of Fort Sam Houston Museum.*

When the remains of seventeen of the executed soldiers of 3-24 Infantry were reinterred in the Fort Sam Houston National Cemetery in 1937, the new graves were marked by headstones that omitted any mention of their military service. Three months after the Army granted clemency to the soldiers in November 2023, new headstones were erected on their graves, correctly reflecting each soldier's name, place of birth, military rank, and regiment. Their graves are the ones decorated by the poppies lying in front of the headstones. *Photo by Dru Benner-Beck.*

The remains of two soldiers, Larnon Brown and Joseph Smith, were claimed by their families. William Nesbit's gravestone now shows his rank as the senior noncommissioned officer among the defendants. *Photo by George Gibson.*

Charles Baltimore's new headstone now correctly displays his personal and military information. At the ceremony marking the installation of the new grave markers in February 2024, a funeral service was conducted for the seventeen soldiers of 3-24 Infantry buried here, rendering them the full military honors they were denied for more than a century. *Photo by George Gibson.*

the Mason and Dixon line in connection with the locating of army camps have been given their answer by the people of Houston and the governing powers of Harris County. They are yet to be answered by the military authorities in the execution of the negro regulars whose murderous assault on Houston resulted in the killing of 17 and the wounding of 21 persons. Such executions will put an end forever to running amuck by negro troops."

The *Chronicle* was casual in its facts, since by that point the casualty list of the violence was clearly established and well known—nineteen people were killed and thirteen wounded—and it was far too quick to congratulate Houstonians on their city's commitment to law and order. The *Houston Press* soon reported that the all-white jury in Sparks's trial deliberated for only "one minute" before acquitting him on all charges. For Black Houstonians, the acquittal was hardly surprising. It was just one more item in the growing ledger of evidence proving that Texas courts did not offer any meaningful justice for them and the law did not regard them as equal when their lives were weighed in the balance. Under segregation, white people had justice. Black people had the law, and the law was written to keep them under Jim Crow's heel.

With each passing week newspapers across the country continued publishing statements by Army officers using language that increased concern in African American communities that the soldiers of 3-24 Infantry were not going to receive any measure of justice. The *Washington Evening Star* printed a story in which members of the Houston Citizens' Commission referred to comments by Brigadier General Chamberlain in which he agreed with allegations of a mutinous conspiracy within Third Battalion. "The committee says that the undisputed and convincing testimony of witnesses prove that the Negro soldiers went forth to slay the white population indiscriminately," the paper reported. "This testimony and the testimony of numerous other circumstances in the record convince us (and our opinion is shared by Inspector General John L. Chamberlain of the United States Army, who so expressed himself to us) that the prior conflicts with the police were mere incidents of the riot; that the riot was unquestionably contemplated prior to that date."[6]

Once again, such reporting drew the attention of James C. Waters Jr., the African American attorney in Hyattsville, Maryland. Waters fired off two more strongly worded letters to General George Bell, who was still the senior Regular Army commander in Houston. "I am advised that many accused men of the 24th Infantry are to be tried for their lives for what took place at Houston," Waters wrote. "Is Inspector General Chamberlain to be a witness? Is anything he has said or written to be received at the trial to be used against the men? I wonder. At all events, it seems to me as a lawyer, the position of Gen. Chamberlain and all other Army officers was such that they had no business to rush into print condemning the men of the 24th Infantry."

In his second letter to Bell, posted the same day, Waters wrote, "No man deplores more than I what took place at Houston. I am as sorry as I would be had some relative of mine been concerned in it. I am, both by training and inclination, an uncompromising defender of law and order. I am equally loyal, however, to fair play, and it seemed to me as I wrote, that if the unfortunate men of the 24th Infantry were to receive anything like a shred of a fair trial, it was as little as Army officers could do to keep silent and do nothing or say nothing to make a fair trial more difficult to procure."[7]

The same day that Waters posted his letters, Colonel Cress updated Brigadier General Chamberlain on the status of the interrogations still being conducted among the soldiers confined in the Fort Bliss stockade. Captain Preston's regimental board of inquiry, he reported, "has progressed apparently very satisfactorily in their investigation. Colonel Hull and his assistant expressed themselves as being highly pleased with the results obtained. . . . The Board has had four confessions and has the identity pretty well established of about 60 men. About the same number of men besides who are unable to account for themselves on the night of August 23rd."[8]

On October 12, the Fort Bliss post commander received a telegram from the Adjutant General's office in Washington, D.C., instructing him to question the Third Battalion soldiers in confinement as to "whether they intend to secure counsel of their own or if they wish counsel detailed by military authorities" in the upcoming court-martial. This was the first time in any of the Army's official communications that any mention was made of defense counsel for the accused soldiers. "If latter method is followed it is proposed to secure services of two competent lawyers probably from National Guard regiments," the telegram concluded.[9]

The question of legal representation was passed on to Major General Ruckman at Fort Sam Houston, who sent a reply back to the AG two days later. In it, he asked that Major Harry S. Grier (whose name he misspelled as "Greer"), then posted to Fort Worth, Texas, to report to Southern Department headquarters to serve as defense counsel for the accused soldiers. The reasons for Grier's selection, as Ruckman explained, were that he had "ample legal knowledge and experience to fill this position, has served with Twenty Fourth Infantry and is well known by the men of that regiment." He also said that Grier was "more available than any other officer," which suggests that his selection was at least as much a matter of convenience as from any real notion that Grier possessed any notable skill as a legal advocate. Ruckman informed the AG that the "order for court will be issued as soon as counsel is consulted as to time he requires to prepare case."[10]

A 1903 graduate of West Point, Grier was originally from Pennsylvania. By that point in his career he had indeed served with both Black infantry regiments, the 24th and 25th Infantry. But that did not mean that the accused soldiers knew him either by name or by reputation, as Ruckman claimed, since Grier had never been assigned to 3rd Battalion of the 24th Infantry. It is even more unlikely that he knew any of the accused soldiers. The accused and their appointed counsel were complete strangers to each other.

The official claims about Grier's legal qualifications are another matter that do not hold up under scrutiny. One newspaper said of him, "Although a graduate of law, and at one time instructor of law at West Point, he is not a judge advocate," a description that contained two correct details and one glaring error. It was true that Grier was not a member of the Judge Advocate General's Corps—he was an infantry officer by branch—and he had indeed taught in the law department at the U.S. Military Academy as a course instructor. But he was not an attorney, and he had never attended nor graduated from any law school. The same newspaper article claimed that Grier had "participated in more than 600 courts-martial, and is considered one of the strongest of counsels in such cases," which was completely untrue.[11] For one thing, if Grier had actually participated in that many courts-martial, that would be an average of 1.2 courts-martial every single week of his fourteen-year career. As far as can be determined from existing military records, Grier had very limited experience with general court-martial cases before 1917. Most critically, it does not appear that he had ever tried a capital case, where the death penalty was on the table.*

Nor was Grier "the unanimous choice of the 118 accused men for their counsel." At the time of his appointment, he was the *only* choice the Army offered them. Something had gone very wrong in A. J. Houston's efforts to offer his services to the NAACP as civilian defense counsel.

Houston's letter to his friend John Milholland, the former treasurer of the NAACP, was written and posted on August 30. In it, he referred to the Brownsville case in 1906, when Black soldiers of the 25th Infantry were accused of rioting in that Texas border town. Houston said he had been asked to represent those soldiers in that investigation, but the request was made too late for him to take any action on their behalf.

"I write this to you for the information of those you can trust with it," Houston told Milholland. "I would gladly appear for the soldiers charged with rioting and mutiny as reported in the enclosed [newspaper] clippings, and devote the necessary time and labor to have a full and fair investigation, which investigation would no doubt prove a revelation to men who . . . have a strong prejudice against the negro race." Houston's experience with the Brownsville affair prompted him to give a warning. If any action was to be taken, he wrote, "it should be prompt as their arraignment before a court-martial will be soon." Everything depended on quick decisions and clear communication.†

Nothing worked out that way. Almost two weeks passed before Milholland even read Houston's letter. In Milholland's own letter to Dr. J. E. Spingarn at the NAACP on September 13, in which he conveyed Houston's offer to the association, Milholland explained that he had just returned after a month's vacation and found Houston's missive waiting on

---

* Major Grier's military records are missing, presumably lost in the catastrophic fire that destroyed more than sixteen million Official Military Personnel Files (OMPFs) in the St. Louis archives in 1973. The only detailed primary sources on his career come from his personal scrapbook and other papers that are in the documents collection of the Army War College at Carlisle Barracks, Pennsylvania. No other military records, most importantly the archived files of the Judge Advocate General or the Adjutant General, support the repeated claims that he had extensive trial experience before the summer of 1917.

† All following quotations from correspondence between A. J. Houston, John Milholland, and various officers of the NAACP are taken from letters preserved in the NAACP's internal archives, listed as File 001527-018-05213.

his desk. He described Houston as "one of the best men I have ever met from Texas. He was United States Marshal for fourteen years. During that time not a single lynching occurred in his district." He urged the association to take Houston up on his offer and assured them that he had "no hesitation in saying no better man can be found in Texas for any work that he would be willing to undertake."

Neither the NAACP's acting chairman or its acting secretary could make decisions about retaining the services of outside civilian counsel without putting the matter to the board of directors, and that process took time. So, days were lost as the matter worked its way through the normal process of decision-making. Unfortunately, nothing about this situation was "normal." The association was at that time inundated with letters and telegrams from all over the country on the issue of the Houston Incident, from people making suggestions, demanding immediate action, and offering their personal, uninformed opinions about the case. The association's officers needed to carefully vet Houston's proposal before making their response. Tragically, no one in the NAACP's headquarters in New York realized how fast the Army was moving to bring the accused mutineers to trial.

Sometime in late September or early October, the NAACP's acting chairman, Mary White Ovington, wrote to A. J. Houston to ask if he would consider defending the soldiers of 3-24 Infantry, and if he thought there was anything he could do on their behalf. It seems that his initial offer to help was not clearly understood as already having been made, and on top of that, her letter may have gone to the wrong address. Houston's reply, written on his personal letterhead, had "Beaumont, Texas," printed at the top of the page, but that line was crossed out and "La Porte, Texas," typewritten underneath. Apparently, he had recently moved from one city to the other. Compounding the problem, he was away from La Porte when the NAACP letter finally reached his office, and that added even more delay to an increasingly urgent matter.

Houston already understood the urgency—he had pointed it out to Milholland when he first offered his services—and when he finally received the association's letter he quickly replied to say that yes, he was willing to take the case. On October 10, Ovington wrote back to him, saying, "Your letter . . . has just reached us. Kindly send us detailed telegram if in your judgment there is anything you can do regarding Houston affair."

Houston replied, "The trial is very near therefore any action along the line of our correspondence must be soon if at all. You will observe that the court-martial, if it appoints counsel, will appoint another officer, who would naturally be prejudiced." In fact, the time that he feared was slipping away was already gone. Houston's letter was dated October 16, two days after Major Grier was appointed as military defense counsel, and a full week after the trial judge advocate, Colonel Hull, informed Major General Ruckman that he had completed his pretrial investigation and was preparing to submit names of accused and witnesses for court-martial.

At the same time the NAACP was communicating with A. J. Houston, W. E. B. Du Bois wrote directly to the Adjutant General of the Army asking when the trial might convene and what options there were for defense counsel. The AG replied by telegram on October 22. "Soldiers Twenty-fourth Infantry charged with Houston riot will be tried by court-martial at Fort Sam Houston San Antonio Texas about November First," it read. "If soldiers do not provide counsel government will detail suitable army officers; outside counsel authorized if soldiers provide it."

Five days later the NAACP formally made a request to A. J. Houston to take on the role of defense counsel. The association would cover his fees and any expenses he incurred in the case. A more detailed letter, written the same day, stated, "The Association is desirous that you should at once take up the case of the accused soldiers, acting as their counsel on behalf of the Association. Will you please communicate with us and let us know the steps that you will take." Houston did not wait for the payment of a retainer, but immediately took the train to San Antonio, where the sixty-four accused soldiers had just been sent to Fort Sam Houston in preparation for the trial.[12] By that point, the court-martial was only five days away from its start.

The NAACP's archives do not contain any detailed notes of Houston's interviews with the soldiers, only the brief summations he wrote in the letters and telegrams he sent to New York. What is clear is that he arrived at Fort Sam Houston ready to take up the defense and that he was filled with ideas of legal strategies and arguments to mount against the government's case, but he never had the chance to stand up in court as counsel for the defense.

All sixty-three soldier defendants refused his offer to represent them.

Someone within the Army had apparently given the soldiers reason to think that if they accepted outside counsel after Major Grier was already officially appointed to act as military defense counsel, it would reflect badly on them during the court-martial. A. J. Houston met with Grier personally after the soldiers rejected his offer, and the two men seem to have discussed the matter in detail. In his next letter to the NAACP, Houston wrote, "The men expressed their gratitude to the Association for the solicitude for their rights but feared that any preference which they might express for special counsel could be construed by the court as a reflection upon counsel whom the court had already appointed from the Army," though Grier apparently assured him he would not have taken it that way. It is not certain who told the accused that they might damage their defense if they accepted the offer of civilian counsel, but comprehensive review of all the departmental records, official reports, and correspondence files strongly suggests that this disingenuous advice most likely came from someone associated with the prosecutorial team—either Colonel Hull, Major Sutphin, or one of the officers on Captain Preston's regimental board of inquiry.

Houston was deeply disappointed and felt that an opportunity had been lost. He wrote to James Weldon Johnson at the NAACP that he had "done all possible but it being upon the eve of the meeting of the court more time was necessary to be in the case than remained. I feel tho that the attempt should be made. If we had not undertaken it even at this late hour we might always have felt that something could have been done if the effort had been made." He concluded, "If it had been possible to have made them the offer before [Grier's] appointment we would have done all that was possible for them."

The association agreed. "It is a matter of regret that we were not able to take steps earlier," the acting secretary wrote in reply, "but the garbling of the telegram to you and the non-delivery of our letter contributed to the delay."

Houston did not drop the matter, because he continued to closely monitor the course of the trial and regularly communicated his suggestions and legal advice to Major Grier, but his absence from the defense counsel's table left a gaping hole in the soldiers' case when their trial began on the first day of November. Captain Haig Shekerjian had been detailed to act as Grier's assistant counsel during the trial, but at the last minute he was pulled from that duty. Grier undertook the defense of sixty-three alone, without any assistance. A single gunshot had changed everything.

Sometime in the evening of October 24, Captain Bartlett James was shot dead in his quarters at the Third Battalion bivouac in Columbus.

———

The night he died, James was just a few days away from taking the train to Fort Sam Houston to serve as a witness for the prosecution in the court-martial. When he was found dead of a gunshot wound to the head with a pistol lying beside his body, it had all the appearances of suicide, which was the verdict quickly rendered by the Army's local investigation.

Bartlett James, however, was an unlikely candidate for suicide. He had just come through an unsettling, perhaps even traumatic, event when Third Battalion fell apart that night in Houston, but his personal conduct in that crisis was beyond reproach. His actions had been thoroughly examined and judged to be exemplary. While other, more senior officers were criticized and excoriated for their failures that night, James was praised. The two IG reports were read at every level of the chain of command, all the way up to the War Department, and James's reputation as a competent, capable young officer was well established. Some commentators have suggested that he was distressed over the prospect of having to testify against his soldiers in court, but that seems unlikely. Most of the sixty-three defendants charged in that first court-martial were men from India Company; only four soldiers from James's own Lima Company were among them. Furthermore, he could only have testified about the chaos that broke out in the camp that night. He personally knew nothing about the violence that occurred in town, and his testimony by itself could not have sent men to the gallows.

Nor did he show signs of the kind of personal strain that might have suggested an inclination to take his own life. His behavior and demeanor had not changed in the weeks and days before his death. He was in regular communication with his family, to whom he was very close, and he was poignantly aware of how hard his brother Russell's alleged suicide just eight months before had impacted his parents and surviving siblings and how the pall of that grief still hung over them.

Several theories have attached themselves to James's death in the years since 1917. His great-nephew Jules James said in 2017, "Our family's folklore had Uncle Bartlett James murdered in his tent by his black troops along the Mexican border." That version of events was rejected with the passing of the decades, and by 2021, as Mr. James firmly stated, the family believed "he was not murdered by his troops." That conclusion is well supported by the evidence. The soldiers of Lima Company stood by Captain James that night when everything fell apart, even rejecting the urging of men from India Company to join Sergeant Henry's doomed sortie. In the investigation that followed the trouble, numerous NCOs and enlisted men in Lima Company expressed their sincere respect and loyalty for their commander.

Another theory suggests that James was murdered by someone who regarded his potential testimony in the court-martial as a personal or professional threat. Two names are often mentioned in this theory—Brigadier General John Chamberlain and Major Kneeland Snow. Chamberlain's alleged involvement can be dismissed out of hand without any serious discussion. There was absolutely nothing that James might have said about the events of August 23 that had any bearing on Chamberlain, personally or professionally.*

Kneeland Snow might seem a slightly more plausible candidate. Everyone was hearing and repeating the story of his abysmal performance in the crisis, and there was Captain James, a man thirteen years his junior who looked like a hero by comparison. But so many other witnesses had already given testimony about Snow's conduct that the voice of one more officer would never make an appreciable difference in that sorry tale of Snow's incompetence. More to the point, it must be noted that not a single piece of evidence has ever indicated that Snow was involved in any way in James's death. By that logic, if Snow had plausible reason to silence James, then so too did Captain Lindsay Silvester, who was James's peer as a fellow company commander and who also was pilloried for his unprofessional conduct on August 23.

No evidence has ever emerged to implicate either Snow or Silvester.

* One recent commentator suggests that since Chamberlain ardently believed Black men were unfit for military service, he may have thought James in some way threatened that position. That idea is a nonstarter. One company-grade officer's opinion on that question would not in the least have threatened a general officer's stance or the Army's official policies on the racial status quo.

The problem is that no answers satisfy the questions surrounding the lingering mystery of Bartlett James's death. His mother lost another of her four sons. The Army lost a promising officer with real leadership potential. His soldiers lost one of the only officers in the battalion who seemed to sincerely care about them as men. It seems very unlikely that he died by suicide, but if he did not die by his own hand, the mystery of who killed him will probably remain unsolved.

James's death had an immediate and far-reaching impact on the trial of the sixty-three soldiers accused in the Houston troubles. The defense, represented by Major Harry Grier, was already operating at a disadvantage—Grier was not a qualified attorney, but he faced a full prosecutorial team of two experienced JAG officers and an Army investigator. Grier was allowed a mere ten days to prepare his case, but the prosecution had been compiling their case for more than two months. The only assistance Grier had going into the trial was from Captain Haig Shekerjian. Third Battalion's adjutant was appointed to act as the defense counsel's assistant during the court-martial. James was scheduled to be a primary witness for the prosecution, since he was considered one of the two most knowledgeable officers who could speak to what happened in the camp when panic broke out that night. Shekerjian was the other most knowledgeable officer, and with James's sudden death, Shekerjian was called to replace him as a primary witness for the prosecution.

The defense of sixty-three men thus fell upon Major Grier alone, without co-counsel or assistance from any other officer.

13. *United States v. Nesbit*

The largest court-martial in American history began on Thursday morning, November 1, 1917. Known as *United States v. Nesbit et al.*, it was named for the lead defendant, Sergeant William Nesbit, who was the senior noncommissioned officer in the group of sixty-three defendants. It was also the largest conjoined murder trial ever held in the United States.*

The court-martial was held in Fort Sam Houston's main post chapel, an elegantly domed building known as the Gift Chapel. Its construction was a gift from the city of San Antonio a few years earlier. The choice of the chapel as the venue for the trial was a matter of practicality—it was the only building on the post large enough to handle the expected numbers of spectators and newspaper reporters, as well as the large group of defendants. It was also conveniently situated near the post guardhouse where the defendants were to be held during the trial, a squat brick building about 140 meters from the chapel.

That Thursday morning the defendants were marched from the guardhouse in column between a cordon of infantrymen from Charlie Company, 19th Infantry, the unit detailed as the guard force for the duration of the court-martial. At the chapel's front steps, onlookers and newspapermen tried to crowd in for a better view of the accused, but soldiers with fixed bayonets kept them at a distance from the main entrance and only allowed the public inside after the defendants were seated.

---

* "Conjoined," in legal terms, means that two or more defendants are tried simultaneously on identical or overlapping charges.

Inside, the religious regalia of a house of worship had been removed to transform the chapel into an ad hoc courtroom. The accused were seated at the front left side of the sanctuary in four rows. As the lead defendant, Sergeant Nesbit sat in the front row closest to the raised dais where the officers of the court's panel would sit. To Nesbit's right sat Corporals Larnon Brown, James Wheatley, Jesse Moore, and Charles Baltimore, an arrangement that grouped the five noncommissioned officers together in a tight, visibly conspicuous group.

The only surviving photograph of the entire courtroom shows just how imbalanced the trial was in terms of prosecution and defense, from its very beginning. A long table just in front of the defendants was Major Grier's position as defense counsel, and the size of that table only underscored the fact that he sat there alone—no other officer to assist him in the defense, no civilian attorney as co-counsel, no investigator to help his case. When Captain Shekerjian was shifted over to the prosecution's side of the trial, the Army took no steps to give Grier another assistant in the defense. Perhaps more damning, there is no indication that Grier ever requested a replacement officer to fill that critical role.

To the right of the defense table were two tables housing the trial judge advocate team of Colonel Hull, Major Sutphin, and Captain Tom Fox from the regimental board of inquiry. The fourth man at their tables was a surprising addition—none other than the Harris County district attorney from Houston, John Crooker. Crooker's ambition of having his name associated with the prosecution of the accused mutineers was achieved after all, even if he was not leading the case.

On the raised dais at the front of the room, the chaplain's pulpit and choir pews were replaced by tables arranged in a U-shape for the thirteen officers of the panel who sat in judgment of the case. The panel consisted of three brigadier generals, seven colonels, and three lieutenant colonels. Seven of them were cavalry officers by branch; the others came from the infantry, field artillery, or medical corps. In terms of their regional backgrounds, five officers were from northern states, four were southerners, and the remaining four were westerners. Brigadier General George Hunter, who was senior among the general officers by his date of rank, served as president of the panel.

The court convened at 10:00 a.m., when the four charges were read aloud with their specifications, in accordance with military trial procedure.

The defendants were charged with violating, in time of war, four separate articles of the Articles of War:

64th Article: Willfully disobeying orders, specifically Major Snow's order that soldiers were to remain in camp the night of August 23, with a separate specification of willfully disobeying the order to turn in their arms and ammunition.

66th Article: Mutiny, in that the defendants "did forcibly subvert and override military authority and break out of camp with the intent of marching upon the city of Houston, Texas, to the injury of persons and property."*

92nd Article: Murder, in that the defendants, "acting jointly and in pursuance of a common intent, with malice aforethought, willfully, deliberately, feloniously, unlawfully and with premeditation," murdered fourteen people "by shooting them with U.S. Rifles loaded with powder and ball."†

93rd Article: Felonious assault, in that the defendants "unlawfully and feloniously" assaulted eight other persons "by shooting at and upon them with U.S. Rifles."

Each soldier was required to stand and state his plea in response to the charges. All sixty-three men pled not guilty to all charges and specifications.

Major Grier then commenced the proceedings by reading to the court a joint statement previously agreed upon by Colonel Hull and himself. This statement, or stipulation, basically listed the facts of the case to which both the defense and the prosecution agreed and would therefore not contest in court. Most critically for the defendants, it minimized the incidents of racist harassment the soldiers endured in Houston. By agreeing

---

* Unless otherwise cited, all quotations in this chapter come from the Record of Trial, *United States v. Nesbit et al.*

† The names listed on the charge sheet as persons killed in the violence of August 23 were: E. A. Thompson, A. R. Carstens; M. Gerado, Fred Winkler, C. W. Wright, Earl Findley, R. H. Daniels, Horace Moody, Captain J. W. Mattes, Corporal M. D. Everton, E. M. Jones, E. S. [*sic*] Meineke, Ira Raney, Senator Satton, and Eli Smith. Police officer Ross Patten, who died of his wounds in September, is not listed. Neither are the Third Battalion soldiers who died that night or died of their wounds a few days later: Vida Henry, Wylie Strong, Bryant Watson, and George Bivens.

to this stipulation, Grier weakened one of the most important arguments in the defendants' case.

"There are certain underlying, contributing causes which, although neither pertinent nor strictly material to the issue about to be tried, nevertheless serve to place the court in possession of more accurate information," Grier read from the stipulation. That slightly convoluted wording meant that Hull and Sutphin had insisted the events leading up to the night of trouble should not be considered as germane or relevant to the case. The weeks of racist insults, harassment, and physical abuse were not going to be presented in a fulsome way for the panel to consider when deciding the fates of the accused. Rather than a comprehensive presentation of all the antecedents, the defense agreed to submit only this bland summary to explain what precipitated the final outbreak of violence. Whether out of loyalty to the Army or because he accepted the prevailing racial views of the time, Grier chose not to raise factors that every impartial observer recognized as highly relevant. By doing so he allowed the prosecution to cut the legs out from under one of the defense's strongest arguments before he even made it. Once that stipulation was entered into the record, he never raised the issue of causative factors in his clients' defense in any effective way.[1]

Whether the list of stipulations that Grier presented to the court was written in consultation with the judge advocate, or whether the judge advocate wrote it and Grier agreed to it after the fact, is unknown. Standard legal practice in military trials in 1917 was much the same as today—the prosecution would never allow the defense counsel to set the scope and tone of the court-martial by letting them write the stipulations. One does not easily give up a tactical advantage, so it seems likely that in the *United States v. Nesbit* court-martial the prosecutor wrote the stipulation and Grier acquiesced to it.

From the first day of the trial, some observers noted the Army seemed to have stacked the deck against the defendants in almost every way that mattered. The prosecution consisted of a team of experienced trial lawyers, while the defense was in the hands of an officer who was not a qualified attorney. Under American military law in 1917, that was not just legal, even in capital cases, but normal. The JAG Corps was very small in the years before the First World War, and there were never enough military attorneys to provide representation to soldiers tried in courts-martial. While the U.S. Army had a total manpower strength of 108,399 men the year before the war, the entire JAG Corps at that time was composed of only seventeen officers who were qualified military attorneys.[2] The vast majority of all courts-martial in that era were conducted without any trained lawyers in the room. Standard practice was for a soldier to be defended by an officer appointed to that duty, who was expected to mount a pragmatic, commonsense defense based on the two guiding regulations of the service—the Articles of War and the Manual of Courts-Martial (MCM). A court-martial was still completely legal even if the defense counsel was not a qualified attorney. The MCM, however, required that any officer acting as a defense representative "perform such duties as usually devolve upon the counsel for a defendant before civil courts in criminal cases."[3] The trial judge advocate, who was usually the only legal professional in the courtroom, was supposed to ensure that the defendant's legal rights were protected under the law, even as he prosecuted the case against him. The inadequacies of that system are self-apparent, and the inherent conflicts of interest are obvious. Nonetheless, while such practices might seem egregiously unfair today, nothing about it was illegal or out of character for courts-martial of that era. It is worth noting, on this point, that Ruckman had specifically requested that Hull and Sutphin be assigned to the prosecution of the Houston case, thereby assuring that he had professional attorneys, not amateurs, to represent the government's case against the accused.

Hull and his investigatory team came to the proceedings with nearly two months of preparation behind them, but Grier had had less than two weeks in which to interview all sixty-three of his clients and construct some semblance of a defense. Major General Ruckman had promised him "all the time he needed" to prepare his case, but Ruckman also made it clear he was keen for the trial to begin as soon as possible, and that was the only priority that seemed to matter in the rush to convene the court-martial. If Grier ever protested the lack of time to prepare, no such objection appears in the record. Furthermore, Grier was never given a copy of the reports that Captain Preston and the two IG officers had compiled in their separate pretrial investigations, so he did not know what statements his clients might have made when they were interrogated without the protection of counsel. The prosecution had all the available information; Grier had almost none.

At the very least, Grier should have requested a delay, or continuance, to better prepare his case. He had both the moral and legal responsibility to do so, and even in that era military law offered numerous precedents that supported such an action. Just a year earlier, Major General Enoch Crowder, the Judge Advocate General of the Army, had testified before the U.S. Senate that continuances were granted liberally in military trials, "for we are a little bit chary of denying applications of an accused. There have been many instances where the reviewing authorities set aside proceedings, instance[s] where it is thought the substantial rights of an accused have not been preserved."[4] The Articles of War stated that continuances ought to be granted "for such time and as often as may appear to be just." After all, the purpose of a trial was supposed to be the pursuit of justice, a tenet that applied to courts-martial as much as to civilian trials. But as has frequently been noted since the nineteenth century, courts-martial often seem to exist only to convict, and right from the beginning the court in *United States v. Nesbit* appeared willing to tilt the field to secure convictions.

Grier perhaps did not ask for a continuance because he assumed such a request would be denied. The thirteen senior officers serving as the panel for the court-martial were all on their way to pressing wartime assignments and were appointed because they were available for temporary duty in the trial.* Even so, Grier was responsible for making every effort that might benefit his clients. Instead of asking for more time to prepare the best case possible, he simply accepted the limitations that were handed to him.

Colonel Hull opened his prosecution by calling his first witness, Major Kneeland Snow. Snow described the night of August 23 as a chaotic scene where lawful military authority in his unit was usurped by soldiers acting in accordance with a prearranged plan to seize weapons and mount an assault on the city. He testified he heard soldiers shouting "Let's go!" and "We've got a job to do!" and claimed they egged each other on and tried to persuade others to join in their mutiny. Snow described it as exactly that—a mutiny—and insisted he had personally done everything he could to prevent it.

When Grier cross examined, he did not seize the opportunity to cast doubt on Snow's credibility as a witness as forcefully as he might

---

* None of the officers appointed to the court-martial panel were JAG officers or military judges. They were serving officers in other branches. It is important to understand, however, that this was both completely legal and normal in courts-martial under the Articles of War, the military law in effect in 1917. Military judges as a professional category did not exist in American military law until 1969.

have. Instead of zeroing in on Snow's questionable conduct that night and highlighting the fact that Snow's testimony could legitimately be described as self-serving, Grier let him off relatively easy. He tried to get Snow to acknowledge that soldiers might have seized their weapons out of legitimate fear of an approaching mob, but all he really succeeded in doing with that line of questioning was to give Snow more opportunity to reinforce the prosecution's contention that the incident was an act of premeditated mutiny.

Even when Snow's testimony opened a gaping hole in his personal credibility, Grier did not rise to the attack. The prosecution's efforts to identify the alleged mutineers depended on an accurate accounting of who left camp that night, and clearly the various head counts were incomplete and unreliable. When Grier asked Snow about the head counts, Snow said he "did not know whether there were any absentees from camp on August 23." If Grier had followed that by pointing out that Snow could not know because he was no longer in camp when those head counts were made, it would have further demonstrated Snow's unreliability as a witness. But Grier never raised the point, and the opportunity passed.

Regarding the panic that overtook the battalion that night, Grier said, "You used the expression 'Stampede or mutiny,' which would indicate that you are not satisfied in your own mind as to which it was?"

"The impression I got was that all the men who were not mutinying were stampeding," Snow replied.

"Are you in a position to state how many were in each class?"

"No, sir."

"Did it occur to you that these men were laboring under some sort of fear?"

"At the time it did not," Snow said. "After I was certain that a number of men had left camp it did. I had the idea that if someone were to say 'boo' the firing would have started."

Grier asked if he was able to identify any of the soldiers who he claimed had interfered with his efforts to stop the seizure of weapons and ammunition. Snow said he could not.

Grier then got Snow to acknowledge that the camp was in almost total darkness when the trouble broke out, "so dark that when you were lying between two men and asked them to cease fire you could not even distinguish who they were," as he put it.

Snow said, "Yes, sir."

This desultory approach to Snow's testimony failed in any way to impeach his credibility or character for truthfulness, which was critical for the defense. Grier never raised Snow's conduct in his cross examination in this first court-martial, nor in either of the two trials that followed. Under extant military regulation and established ethics requirements of American law, Grier was required to perform his defense duties in a court-martial just as zealously and effectively as a civilian attorney would be expected to do in a criminal case before a civil court.[5]

This obligation applied to Grier even though he was not an attorney. With his lack of legal training and courtroom experience, it was entirely possible that Grier did not understand the ethical requirements arising from this, but that ignorance did not excuse him. This insufficiency hampered almost every aspect of his work as defense counsel in every one of the trials related to the Houston Incident. Grier's ignorance of the statutory requirements all but guaranteed that he was unable to meet them, and Colonel Hull never fulfilled his legal duty as the judge advocate to protect the defendants from their counsel's lack of expertise.[6]

One of the peculiarities of a military court appeared at this point in the trial. Officers of court-martial panels were free to directly question witnesses as often as they liked, and several officers now did so, calling Snow into question in a way Grier never did. Lieutenant Colonel O. B. Myer asked Snow, "How many men were away without leave?"

"I don't know how many," Snow answered.

Another panel member said, "I haven't heard the names of anyone mentioned yet. I would like to know if you know the names of any of the men you met that night?"

Snow said that he did not.

When the court recessed on that first day of the trial, Grier stepped out onto the steps of Gift Chapel and spoke with the reporters congregated there. Grier told the journalists that "the testimony of Major Snow, unless rebutted, established the fact that a mutiny occurred, although the participants were not identified." That statement was an outright violation of his duties as defense counsel, duties clearly defined in the Manual of Courts-Martial, because he publicly declared that the prosecution had proven its most important charge before the trial had hardly begun. More importantly, it was a betrayal of the sixty-three soldiers who were depending on him for their lives.[7]

On the second day of the trial, the inadequacies of the head counts came up again in the testimony of several witnesses. The prosecution interpreted the head counts as meaning that any man whose name was not on one of those lists must have been out of camp and was therefore assumed to be an active mutineer who joined Sergeant Henry's column. Grier tried to counter that by showing the court just how disorganized the battalion's officers were in their counts and how often they had failed to identify specific soldiers by name. Lieutenant Snider testified that his first head count of Kilo Company indicated twenty-nine men were missing, but his original record of that tally was missing as well. He had written soldiers' names in his notebook, he said, and then tore the pages out and recopied them. He had since lost those notes, but he said he was confident that the paper he displayed to the court, a paper on which he had written the names he remembered from the original list, was accurate. Grier never challenged him on that assertion.

When Lieutenant John Jack took the stand, he said five soldiers were turned over to his custody after they were arrested in town the morning after the violence. He had not bothered to write down their names, he said, and he did not know any of them by sight. Now, two months after the event, he had no idea who those men were.

Another problem with the head counts, one that Grier never brought up as clearly as he should have, was the profusion of similar names in the battalion. India Company had four men named Johnson, four Jacksons, five named Davis, and three Browns. Kilo Company had six men with the surname of Jones, four who were named Williams, and four Smiths. Mike Company had four more Jacksons and another four Smiths. Three more Jacksons, three more Johnsons, and another four men named Davis were in Lima Company. Even the relatively unique name of Hawkins appeared twice—Thomas C. Hawkins and James R. Hawkins, both assigned to India Company. At different points in the trial, men with the same last name were repeatedly confused with each other. Since in both written records and witness testimony soldiers were often referred to by their last names only, identification was repeatedly uncertain and inaccurate.

When Captain Shekerjian took the stand as a primary witness for the prosecution, Hull asked if he could remember the name of any soldier "who came to your attention that night whether favorably or unfavorably." Shekerjian testified that Sergeant William Nesbit had warned him, "Lie down, captain, they're shooting all over," rendering a positive statement about the trial's lead defendant.

During the following days, several names came up in testimony that would prove particularly significant. A few days before the violence broke out in Houston, Private Pat McWhorter had gotten himself into trouble over his hot-tempered outburst when an automobile bumped into a boy at Camp Logan. Now, in the courtroom, the testimony of several witnesses put him squarely in the middle of the troubles. Captain Silvester told the court that at about 1:00 a.m. that night he had found McWhorter in his tent with a bullet wound in his leg. McWhorter, he said, had apparently just returned to camp.

"Did it ever occur to you that McWhorter's injuries might have been contracted in the same manner as Private Strong's," Grier asked him, "that they were received in camp?"

"Yes, sir," Silvester said, "at first it did, but I was satisfied that it did not." A moment later, though, he contradicted himself. Referring to McWhorter and another soldier, Private Thomas Jackson, who was also wounded by a gunshot wound in the leg, Silvester told Grier that McWhorter "said he had been shot over in Company L. Jackson told me he had been shot in the company street. It led me to believe that they were both shot in camp." Actually, both men had gone out with Sergeant Vida Henry's sortie.

During the testimony of First Sergeant Parker of Mike Company, he repeatedly mentioned McWhorter in his testimony. In a pointed cross-examination, Grier raised the possibility of personal bias in Parker's testimony.

"As a matter of fact, you don't think much of McWhorter?" Grier asked him.

"No, sir," Parker admitted. McWhorter had a reputation as a hothead who tended to let his mouth get him into trouble, and Parker, as the company's senior NCO, had had to deal with him in a disciplinary capacity several times, but this was a deadly serious business now and Grier sought to call attention to personal animosities that might color Parker's testimony.

Hull rose for redirect. "Counsel asked you whether you didn't think much of McWhorter," he said to Parker. "Why didn't you think much of him?"

"Because before we left Columbus, the first sergeant had trouble with McWhorter and he was confined," Parker replied, meaning that he was confined to the battalion guardhouse, the standard punishment for minor offenses. "I recall in Houston he had trouble on a car and he was tried and put into confinement. His general conduct in the company was such as to not make me think much of him as a soldier."

That prompted Grier to make one of his first objections. "I move the court to strike out all the testimony regarding the character of McWhorter," he said. "The defense has not put the character of the accused in question." The panel recessed for a full five minutes to discuss the motion, then returned to overrule Grier's objection. Parker's testimony was allowed to stand.

McWhorter also came up in the testimony of Private John Denty. Hull asked if Denty knew the names of any Mike Company men who refused to turn in their rifles that night, and Denty named McWhorter, along with Privates William Burkett, Dean New, Jessie Sullivan, Thomas Jackson, and Walter Johnson. Hull asked if he overheard them making any remarks.

"McWhorter was in the company street, so the Company Commander told them he would give them two minutes to turn in their rifles," Denty replied. "McWhorter said, 'Shit,' he wasn't going to do nothing, he was going to town and 'shoot the God damned son of a bitch up,' he was tired of seeing soldiers coming in there with their heads all beat up."

Corporal Larnon Brown had already been mentioned in Shekerjian's testimony because he was one of the few men Shekerjian said he had personally spoken to during the chaos, when he tried to convince Brown not to leave camp with Sergeant Henry's column. When India Company's supply sergeant, Rhoden Bond, took the stand, Hull asked him, "Did any member of Company I say anything to you about issuing ammunition?"

"Yes, sir," Bond said. "Corporal Brown asked me whether we were going to issue any ammunition. I said, 'No, I had no orders to do so.' He said, 'Well, you better be gone when we come.'" Another NCO witness also placed Brown with the ammunition a short time later. Sergeant Fox reported being overwhelmed when men rushed the supply tent. "I tried to stop them," he said. "They pushed me out of the way. Some tall man reached over me. I took him to be Corporal Brown. He got a box which proved to be pistol ammunition."

Another NCO among the defendants, Corporal James Wheatley, was pointed out in the testimony of two military witnesses. Private Lark Jamison, a soldier from Mike Company who was at Camp Logan on August 23, testified that the morning after the violence Wheatley came in with Private Gerald Dixon. "We asked them where they had been," Jamison said, "and they said, 'Down in the Fourth Ward, raising hell. We shot all the lights out.'" When asked if he could identify Wheatley and Dixon among the defendants, he did so. Another witness, Private George Burrus from India Company, testified that shortly after rumor reached Third Battalion's camp that Corporal Baltimore had been shot, he overheard Corporal Wheatley tell a group of soldiers, "Something should be done about this."

Private Robinson, who was on duty in India Company's supply tent when the trouble broke out, said that when the tent was rushed in the panic he recognized several voices, notably those of Vida Henry, Frank Johnson, and James Divins.

"What did they say?" Hull asked.

"I heard Sergeant Henry tell them to save their ammunition and not waste it," Robinson said. "He said, 'Hurry up, the mob is coming.'" Robinson also testified that Sergeant Henry had threatened to shoot any man who did not go out with him.

"Did you believe a mob was coming?" Grier asked on cross-examination.

"I don't know," Robinson said. "I knew the police had been beating the soldiers, so I didn't know what they were likely to do. The men had no guns and I thought that made them that much afraid."

"Well, what had the soldiers done to make them think the mob was coming?" Grier asked.

"The soldiers didn't believe they had done nothing," Robinson answered. "The police had beat up one man [Baltimore]. I suppose they would beat up a thousand if they could get their hands on them."

Robinson concluded his testimony by insisting there was no inkling of a conspiracy to mutiny in Third Battalion that night. "There was nothing to make me believe that anything was going to happen whatever," he insisted.

The last witness of that day was Private Goode from Lima Company, and his testimony returned to the difficulties encountered in conducting accurate head counts in the camp. He testified he was ordered to search all the company area, not just the skirmish line where most of the soldiers were. He said he found men hiding behind the tents, behind the camp kitchen, and scattered around in other places. At about 1:45 that morning, he said, Private Peacock came back into camp with a group of soldiers. Peacock had a rifle and said he had been in town with Sergeant Henry, and that about thirty men had returned with him. A couple of hours later, Private Parham straggled in. "He said he had been down the railroad with Sergeant Henry," Goode said, and that Parham had reported Henry's death.

One of the panel members asked, "Did he say that Sergeant Henry was killed or that he had killed himself?"

"He said he was killed," Goode said.

———

Local newspapers followed the court-martial closely, and more than one reporter commented on the stark differences between civilian trial procedures and the more spartan, stripped-down characteristics of military law. "Technicality in military jurisprudence is unknown, judging from the trial now in progress," a writer for the *Post* declared. "Rules of evidence, as they are known to every lawyer in Texas, who [has] practiced only under civil law, are disregarded. Only one thing is sought—and obtained—truth. For three days since the court-martial convened, witnesses have been examined and cross-examined—and the first objection, legal or otherwise, is yet to be raised by counsel." A court-martial, he told his readers, "is the last place on earth for a guilty man to be tried and the safest place for an innocent man. It is a shorthand rendering of the facts."[8] Perhaps that was true in ideal circumstances, but it was also true that a defendant could be steamrolled in a court-martial, if all the protections of law and due process were not scrupulously followed.

On November 5, the prosecution shifted from its military witnesses to Houston residents who were called to the stand to give their versions of what had happened. "Their testimony was an appeal for justice," a reporter wrote. "Little by little, too, such possible defenses as might have been offered by the accused are being shattered by the evidence of the prosecution's witnesses. Identification of the particular defendants who composed the invading party, and especially who fired the specific shots which caused the death of innocent men and women is still to be made, and on the difficulty of such identification the accused strongly rely. But they will be disclosed, it is understood," the writer promised, "and that will be the final link in the chain of evidence."[9]

Most of this civilian testimony came from people who had direct, personal knowledge of the violence—several of them either saw family or friends killed or wounded or were themselves injured in the shooting. Reporters noted that Major Grier seemed reluctant to subject these witnesses to stringent cross-examination. Most of the time, one wrote, "he is satisfied to let the testimony remain as given."

That choice was perhaps a sensible one. These witnesses were more likely to have the court's sympathy, and Grier probably knew he could gain no advantage by being aggressive in his questioning of them. However, Grier surely grasped the most critical fact about their testimony—none of the civilian witnesses were able to identify a single man among the defendants as any soldier they saw in the city streets that night, so he did not need to undertake an intensive cross-examination.

Misidentification was a continuing problem for the prosecution's witnesses. In one exchange, a police officer witness was asked if he could point out Private Jessie Sullivan among the defendants, since he had arrested Sullivan the morning after the troubles. The witness identified a soldier among the defendants, whom Grier asked to stand and say his name, which turned out to be Private Fred Brown. Sullivan remained seated in a completely different row.

The witness then said he was sure he could identify Sullivan by a process of elimination, and Hull asked the court that he be allowed to do so. Grier objected strenuously to this method of identification, but the panel once again overruled Grier's objection, and the witness was allowed to go over to the defendants' gallery and speak directly to the accused men. He had one man in the back row stand up and asked him several questions. Even after all that, he told the court, he still was not able to positively identify Private Sullivan. Hull and Grier both knew that the soldier the witness had just spoken to, the man whom he said he could not identify, was in fact Sullivan himself. Hull now asked that Sullivan be ordered to step forward so the witness could have another look at him, obviously signaling to the witness that this was the man he was supposed to identify. That was going too far, even for that court. A member of the panel objected to the impropriety of the prosecution's request, and Hull was overruled.

It was not the only time Hull crossed the line of legal propriety in his efforts to manipulate the identification of the accused. When a civilian witness tried to identify Private Terry Smith and instead pointed to Private Douglas Bolden, Hull had the two soldiers stand next to each other so the members of the panel could decide "whether they looked alike." His implication was a subtle invocation of a tired old racist trope—the witnesses could be excused for being unable to make accurate identifications when so many of the accused Black men looked so similar, according to white observers. The court did not object in this instance, and Grier once again did not protest as he should have.

Knox Polk, a sergeant in the Houston police department, took the stand and testified that he had been on duty as the desk sergeant the morning after the riot and that he wrote the names of several soldiers into the police blotter when they were brought to the station. Among the names he read aloud to the court were Private Risley Young, Corporal Larnon Brown, and Private William Breckenridge. All three men were reported as having been detained in town in the hours after the troubles. Young and Brown were unarmed when they were arrested, but Breckenridge was described as practically being a walking arsenal when he was taken into custody, having an Army-issue M1903 Springfield rifle, a Model 1911 Colt .45 pistol, a .32 pocket pistol, and three belts of rifle ammunition in his possession. That profusion of weaponry alone should have made him easy to remember.

When Polk was asked if he could identify any of these men, he said he was pretty sure he could pick Breckenridge out of the crowd. He pointed to one of the defendants and said he thought the man "looked like" Breckenridge. Grier immediately informed the court that the man Polk singled out was not Breckenridge. It was one more embarrassing misidentification added to the prosecution's tally.

Colonel Hull shifted tactics at this point in the trial because none of his witnesses had proven able to positively identify a single defendant. "Judge Advocate Hull is not inviting his witnesses to identify any of those arrested by them," a reporter wrote. "It is contended by the prosecution that the giving of a name by one of the accused at the time he was arrested or registered at the police station is prima facie evidence as to his identity. . . . The prosecution does not want to assume the burden of picking out the particular man from among the accused."[10] The problem was more serious than that. The fact was that not a single witness had yet managed to positively identify any defendant as a participant in the violence.

E ven though Grier sat alone at the defense table each day of the trial, he could have consulted with another, far more experienced legal mind had he chosen to. Even though the soldier defendants had rejected A. J. Houston's offer of legal services, Houston remained in San Antonio for the first week of the trial, and he was in the courtroom every day as an observer. At several points in the proceedings, he advised Grier to suggest a tactic or point out vulnerabilities in the prosecution's case. Grier never acted on any of his advice.

One of the legal issues Houston mentioned, which Grier never raised during the trial, was the composition of the court—all the defendants were Black, and every member of the panel sitting in judgment of them was white. "I would not have challenged any member of the court as is provided for by law," Houston wrote in a letter he sent to the NAACP, "but would have filed an exception to the order appointing the court, in that no member of it is of the same race as that of the accused." The law already established this argument, he said. "The Supreme Court of the United States has several times held that an indictment upon which a colored man is tried for a capital offense must have been presented by a grand jury upon which was at least one colored member." Although it would have required an extension of this case law to military courts, the legal argument was well supported and the Equal Protection Clause absolutely could have been applied to this court-martial. Furthermore, qualified Black officers were available to serve at that time and in that trial. Houston pointed out that Colonel Charles Young "by virtue of his rank as a field-grade officer is eligible to membership of a general court-martial" and that the 8th Illinois National Guard then training at Camp Logan had "a full complement of colored field-[grade] officers" who were equally eligible to sit on a general court-martial panel.

Houston also believed that the defense should emphasize the degree to which the soldiers believed a race mob was coming, and how that belief affected their behavior that night. "By the same kind of cross examination of the civilian witnesses for the prosecution the proof could easily have been made that there was a pronounced mob sentiment which had been growing among the irresponsible element of the white men in the city," he wrote. He believed Grier should have shown "by all the colored witnesses, on both sides of the case, the influence upon their minds of the possibility or the probability of coming directly under the power of the American mob in all of its frightfulness."[11]

When Third Battalion soldiers began testifying to their experiences at the hands of Captain Preston's regimental board of inquiry, with its "various and devious" means of interrogation, Houston thought Grier missed yet another opportunity to knock holes in Hull's prosecution. "In the testimony of Harry Richardson," he wrote to the acting secretary of the NAACP, "is revealed for the first time the character of the inquisition of cruelty to helpless prisoners, some of whom must have been innocent, to prepare to entrap them at the trial, in the effort to make those confess who would, and to use their testimony to convict their fellows, some of whom may be less guilty than those who thus purchased their own immunity from punishment." Houston was incredulous that Grier allowed those facts to emerge in testimony without pursuing the matter in cross-examination, which might have greatly benefited his clients' case. "This was revealed without any examination of any witnesses upon so vital a question," he wrote. He was baffled by Grier's lassitude in the courtroom.

In one relatively rare instance where the record offers a limited defense of Grier's conduct in the trial, he did attempt a follow-on question when Lieutenant Levie, one of the members of that Regimental Board of Inquiry, was on the stand for the prosecution. Levie had stated that he and other members of the board received instructions from the Army Inspector General, Brigadier General John Chamberlain, on how they should conduct their interrogations of the accused soldiers. Grier asked him what those instructions were, and Hull was immediately on his feet, objecting that the question was irrelevant. The panel supported Hull's objection, Grier's question was never answered, and to this day no one knows what instructions the Army's senior investigator gave the board of inquiry during their interrogations of the Third Battalion men.

On November 14, Hull called the first of his seven immunity witnesses. These were soldiers from Third Battalion who had agreed to turn state's witness and testify for the prosecution. Under questioning by

Preston's board or the trial judge advocates, five of the seven had already admitted their participation in some phase of the alleged mutiny. Whether that admission was truly voluntary or was coerced was a question that Hull skipped over and Grier, inexplicably, never pursued.

Each of these witnesses was promised immunity from the most severe punishments—death or life imprisonment—but to ensure their cooperation, that protection was not officially granted until the day they took the stand in court and testified against their fellow soldiers. "This required," former JAG officer Dru Brenner-Beck says, "both that Major General Ruckman as the convening authority grant immunity, [and] that John Crooker obtain a similar grant from the State of Texas."[12]

The testimony of these witnesses was not surprising or even revelatory. Each of them recited the names of soldiers he remembered seeing in the column that marched out with Sergeant Henry, but most of these men, even though they were veterans who had been with the battalion for some time, only admitted to knowing a dozen or so soldiers in that group. This resulted in repeated instances of outright chicanery on the part of the prosecutors. When Private Lloyd Shorter seemed able to only remember a few men who had joined the alleged mutiny, Colonel Hull began reading off the names of the defendants present in the courtroom and asked Shorter if he knew anything about their participation. Grier objected to this, and Hull in a show of disingenuous magnanimity settled for asking about those names in "a broad general way." But the damage was already done—by that point the witness had been led to say what the prosecutor wanted, and Shorter was suddenly able to remember twenty-one names he had previously been unable to recall.

Hull and Sutphin repeatedly asked their witnesses leading questions, steering them through their testimony by phrasing their inquires in such a way that the prosecution's version of events entered the record in their words, rather than that of the witnesses. Grier rarely objected to this irregularity, and what objections he did raise were tepid at best. The officers of the panel allowed the prosecution to lead the witnesses again and again, while the defendants' counsel simply sat there at his solitary table, silent and acquiescent to the trampling of his clients' rights.

Even with those perfidious tactics, the inherent weaknesses of the prosecution's immunity witnesses were plain to see. Private Joseph Alexander was only able to name fifteen men out of the more than a hundred who were in the column; Private Elmer Bandy remembered just seventeen of them. Private First Class Henry Peacock identified twenty men, but all of the names he provided had already been given by at least one of the prosecution witnesses who preceded him. Peacock did, however, admit to clubbing police officer John Richardson with his rifle so hard that he broke the stock. He told the court, "I was very sorry I did that. I have been worrying more about that than anything else since it happened."

Hull's star witness was Private Cleda Love, a recruit in India Company who had only joined the battalion three short months before the troubles. Nonetheless, Love recited the names of forty-one men who he claimed were active participants in the violence that night. His memory, as one commentator noted, "was nothing short of incredible." "Incredible" can mean very different things, not all of them complimentary, and Love's testimony was demonstrably unreliable. Five of the men he said he saw in Henry's column were soldiers who either could conclusively prove they had never left camp that night or were picked up in town the day after because they had already been in the city and had nothing to do with Henry's sortie.

Grier challenged Love's testimony more aggressively than he did that of any other witness and cross-examined him on the stand for more than an hour. Besides being a newcomer to Third Battalion and therefore still something of an outsider, Love had somehow managed to make himself unpopular in his unit almost from the first day he joined it. The soldiers in his own company disliked him on a deeply personal level, and Grier used that fact to question whether this astonishing feat of recollection and damning testimony was driven by Love's desire to get back at men who had made it clear they detested him. Love insisted that his recall was accurate and in no way influenced by vindictiveness nor even an effort to save himself from the noose. In the end, Grier failed to discredit his testimony as completely as he might have.

Grier began his defense of his sixty-three clients on Monday morning, November 19. The limited time he had to prepare his case before the court-martial, combined with the fact that few men among the defendants seemed to truly trust him enough to confide in him, meant his efforts were hamstrung from the start. Few of his clients were willing to take the stand. The accused soldiers had endured nearly two months of aggressive interrogations before the trial even began, interrogations by various Army officers who refused to accept their statements and threatened to see them hanged unless they changed their stories. Consequentially, few of the defendants were willing to subject themselves to more of that verbal assault in open court. Anything they might say on the stand, many of them seemed to believe, would just be twisted around to make them appear guilty. A few men may have been fatalistic in their outlook. From their perspective, the verdict was already a foregone conclusion, and the court was probably going to convict them no matter what defense they offered. As a result, only nineteen men out of the sixty-three defendants took the stand to testify on their own behalf.

Private First Class John Hudson said he left camp only because he was frightened in all the chaos and shooting and did not know what else to do when Sergeant Henry ordered India Company to fall in. If he had heard any officer countermand that order, he said, he would never have marched out that night. "I didn't hear any officer's command of no kind," he said. "I didn't know what to think. . . . If I could have heard any officer's voice I would never have been here now."

Several of the prosecution's immunity witnesses identified Private Grover Burns as being one of the soldiers who marched out with Henry's column, but Grier produced three alibi witnesses to corroborate Burns's testimony that he had remained in camp with Lina Company's skirmish line. When Burns took the stand to testify in his own defense, General Hunter pointedly asked him why so many witnesses claimed to have seen him with Henry's group. Burns replied that "those men were doing that to save their lives . . . They would do anything the investigation board told them to do, even if they would have mentioned men in the Tenth Cavalry, they would have said they were there, too."[13] That was a more effective refutation of the prosecution's witnesses than any argument Grier offered.

Private Douglass Lumpkins told the court that he did not have a weapon when the shooting broke out, so he ran to his tent and hid under his cot. He remained there for several hours, he said, and that was why his name never got on any of the head counts—anyone who checked the tent would not have seen him under his bunk in the darkness. A brief interlude of legal theater ensued when the prosecution insisted that a grown man of Lumpkin's size could never have gotten himself under a military-issue cot far enough to be hidden from view, and Grier had a cot brought into the courtroom and assembled in the middle of the floor. Lumpkins then crawled under it, demonstrating to the officers of the panel that he could indeed fit.

Private Douglas T. Bolden's testimony was particularly important, because he alibied several of his fellow defendants, specifically Private First Class Thomas C. Hawkins. Bolden said that he saw Hawkins in the skirmish line of soldiers who had taken up defensive positions on the camp perimeter, and he a had clear memory of that because he had stepped on Hawkins's foot in the darkness and the two men exchanged words.

Private Roy Tyler testified that he had not gone out with Sergeant Henry's column because he was suffering from an infected foot and was on limited duty. He was able to show that he had attended sick call for the ailment earlier that day and that Lieutenant Chaffin, the battalion medical officer, had placed him on profile, meaning he was limited to light duty because of a medical issue.

Other soldiers testified that they never got on the head count lists because they had hidden and not come out until long after the chaos. One man said he spent the night in the drainage ditch that bordered the camp; another told of hiding between the kitchen tent and a large ice box.

The prosecution had argued that because the soldiers who left camp with Vida Henry moved out in an orderly, organized column, this should be taken as proof of a preexisting conspiracy among men who seized the opportunity to wreak their unlawful vengeance on Houston's defenseless population. Grier argued it was nothing of the sort. The fact that the soldiers who marched out did so in column, with an advance party and a rear guard of NCOs, actually demonstrated that those men were acting under the leadership of the senior military authority present at that time, he insisted. They went out as an organized unit, not as a riotous mob or rabble, and if they obeyed the wrong orders, the fault for that lay with Sergeant Henry, who gave those orders.

The fact that at least two of the civilians killed or wounded that night—G. W. Butcher and A. R. Carstens—were initially shot on streets that were not part of that column's route of march added some weight to Grier's argument that the prosecution had still not proven that any individual defendant could be shown to have killed any particular victim. There was also the matter of the ambush of the jitney near Camp Logan that resulted in the death of E. M. Jones and the wounding of Charles Clayton. None of the soldiers who went out with Sergeant Henry had been implicated in that incident, and they were nowhere near it, a fact that Grier pointed out to the court.

Grier also tried to gain some traction from how inconsistent the prosecution witnesses had been in their widely varying estimates of just how many men were in Henry's sortie. If they were so unsure of that basic fact, Grier argued, and if Hull and Sutphin had found it necessary to so egregiously coach and lead them through their statements on the stand, surely that cast the accuracy of their testimony in serious doubt. The prosecution's case was built on assumption, not evidence. It was an absolutely valid argument, but those were points that Grier should have raised in forceful objections and cross-examination when those witnesses were testifying, not days later as rebuttal against testimony that he had already allowed into the record unchallenged.

The inadequacies of the defense Grier mounted were self-apparent, but it was also true that he was in an impossible situation. As counsel for the defense, a basic strategy would be to establish an alibi defense for each of his clients. But as the single officer tasked with representing sixty-three men simultaneously, he was handicapped by a fatal conflict of interest. He was duty-bound to defend each soldier equally well, but one soldier's defense could easily implicate a fellow defendant. That was a scenario that could play out dozens of times if he tried to build a case in defense of individual men. If, for example, he attempted to show the court that Abner Davis was mistaken for Ira Davis, both of whom sat among the defendants in the courtroom, he might alibi Abner Davis by dooming Ira Davis. If he had had enough time before the court-martial began, and if he had been given the support of an investigator, Grier might have been able to build individual defenses for many of his clients, but time and adequate support were two things Ruckman had denied him in the headlong rush to start the trial. As the American Bar Association had already noted in 1908, a lawyer was in an inescapable conflict of interest "when, in behalf of one client, it is his duty to contend for that which duty to another client requires him to oppose."[14] The Army's JAG Corps in 1917 understood that legal reality just as well as it was understood by their civilian counterparts, but they nonetheless allowed the court-martial to proceed under that fatally flawed contradiction.

Grier rested his defense on November 25, and at 11:00 that morning Major Dudley Sutphin, the assistant trial judge advocate, commenced the prosecution's closing arguments. The government's entire case was predicated on the legal concept of collective guilt—any man proven to have participated in the alleged mutiny was considered equally guilty of all acts of murder, or assault with intent to commit murder, that occurred during the mutiny. Participation in mutiny established full conspiratorial liability. If the court accepted the prosecution's argument that the events of August 23 were a mutiny, then Hull and Sutphin did not need to prove the individual culpability of any defendant. As far as the Army was concerned, mutiny was a crime without excuse or exculpation, and Sutphin argued the court need not trouble itself over which soldier might have fired the fatal shot that killed any particular victim or was present when any named individual was wounded. They were all guilty, he declared, simply by their presence and participation in the act of mutiny. One great, gaping hole remained in that argument, however—under military law a charge of mutiny required proof of a preexisting conspiracy, and the prosecution never actually proved the existence of any conspiracy to commit mutiny.

Grier knew that. When he delivered his closing arguments, he told the court that "not one iota of evidence" had proved the existence of a conspiracy to subvert lawful military authority prior to the moment the battalion was overtaken by panic. It was a spontaneous outburst, he insisted, one triggered by preceding weeks of harassment by the police and precipitated by the soldiers' very real fear that night that they were under threat from a race mob. He pointed out that numerous witnesses had testified that many soldiers dropped out of Henry's column as soon as it became apparent there was no mob for them to fight. Fewer than fifty men, by Grier's count, could be assumed to have still been in the group when the killings in the San Felipe District occurred. He then argued that the testimony of prosecution witnesses who were themselves complicit in the violence should be considered very cautiously, and the panel should not take their version of events as truth incarnate.

Colonel Hull made the final statements in the trial. He focused on Grier's argument that panic and fear were behind the soldiers' decision to leave camp and march into the city. When the firing broke out in camp that night, Hull claimed, soldiers deliberately refrained from firing in the direction in which Henry's column marched out into the city, suggesting that even men who remained in camp were involved in a battalion-wide conspiracy. "It might seem from the remarks that fear was incidentally being presented to this court as a defense for military offenses," he declared, and he derided the supposed fear of an advancing mob as little more than the

sort of panic "that might stampede a crowd of nine-year-old school girls."
His sarcastic derision did not end there. "The exigencies of the service,
as far as I know," he told the panel, "have not produced fear as a proper
defense for military offenses. Fear to a soldier is a crime itself."[15]

As a prosecutor, Hull was supremely self-confident, but his closing
statement revealed the limits of his personal military experience. He was a
skilled attorney who had spent years arguing in courtrooms, but he himself
had never heard a shot fired in anger and his claim that "fear to a soldier
is a crime itself" was not just an aspersion on the combat veterans among
the defendants; it was an outright distortion of the legal facts. Cowardice
truly is a crime under military law. Fear, on the other hand, is a natural,
ever-present reality of soldiers' experience, and most soldiers manage to
function and go forward into harm's way despite their fear of being killed
or injured. Fear and cowardice are not at all the same thing. Hull's dishon-
est claim that they were was just so much courtroom hyperbole uttered by
a man who had only ever faced the threat of angry words, never bullets.

———

The court-martial adjourned late on the afternoon of November 27.
In three and a half weeks of trial the court had heard the testimony
of 194 witnesses, the vast majority of them called by the prosecution. The
thirteen officers of the panel spent most of the next day in deliberation. The
records of that deliberation were secret and remain so, because the processes of court-martial deliberations are never disclosed. Only the results
are made public in the final verdict. It is impossible to say if the panel agreed
unanimously on each defendant's guilt or innocence, or if the members
of the panel argued with each other over their conclusions. Nonetheless,
a certain protocol was always followed in these deliberations. Each defendant's name was taken in turn, and each member of the panel was polled
as to his determination of that man's guilt or innocence on each charge.
The most junior member of the panel, in this case one of the lieutenant
colonels, stated his verdict first so that he was not unduly influenced
by the opinions of the more senior officers. The other members of
the panel then gave their verdicts in order of rising seniority. The panel
reached their decisions on all sixty-three defendants in less than twelve
hours of deliberation.

Some observers who had followed the course of the trial from the beginning thought they knew which way the balance of judgment was tilting, and they feared it was not toward justice. The day before the officers of the panel began their deliberations, A. J. Houston sent a letter to James Weldon Johnson at the NAACP. "The fact is too historic not to be recognized that there is hardly such a thing as military mercy," Houston wrote. Everything he had seen in the court-martial led him to believe that the verdicts were going to go against the defendants. He acknowledged the severity of the charges, especially mutiny, but there was more to the case than that charge. "Yet, for any of these men to be executed for that offense, it would be a crime against the nation," he concluded. The men of 3-24 Infantry had not received the full process of justice, he believed, and he feared what he thought was coming next.[16]

At 10:00 on Thursday morning, November 28, the defendants were brought back into court to hear the verdicts announced. Fifty-four of the sixty-three were found guilty on all charges and specifications. Four other men were found guilty only of disobeying orders by leaving camp, and the remaining five defendants were acquitted. None of those convicted, however, knew what sentences the panel had settled on. All defendants were then removed from the courtroom, and in their absence Brigadier General Hunter announced the sentences: thirteen men were sentenced "to be hanged by the neck until dead"; the other forty-one who were found guilty of mutiny and murder were sentenced to life imprisonment "at hard labor for the term of their natural lives." The four men convicted of disobeying orders were sentenced to prison for terms ranging from two to two and a half years.

One recurring question is why the court decided that the thirteen men whom it sentenced to death were deserving of that harshest punishment. The records provide no absolute answer, but a close analysis of the case offers some logical conclusions. The court sentenced to death every noncommissioned officer among the defendants: Sergeant Nesbit and Corporals Brown, Wheatley, Moore, and Baltimore. They were seen as having more responsibility for what happened that night, on account of their rank and roles as leaders. The junior enlisted men—Privates First Class Snodgrass, Hawkins, and Breckenridge, and Privates Divins, Johnson, Young, McWhorter, and Ira Davis—were all accused of making statements in the hours before the violence that the court interpreted as advocating mutiny. Johnson was furthermore identified by several witnesses as the man who first raised the shout that a mob was approaching the camp, but it was never proven that that was a prearranged signal for a mutinous uprising, as the prosecution alleged.

At that point, all sixty-three defendants knew whether they had been acquitted or convicted. Those acquitted were immediately released from confinement and returned to duty with their regiment, but the men who heard the court pronounce them guilty could only wait. Sentences in a general court-martial could not be imposed until the convening authority—Major General Ruckman, in this case—approved them. Ruckman would not render a decision until his staff judge advocate (SJA), the senior legal advisor on his command, read the entire record of trial and made his recommendations on the sentences. The Southern Department's SJA was Colonel George Dunn, and most observers familiar with military law expected that it would take him some time to carefully read and consider the 2,169 pages of the *United States v. Nesbit* record.

A. J. Houston summarized the case in his November 26 letter to the NAACP, and he did not hesitate to criticize what he saw as the trial's inadequacies. "It is purely a race issue," he wrote. "The white murderers at East St. Louis had no reason to fear a negro mob, nor have been, are likely to be, punished for the brutality to the negro race, under the white man's administration of *his* laws in *his* courts. In the case at Houston, members of their race had warned the negro soldiers that there was a probability of a white mob attacking the camp." As a Texan, Houston believed the soldiers' fear of a race mob was absolutely legitimate. He enclosed a clipping from a local newspaper, which he said "indicates that the department commander [Major General Ruckman] has intimated to the press that he will not exercise his full authority, to take final action upon the findings of the court-martial, but with his endorsement will send it up to the president, which means that the recommendation of the secretary of war will doubtless be followed by the president." That was the only note of hope Houston could find in the situation as the nation waited to learn the decisions of the court.[17]

The wheels of justice, the old cliché says, grind slowly, but nothing about this trial had been characterized by a slow, careful quest for the truth. The Army had moved with precipitous haste almost from the beginning of the judicial process, and now that headlong rush continued as fifty-eight men waited to learn if they were going to live or die. Contrary to expectations and regulatory guidelines, Colonel Dunn was not conducting a careful, methodical review of the record of trial. His mind was already made up, and he was taking inexcusable shortcuts in the review process. He already knew what recommendations he would make to General Ruckman.

14. GALLOWS

In Henderson, North Carolina, the Hawkins family were anxiously waiting for news from Texas. Coleman and Cassie Hawkins had two sons then serving in the Army.* Their younger son, Thomas Coleman Hawkins, was in India Company, 3-24 Infantry, and the family had heard nothing from him for more than two months. That was highly unusual. Hawkins had always written home regularly, even while he was posted overseas in the Philippines. He had returned to the United States a year earlier in time to serve in the Punitive Expedition into Mexico, and that July he had arrived in Houston with 3-24 Infantry. Suddenly at the end of August there were no more letters, and his parents lost contact with him. In mid-October Cassie wrote to the War Department asking for information on her son. The only reply she received was a terse, officious note informing her that he was on duty with his unit. She was not told her son was at that time confined in the guardhouse, facing a court-martial on the capital charges of mutiny and murder.

T. C. Hawkins had originally enlisted on October 19, 1914. Joining the Army was not a spontaneous decision—his older brother Lewis Henry was already a soldier, serving in the 10th Cavalry Regiment. In September 1914 Lewis wrote home to encourage his younger brother to enlist in the Army. It was the manly thing to do, Lewis said, and the Army offered the sort of health and education benefits hard to come by in rural North Carolina. In addition to the material advantages, Lewis told his brother, a young Black man was far safer in the Army than he could ever be in a southern state.

---

* Material on Thomas C. Hawkins, including transcripts and quotations from letters, come from his great-nephew, Jason Holt, Esq., who generously shared them with the author.

T. C. Hawkins followed his brother's advice, enlisting with the 24th Infantry and shipping out for the Philippines. The decision seemed to be a good one, and Hawkins took to soldiering with enthusiasm and real ability. His talents were quickly noted by his superiors, and his personnel records indicated official evaluations that described him as a soldier of high intelligence with good language skills, especially in writing.

His letters home to his parents were filled with descriptions of tough conditions in the tropics, describing steady attrition in his unit from fever and unspecified disease, as well as sporadic combat engagements. Whether these small-unit actions were fights with Filipino bandits or holdout elements of the Filipino nationalists that resisted American rule in the islands is unclear, because the Philippine-American War was over by then and American control of the islands was largely consolidated, but it was still tough duty in hazardous conditions. In a letter to his father on August 24, 1915, Hawkins wrote, "You would not have an idea what trouble these natives give us here. I never said anything about it because it would upset mother, but the rougher they come the better I like them." He also told his father he was going to school, taking advantage of the chance the Army offered to continue his education. He liked the Army, even when it was hard and dangerous.

Though Hawkins enjoyed his experiences in the Philippines, even with all the challenges, and soldiering suited him, family problems at home made him consider getting out before his full enlistment was up. His father's health seems to have taken a turn for the worse, and working the family's tobacco farm was increasingly difficult for the older man. In a letter to his father, Hawkins wrote, "I like the army alright but how would a man with a heart feel in the army with a father in your condition and he had [nine] in the family to look out for." He had been sending a regular portion of his pay home to his parents as a monthly allotment, and his father suggested he should stop the allotment and save his money in order to buy out his enlistment contract when the regiment returned to the United States. Hawkins rejected that idea. His family needed the money, and he told his father, "If I did not want you to have it I would not have made it." He felt his familial responsibilities very deeply. As he weighed the decision of whether he should stay in the Army or take his discharge, he told his father that if he left the Army he would immediately return home to North Carolina, "because I could not be any good to you all [if he did not return] because I know the state is panic stricken." In the end, Hawkins decided to stay with his regiment when it returned to the States. He was promoted to private first class on July 24, 1916, just a year before he arrived in Houston with Third Battalion.

Now, in the early days of December 1917, Hawkins was confined in the cramped basement of the Fort Sam Houston guardhouse with the fifty-seven other men who had just been convicted in the *United States v. Nesbit* court-martial. All of them knew that the verdict of guilt carried with it the potential of serious prison sentences or, even worse, the death penalty, and they knew the court had already decided on those sentences. There was nothing any of them could do except wait while the sentences were reviewed, wondering which of them would live and who among them would die. They were under no illusion about the danger looming over them, and they made a request to the court that if they were sentenced to death, they would be permitted to die by firing squad rather than be executed by hanging. In military culture, facing a firing squad was considered a more honorable way for a soldier to die.

Hawkins's parents back in North Carolina knew nothing of this. As the silence drew out and their anxiety deepened, they continued hoping for news of their son, and they waited for letters that did not come.

———

Newspaper reporters who had followed the course of the trial lost no time filling their dispatches with their guesses as to the possible outcome of Colonel Dunn's review of the case. Many of them had repeatedly written wild speculations whenever they had no concrete details to report on, and they continued to do so. Many commentators took it as a given that the death penalty would be imposed on the convicted men. It only remained to be seen how many of the defendants might be executed and what method of execution the Army would use. As the reporter for the *Houston Post* pointed out, Ruckman could not increase the severity of any sentence, but he was fully empowered to mitigate the court's decisions to less severe punishments if he chose to do so. "A sentence of death by hanging is subject to change to sentence of death by shooting," he wrote, "but a sentence of death by shooting could not be changed to one of death by hanging, hanging being held a more severe penalty." The reporter did not bother to mention that Ruckman also had the power to commute any sentence of death to a prison sentence. The *Post*'s correspondent may not have considered it a possibility, or he may have thought such a detail would not be well received by his Houston readers. At any rate, he concluded his piece by pointing out one detail of military law that was to cause intense controversy and outrage a few days later. "No appeal will be possible from the findings and approval of General Ruckman," he wrote. "Ordinarily approval of the president would be required if a death penalty were called for. In time of war, it is said, that is not required."[1] In December 1917, the United States was in a state of war.

Army chaplains and representatives of the military chapter of the YMCA visited the guardhouse several times to minister to any of the prisoners who wanted religious support. Most of the men responded to the opportunity; fifty of them made professions of faith and signed pledge cards. "I hereby pledge my allegiance to the Lord Jesus Christ as my Savior and King," each card read, "and by God's help will henceforth fight the battles for the victory of His Kingdom." Corporal Larnon Brown and Private James Divins did not make any such declaration. Private Frank Johnson said that since he had no particular interest in religion and espoused no religious faith, it would be hypocritical of him to make such claims now, but the sources describe him making that statement in an affable sort of way, his tone not at all bitter or anti-religious. In addition to the military chaplains, the Army permitted a local African American clergyman, Reverend L. H. Richardson of the Methodist Episcopal Church in San Antonio, to visit the guardhouse and talk with the prisoners.

As the Southern Department's staff judge advocate, Colonel Dunn had a critical part in the process of military justice. Major General Ruckman was no more of a trained lawyer or a legal expert than was Major Grier, and though Ruckman had the authority to approve the court's verdicts and sentences in the court-martial, it was expected that in making that decision he would rely on the professional advice of his staff judge advocate.

Dunn was perhaps the last person a soldier convicted by court-martial would want to have as the reviewing officer of his case, particularly if that soldier was Black and innocent of the charges. Dunn had come into the Army during the Spanish-American War, more on the basis of his personal connections than because of any innate talents or qualifications as a soldier. He was a personal acquaintance of Theodore Roosevelt, who in 1898 was Assistant Secretary of the Navy. When Roosevelt resigned his political office to form the Rough Riders, Dunn secured a commission as a staff officer and accompanied the future president during the campaign in Cuba. After that short, confused farce of a war, Dunn retained his commission and stayed on in the Regular Army as a JAG officer. His fellow military attorneys were less than impressed by his legal skills. When Dunn was sent to Europe to observe the functioning of the legal branches in the British and French armies, a senior officer in the JAG Corps wrote that he seemed to spend more time patronizing the tailors of London and Paris than he did performing any military duties. He was also on record as a committed proponent of racial segregation, and he repeatedly espoused conspiracy theories about the unreliability of Black soldiers.

Now he was tasked with conducting a close legal review of the voluminous transcripts of the *Nesbit* court-martial. Dunn did not approach that duty with the degree of professional thoroughness that one might expect when men's lives were in the balance. Colonel Hull later testified that at the end of each day of the trial he had sent Dunn a copy of the transcript of that day's proceedings so that he might review it as the trial went forward. It is unclear if Dunn ever actually read the daily record. What is certain is that once the court-martial was over and the review process began, he never read the complete record of trial.

Instead, Dunn detailed a junior officer in his section, "a lawyer from civilian life," to review the record of trial. It was an appalling dereliction of his duty that he would delegate this vital task to a newly commissioned officer who had almost no experience with the unique peculiarities of military law. As a result, the sentences of the largest court-martial in American history were in the hands of a racist staff officer and an inexperienced lawyer who was still learning to find his way through the Articles of War and the Manual of Courts-Martial.

Dunn declared his review of the case completed on December 3, just three days after he received it, and he passed it on up to Ruckman with the recommendation that the court's verdicts and sentences should be accepted and executed without any alteration. Ruckman, for his part, made only one decision contrary to the court's recommendation. The court had convicted Private First Class John Hudson and sentenced him to life imprisonment at hard labor, but eleven of the thirteen members of the court panel recommended clemency for him. Ruckman rejected the clemency. He approved all findings and sentences adjudged by the court-martial and ordered the thirteen death sentences carried out as soon as gallows could be constructed. No one outside of his immediate command knew of his decision, or that he was arranging a hasty, secret execution.

The soldiers in the post guardhouse did not know of it until Saturday evening on December 8. The guard detail from Charlie Company, 19th Infantry, came into the guardhouse and read out a list of names: Sergeant William Nesbit; Corporals Larnon Brown, James Wheatley, Jesse Moore, and Charles Baltimore; Privates First Class William Breckenridge, Carlos Snodgrass, and Thomas Coleman Hawkins; and Privates Ira Davis, James Divins, Frank Johnson, Risley Young, and Pat McWhorter. Those thirteen men were taken out of the guardhouse and marched across the street to one of the cavalry barracks on Stanley Road. There they were placed in a single room under close guard. No official announcement of the sentences that Ruckman had approved had yet been made, but the thirteen men knew their separation from their comrades could only mean one of two things—either the other forty-five men left in the guardhouse were facing execution or they were.

———

Very little reliable information exists to relate what happened in the time between the night of December 8 and the morning of December 11. Ruckman had clamped a cover of secrecy over the entire case, and no one beyond his immediate staff knew exactly what was going on in those two days and three nights. The few available details come from a couple of first-person accounts written long after the event, one newspaper article of uncertain reliability, one letter from a Black clergyman, and several short letters written by the condemned men the night before they were executed.*

The newspaper article is an extensive piece in the December 28 issue of the *San Antonio Light*. Some of its details are supported by other accounts, but too much of it takes a highly imaginative tone invoking familiar racist tropes to allow a researcher to place too much confidence in its accuracy. That problem is made clear in the article's title. "Veil of Secrecy Is Drawn to Reveal Strange Scenes in Death Chamber of Men Hanged for Houston Riot," it declared and added, "Vigil during their last

---

* The newspaper article appeared in the *San Antonio Light* on December 28, 1917. All quotations referring to newspaper accounts are drawn from that source.

night on earth is turned into an old-fashioned 'revival meetin',' chains on swaying bodies clinking with the rhythm of songs."

According to this article, after the thirteen men were separated from the other prisoners in the guardhouse and removed to the cavalry barracks, Sergeant Nesbit told one of their visitors what he and his companions felt. "We thought the end had come," he allegedly said. "We all thought we were to be shot the next morning. Nobody told us anything, but we all got ready to die. We spent the night praying and singing. We got a lot of comfort out of the meetings that had been held with us by the Y.M.C.A. men. Morning came. That was Sunday morning, and they didn't shoot us. Our spirits rose and we got hopeful that our lives were spared. We thought maybe the others had been shot and we had been separated from them to be given jail sentences or set free."

On Sunday morning, an Army chaplain named B. W. Perry came to minister to the prisoners. "Something in his solicitude for their spiritual welfare, and the soberness of his message to them," the newspaper declared, "brought intimations of something other than prison sentences and freedom." Sunday night passed without incident, and Monday dawned with the prisoners daring to hope "they had gained a new lease on life."

Those hopes were extinguished shortly before noon when Chaplain Perry returned accompanied by another chaplain, R. R. Fleming, who had been tasked with informing the prisoners they were sentenced to death, and they would be executed in the morning. "I come to bring you news of your fate," Fleming told them. "I have been told by the commanding officer that each of you will be hanged tomorrow morning at sunrise."

"There was no 'right' way of telling them," Fleming later said. "Any way I tried to shape the announcement beforehand, it seemed to be all wrong. I decided to tell them frankly and briefly, and as simply as I knew how."

It was the right decision. None of the condemned men reacted to that grim announcement with shock or protestations. It was as if they had expected it and had already prepared themselves for it. Nesbit's and Larnon Brown's only reaction was to light cigarettes—"coolly and indifferently, it seemed"—and have a quiet smoke.

The newspaper writer claimed that Risley Young spoke up to encourage his fellow condemned, but the degree to which the writer claimed Young supposedly asserted that they had received a "fair trial" and "that there had been no effort to 'railroad them'" rings a bit false. That he tried to encourage his comrades is entirely plausible, but that he enthusiastically exonerated the judicial process that had condemned him and his fellows seems highly unlikely.

The chaplains asked the prisoners if there was anything they wanted in their remaining hours. Most of the men asked that messages be conveyed to their families and took the opportunity to write their last letters to friends and family.

Charles Baltimore's parents had died some years earlier, so he wrote to his brother Frederick in Chambersburg, Pennsylvania. "Dear Brother," he wrote,

> *I write you for the last time in this world. I am to be executed tomorrow morning. I know this is shocking news, but don't worry too much, as it is God's will. Meet me in heaven. I was convicted in the general court-martial held here last month; was tried for mutiny and murder. It is true I went downtown with the men that marched out of camp. But I am innocent of shedding any blood. "For God so loved the world that he gave his only begotten son, that whosoever believeth on him shall not perish, but have everlasting life." I am going to meet father and mother and all the rest of the family gone before. Good-by; meet me in heaven.*
> *Your brother,*
> *Charles Baltimore.*[2]*

Chaplains Perry and Fleming asked the prisoners if they wanted any visitor to spend their final hours with them. "They asked, with one accord, for a negro preacher named Ford," the reporter wrote in the *Light*. "Ford is a typical negro 'parson' of the old school whose 'camp meeting' style of old-time religion evidently suited the thirteen negroes." Unfortunately, Reverend Ford was not in San Antonio that night, so Reverend Richardson came to Fort Sam Houston to spend a few hours with the condemned men.

At about 8:00 that evening, the prisoners requested that the Army chaplains ask another local minister, Reverend G. F. C. Curry, if he would be willing to come and spend their last night with them. When

---

* The Bible verse Baltimore quoted in his letter is John 3:16.

Curry arrived at the barracks, he told the men, "'Tisn't for me to accuse you or clear you. I didn't come here to discuss the merits of the trial, but to get you right with God before you go." The rest of the night, according to the newspaper's account, was passed in prayer and the singing of hymns.

At 5:00 the next morning the guard detail from the 19th Infantry came in to say their farewells to the condemned men. All accounts agree that the men from these two different regiments—one a unit of Black soldiers and the other of white soldiers—had got on very well with each other during the weeks of pretrial confinement and the trial itself, and a mutual respect and friendship had developed between them. "It was a touching scene," the newspaper article said. "The color line disappeared, and there were tears in the eyes of the guards as they bade their charges farewell."

At 6:00 Sergeant Nesbit and the other twelve prisoners were taken out of the cavalry barracks and driven out to the spot on the edge of Camp Travis where the post engineers had worked all night building a large gallows not far from Salado Creek. The engineers had worked by the light of several large bonfires, and the execution site was secured by a cordon of mounted cavalrymen and the 19th Infantry's Charlie Company. The Bexar County sheriff, John Tobin, and several of his deputies were the only civilians present, except for Reverend Curry, who was permitted to accompany the condemned men to the place of execution. The civilian lawmen were asked to attend because they had one particular skill that the military personnel lacked—apparently the Army had no one at Fort Sam Houston who knew how to tie hangman's knots for the nooses, so the sheriff's deputies tied the knots in the ropes that were draped over the crossbar of the gallows.

When the condemned men arrived at the execution site, Chaplain Fleming mounted the steps to stand with them in their final moments, but Reverend Curry remained below the scaffold, bearing witness to it all and praying as the eastern sky tinted with the approaching dawn.

The thirteen prisoners were seated in chairs arranged along a single large trapdoor, seven on one side and six on the other. The soldiers detailed as executioners placed the nooses over their heads and tightened them around their necks. One prisoner supposedly thought the rope around his neck was a bit too loose and asked for it to be tightened "just a little," smiling as if his request was of no particular consequence.

The 13th Infantry's regimental commander, Colonel Millard Waltz, was assigned the grim duty of overseeing the execution. Waltz was the same officer who had gone into 3-24 Infantry's camp in Houston the morning after the trouble to disarm the battalion. Thirteen of the soldiers who had looked up at him that morning as he stood on an ammunition box to talk to them could not have known that they were seeing the man who, fifteen weeks later, would be ordered to preside over their deaths. At precisely 7:17 that morning, as the rising sun touched the eastern horizon, the trap was sprung and the thirteen men dropped to their deaths.

After half an hour, the bodies were taken down from the gallows and placed in plain pine coffins. They were not buried with their identification tags, as military custom dictated, but were identified only by slips of paper on which were written their names and date of death. These were inserted into glass soda bottles that were placed in the coffins before the lids were nailed shut. Then the thirteen coffins were taken down near the bank of Salado Creek and buried in a row of thirteen waiting graves. The graves were marked by small, numbered blocks at the head of each mound of earth. Charles Baltimore's grave was number one, Jesse Moore was interred in grave number seven, William Nesbit was placed in grave number ten, and T. C. Hawkins was buried in grave number eleven.

By noon the gallows had been disassembled and all traces of the hanging were eradicated. Only the cold ashes of bonfires, thirteen mounds of freshly turned earth, and the presence of a military guard indicated that something tragic had happened in the first light of dawn. No one in the public, the press, the government, or even the Army knew that thirteen soldiers had been put to death in Texas without any chance of appeal or higher review. No one knew anything about it until later that day when Ruckman sent a terse telegram to Washington announcing that he had ordered the execution of the men condemned in the *Nesbit* trial.

It is not certain how most of the families of the executed men first learned of their deaths. Some of them may have read of it in one of the newspapers that rushed to print the news after Ruckman's telegram was released to the public. At least two families only found out when their soldiers' final letters arrived in the mail.

T. C. Hawkins's parents knew nothing of what had happened until a small box arrived at their home in North Carolina a few days later. The parcel contained his personal effects, the charge sheet from the court-martial, and his last letter, which is reproduced here with its original punctuation. "Dear Mother & Father," he wrote,

> *When this letter reaches you I will be beyond the veil of sorrow I will be in heaven with the angels. Mother don't worry over your son because it is heaven's gain look not upon my body as one that must fill a watery grave but one that is asleep in Jesus. I fear not death, did not Jesus ask death, "where art thy sting?" Don't regret my seat in heaven by mourning over me. I now can imagine seeing my dear Grandmother and Grandfather and the dear girl Miss Bessie Henderson that I once loved in this world standing at the river of Jordan beckoning to me to come, and O! Mother should they be sensitive of my coming don't you think that they are anxious for tomorrow morning to come when I will come unto them. I am sentenced to be hanged for the trouble that happen in Houston Texas although I am not guilty of the crime that I am accused of but Mother it is God's will that I go now and in this way and Mother I am going to look for you and the family if possible I will meet you at the river. "Come unto me all ye that are heavy laden and I will give the rest" [sic]. Bless His holy name. This is the happiest day I met with since Jesus spoke peace to my soul in Brookstone Church from my promise to God I have strayed away but I am with Him now. Send Mr. Harris a copy of this letter. I am*
>
>

Your Son
TC Hawkins

>
> *P.S. Show this to Rev. Shaw. Rev. Shaw I am with Jesus and I will look for you in that great morning.**

That was how Cassie Hawkins learned that her son would never come home.

---

* Hawkins's letter has been given minor grammatical edits for clarity. The Bible verse he quoted is Matthew 11:28.

15. OUTRAGE

The first official news of the execution came in the form of a short, curt telegram that arrived in the Adjutant General's office in Washington, D.C., just before noon on December 11. "The proceedings, findings, and sentences of the General Court-Martial which tried the 63 members of the Twenty-Fourth Infantry for participating in Houston riots August 23rd were approved by me December 10th," Major General Ruckman wrote. "The court sentenced Sergeant William C. Nesbit, Corporal Larnon J. Brown, Corporal James Wheatley, Corporal Jesse Moore, Corporal Charles W. Baltimore, Private (First Class) William Breckinridge, Private (First Class) Thomas C. Hawkins, Private (First Class) Carlos Snodgrass, Private Ira B. Davis, Private James Divins, Private Frank Johnson, and Private Risley W. Young, all Company I, and Private Pat McWhorter, Company M, to capital punishment. The sentence has been executed."[1]

From the very beginning of the affair, given the racial and political climate of the era, most Black citizens had expected that some of the men accused of involvement in the Houston Incident would face severe punishment. But a few developments after that night of violence in August had caused some people to allow themselves small flickers of hope that perhaps this time their worst fears would not be realized. When the Army moved quickly to get all the men of 3-24 Infantry out of the reach of vengeful Texans, it looked to some as if the government was not going to allow southern segregationists to determine the course of events. As September and October passed without the drumhead courts-martial and summary executions that many feared might follow the incident, some dared to hope that perhaps real justice was going to be applied to the case.

Before the court-martial began, W. E. B. Du Bois had written of the defendants, "We ask no mitigation of their punishment. They broke the law." African American citizens agreed with the essence of that idea, but only as long as whatever punishment those soldiers faced was fair and represented the culmination of real justice and that the court that tried them took into account all the provocations and injustices those men and other Black men had so long endured in a nation that judged their race before it acknowledged their citizenship. Even if the judges that weighed their fates handed down harsh sentences, the appeals process might still offer hope of obtaining a measure of mercy.

Ruckman's announcement that the sentences were already carried out crushed that hope.

Du Bois, again, gave voice to the grief of many. "They have gone to their death—thirteen young, strong men," he wrote when the news of the hanging was released, "soldiers who have fought for a country which never was wholly theirs, men born to suffer ridicule, injustice, and, at last, death itself . . . They broke the law. Against them punishment, if it was legal, we cannot protest." But Du Bois saw the whole picture, not just the coldly impersonal legalities of the case, and his own emotions blazed through the words on the page. The thirteen soldiers hanged in the cold light of dawn represented more than themselves, he told his readers—they represented their fathers and mothers and brothers and sisters and untold others before them who died at the hands of people who hated them simply because they were Black. Du Bois condemned "the shameful treatment which these men, and which we, their brothers, receive all our lives, and which our fathers received, and our children await; and above all we raise our clenched hands against the hundreds of thousands of white murderers, rapists, and scoundrels."[2]

Grief and anger were the reactions in many African American neighborhoods, homes, and congregations when the news broke. One prominent Black paper, the *New York Age*, denounced the execution as an outrage, declaring in an editorial, "Strict justice has been done, but full justice has not been done. And so sure as there is a God in heaven, at some time and some way full justice will be done."[3] The fact that all the blame, and all the consequences, were borne only by Black men was undeniable. In another article in the *New York Age*, James Weldon Johnson made that point forcefully. The ultimate responsibility, Johnson insisted, "must be laid directly upon the shoulders of the Administration in Washington. If in the beginning an authoritative and definite order had gone out from Washington that every man in the service of the army should receive the same treatment as every other man of like rank and that the Government would not tolerate anything else, none of the serious troubles, including the affair at Houston, would ever have happened."[4]

A week after the hangings, the Baltimore *Afro-American* reported on a sermon delivered by Reverend George Frazier Miller in St. Augustine's Episcopal Church in Brooklyn, New York. Reverend Miller "referred to the soldiers executed as 'the thirteen martyrs,' and intimated that their 'sacrifice to appease the people of Houston' would undermine the patriotism of American Negroes." Miller went on to denounce Ruckman's handling of the case. "The military commander who carried out that order was guilty of military lynching," he declared from the pulpit. "The commander took advantage of the state-of-war situation. . . . If this thing had been reported to Washington, we in this country would have had a chance to plead for mercy. Thirteen men of the United States army were denied the right of appeal which is accorded to any criminal. We want the entire country to know that we of the Negro race have been seriously wronged, not because the thirteen were killed, but because they were denied the right to appeal— to appease Houston. Those thirteen were sacrificed on the infamous altar of Southern prejudice. Yet we are still expected to glory in patriotism." He concluded, "That deed is not calculated to enhance the patriotism of American Negroes, but to destroy it."[5]

The reactions were markedly different in most white communities. The evening edition of the *Princeton Daily Democrat* in New Jersey on December 11 told its readers, "Execution of sentences passed on negro soldiers who figured in the Houston riots was in full accord with the law, the Department of War admitted this afternoon. While refusing to give out official reports the department said the commander has power to act without orders from Washington. The court-martial had been carefully selected. It consisted practically entirely of general officers to avoid injustice which might have occurred."[6] This choice to focus on the technical legality of the court-martial and executions, while overlooking the deeper questions of fairness and justice in the process, was repeated by most journalists and government officials in the weeks following the hanging.

Although technically authorized by the Articles of War, this rush to execution was not mandated; as specifically stated in the Manual of Courts-Martial, commanders were authorized to suspend any execution

of a death sentence "until the pleasure of the President shall be known."
The provision for hasty executions was never intended to operate outside
a theater of war, and certainly not within the domestic boundaries of the
United States. Its use in this secretive, summary manner struck many in
the Army as a blackhearted twisting of military law and service traditions.
The day after Ruckman announced he had executed the thirteen soldiers,
a senior JAG officer, Lieutenant Colonel Samuel Ansell, wrote an outraged
letter to the Judge Advocate General. Ansell held nothing back in castigat-
ing General Ruckman and Colonel Dunn and what he regarded as their
indefensible mishandling of the case:

> Subject: Evidence of inefficiency of Maj. Gen. John W. Ruckman,
> commanding the Southern Department, headquarters at San
> Antonio, Tex., and of Col. George M. Dunn, Judge Advocate
> General's Department, the judge advocate upon the staff of
> Gen. Ruckman . . .
>
> 1. I feel it my duty to call your attention to what I conceive to be
>   evidence of the incompetency of the two officers of the Army
>   who are the subject of this memorandum with the intention
>   and purpose that these views be brought by you to the atten-
>   tion of the Chief of Staff and the Secretary of War . . .
> 3. Yesterday we were apprised, through the public press and for
>   the first time, that Gen. Ruckman had proceeded summar-
>   ily to execute the sentences of death in the case of 13 negro
>   soldiers recently tried in his department. I shall not allude to
>   this case further than to say that, under the circumstances
>   surrounding this case which were such as to reveal them-
>   selves in all their bearings to a man of ordinary prudence
>   and care, a man possessing the poise and sanity of judgment
>   that should be necessary concomitants of the rank which this
>   officer holds, could not have summarily carried into execu-
>   tion those sentences. Under the circumstances of this case
>   the action taken by this commander was such a gross abuse
>   of power as justly to merit the forfeiture of his commission.
> 4. I must assume that this general has sought and acted upon
>   the advice of his judge advocate, Col. Dunn, and that this

officer therefor has, in the same degree with Gen. Ruckman, manifested his incompetence at a critical time.[7]

While the telegraph lines and newspaper presses were busy with the news from Texas, the Army prepared for the second trial of accused mutineers. No one was in any doubt that another trial was coming, because Ruckman had already issued the order for that trial back on October 20. Before that trial began, however, another court-martial convened at Fort Sam Houston on December 15, and that one was not focused on the soldiers of the 24th Infantry.

Major Kneeland Snow was to have his own day in court.

At about 9:30 on the night of November 23, while the *United States v. Nesbit* court-martial was still underway, a plainclothes detective with the San Antonio police vice squad saw a soldier and a civilian woman entering the Fairmount Hotel. San Antonio had recently stepped up enforcement of the city's anti-vice laws, because prostitution had increased with the influx of thousands of soldiers coming into the city for training at Fort Sam Houston. As far as the police were concerned, a woman in the company of a soldier going to a hotel at night prompted an immediate suspicion of immoral activity. When the detective checked with the hotel's night clerk, he grew increasingly certain that the couple were not husband and wife. Because the man in question was a soldier, a military policeman was summoned to investigate.

An MP sergeant arrived at the Fairmount a short time later and accompanied the police detective upstairs, where they found the man and woman occupying a room together. When they asked the man if he really was married to the woman he claimed as his wife, he reluctantly confessed he was not. The MP took them both into custody. At the city police station, the man identified himself as Major Kneeland Snow. Snow said that he was in San Antonio as witness "against the colored soldiers of the 24th Infantry, tried at Fort Sam Houston at the present time." Snow's name, however, was not to be found in the hotel's registry because he had registered under a false name.

Snow told a deputy U.S. marshal at the station that he had registered as "G. W. Smith and wife," and admitted that the woman with him was not actually his wife. He identified her as Marjorie Vernon from El Paso, Texas, who had recently arrived in San Antonio on or about the first of November. Miss Vernon, for her part, said she was twenty years old (seventeen years younger than Snow) and that she had been staying at the Fairmount Hotel since November 1. Snow had covered the cost of her lodging and spent each night there with her.

The marshal decided not to pursue the matter after Snow promised him that he would "advise the woman that she better leave San Antonio on the first train that she could leave the city, which she agreed to do." He explicitly told Snow that he was not to return to the Fairmount with her. Snow assured the authorities that he had another room at the Gunter Hotel, which was apparently his official billet provided by the Army, and that he would see to it that Miss Vernon left town that day.

The next morning, a San Antonio police detective arrested Snow and Vernon at the Fairmount, in the same room they had occupied the night before. This time the matter was not going to be dropped and the pair were formally charged—Vernon with being a "common prostitute," and Snow for "associating with a common prostitute." Because Snow was a serving Army officer, military regulations interpreted such a charge as "conduct unbecoming an officer and gentleman," which was a violation of Article 95 of the Articles of War. That warranted a court-martial.

On Saturday morning, December 15, four days after the hanging of the thirteen soldiers condemned in the *United States v. Nesbit* trial, a general court-martial convened at Fort Sam Houston to try Snow's case. When the court opened its proceedings, Snow introduced his defense counsel—none other than Major Harry Grier. That seemingly insignificant detail in the record of trial, Snow's act of introducing Grier to the court, meant that Grier was not officially appointed to the role of defense. He was serving voluntarily. Apparently, Snow personally requested Grier to defend him in the trial, and Grier agreed. The two officers probably had a long acquaintance with each other, since they had served in the same regiment at different points in their careers. The Army's prosecution was brought by two very junior officers—Captain Clyde McConkey and Second Lieutenant R. S. Sanford, neither of whom was a JAG officer, and neither of whom had much experience in military trials.

The nine-member panel of the court-martial included one officer in the rank of captain and a major who was apparently junior to Snow by date of rank. Their presence on the panel contradicted the military regulation that an officer could only be tried by officers of equal or higher rank. Grier's first words in the trial were to say, "It is apparent that there are two members of the court that are junior to the accused; nevertheless with the view of serving the interests of the Government, and with proceeding this case, the accused waives his objections to those members, and goes to trial." The Army wanted the court-martial concluded as quickly as possible, particularly since the accused in this trial was the government's star witness in the prosecution of the accused mutineers in the infamous Houston case. That desire for haste suited Snow just fine.

The first and third specifications of the charge against Snow stated that he, "in company with a lewd woman named Marjorie Vernon, did register at the Fairmont [sic] Hotel . . . under the name of G. W. Smith and wife . . . and did occupy said room with said lewd woman until he was arrested by the civil authorities." Compounding the seriousness of that offense, according to the specification, was that Snow's actions occurred "at a time when the Federal and Municipal authorities were using every effort to control the vice conditions in the City of San Antonio." In other words, Snow's actions did not just violate the 95th Article but also brought disrepute upon the Army. The second specification of the charge focused on the fact that Snow had "broken his parole" by returning to the hotel with the woman in question after he promised the civil authorities he would not do so.

Snow pled not guilty to the charge and all specifications.

As the first witness for prosecution, Captain McConkey called to the stand the night clerk of the Fairmount Hotel, who identified Snow as the man who registered under the name G. W. Smith. The clerk said that Snow had occupied the room with the woman he claimed was his wife for about three weeks beginning on November 1. Snow spent every evening there, he said, "until he was arrested." He had seen Snow enter the hotel each night at about 10:00 p.m., always in the uniform of an Army officer.

The next witness was Sergeant Edward Pickens, the military police NCO who first detained Snow and Vernon at the hotel. Pickens told the court that his instructions from the federal marshal were to go to the Fairmount and question the man in the hotel room; if he found that the man was not married to the woman he was with, he was to arrest them both and bring them to the station.

"I asked him if he was married and he did not make any answer at all, right then," Pickens said, and added that when he pressed Snow on the question, Snow only said that his "intentions were good." After three or four minutes, Snow finally admitted he was not married to the woman with whom he was sharing the hotel room.

The court discussed this for several minutes, debating what Snow's prevarications really meant. A member of the panel asked Pickens, "Was the object of your question to ascertain if he was married to this woman?"

"Yes, sir," the sergeant replied. "If he was married I had no right to arrest him, but if he was not, I did."

When the federal marshal, A. E. Farland, was called to the stand, Grier pressed him on whether he had thought Marjorie Vernon was a "good woman or bad." Farland said he thought she was a good woman. Why then, Grier asked, had he ordered Snow to get her out of town? "You stated that you thought she was a good woman, and yet you wanted to get her out of town," he said. "You must have been satisfied in your own mind that she was not a pretty good woman."

"I said I did not consider her a common prostitute or a streetwalker," Farland clarified. As far he was concerned, Snow's duplicity in registering under a false name and claiming Miss Vernon was his wife when she was nothing of the kind indicated that things were not aboveboard, regardless of whether she was a good woman or bad.

J. Edward Wilkens, a judge of the Corporation Court of the City of San Antonio, testified that on November 26 he had presided over the trials of several cases, one of which accused a Marguerite Vernon of vagrancy, to which a plea of guilty was entered into the record and a fine of twenty-five dollars imposed. Wilkens had trouble reading the spelling of the defendant's name, which was "not very distinctly written" in the original record.

"What offenses do you include under the charge of vagrancy?" the prosecutor asked.

"Well, if Marguerite Vernon was a female," Wilkens said, "she would be, under the State law and under which we tried her—she would be either a common prostitute or a wandering Gypsy or a fortune teller, in order to be a vagrant, if she was female."

On cross-examination, Grier established that Vernon herself had not actually appeared in court that day, and that the guilty plea was lodged by someone who claimed to be there on her behalf. Grier then wanted to know if it was normal procedure in Wilkens's court for a proxy to plead guilty for a defendant without the judge determining if the person making the plea was authorized to speak for the defendant. Wilkens said it was absolutely normal, but only in cases where a fine would be adjudged, rather than jail time. He did not recall who it was that appeared in his court on Vernon's behalf, and no name appeared in the record. The only person Vernon knew in San Antonio was Kneeland Snow, and it was in Snow's personal interest to make her involvement disappear as quickly as possible. Snow was likely the unnamed person who lodged the guilty plea in her absence.

At this point, Captain McConkey asked the court for a continuance to give federal authorities time to locate Vernon, because her whereabouts were unknown and Snow refused to divulge them. Grier argued strenuously that the court should not waste time procuring her testimony, and after a short recess for deliberation the court agreed. McConkey, outmaneuvered, rested the prosecution's case without further argument.

Grier called two character witnesses for the defense. The first, Colonel E. C. Carey, testified that he had known Snow in different assignments since 1911. "I consider Major Snow to be an excellent officer in every respect," Carey told the court, and that was the extent of his testimony, because McConkey never asked him a single question in cross-examination.

The other witness for the defense, perhaps surprisingly, was none other than Captain Haig Shekerjian, Snow's former adjutant in 3-24 Infantry. Shekerjian's personal acquaintance with Snow also went back to 1911, when both men were assigned to the First Infantry, and of course included their time in 3-24 Infantry dating from March 1917. One might have expected Shekerjian to produce testimony of a less complimentary nature, because he had not only observed Snow as a fellow company-grade officer and battalion commander but had also been left in the lurch the night of August 23 when Snow abandoned the battalion and fled in panic. He, perhaps better than anyone, could speak to Snow's failure of command responsibility. When Grier called him to the stand, however, Shekerjian limited himself to saying that Snow was an officer of "excellent character" and that he had "always considered him a moral man."

Shekerjian had apparently decided that he would take the official line and say nothing about Snow's actions in Houston, but McConkey still had the opportunity to directly question him on those matters, as Snow was on trial for moral failings and deficiencies in his character, and any evidence that knocked holes in the shiny veneer he presented in court was well within bounds for the prosecutor to raise. Inexplicably, McConkey declined to ask Shekerjian any questions at all. In light of the fact that McConkey was not trained as a JAG officer and may not have been aware of all the controversies surrounding Snow's actions in Houston, he does not seem to have recognized the opportunity presented by Shekerjian's presence on the witness stand. It is also within the realm of possibility that the convening authority, Major General Ruckman, had made it clear to all parties that this court-martial, just like the trial of the accused mutineers, was to move along quickly, with no unnecessary complications. Whatever the reason, McConkey allowed Shekerjian to depart the courtroom without a single question challenging his description of Snow as a man of unsullied reputation.

When Grier made his closing arguments to the court, he focused on the definitions of the words the government used in the specifications against his client. The word "lewd" drew his particular attention, which, he told the court. was legally defined as "given to the unlawful indulgence for lust, eager for sexual indulgence." As far as Marjorie Vernon was concerned, he insisted, "there has been absolutely nothing submitted in evidence before this court" to prove she was a prostitute. He did not mention the fact that a guilty plea had been lodged in her name on the charge of vagrancy and that he had worked very hard as defense counsel to keep Vernon out of court so that she could not be directly questioned on her character. He went on to question the motivations behind the police decision to arrest Major Snow the next morning when he was found to have returned to the Fairmount Hotel. It was all an attempt to impugn the reputation of an officer "of good moral character," he told the court, and much was being made out of nothing. As he described it, the entire court-martial was a waste of the government's time.

Captain McConkey's response was described in a single anemic sentence in the record of trial: "The Prosecution submitted the case without remark." McConkey did not even bother to make a closing argument in support of his case for the prosecution.

The court retired for a very brief deliberation, then returned to announce that they found Snow guilty of the first specification, "except for the words 'lewd,' and 'he was arrested by the civil authorities.'" They also disallowed all reference to the fact that San Antonio was attempting to curb vice in the city at the time Snow was arrested. He was found not guilty of the second and third specifications on the charge. He was, however, found guilty of violating the 96th Article of War, meaning that the court believed his actions were "of a nature to bring discredit upon the military service," though not conduct unbecoming. Snow was sentenced to forfeit twenty-five dollars of pay each month for a period of six months.

As with all general courts-martial in the Southern Department, the record of trial had to go to Major General Ruckman for review. Ruckman delivered his decision eleven days later and approved the proceedings of the court-martial. He wrote that the evidence "establishes the guilt of the accused" as far as the first specification of the charge, but then he overturned the whole matter in two short sentences. Because the court-martial panel had excepted the words that it did in its verdict, Ruckman wrote, it had therefore "eliminated the gist of the offense." Ruckman summarily disapproved the court's verdict of guilty on the first specification and the sentence of a fine. Major Snow was returned to duty as if the trial had never taken place.

It bears noting that the perfunctory, blink-and-you-miss-it nature of Snow's court-martial was problematic for another reason. Military regulation and practice required the bringing together of all known charges for a single trial. Two separate inspectors general had recommended that Snow should be charged with dereliction of duty in the August 23 incident, and Ruckman had told the Chief of Staff of the Army that Snow would be tried on those charges. This never happened. Ruckman's continued willingness to ignore Snow's misconduct and failures while aggressively pursuing the harshest punishments for 3-24 Infantry's enlisted men suggests a determination to stack the deck against the soldiers. Serious misconduct by the prosecution's primary witness would usually be enough to undermine the government's case, but Snow's wrongdoing was ignored in every one of the three Houston Incident courts-martial.

Two days after Snow's court-martial wrapped up its business in less than six hours, the second trial of accused mutineers from the 24th Infantry began at Fort Sam Houston. Named *United States v. Washington et al.*, this court-martial convened to try the case of the fifteen soldiers from the Camp Logan guard detail who were not members of Vida

Henry's ill-conceived sortie into the city. These men were accused of carrying out a specific act of violence that night, the ambush of the civilian jitney that resulted in the killing of E. M. Jones and the severe wounding of Charles Clayton. The accused were charged with "the murder of E. M. Jones, by shooting him with U.S. Rifles, loaded with powder and ball, on or about the 23d of August, 1917," in violation of the 92nd Article of War. They were also charged with violating the 96th Article of War, the general article, known to soldiers as "the Devil's Article," because it allowed charging of conduct if it was considered prejudicial to good order and military discipline, or if it was of a nature to bring discredit upon the military service, or if the offense was any other crime not capital. The latter specifications accused them of "leaving post and proceeding towards the camp of the Third Battalion, 24th Infantry . . . with the intent to join with various other members of the Third Battalion . . . and in marching upon the city of Houston, Texas, to the injury of persons and property therein situated, and of quitting their guard and marching along a public highway adjoining said Camp Logan in a riotous manner, threatening the lives of white persons whom they met and causing injury to other white persons." The specific reference to the victims of the crime as "white persons" explicitly underscored the racial attitudes that marred the trial.* This was a much smaller and much less publicized trial than the first one. This one was held in the building that is today the practice room of the Fort Sam Houston Post Band, farther away from the public's gaze.

Once again, Colonel John Hull and Major Dudley Sutphin prosecuted the case as judge advocates, and Major Grier served as the sole defense counsel for the fifteen joint defendants. Grier's defense was compromised by the fact that he could not effectively represent multiple clients simultaneously without implicating some of his clients while trying to alibi others, as had been true also of the earlier trial. Furthermore, Grier still had not been provided with the pretrial investigation reports that the prosecution was using to build its case, so he was operating as blindly as he did during the first court-martial. The officers who formed the panel of this second court-martial were also the same thirteen men who had served as the panel of the *United States v. Nesbit* trial.

---

* All quotations referring to the *Washington* court-martial are drawn from *United States v. Washington* et al., Trial Summation Memorandum, Records Group 153.

Unlike the first court-martial, the *Washington* trial was a much more straightforward affair, at least as far as the salient elements of the case were concerned. Whether or not the defendants in this trial had gone into Houston that night was never really in question (as long as one was willing to believe the prosecution's immunized witnesses), and they were the only soldiers who were known to be in the vicinity when the Jones jitney was shot up. Because of those facts, this trial focused on establishing each defendant's personal involvement in the shooting.

The official investigations that followed the August 23 incident had already characterized the shooting near Camp Logan in prejudicial language that colored the government's portrayal of the event. Brigadier General Chamberlain, the Army IG, had written in his report, "The men doing this shooting must have come from Camp Logan and must have been members of the guard." That much was true, but Chamberlain's next sentence bordered on imaginative exaggeration that was not supported by evidence. "Furthermore," he wrote, "it shows that these men, at least, were not hunting policemen but were shooting everybody that came along."[8]

One of the prosecution's primary witnesses was Private Ezekiel Bullock of Kilo Company, who had been a member of the guard detail at Camp Logan the night of August 23. Bullock testified that the men of the guard detail had been agitated over the events in town that day, and that when the gunfire broke out at their battalion camp later that night, he heard men say, "They are shooting up the camp," and "They are killing our men over [at] the camp." Most of the soldiers argued they should move to the camp and aid in its defense.

When Hull asked Bullock if he particularly remembered any soldier arguing that they should desert their post and head to the battalion camp, the witness named Privates Thomas McDonald and Albert Wright. McDonald, he said, had shouted, "I will shoot up every white son of a bitch on Washington Street," and he remembered Wright saying, "We will show these damn sons of bitches who we are." At that point, according to Bullock, the group of fifteen men, including himself, left Camp Logan and moved out into the civilian streets. He said Privates Babe Collier, James Robinson, Wright, Joseph Smith, McDonald, and himself were at the head of the small column. When the group encountered the Jones jitney, Bullock said, McDonald and Wright were the first to open fire on the vehicle. Bullock claimed that he himself never fired but had dropped into a ditch to avoid being hit by the fire of the men who were behind him.

Hull asked Bullock if any of his comrades said anything to him after the shooting. "Yes, sir . . . Private Wright," Bullock said. "He said I was a damn fool and scared to death . . . I should be shot myself." He went on to claim that several soldiers wanted to fire on a group of civilians they saw at a restaurant as they moved down the street, but that he had argued against it and the civilians were not harmed. Whether his claim was true or not, it was true that the soldiers never fired on the numerous white people they saw that night—that fact was corroborated by several civilian witnesses.

Bullock further testified that when Third Battalion was relocated back to Columbus, New Mexico, he was approached by McDonald in the mess hall one day. Hull asked him if McDonald had said anything to him.

"He asked me had I been doing any talking [to the investigators], and I told him no," Bullock said. "He said, 'Well, if you haven't done any talking, we won't get any time out of this, we will only get about two months, probably discharged or restored to duty.'"

Another prosecution witness, Private Willie Blunt of India Company, testified that while they were confined at Fort Bliss, McDonald said, "This damned stool pigeon got me in trouble like I am in now."

"Did McDonald say anything to you about not telling what happened that night?" he was asked.

"All I heard said was nobody ought to have any big mouth," Blunt said.

The trial proceeded quickly, and it did not take the prosecution very long to identify who did what and the degree of individual culpability, at least to the court's satisfaction, and Grier's efforts in the defense were as uninspired and lackluster as they had been in the first trial. When the court-martial adjourned after five days of testimony, the panel found all fifteen defendants guilty as charged. Five men, Privates Babe Collier, Thomas McDonald, James Robinson, Joseph Smith, and Albert Wright, were sentenced to death by hanging. The other ten soldiers were sentenced to imprisonment at hard labor for terms ranging from seven to ten years.

At this point, the apparently repetitive patterns of the *Nesbit* court-martial took a turn in a different direction. Ruckman's secretive, hasty execution of the death sentences in that first trial was not going to be allowed this time. The hanging of the first thirteen men without allowing them any chance for outside review or an opportunity to appeal for clemency had so infuriated senior officers in the War Department that they had quickly issued orders that henceforth no death sentences were to be carried out without being sent up the chain of command for review by the Secretary of War and the approval of the president of the United States. Never again would any American soldiers be put to death without the explicit approval of the national executive authority.

This was made immediately clear in written orders and reiterated more than once. In January 1918, the Army Adjutant General sent a telegram to Ruckman. The Secretary of War wanted it clearly understood, the AG said, that "there must be no exceptions made to the rules prescribed by the President. In the cases of the members of the Twenty-fourth Infantry lately tried at Fort Sam Houston, no part of the sentence will be executed until notification from the Judge Advocate General that there is no legal objection to the execution of the sentence."[9] These restrictions applied not only to the soldiers condemned by the Houston courts-martial but also to the entire Army. The two General Orders issued in January 1918, which prohibited any executions or dishonorable discharges without review by the Judge Advocate General, would be incorporated into the post–World War I Articles of War and form the basis of the first military appellate procedure in American military law.

The five condemned men remained in confinement in the Fort Sam Houston guardhouse while they waited to learn if President Woodrow Wilson would commute their sentences to imprisonment or if they, too, would die on a gallows in the dawn of a morning yet to come.

16. THE LAST COURT-MARTIAL

As 1917 turned over to 1918, much of the public's attention on the Houston case was beginning to fade as American involvement in the Great War occupied ever more inches of newsprint. Young Americans were fighting and dying in France, and that seemed a far more immediate and pressing matter than the Houston Incident, which as far as most people knew had been concluded by the second court-martial. The names of the thirteen men hanged on December 11, the fifty-five who were then beginning to serve long prison sentences at Fort Leavenworth, and the five soldiers then confined under sentence of death were increasingly fading from the awareness of most people in the United States.

African American citizens were still deeply concerned with those men, however, and so too was Texas attorney A. J. Houston. He had not succeeded in his efforts to defend the sixty-three soldier defendants in the *Nesbit* court-martial, and that failure haunted him. He continued to monitor the government's case against the remaining soldiers accused in the Houston Incident, and he maintained a regular correspondence with the NAACP about their situation.

On January 14, 1918, Houston wrote to the association's acting secretary, James Weldon Johnson, to lament the deaths of the thirteen executed men, which he characterized as a terrible injustice. Those men had been denied the due process of law, Houston wrote, and he expressed the same shock shared by many at the fact that they were hanged in secret with no chance to appeal the death sentence. "There was nothing more to do but await the decision of the court-martial being received by the War Department for review, when the case could have been fully presented to the Secretary, but when the right of appeal was cut off by such unreasonable hurry in the carrying out of the sentence of the court one's horror cannot be expressed," he wrote.[1]

He could do nothing for the men now buried in the thirteen graves down by Salado Creek, but he hoped to help the living men sentenced by the *Nesbit* and *Washington* courts-martial. In another letter to Johnson on February 8, Houston wrote, "Those, or some of them, even one, now in the penitentiary at Leavenworth, Kansas, would certainly be willing to have habeas corpus proceedings instituted in their behalf, before some United States judge, then I believe that the precedent would be established for the trial of colored soldiers by courts-martial, for capital offenses, that they are entitled to a member on the court, of their own race." Houston was still troubled by Grier's failure to raise the issue of an all-white panel in the *Nesbit* trial, and he felt the issue was worth raising in an appeal.[2]

Johnson replied in a letter to Houston on February 14. "We have taken steps to try and save the five men now under death sentence," he wrote. "The New York Branch is making an effort to secure a petition of ten thousand signers urging the President to extend executive clemency to those men. Other branches all over the United States have been instructed to take similar action and undoubtedly the majority of them will do so." He then mentioned the disturbing news that prosecution of the 24th Infantry soldiers was not yet ended. A third court-martial was about to convene. "We have also noted that not only are these five additional men under death sentence but that forty more are to be tried on the same old charges," Johnson wrote. "We want to do everything we can to arouse the country and the administration to the fact that a halt should at some time be called on these wholesale prosecutions until something is done to punish the men who are primarily responsible." He did not name the persons he thought were "primarily responsible," but it was clear that he cast the net of blame beyond the limits of 3-24 Infantry's soldiers.[3]

Johnson was correct that another court-martial was coming—in fact, that trial convened just four days after he wrote his letter to Houston—but announcement of the court-martial may have come as a surprise to the Army and the War Department. When the *Washington* court-martial concluded its business on December 22, Colonel Hull informed his superiors that the Houston case was finished. The government had identified and prosecuted the men it felt were most culpable in the incident, and as far as Hull was concerned, the process was ended. The Army agreed. The thirteen officers who served as the panel of the *Nesbit* and *Washington* courts-martial were thanked for their service and allowed to depart for other wartime assignments. Hull congratulated himself on the successful completion of a career-making case and left Texas for a posting with the JAG department of the American Expeditionary Force in France. His assistant judge advocate in those trials, however, was not yet ready to see the Houston case wrapped up.

Major Dudley Sutphin had been second chair to Hull during the first two courts-martial, and he was not satisfied with that understudy role. In his opinion the Houston case still offered some mileage for an ambitious JAG officer with an eye on his career advancement, and Sutphin was nothing if not ambitious. He was determined to have his turn in the prosecution's first chair and see his name in newspaper headlines.

Sutphin himself did not have the authority to convene a court-martial, but as long as John Ruckman was the commanding general of the Southern Department, he had no trouble getting the trial he so fervently desired. Thus, on February 18 the trial known as *United States v. Tillman* convened with Sutphin as the leading judge advocate. Forty more soldiers were arraigned on capital charges of mutiny and murder. Once more, Major Harry Grier served as the sole defense counsel for all defendants.

Right from the beginning, it was clear that Sutphin's prosecution of the *Tillman* court-martial was so biased as to almost make *United States v. Nesbit*, with all its judicial shortcomings, look like a model of judicial propriety by contrast. The real discrepancies in the third court-martial, however, are only apparent if one reads the records of all three trials in comparison with each other.

All three courts-martial relied heavily upon the testimony of immunized cooperating military witnesses, but between the first and third trials those witnesses changed their testimony in marked ways. Because the panel of the *Tillman* court-martial consisted of a different group of officers who did not have the record of the previous two trials to refer to, this mass of perjured testimony would not have been immediately obvious to the members of the court. But the deviations in testimony between the trials are so significant as to suggest deliberate prosecutorial misconduct. Sutphin was intimately familiar with the record of the first two trials, since he had sat through a month's worth of testimony in those prosecutions and acted as a full co-prosecutor in those cases, so it defies plausibility to ascribe any innocent agency to his presentation of such different testimony from the same witness regarding the same events.

The vast majority of evidence identifying those soldiers who departed the camp with Sergeant Vida Henry's column, identifying those who committed specific violent acts, or detailing the alleged existence or content of a preexisting conspiracy among the members of the 3rd Battalion was based almost exclusively on immunized witnesses' testimony, just as in the *Nesbit* trial. For example, Private Cleda Love had been the only prosecution witness to claim knowledge of a preexisting agreement to leave camp at 9:00 p.m. on the night of August 23, supposed evidence of a conspiracy to commit mutiny. In the third court-martial, he greatly enlarged on his testimony in the first trial. Given the dependence of the prosecution's case on Love and the other immunized witnesses, these major changes in witness testimony between the different trials should have raised significant questions on their credibility. The testimony of Private Love, described as "completely unreliable" by later senior JAG reviews conducted in the decade after the trial, was particularly problematic. But an examination of the testimony of Privates Lloyd Shorter, Frank Draper, and John Denty also reveals significant changes in what they said between the first and third trials. An additional cooperating witness in the *Tillman* trial, Private William Kane, who was convicted and sentenced to life in the *Nesbit* case, cooperated with the prosecution in exchange for a clemency recommendation.

As a result of Kane's revised and enlarged testimony, he served no time in prison. His testimony included statements purportedly made by the thirteen convicted soldiers who were executed on December 11, 1917, statements that could not be rebutted or even investigated by the defense in the later trial. Dead men cannot refute false testimony. That did not stop Sutphin from using that unverifiable testimony against the forty defendants in his prosecution.

The circumstances leading to Private Kane's cooperation are a further example of a pattern of prosecutorial misconduct that began with Colonel Hull and continued with Major Sutphin. When the *Nesbit* trial concluded, Kane was escorted to the judge advocate's office at the Old Post Quadrangle at Fort Sam Houston to be formally served his copy of the record of trial in which he was convicted. There he was questioned by Colonel Hull without the presence of his defense counsel. Hull assured Kane that nothing he said would be used against him; he was only seeking information that could be used against other 3-24 Infantry soldiers who deserved to be prosecuted but who had not yet been identified. Sutphin also assured Kane that his statements could not be used without his permission. A comprehensive review of the records shows that this was not an isolated incident. After the first trial Hull, as the prosecuting judge advocate, admitted that he "interviewed all the soldiers who had been tried, and secured considerable information" to use against the defendants of the next two courts-martial. As a result of this questioning, Private Kane subsequently agreed to testify in exchange for a clemency recommendation.

Further impugning the credibility of the cooperating witnesses, Private Samuel Riddle, a defendant in the *Tillman* case, testified that he was called before Major Preston's investigation board at Fort Bliss prior to the third trial. The board pressured him to change the statement he had made during the initial investigation after the Houston Incident. One of the board members told him that if he would alter his testimony, he could rejoin his battalion as a free man. Riddle stuck to his story, at which point the board told one of its cooperating immunity witnesses, Private Frank Draper, to take Riddle out of the room and urge him to change his story.

"They all know you did not go downtown," Draper allegedly told him. "Riddle, the things these people want to know—they want to know something about somebody, and just state anything you know that will help them."

When Riddle protested that he did not know anything that would help them, Draper replied, "Well get somebody in there that can't give a good account of themselves—you pick around in there and find out about it and get somebody that can't give a good account of themselves, and you can go." Draper also approached a Black civilian witness, named Mrs. Crowell, and warned her that the board thought she should change her testimony supporting defendant soldiers' alibis. Draper conveyed the board's threat to charge her with perjury if she did not change her testimony.

The discrepancies in the testimony of cooperating witnesses between the *Nesbit* and *Tillman* trials seriously undermine the legitimacy of Sutphin's prosecution in that third trial. In the *Nesbit* trial, Private Lloyd Shorter testified as to the sequence of events in Third Battalion's camp during the afternoon of August 23. He was short on details of the activities in camp that afternoon and early evening, and instead focused on the activities of

Henry's column as it left the camp later that night. In both trials, Shorter testified that he was with the column until it reached the cemetery, at which point he jumped out of the column and hid in a house with two other soldiers until the next morning. In the *Tillman* trial, however, Shorter suddenly seemed to have remembered a trove of details he had never mentioned in the first court-martial. He identified a different group of soldiers leaving the camp much earlier in the evening while the weapons were being collected. This group, he claimed, attacked an ambulance before the shooting broke out in camp.

Between the two trials, Shorter also more than doubled the number of soldiers who he claimed left the camp in Henry's column, from eighty-five to at least two hundred men. In the *Tillman* trial, Shorter testified that he left the camp before the departure of the column and was out on Washington Avenue, a change in his story that made it possible for him to have observed the alleged attack on the ambulance at that location prior to the firing in camp.

As was true of other prosecution witnesses, Shorter's testimony in the *Tillman* trial directly and repeatedly contradicted his testimony in the *Nesbit* court-martial. In *Tillman*, Shorter testified he left the camp prior to the panicked firing and then observed the attack on the ambulance, after which he ran to lie at the corner of the field until the column passed him. He then came out of his hiding place to join the rear of the column after it left camp and passed his location. In *Nesbit*, however, Shorter had testified that he was in India Company's street, participating in the rush on the supply tent and panicked firing, and that he then fell in with Henry's column before it marched from camp. Those alterations raise significant questions about Shorter's credibility.

One more detail in the *Tillman* record of trial indicates how far-reaching the government's duplicitous handling of the case really was. Corporal Tillman's wife was staying in a house near the battalion camp, and in his statements to Army investigators after the troubles, Tillman said that when things began to calm down after the panicked shooting, he had requested permission from Shekerjian to go and check that his wife was safe. Shekerjian had told him he could go and confirmed this in his own statement during the investigations. Tillman thus would seem to have had a solid alibi to show that he did not leave camp with Henry's group. Sutphin, however, characterized the other periods of time when Tillman was not specifically accounted for as opportunities for him to have left camp for criminal purposes, once again reversing the burden of proof. Shekerjian could have spoken up in support of Tillman's alibi, and absolutely should have, but he never did. For whatever reason, Shekerjian chose to throw his lot in with the prosecution and left Tillman in jeopardy of his life. The panel of the *Tillman* court-martial dropped the charges against one man, Private Wilder Baker, who was determined to be incompetent to stand trial by reason of insanity. Baker was committed to the St. Elizabeth Government Hospital for the Insane in Washington D.C. Two men were acquitted, and the remaining thirty-seven defendants were convicted. Twelve of them were sentenced to life imprisonment at hard labor. Nine defendants were found guilty of mutiny, but not guilty of murder and felonious assault—a finding that is logically inconsistent. If a soldier was guilty of mutiny, then under military law's doctrine of joint conspiratorial liability he was also guilty of any offense committed in the course of the mutiny. For the panel to find these soldiers guilty of mutiny but not guilty of the associated violence that occurred in the mutiny is not logical or legally consistent, and military law absolutely requires a consistent finding.

As a result of the post-trial disapproval of the findings of guilt on the mutiny charge for Privates Glen Hedrick, Henry Thomas, and James Wofford, their sentences of fifteen years' confinement were reduced to two years because the judge advocate review determined that there was insufficient evidence to sustain the mutiny finding. The other five defendants who were found guilty of mutiny but not murder or assault had the findings of guilt and sentences to fifteen years' confinement approved in full. The difference in the quality and quantity of evidence between the four whose findings were disapproved and the five whose findings on mutiny were approved is marginal. The record of this trial contains no rationale to explain this different treatment. The only plausible conclusion is that it was a compromise to convict soldiers based on insufficient evidence of guilt for any of the offenses. At best, these inconsistent findings represent a compromise verdict; at worst, they indicate that the panel of the *Tillman* court-martial failed to base its findings on sufficient evidence for all nine soldiers, raising doubts about the evidentiary basis for the conviction of all defendants.

Eleven men—Corporals Robert Tillman, John Geter, and James Mitchell, Privates First Class William Boone and James Gould, and

Privates Henry Chenault, Edward Porter Jr., Robert Smith, Hesekiah Turner, Quiller Walker, and Charlie Banks—were sentenced to death.

Sutphin had succeeded in his ambition to prosecute a major capital criminal case, even if he had to suborn perjured testimony to get his convictions. Twenty-six men went to prison. Eleven more joined the five condemned soldiers from the *Washington* trial in the Fort Sam Houston guardhouse, where they waited to learn if the president would commute their sentences or send them on to their deaths at the end of a rope.

On February 20, just two days after Sutphin began his efforts to manipulate the *Tillman* court-martial to a wholesale slate of convictions, a delegation representing the NAACP arrived at the White House for a meeting with President Wilson. They were there to present a petition signed by more than twelve thousand people asking for executive clemency for the five soldiers sentenced to death by the *Washington* court-martial. The delegation also asked that the president review the cases of the forty-one soldiers sentenced to life imprisonment in *United States v. Nesbit*.

"We come not only as the representatives of those who signed this petition, but we come representing the sentiments and aspirations and sorrows, too, of the great mass of the Negro population of the United States," James Weldon Johnson told Wilson. "We make it not only in the name of their loyalty, but also in the name of the unquestioned loyalty to the nation of twelve million Negroes. . . . The hanging of the thirteen men without the opportunity of appeal to the Secretary of War or to their Commander-in-Chief, the President of the United States, was a punishment so drastic and so unusual in the history of the nation that the execution of additional members of the Twenty-fourth Infantry would to the colored people of the country savor of vengeance rather than justice."*

The injustice of the *Nesbit* court-martial, the NAACP representatives said, was exacerbated by the taint of racism, which was all too obvious if only one bothered to acknowledge it. As Johnson told the president, "Although

---

* What Johnson meant was that all the officers of 3-24 Infantry were white men, all the enlisted men were Black, but only Black men had been prosecuted by courts-martial. No white officer had been held responsible for what happened in Houston.

white persons were involved in the Houston affair and the regiment to which the colored men belonged was officered entirely by white men, none but colored men, so far as we have been able to learn, have been prosecuted or condemned."

The NAACP's delegation concluded its presentation to Wilson by drawing his attention to the injustices that Black Americans had endured long before the Houston Incident ever made national news. Before they left the White House, they told the president of "the terrible outrages against our people that have taken place in the last three quarters of a year; outrages that are not only unspeakable wrongs against them, but blots upon the fair name of our common country. We mention the riots at East St. Louis, in which the colored people bore the brunt of both the cruelty of the mob and the processes of law. . . . And we ask that you, who have spoken so nobly to the whole world for the cause of humanity, speak against these specific wrongs." Other people had made the same appeal to Wilson since the beginning of his term as president and been disappointed by his lack of action on the issue, but events were coalescing that would finally force Wilson to acknowledge the nation's racial trauma.

The association's delegates did succeed in achieving one immediate goal, however. After their visit and the presentation of their petition, Wilson could not ignore the fact that African American citizens were intensely focused on the fate of the sixteen men now under sentence of death from the *Washington* and *Tillman* courts-martial. Those men would receive a thorough review of their death sentences. There would be no more secret executions.

Sutphin was not quite finished with his particular brand of vindictiveness, however. One week after he completed his prosecution of the defendants in *United States v. Tillman*, he wrote a long memorandum to Major General Ruckman. "I beg to submit herewith recommendations with reference to certain members of the 24th Infantry whose conduct on the night of August 23, 1917, has been under investigation," Sutphin wrote. He listed ten names—eight NCOs and two enlisted men—and argued that they should all be discharged immediately or, in the case of the NCOs, at least reduced in rank.

Referring to Battalion Sergeant Major William Washington, Sutphin wrote, "His conduct was cowardly in the extreme and he does not deserve to hold a position of responsibility in any organization." That criticism had some merit, because several military commentators held the same opinion of Washington—his actions the night of the violence were at best utterly incompetent and at worst a clear demonstration of cowardice. When Sutphin turned his attention to the other men on his list, however, it quickly became clear that he bore a grudge against them for not cooperating with his prosecution as enthusiastically as he thought they should have.

Sutphin told Ruckman that Sergeant William Fox "should have been of great assistance to the Government in these cases, whereas, he not only refused to give information but did all in his power to protect men whom he knew were guilty of murder and mutiny that night. There is little question but that the testimony which he gave in the last trial in support of certain of the accused was untrue." He complained that Sergeant Gardner Davis "has persistently refused to give any information to the Government and during the last trial showed a marked disposition to protect those who were guilty."

Turning his attention to the junior enlisted men, Sutphin pointed his denouncing finger at Privates First Class Henry Peacock and Joseph Alexander and Private Elmer Bandy. "All three of these men turned States Evidence and testified on behalf of the Government in the trial of the 63 members of the 24th Infantry last November," he wrote. "By authority of the Department Commander these men were granted immunity before taking the stand. Neither one of these men was of assistance to the Government in the last trial, just completed. I am of the opinion that they took advantage of immunity that have previously been granted them and simply refused to give any further information. . . . I would recommend that these three men be discharged from service."[4]

Ruckman referred the matter to the soldiers' newly appointed regimental commander, Colonel Wilson Chase. Chase concurred with Sutphin's criticisms. On April 5 Chase recommended that all ten be discharged from the service with a prohibition against reenlistment. "It is apparent that they failed to perform their duty at the time of the Houston riot, and since have not given their full support to the government as evidenced by their failure to supply the trial judge advocate with full and complete information leading to the conviction of the guilty parties," he wrote. "It is believed that an example should be made . . . of such a nature as to discourage other men from similar conduct in the future. . . . There are only ten of them and it is believed the government could well dispense with their services."[5]

Ruckman was never one to take a merciful view on matters of punishment, and he agreed with Sutphin's recommendation. In one of his last official acts before he was relieved of his command of the Southern Department, on May 1, 1918, he ordered the soldiers on Sutphin's list to be discharged from the Army with a prohibition against any future reenlistment.

17. FAILURES OF JUSTICE

When the *United States v. Tillman* court-martial adjourned in March 1918, Major Harry Grier had by that point appeared as counsel for the defense in four separate courts-martial. He had defended 119 men—sixty-three in the *Nesbit* trial, fifteen in *Washington*, 40 in *Tillman*, and one in *Snow.*

Throughout the trials, Grier kept a personal scrapbook in which he pasted clippings of newspaper stories about the cases.* He seems to have regarded his role in the courts-martial as the pinnacle of his experience in the practice of military law. In that scrapbook, Grier also preserved one souvenir that never appeared in any newspaper.

Pasted into the yellowing pages of the scrapbook is a cutting from a typewritten memorandum. In a penciled notation he wrote above and below the clipping, Grier described it as "Extract copy from a letter written by Colonel J. A. Hull, Judge Advocate of the court which tried the 'Houston Rioters.'" Grier identified the date of the original letter as January 11, 1918, and that it was originally sent to the department judge advocate, Colonel Dunn. The text of the clipping is startling.

"I intended to make a recommendation that a strong letter be given to Major Grier," Hull wrote. "He is one of the ablest, most conscientious and high classed officers of his rank in the Service. He never loses sight of his obligations to the Government, and wherever he may be placed, he will bring to the discharge of his duties, experience, a right discretion and a pleasing personality. You of course appreciate fully the opportunities he had

---

* The existence of Grier's personal scrapbook was unknown for most of the century following the Houston trials. It was located in the archives of the U.S. Army Command and General Staff College at Carlisle Barracks, Pennsylvania, by Dru Brenner-Beck in 2020.

as counsel to raise race questions and so forth, which, while they might not have helped his clients, certainly would not have helped the interests of the Service." In other words, the JAG officer who prosecuted the case against Grier's clients commended him for placing his loyalty to the Army over his duties to the defendants and for not bringing up the critically important fact of racist provocations that might have mitigated his clients' sentences.

This loyalty to the Army had a direct, detrimental effect on the defense in several ways. Grier only superficially raised the racial animus and violence faced by the soldiers during their deployment to Houston in their defense, limiting himself to the prosecution's anemic stipulation that he read out on the first day of the *Nesbit* trial. He also declined the offer of assistance from attorney A. J. Houston in his representation of the soldier defendants and failed to raise any of the pertinent legal issues that Houston advised him of. These failings violated established American legal ethics. In 1908, the American Bar Association adopted its first Canon of Professional Ethics, in which Canon 5 required that a lawyer, having undertaken the defense of a criminal case, "is bound by all fair and honorable means, to present every defense that the law of the land permits, to the end that no person may be deprived of life or liberty without due process of law."[1] This conduct required of civilian attorneys equally applied to practitioners of military law in courts-martial because it was required by Paragraph 109 of the Army's Manual for Courts-Martial.

Finally, Grier failed to understand the ethical prohibitions that should have prevented him from representing Major Snow in his court-martial between the *Nesbit* and *Washington* trials. Given his lack of formal legal education, it is unlikely that Grier even knew of the decade-old rule on representing a subsequent client who had conflicting interests to his current clients, clearly expressed in a provision of the 1908 American Bar Association's Canons of Professional Ethics: "It is unprofessional to represent conflicting interests . . . The obligation to represent the client with undivided fidelity and not to divulge his secrets or confidences forbids also the subsequent acceptance of retainers or employment from others in matters adversely affecting any interest of the client with respect to which confidence has been reposed." That regulation applied to Grier's representation because of the force of Army regulations.[2]

Because Snow was the key prosecution witness in the three courts-martial, impeachment of his credibility or character for truthfulness was critical for the defense. Yet Grier never brought up the issue of Snow's conduct—neither his professional incompetence the night of the violence in Houston nor his personal improprieties that led to his court-martial on charges of conduct unbecoming an officer—in his cross-examination in any of the three Houston case trials. By representing both Snow and the soldiers of Third Battalion, Grier placed himself in an inextricable conflict of interest that was utterly contrary to established rules of legal ethics, and he put his loyalty to the Army far ahead of his duty to the men he was supposed to defend, in direct violation of the MCM and military law.

Major General Ruckman's handling of the *Nesbit* court-martial had drawn immediate criticism and condemnation from many observers, and his decision to secretly hang the thirteen men condemned in that trial outraged people all over the country. The Army, for reasons that can be interpreted in different ways, chose not to make any official or public criticism of Ruckman's actions. Lieutenant Colonel Ansell's bitter denunciation of Ruckman the day after the executions was an internal memorandum that was never released to the public and was buried in the records of the Judge Advocate General's Corps and the *Congressional Record*. It would not come to light until decades later. But the issuance of General Orders Number 7 on January 17, 1918, meant that commanders such as Major General Ruckman would not be able to act so precipitously again.

That was a critically important detail, because Ruckman was allowed to remain in his position as commanding general of the Southern Department, and in that role he was the convening authority for the subsequent trials related to the Houston case. In addition to the TJAG's criticism of his rush to execute the thirteen men condemned in the first trial, Ruckman's handling of Snow's court-martial had prompted the Secretary of War, Newton Baker, and the Chief of Staff of the Army to personally take him to task for his decision that Snow's actions did not constitute conduct unbecoming of an officer. Furthermore, Ruckman had attempted to prevent African American soldiers from subscribing to or reading *The Crisis*, the NAACP's news magazine. In his written comments, Ruckman had blamed the trouble in Houston on the failure of officer leadership, a fact which underscored his hypocrisy in never holding any of the battalion's officers accountable for that failure. All of these factors were mounting against him, and when the third court-martial completed its questionable prosecution on March 27, 1918, the Army finally moved to deal with Ruckman.

In April of that year, Ruckman was required to undergo a medical examination to clear him for overseas service with the American Expeditionary Force in France. He failed the physical because he was found to have high blood pressure. On May 1, Ruckman was medically retired from the Army. He was reverted to the rank of brigadier general and honorably discharged.

That speaks volumes to anyone familiar with military culture and norms. General officers do not lose their stars just because of high blood pressure, and even if such a medical condition disqualified Ruckman from deploying for active service in the theater of war, he could still have continued to serve in an administrative position in the United States. The medical disqualification was a pretext, seized upon by the Army to divest itself of an officer whose judgment and handling of justice had caused the military a considerable degree of public condemnation and embarrassment. In the 1918 issue of the *Army Register*, Ruckman's terminal rank is listed as brigadier general—his eight-month tenure as a two-star major general appears only in the fine print of his biographical entry. The Army could well have relieved him of his command for reasons of "loss of confidence in his abilities," which is the standard language the military uses in such cases, but instead Ruckman was simply put out to pasture with no publicity or official condemnation. The implied disgrace of his removal, however, was clearly apparent to anyone who understood how the military worked.

———

By the time Ruckman was shuffled off the stage, sixteen men—five from the *Washington* trial and eleven from *Tillman*—were under sentence of death, waiting for their cases to work through the review process now required by General Orders Number 7. Whereas the thirteen soldiers condemned in the *Nesbit* court-martial had gone to the gallows twelve hours after they were informed of their death sentences, these other sixteen men waited while weeks turned into months.

The records of their trials went first to the Army JAG for review to determine if the proceedings were conducted in accordance with the

Articles of War and the Manual of Courts-Martial. The acting TJAG, Colonel James J. Mayes, found the verdicts and sentences of the *Tillman* trial to be "unduly severe." He focused particularly on the death sentences handed down on Corporals Robert Tillman, John Geter, and James Mitchell, along with Private First Class James Gould and Privates Henry Chenault, Edward Porter Jr., Robert Smith, Hesekiah Turner, and Quiller Walker. Those sentences, he believed, were not supported by the evidence that Major Sutphin had produced in his prosecution. Mayes passed the records, with his recommendations for reduced sentences, over to the War Department.

A few days later, Secretary of War Newton Baker returned the files to the TJAG with a specific instruction. Mayes was ordered to "determine the comparative character and extent of the participation" of the condemned men with regards to the killing or wounding of people during the violence of August 23. Mayes again carried out a thorough, painstaking review of the records and separated the sixteen cases into two separate groups—those who he believed could be proven to be guilty of the killing of at least one civilian, and those who he felt were not explicitly responsible for those crimes. He determined that all five men from the *Washington* trial were guilty by that standard, and six from the *Tillman* court-martial. In his report to Baker, Mayes wrote, "The punishments already imposed have been heavy and have fallen upon a number of individuals." Furthermore, he said, the "American people are prone to consider a measure of atonement by death as being sufficient and to tire of continued executions, intermittent and after long delay." With that in mind, he recommended the government should commute the death sentences of Corporals Tillman, Geter, and Walker and Privates Banks and Chenault. He felt the death sentences of the remaining eleven soldiers should be carried out.

Baker was inclined to the exercise of more mercy. He agreed with Mayes's finding on the appropriateness of the death sentences in the *Washington* trial but believed that only one death sentence from the *Tillman* court-martial should be approved. Baker wrote to President Wilson and recommended that the president approve the death sentences of McDonald, Robinson, Smith, Collier, and Wright. Of the *Tillman* convictions, Baker said he believed only Boone was shown to have deliberately shot a civilian victim, and so should be hanged. Wilson concurred with that finding and signed his executive approval of the death sentences of those six men.

The death sentences of the remaining ten soldiers were commuted to life imprisonment.

Once more, a gallows was constructed under cover of night out on the edge of the Fort Sam Houston post acreage, at the same spot where William Nesbit, Charles Baltimore, Jesse Moore, and the other ten men from the *Nesbit* court-martial had been hanged the previous December. The prisoners were awakened before dawn on September 16 and driven out to the execution site. They had been informed of the execution order a few days before, and they knew their time had come. As before, the hanging was carried out under heavy military security and no civilian witnesses were permitted to attend. Only a Catholic priest, Father H. F. Kane, the parish priest of St. Peter's Church in San Antonio, who had spent many hours with the prisoners during their confinement, accompanied them to the place of execution. Mounting the gallows with the doomed men, Father Kane conducted an impassioned "service for the departure of a condemned soul." Once again, the trap was sprung at the moment of sunrise, and five more graves were added to the thirteen now covered by grass down by the banks of Salado Creek.

But there should have been six new graves, not five.

A few days after the execution, a telegram from the War Department arrived at the headquarters of the Southern Department. "Received notice of execution of five," the telegram read. "Where is the sixth?" Private First Class William Boone had somehow been omitted from the hangings carried out that morning.

It is unclear as to how it happened, but Boone had not been taken from the guardhouse with the other men, which led him to believe that his death sentence had been commuted at the last minute. One can only imagine his reaction when he was informed that his survival was only the result of an administrative error and he was going to die after all. Father L. J. Welberg, priest at the Holy Redeemer Catholic Church, went to the post guardhouse on Monday afternoon, September 23, after Boone had received the grim news. Welberg said that he found Boone "pacing the floor and raving."[3] After talking with the condemned man for a time, Welberg managed to calm him down a bit. Boone asked to be baptized, and the priest performed the ritual for him.

The next morning, Boone was hanged at the same spot where the other eighteen soldiers had died. He may have been more personally culpable in one of the homicides that occurred that night in Houston, but his death was perhaps harder than those of the other Third Battalion men. They went to their deaths together in the company of their brothers in arms, but Boone faced the noose alone.

His execution, as the *Houston Post* noted in an article that appeared on September 25, "brings to a close the punitive measure taken against the instigators of the Houston mutiny of August 23, 1917."[4] That final execution did indeed close the capital punishment part of the three trials related to the Houston Incident, but the newspaper overlooked the dozens of men who were then facing untold years of imprisonment, sentences that stretched out across decades to come.

The final number of executed soldiers—nineteen—exactly mirrors the number of people who died in the violence in Houston, and it might be tempting to ascribe some deliberate intent or agency to that number, as if the government chose to exert a sort of "eye-for-an-eye" or "life for a life" punishment for what had happened. That would be to attempt to read too much into the history. It was simply a coincidence, grim and troubling perhaps, but coincidence nonetheless.

18. THE PRISONERS

Fort Leavenworth is a small, bucolic Army installation not far from where the Missouri River forms the state line between Kansas and Missouri. In the Army, the name carries a special, and not necessarily positive, cachet. When soldiers say "Leavenworth," they do not usually mean the military post, nor the small, adjacent Kansas town of the same name; they mean the military prison facilities that have been the most infamous features of the installation since the nineteenth century.

In 1918 the United States Disciplinary Barrack (USDB), often called "the Castle," had been on the site since its construction began in 1875. It was a huge, red-brick monolith topped by a small dome, which gave it its other nickname, "Little Top"—distinguishing it from the federal penitentiary a couple of miles away known as "Big Top." Soldiers convicted by courts-martial who were sentenced to incarceration at hard labor were put to work constructing both facilities, and when the Third Battalion men convicted in the three Houston case trials arrived there to begin serving out their sentences, they joined the labor crews of prisoners that were then finally completing the work on the USDB complex.

Forty-five men were sent to Leavenworth after the *Nesbit* court-martial in December 1917. All but four of them were there on life sentences. Ten more men joined them after the *Washington* court-martial. Finally, thirty-six more men who were sentenced in the *Tillman* trial arrived at the prison in two separate groups. The second contingent of eight men who arrived at the prison in September 1918 were the soldiers originally sentenced to death in the *Tillman* trial with William Boone, but whose sentences were commuted to life imprisonment by President Wilson's review earlier that summer.

As occurs in all prison intakes, the new prisoners were administratively processed into the inmate population. Their personal biographical details were filled out on standardized government forms that listed their places of birth, highest levels of education, former occupations, years of military service, and next of kin. On a form that began with the phrase "In the event of my death while in the Federal Penitentiary" they were required to designate a person to receive their personal effects. Most of them named parents or siblings. Their fingerprints were placed in the files, and their identification photographs were taken—one picture taken face-on, and another in profile from the right side. Most of them were photographed in their issued prison uniforms with the plain woolen shirts buttoned to the collar in accordance with prison regulations. A couple of men, uncharacteristically, were still wearing their Army uniforms when they were photographed, and the subdued brass discs with the 24th Infantry Regiment's distinctive "24" over crossed rifles on their left collar points, and the "US" disc on the right, are clearly visible in the photos. Most men look into the camera stoically, with no expression on their faces. Others reveal something of their emotions as the camera recorded the beginning of their time in prison. Some men, such as Callie Glenn, look almost bereft, as if still trying to understand how they had come to such a pass. A few, like Abner Davis and Robert Tillman, appear unabashedly angry, and they stare into the camera lens with undisguised animosity.

The Third Battalion prisoners did not settle quietly into their incarceration, resigned to the loss of their freedom and the besmirchment of the military service that meant so much to them. Almost from the first weeks of their imprisonment, they began appealing their case, not only through the formal legal process but also in the public forum. The soldiers wrote to almost everyone and every organization they thought might help them: senior officers of the NAACP, Marcus Garvey's Universal Negro Improvement Association, the Negro Civic Welfare Committee in Cincinnati, and the National Equal Rights League. They appealed to veterans' organizations such as the American Legion. They wrote to newspapers and popular journals; directly to the Army, sending letters to the Judge Advocate General and the Adjutant General; and to their individual congressmen and senators. Warsaw Lindsey, who was convicted in the *Tillman* trial, wrote to W. E. B. Du Bois and told him, "I, like everyone concerned—believe that we shall gain our freedom if a wide range of publicity is given to our cases. I cannot emphasize our need of publicity too much. WE CANNOT HAVE TOO MUCH PUBLICITY. I advocate this with all my heart: show to all the world, in a true and unexaggerated public exposition, just the correct state of the War Department's perfidy."[1]

George Hobbs, one of the first sixty-three defendants in the *Nesbit* trial, wrote to New York congressman James Wadsworth. Hobbs was not a well-educated man, but he was a long-service soldier and a veteran of service in the Philippines and the Mexican Expedition, and his appeal was eloquent in its passion:

> Kind Sir: I volunteered for the United States Army and was sent from the recruiting barracks to the Philippine Islands. Later I returned to the United States and then remained in service until the Houston Riots of which I am accused of being a participant. Sir, I am now confined in the US Petitionary [*sic*] by general court martial order but for a surety of fact, I am Innocent of the crimes and never took any part at all in the Houston trouble. By a careful review of this case, you will note that there was an undue prejudice against us or we would not have been sentenced to these long sentences If this had not been the case. Prior to the time of sentence I was a soldier of excellent character therefore it is my earnest desire to be restored to duty so that I may regain my good name which I had in the service and for my country and colors which I have always and will always loyally support.[2]

Another veteran incarcerated at Leavenworth was Isaac Deyo, the oldest man among the defendants in the three courts-martial. He had more campaign credits on his record than almost any other soldier, having begun his military career during the Spanish-American War. Deyo wrote to Iowa senator William S. Kenyon to appeal for his help in obtaining clemency:

> Since the time of my conviction I have received no consideration whatsoever. I have been informed by the military boards upon several occasions that they could not do anything for me, or for any military prisoner who was sentenced to life imprisonment. Now I am innocent of all the charges and specifications, as is asserted by my pleas. Therefore, I appeal to you to have this wrong right. I do not want to be punished for the misdeeds of another—or perchance for a crime that never had commission.

I enlisted in the United States Army April 1, 1898. I served continuously until the time this difficulty arose. I had never been involved into—not even the slightest difficulty. Hence, I feel proud of my Army record. I believe that these things ought to be take more into consideration. I am merely seeking a fair trial. The Constitution of the United States requires that every man shall be tried before all courts thereof fairly and impartially. So far, I have had neither a fair trial nor an impartial one. I am asking for that now. And moreover, I believe that Justice, Humanity and all concerned would be materially benefitted by giving me such a trial as is aforementioned.[3]

Kenyon passed Deyo's letter on to the Army JAG, and a short time later he was informed that clemency was denied in Deyo's case. Undeterred, Deyo wrote to the editor of the *Kansas City Post*, Burris Jenkins, lamenting that he "entered a plea of: 'NOT GUILTY'" at the court-martial. "But for the good accomplished, I might just as well entered no plea at all," he wrote. "*I was tried by a General Court Martial.* Do I need to explain further?" He then reiterated his statements about justice, humanity, and the constitutional guarantee of a fair and impartial trial. "It isn't very much that I am asking the country in return for some twenty years faithful service," he continued, "just that they remit the unexecuted portion of my sentence: that they return the life that belongs to me, which they have taken away. Now a little thing like that doesn't amount to a whole lot to the country. I know it is a small thing; but to me, it is different. It is all I have."[4]

Not everyone in the government was sympathetic to such appeals. When Ben McDaniel, convicted in the *Nesbit* trial, wrote to Senator John Sharp Williams of Mississippi to ask for his help, Williams gave him short shrift. "In my own private opinion, instead of having been sent to the penitentiary for life, you people who took advantage of the fact that you were in the United States Army and had guns and munitions, and undertook to terrorize the city of Houston, ought, every one of you, to have been put to death," Williams wrote in a short, angry reply. "I shall certainly not ask clemency for you, or any of the balance of the crowd." Considering Williams's record of racist statements, his attitude toward the Black soldiers convicted in the Houston case was hardly surprising.[5]

If some of the Third Battalion prisoners were not educated men, others were, such as James R. Hawkins. Hawkins had served in India Company along with T. C. Hawkins and was sentenced to life imprisonment at hard labor in the same court-martial that sent T. C. Hawkins to the gallows. James Hawkins wrote directly to Lieutenant Colonel Samuel Ansell, the TJAG, in May 1919. He began by saying that he was not writing solely on his own behalf but was also speaking for all the Third Battalion men imprisoned with him. "We ask you to consider the fact that we were in the south, in the State of Texas," he wrote, "where the negro is unanimously hated whether in uniform or not. . . . [E]ach time we went on the street we were greeted with the vulgar word 'nigger.'" The situation in Houston was intolerable, Hawkins said, and he detailed the litany of repeated harassment and physical abuse Third Battalion had endured in the weeks leading up to that August night. He asked Ansell, "What soldier would not feel resentful upon seeing his comrades come to camp beaten up by a policeman, just because he is a negro?"

"Had we committed a dastardly crime, we would have no grievance," Hawkins continued, and he assured the TJAG "that every man in this body would rather be lying beneath the sod in the 'Argonne Forest' than be a prisoner for this alleged crime . . . * To be kept out of the war has punished us. We would rather of had a headboard mark our resting place in a soldier's grave, marked 'killed in action,' than have a court determine our living grave."

Hawkins summed up his appeal by saying that he and his fellow prisoners "asked once more the privilege of donning the uniform that we adore, that we may once more regain the good name we once had." It was not just their personal honor to which he was referring—it was the honor of their regiment, which had earned a reputation that "was not excellent—it was magnificent." He appealed to the TJAG and the Army to "give us a chance to be in the future what we have been in the past, honorable soldiers."[6]

Many of the prisoners had family and friends on the outside who quickly took up their men's case in correspondence. Henry Lee Chenault, one of the few married men in Third Battalion, had been convicted in *United States v. Tillman* and was originally sentenced to death. President Wilson's

---

* The Argonne, in northern France, was the sector most American forces served in when they arrived in France in late 1917. It was brutally hard terrain for infantry combat.

review had commuted that sentence to life imprisonment. Chenault had maintained his innocence from the beginning of the case, and he never changed his story during his incarceration. His wife, Willie Bernice, wrote to the JAG a few months after he was sent to Leavenworth.

"Dear Sir," she wrote, "I am writing to you in regard to my husband who is confined in Leavenworth prison. . . . I have a little child and haven't any support and I am now living with my mother at the present. So I would like to know if there is anything that could be done to get him out."

The acting TJAG replied personally to her letter. "It is, of course, much to be regretted that your husband, by his conduct, has brought upon himself the penalties of the law, but in view of the facts disclosed by the evidence in his case, clemency cannot consistently be recommended— certainly not at this time."

Chenault's case was examined in a regular clemency review the year after he began his sentence at Leavenworth, and the examiner's comments underscore the casual, blatant racism that marred the judicial system. "This man appears to be a good average type of negro," the record states, before going on to deny clemency on account of the nature of the crime for which he was convicted.

Under military law, sentences handed down by military courts are required to undergo regular reviews, and this was done repeatedly for the cases of the Third Battalion men incarcerated at Fort Leavenworth. One of the earliest reviews, conducted by JAG officer Lieutenant Colonel Edward A. Kreger in the summer of 1919, quickly fastened on egregious shortcomings in the trials that had sent some of those men to prison. Kreger was a remarkable soldier. A former infantryman and veteran of combat in the Philippines, he was awarded the Distinguished Service Cross for valor. When he transferred to the Judge Advocate General's Corps, he distinguished himself as an attorney of considerable skill. Major General Samuel Crowder, the TJAG, once referred to Kreger as "unquestionably the best lawyer in the Department."*

* Kreger rose to the rank of major general and served as the judge advocate general in 1928.

Kreger was particularly struck by the case of Abner Davis, and he wrote a scathing critique of the prosecution that convicted him:

> From the fact that Davis participated in the rush on the supply tent, it does not necessarily follow that he did so with intention to march upon the city of Houston. When the cry was raised that a mob was coming, practically all the members of his company rushed and got their rifles and ammunition. It is not contended that they all had the intention of going to Houston at this time, and in fact less than one-fourth of the members of the company left the camp according to the check which was made. The mere fact that he got his rifle then is not enough to show that he did so with the intention of committing any unlawful acts. It is just as reasonable to say that his intention was to protect the camp and himself from a mob, as did three-fourths of the men in the other company. There must be some evidence of an intention. The finding therefore that the act was with the intention to march upon the city of Houston to the injury of persons or property located therein, is not sustained by the evidence.
>
> Any soldier who participated in the mutiny with the intention of marching upon the city and committing unlawful acts was responsible for all the acts committed by those who actually did visit the city, even though he himself did not leave the camp. If he did not have such intention, then he is not responsible for the acts of the others. Having failed to produce any evidence to show such intention on the part of Davis, it was then [incumbent] on the prosecution to show that he did actually participate in the murders and assault. This it failed to do, and there is therefore no evidence to support the finding.
>
> Nor can the fact that the story of the accused was proved to the satisfaction of the court to be false, supply the deficiencies in the evidence produced by the prosecution. The prosecution must show beyond a reasonable doubt that the accused was present in the column, and while the court might consider the fact that his statement was shown to be false, it could not use his statement that he was at one place as affirmative evidence that he was at another particular place. No matter

how improbable his story as to where he was might appear, the court may not say he was not there, therefore, he was in the column, where he was charged with being. This would be using the charge as evidence, and throwing the burden on the accused to show affirmatively that he was not where he was charged with being.[7]

Contemporaneous legal reviews conducted by two separate reviewing judge advocates also identified many of the same flaws. The criticisms that Kreger raised were in fact applicable to the prosecution's presentation of the case against all 118 defendants in the three trials. That raises substantial doubts that those courts-martial resulted in any justice under the military law of the day.

Kreger's analysis highlighted one of the most important deficiencies in Hull and Sutphin's prosecution of the accused mutineers of Third Battalion. In 1917, just as today, military law held that the offense of mutiny requires specific intent, "defined as consisting in an unlawful opposition or resistance to, or defiance of superior military authority, with a deliberate purpose to usurp, subvert, or override the same, or to eject with authority from office." Military law has long differentiated even violent acts, insubordination, or willful disobedience from the greater, heightened intent required for the government to substantiate a charge of mutiny. A soldier could not be guilty of mutiny absent proof beyond a reasonable doubt of this specific intent. As argued by the prosecution in the Houston courts-martial, mutiny "is not mere insubordination itself, but consists of an act or collective acts of insubordination committed with the intention of overriding military authority, in other words, it is the intent which distinguishes it from other offenses which combine to constitute it; this intent may be openly declared by words or it may be implied from acts committed; intent alone, however is not sufficient and therefore the offense of mutiny is not complete until the opposition or resistance to military authority has manifested by overt acts and specific conduct."[8]

In the aftermath of the national outrage that erupted after the execution of the first thirteen soldiers without outside review, the Army conducted full reviews of the records of trial in the three courts-martial. These reviews repeatedly stated that "the record is singularly free from evidence that is irrelevant or of doubtful competency, that the record shows no grounds for the apprehension that there has been or will be in the proceedings some discrimination against the negro race," and that "the rulings of the court are without trace of race prejudice or other bias."[9] But a close reading of even these early reviews shows that the Army deliberately disregarded evidence that would have raised substantial doubts about the legal sufficiency of the charges and the degree to which the charge of mutiny implicated all the soldiers accused, or which otherwise should have merited relief in their defense.

The Army similarly failed to complete clemency reviews in good faith in compliance with its own procedures. The case of Private Abner Davis is a concrete example of this failure. Lieutenant Colonel Kreger identified significant deficiencies in the case against Private Davis, and concluded, "In view of the fact that the evidence does not sustain the findings of guilty of murder and assault to commit murder, it is recommended that all of the unexecuted portion of the sentence in this case, in excess of confinement for 7 years, be remitted." In a note to this recommendation, Colonel King, a fellow reviewing judge advocate, stated, "It is believed that this man should be punished about equally with the others convicted of mutiny only, as Love's testimony is so unreliable and there is no evidence that he went to town. Recommendation should be made for reduction when he has served sufficient time." And in a follow-on memo from Colonel King to Colonel Ely, King concluded: "Because of the meagre evidence it is believed that [Davis] might be punished about the same as the men convicted of mutiny only, but if recommendation for reduction is made now it will precipitate an avalanche of applications from the others. It is believed that when he has been sufficiently punished the sentence may then be remitted, or at least, at some later date." In other words, JAG reviewers acknowledged the indefensible flaws in the government's case for a soldier who was wrongfully convicted, but argued that to extend clemency to him would open a floodgate of appeals for clemency from the other men convicted in the Houston Incident courts-martial. Better to let him sit in prison for a while longer, the Army decided, rather than have to deal with a tsunami of legal paperwork.

Abner Davis remained incarcerated. In 1924, the Army approved a limited reduction in his sentence from life imprisonment to twenty-three years and seven months, and more than twelve years later, the reviewing judge advocate, responding to a 1931 Army Adjutant General request for a "remark and recommendation . . . relative to clemency in behalf of Abner Davis," referred to Lieutenant Colonel Kreger's 1919 review and stated, "As Davis was convicted of participating in the murder of fourteen people and assault with intent to kill eight other persons, this office does not feel warranted in recommending any further extension of clemency than has heretofore been granted."[10] The Army therefore persisted in mischaracterizing the record and denying clemency based on a conviction which it had, in fact, determined there was insufficient evidence to sustain. And given that the deficiencies in evidence Kreger identified applied to more defendants than just Davis, the Army's clemency reviews, a specific statutory right of soldiers, failed to meet the Army's own standards under the law.

Even in the clemency petitions submitted to President Wilson for those soldiers who were condemned to death in the second and third trials, the Army stated that "commutation of the death sentences may not properly be recommended in any case in which the finding of guilty is supported by competent evidence showing actual participation in any such wounding or killing."[11] Yet, referring to the *Nesbit* case, the Army only stated that "thirteen of the accused have been hanged."[12] Because the Army's own review of the *Nesbit* trial failed to identify any actual participation in any wounding or shooting by the original thirteen executed soldiers, with the possible exception of McWhorter, this statement intimating that those thirteen soldiers participated in the actual wounding or killing was at best misleading and at worst false. This fact demonstrates the degree to which Major General Ruckman's decision to immediately execute the sentence of the *Nesbit* court-martial upon his personal approval, without outside review, substantially impacted the ability of these thirteen soldiers to present evidence for consideration as to whether the sentence of death should be approved, as was their right under long-standing military law. Although the 1916 Articles of War authorized immediate execution in time of war, it did not mandate it, nor was that provision ever intended for implementation within the limits of the continental United States.

The Army conducted the original reviews of the record of trial, albeit after the executions in the *Nesbit* case had taken place, in 1918, when it prepared the records of the second and third trials for presentation to President Wilson for confirmation. The War Department, in its response to a November 1921 letter forwarding a proposed congressional resolution that requested the Army to "transmit information to the House of

Representatives relative to soldiers of the United States alleged to have been implicated at the riot at Houston, Tex, on the 23d day of August, 1917," provided a report that summarized the subsequent clemency reviews conducted between 1918 and 1920 and the limited clemency that had then been granted by the Army.[13] The War Department report concluded, "The only reason clemency has not been extended and is not now recommended is that on account of the offenses of which these men were clearly guilty they are not entitled to any clemency."* Clemency, when it was granted, was in the form of reduced years of the prison sentences, not actual commutation or release from prison.

This War Department report illustrates three fundamental concerns. It disregarded the significant flaws identified by Lieutenant Colonel Kreger in his 1919 review, flaws that should have raised some concern on the evidence supporting the convictions for a significant number of the accused soldiers. It falsely informed Congress that "in each of these three trials the defendants were represented by Major H. S. Grier, of Pennsylvania, Inspector General of the 36th Division, a lawyer of experience, specially assigned by the Government as counsel for the defendants," perpetuating the false assertion of Grier's legal training and qualifications, which also appeared in all three 1918 reviews of the records of trial for the courts-martial. Finally, it incorporated a comment from the January 29, 1918, written review of the *Nesbit* trial, "The evidence of guilt (of those sentenced to death) was overwhelming and stands without explanation or contradiction," a statement in the original that immediately followed the comment "None of these men took the stand on his own behalf, neither did any of them make an unsworn statement as might have been done without being subject to cross examination."[14] The incorporation of this comment, in the original reviews of the record of trial and in this report to Congress, points to the failure of the court to protect both the constitutional and military law protections against self-incrimination.

This was not the only instance in which falsehoods were told to defend the trials of the Third Battalion soldiers. In January 1919, Ruckman, still smarting over his forced retirement from the Army, issued a statement in

* Letter of Secretary John Weeks, Secretary, War Dep't, to Representative Julius Kahn, December. 6, 1921, at 5.

which he responded to criticisms of the military justice system in general, and specifically to his decision to hastily execute the thirteen soldiers. Ruckman falsely asserted that each of the thirteen men had been represented by qualified legal counsel, and Colonel George M. Dunn, his staff judge advocate, claimed that "each of the 13 men executed had confessed his guilt on the morning of the hanging." That was an outright lie. All the executed men steadfastly asserted their innocence throughout the court-martial and did so on the morning of the hanging. Yet this false assertion entered the narrative, denying those soldiers their rights even after death. Such a deliberate distortion of the record by the two men responsible for the hasty execution speaks volumes about their perfidy—having denied thirteen soldiers their rights to due process of law, Ruckman and Dunn now sought to excuse their actions.[15]

The disregard of identified flaws in the evidence supporting a significant number of convictions and the false assertions that the soldiers were represented by "a lawyer of experience" were all contrary to the Army's own regulatory requirements for a good-faith clemency review. The sole rationale given for the denial of clemency was the seriousness of the crimes, and the evidence for that had already been thoroughly undermined.

In the face of continued requests for clemency, in December 1921 the undersecretary of war directed Colonel John A. Hull, who had served as the prosecutor of the *Nesbit* and *Washington* courts-martial, "to study the individual cases and records and to submit such recommendations in each case as my [Hull's] knowledge and judgment dictated." Assigning the prosecutor of these cases to conduct the review demonstrated a clear lack of impartiality and a lack of good faith on the part of the Army in the conduct of the review. It was an inexcusable conflict of interest, because if Hull were to report that any defendant had been overcharged, convicted on insufficient evidence, or denied the due process of law, such a conclusion would also be a criticism of his own actions in the trial. Hull should have recused himself from the task of conducting a clemency review for men he himself had prosecuted, but he never did. When he drafted a demonstrably misleading and inaccurate report of his review to Congress in December 1921, it only underscored his self-serving lack of professional integrity.

In that report, Hull declared, "Of the 57 men who were in confinement at the commencement of this year, under sentences of life imprisonment, it must be remembered that while each and every one was guilty of actively participating in the mutiny and ensuing murders, that all those against whom there was affirmative proof of taking a personal part in an actual killing have been executed."* He assured Congress that the Third Battalion defendants had been represented by a qualified, experienced attorney, while he knew very well that Major Grier was nothing of the sort. He dismissed Lieutenant Colonel Kreger's 1919 assessment of the evidentiary flaws in the case, saying, "Different minds must arrive at different estimations of the degree of personal responsibility of the men now in confinement, though they are all equally responsible in the eyes of the law." Even so, Hull admitted, "we find here men, who, by the nature of their offenses, have merited the most severe punishment but have as a group had less clemency extended to them than any other group of prisoners that the United States now has in custody."

After stubbornly insisting that the cases against the Third Battalion prisoners had been accurate, the sentences appropriate, and their trials the correct exercise of justice, Hull completely contradicted himself when he considered four prisoners in detail. "Tillman and Mitchell, and probably Corporal Geter, if they actually left the camp that night with the Henry Column promptly had a change of heart and returned to camp long before the column reached town," Hull wrote. "Turner, while repeatedly identified as being with the column, was always mentioned as first aid man to the injured and, from his general character, I have reason to believe that he was more exercised in trying to help his wounded comrades than inflicting injury upon the civil population of Houston."

That statement revealed a troubling fact about Hull's already conflicted review of the 24th Infantry court-martial convictions. After concluding that those four soldiers had had no part in the criminal violence that occurred in Houston, he only recommended a reduction of life sentences to twenty years, even as he acknowledged that the government's case against them could not be sustained under a full review of the evidence. He completely ignored the fact that Tillman, Mitchell, Geter, and Turner were all originally sentenced to death even as significant evidence showed

* Hull's reference to "57 men who were in confinement . . . under sentences of life imprisonment" referred to the prisoners whose sentences had not yet been reduced to term less than life in prison.

they had not left camp that night, and only President Wilson's decision to commute their punishment to life imprisonment had saved their lives. The very fact that Hull was given the task of assessing clemency for soldiers that he prosecuted raises grave doubts that the Army ever properly evaluated the numerous clemency petitions submitted by, and on behalf of, the soldiers of 3-24 Infantry.

Hull continued to insist that the prosecutions and convictions of the Third Battalion prisoners were legally and morally correct in every respect. In 1922 he received a letter from a representative of the American Legion in Minnesota, inquiring about Charles Hattan, who was convicted in *US v. Tillman*. Hattan had written to the Legion in his home state, appealing for help, and described the case against him and his fellow soldiers as "unfortunate for the reason that the innocent and guilty were made to suffer alike. My purpose in making this outline or brief biography is not to convince you of my innosense [*sic*] but, in the hope of enlisting your co-operation in securing a fair and impartial investigation of my case." Hattan had tried other avenues in search of support, all without success; now he wrote, "I am without means to employ counsil [*sic*], consequently my plea to you is made in the hope that it may find response from purely humanitarian impulse."

Hull's response was a self-assured misrepresentation of the case. "I am thoroughly familiar with the case," he wrote back to the Legion, "and can assure you that there is no possibility that an innocent man is being punished, as his participation in the mutiny and riot is clearly established by the evidence." He did not mention that several other officers' reviews of the case were already casting serious doubts on the reliability of that evidence, or the fairness of the punishment.

———

As the country prepared for the inauguration of President Warren G. Harding, the national headquarters of the NAACP sent a letter out to the association's branch presidents and secretaries. "Three years ago the whole country was shocked and the colored people stunned by the news that thirteen soldiers of the Twenty-fourth U.S. Infantry, charged with rioting in Houston, Texas, had been summarily and secretly hanged without being granted their right of appeal to the Secretary of War or to their Commander in Chief, the President," the letter declared. "Sixty-one

ex-members of this same regiment, tried on the same charges, are now serving life and long term sentences in Leavenworth Prison. The men, hanged
and in prison, were not guilty of treason in any degree, to the army, to the
nation, or to the flag. They belonged to a regiment with a long record for
discipline, loyalty and bravery, and at the time of the commission of the
acts for which they were punished. They were still as loyal as any soldiers
in the country's service." The association believed that they should put
their appeal for clemency to the new president without delay. "We must
make an effort to secure the liberty of those now in prison," the letter said.
"We should do this by securing a petition of 100,000 bona fide signers, to
be presented to the incoming President of the United States."[16]

Public efforts to secure clemency for the Third Battalion prisoners
continued, and the reaction to those efforts was sometimes hostile. Several
newspapers, usually in southern states, denounced the attempt and its supporters in blatantly racist terms. Their reporting and editorials described
the prisoners as bloodthirsty criminals who had tried to kill every white
person they encountered in Houston that night in 1917, men for whom no
reasonable person could entertain ideas of mercy or mitigation. It was a
commonly expressed attitude, but at least one Houston paper, the *Informer*,
pushed back against it.

Its editorial acknowledged that criminal violence had occurred in
Houston, and frankly stated its belief that "while some of these soldiers . . .
did not conduct themselves as defenders of their country, neither does
this paper justify their actions in killing and maiming the citizens of this
community; for two wrongs never did make a right." Having conceded
that point, the paper then proceeded to excoriate the racist abuse that
had characterized the city policemen's treatment of the Black soldiers and
blamed the Houston Police Department for the outbreak of violence. "The
Informer stands for law and order," the editorial continued. "But if the
criminal courts of the land can take into consideration extenuating and
mitigating circumstances . . . and if citizens are within their rights to petition the governors and pardon boards of the several states for the releas-
ing pardon of prisoners . . . why condemn, vilify, and excoriate a body of
American citizens who are merely pursuing a similar course in this cause?"
The *Informer* might have been a southern paper, but it took a broader view
than most of its contemporaries. "But whether the president pardons the
24th Infantrymen or not," it urged its readers, "let both sides tell the truth

and let principle and not prejudice be the guiding and determining factor both among the proponents and opponents of this agitation and movement for these black troopers' release from federal prison."[17]

Other commentators made the same appeal for reasoned, balanced discussion of the case. Hamilton Fish III, a newly elected congressman from New York, wrote to Major General W. A. Bethel, who was then the Judge Advocate General. "Having served with colored troops in the South I know something of the difficulty of their situation," Fish wrote, "at least enough to appreciate that the wrong was not all on their side. In view of the recent amnesty to political prisoners who obstructed the draft, poisoned the minds of our people, and lawbreakers and draft dodgers out of thousands . . . might not these colored soldiers also be granted clemency whose only offense was to take part in a race riot where evidence has been produced to show that a large part of the responsibility should be borne by the white civilian population?" Fish's perspective carried some weight, because he was not just a politician. He was an officer in the Army Reserve, and as an infantry officer during World War I he was awarded the Silver Star for valor while serving with the 93rd Infantry Division, the famous all-Black division known as the "Harlem Hellfighters." After the war he had immediately taken up the causes of veterans' issues and supported the national anti-lynching campaign. "I make no apologies or hold no brief for the colored noncommissioned officers and leaders in the riot who have been executed," he wrote, "but have not the others who participated in the riot without premeditation been sufficiently punished?" Fish then requested copies of the records of trial of the courts-martial so that he could prepare a petition to President Calvin Coolidge on the soldiers' behalf.[18]

Henry J. Dannenbaum, a Texas judge who had been a member of the Houston Citizens' Commission in 1917, objected to any clemency and protested the NAACP's efforts on the soldiers' behalf. "It was undoubtedly the purpose of the Battalion upon leaving the camp to go to the Police Station and kill as many officers as they could find," Dannenbaum wrote. "They were only stopped by the interference of some of the soldiers from Camp Logan who were rushed to the defense of the town." That was a distortion of what actually happened that night, because Sergeant Henry's sortie fell apart on its own well before any organized resistance was mounted against it, but that was not Dannenbaum's last word on the matter. "The pardon of these men at this time would be very damaging to the best interests of the Colored people in the South," he continued. "The Ku Klux Klan is now in the saddle politically in most of the southern states. . . . If the Association finds itself unable to withdraw its appeal for the pardon of these men I would suggest that it at least withdraw such appeal temporarily with the public statement that it is done without prejudice with the right to present it at some future time." He closed his letter by saying, "Of course you understand that for the reasons stated above I shall always oppose any pardon of these men. I have no personal interest in their punishment; no member of my family and none of my friends were injured in the riot; but as a good citizen and particularly as a friend of the colored people, I think that the men should suffer the penalty which has been imposed on them."[19]

Meanwhile, as petitions circulated, different organizations appealed to different agencies of the U.S. government in an effort to secure some clemency for the Third Battalion prisoners and other individuals argued just as forcefully against it, the men in Leavenworth were experiencing the strain of an interminable incarceration. One prisoner, James Coker, wrote to the NAACP's national headquarters in 1920 with a plaintive request. "Have the members of the Fort Sam, Houston, Trial been forgotten and are you willing to help those who cannot help themselves?" he wrote. "We would respectfully solicit your aid in securing papers, magazines, and other up to date literature, published by Colored people." He and his fellow prisoners wanted to be kept informed about the efforts to secure their release, and he felt that access to a range of reading material could have wider benefits in the prison. "No greater opportunity than this to educate our race men confined in prison here . . . has ever presented itself," Coker concluded.[20]

William Burnette, who was convicted in the *Tillman* trial, wrote to the NAACP in February 1922. "Dear sir as we are unable to learn wheather or not the petition which was sent in to President Harding was denied or will there be any actions taking . . . we are awful tired. I gave my all for this country. I have been paid in awful poor gratitude. Sir please inform me if any actions has been promised or taking in our case." Burnette's spelling might have been a little inconsistent, but he had a beautiful, elegant handwriting, and he spoke for himself better than anyone else could.[21] Gerald Dixon, who had been incarcerated even longer since he was one of the men convicted in the first court-martial, wrote his own letter to the NAACP that year. "It is very hard work for a fellow to stay in prison expecting something to be done for him any day," he wrote. "I should not be in to[o] big of a hurry about this case. But I do wish to get your views on this case."[22]

Some of the Third Battalion prisoners began to receive some clemency, but it came in small dribbles rather than a torrent, and so did little to raise the hopes of most of the men. By the summer of 1922, the first reviews of their cases produced reduction of life sentences for a few men, to twenty, eleven, or ten years. Other prisoners did not receive even those limited measures of relief.

For the men behind bars, it might have seemed that the NAACP and other African American organizations had begun to lose enthusiasm in their advocacy. The truth of the matter was far grimmer. The former members of the 24th Infantry might have been in prison, but at least they were relatively safe in confinement. In the years immediately following the end of the Great War, a wave of horrific racial violence swept across America, and during those months Black people were dying in massacres and mob violence. The attention and resources of the African American community, understandably, were focused on lives that were in immediate danger.

On September 30, 1919, in the small cotton-growing town of Elaine, Arkansas, Black sharecropper tenant farmers who were living in conditions of virtual peonage and serfdom attempted to form a labor union. When they met to discuss that goal, local landowners and law enforcement viewed their meeting as a plot to launch a violent uprising, and they moved to break it up. In the confrontation, someone fired a single shot. That precipitated an outright massacre in which five white men and some two hundred Black people were killed. It was the worst racial violence in the United States to that date, coming just two years after the East St. Louis race riot that had been so much on the minds of the Third Battalion soldiers when they arrived in Houston.

After the killing stopped, authorities in Arkansas charged 122 Black citizens with various crimes such as insurrection and conspiracy. Seventy-three men were also arraigned on capital charges for murder. When the cases went to trial in 1920, counsel for the defense called no witnesses and the African American defendants were not permitted to take the stand in their own defense. Some of the trials, even on the capital charges, were reported to last less than an hour each, and the juries deliberated barely ten minutes before returning guilty verdicts. Most of the defendants were convicted and sentenced to prison, but twelve men were sentenced to die in the state's electric chair.

The NAACP was closely involved in the task of trying to organize and assist the appeals process for those men, who became known as the "Arkansas Twelve." The association launched a fundraising campaign to hire Scipio Africanus Jones, a leading African American attorney in Arkansas, and George Murphy, a former Arkansas state attorney general. For the next five years, the association was closely involved in efforts to save the Arkansas Twelve from execution, efforts that were ultimately successful. But that expenditure of resources and time meant that clemency appeals for the prisoners incarcerated at Leavenworth became a matter of lesser priority. In January 1920, the assistant secretary of the association replied to a letter received from the sister of Sherman Vetelcer, who was sentenced to life imprisonment in the *Tillman* trial. "Due to the pressure of other matters, particularly the defense of victims in Arkansas and in Chicago . . . it has been absolutely impossible for us to take this matter up and secure a reopening of these cases," he wrote, and assured her, "We shall be very glad to do all that we can towards securing a release of the men who are now in prison. . . . I am sorry that we are not able to take the matter up now as we would like to do."[23]

He made the same observation in a letter to the Negro Factories Corporation, which had requested information about the association's efforts to aid the Third Battalion prisoners. "As you probably know, we worked on the Houston riot case at the time it came up," the assistant secretary wrote. "We have attempted to secure action at Washington leading towards the release of the prisoners after they had been given a new trial. Our every effort, however, in this direction was blocked and because of tremendous expenditures in connection with other cases which we were handling, it was necessary for us to defer action until a more favorable administration attained power. We expect within a very short time to take up the Houston riot case and shall do as soon as handling of other cases will permit us to do so."[24]

The year after the Elaine Massacre, the thriving African American community in Tulsa, Oklahoma, was attacked in an orgy of mob violence that totally destroyed the Greenwood neighborhood of the city, known as the "Black Wall Street" for its prosperity. Property damage far eclipsed what was destroyed in Arkansas, but the death toll may also have been higher as well. As in the Arkansas case, the NAACP and other African American organizations marshaled what resources they could in response, and again the cases of the Houston courts-martial were eclipsed by greater tragedies.

At the same time that Black Americans were dying in the racial violence in Arkansas, Oklahoma, and other states, senior leaders of the NAACP were working to generate support of the Dyer anti-lynching bill that was then slowly making its way through the legislative process in Congress. The first major effort to make lynching a federal crime, it faced entrenched political opposition from the outset. The prisoners at Leavenworth were well aware of the proposed legislation, because it came up frequently in their letters. They, like African American citizens everywhere in the country, hoped that this might represent a step out of the maelstrom of unfettered racial violence that the federal government had for so long refused to do anything about. The Dyer bill was first attempted in 1918 but failed to get out of committee; when it was reintroduced in 1922 it passed by a majority vote in the House of Representatives, but determined efforts by hard-line segregationist southern Democrats in the Senate prevented it from coming to a vote in that chamber in 1922, 1923, and 1924. The bill was finally withdrawn and not reintroduced.*

That news also reached the men in Leavenworth. When George Hobbs wrote another letter to James Weldon Johnson in December 1922, he apologized for taking some of Johnson's time when other matters were more pressing. "We have been reluctant to ask the N.A.A.C.P. to worry about aiding us," Hobbs wrote, "because the fate of the Arkansas men and the Dyer bill needed attention. I am, indeed, sorry to know that the Dyer bill was put aside, it is greatly needed."

Hobbs inquired whether time and resources were available for the NAACP to resume its efforts on behalf of the Third Battalion prisoners. He reported that "six more of the boys have received reductions of twenty years from life," but that forty-five other men were still under sentences of life imprisonment "and have no future to look forward to." Hobbs felt the

---

* Another attempt to pass a federal anti-lynching law came in 1934 with the Costigan-Wagner bill, which also was blocked by opposition from the southern Caucus in the U.S. Senate. Not until 2022 did both houses of the U.S. Congress finally make lynching a federal crime with passage of the Emmett Till Anti-Lynching Act.

injustice of it all very deeply. "If we had started the trouble, or if our records were bad, we could not ask the good people to back us, but such is not the case. Everybody admits that something should be done for us, but we will need help to pull through."[25] Unfortunately, a combination of politics and national crises meant that Hobbs and the other men in Leavenworth would receive less and less help as the next few years went by.

The troubles of the Red Summer of 1919, when Black soldiers returning from France were targeted by racist violence; the race riots in New York, Chicago, and other cities; and the pogroms of violence that murdered hundreds of African Americans in Elaine and Tulsa constituted a continuous sequence of catastrophes that were more pressing than the ninety-one men incarcerated in the Leavenworth prison. Some of the prisoners were paroled starting in 1924, but that was always a matter of regular administrative process and never because of any outside advocacy. When the stock market crash of 1929 plunged the United States into the Great Depression, the cases of the men caught up in the Houston Incident faded very far from the thoughts of most of the public.

African Americans, however, had not forgotten their plight. As the anniversary of the 1917 execution approached, the *Chicago Defender* published an article in which it declared, "Thirteen soldier martyrs of the 24th U.S. Infantry were ushered into eternity six years ago, Dec 11, 1917, with the bravest of hearts and like warriors bold. Their death traps were sprung by their Caucasian comrades, and without a tremor they hung suspended until announced 'officially dead' by an ungrateful military authority backed up by a prejudiced Democratic administration." The *Defender* called the thirteen executed men "dead martyrs to Southern race prejudice" and concluded, "This day, Dec 11, although a day of sadness, should also be set apart as a happy reminder that soldiers who loved their Race and country were willing to die as martyrs for a cause that was and is now sapping the vitals of the nation where exasperating, prejudicial racial animosities are destroying the fabric of our national honor."[26]

For some of the men in Leavenworth, the inevitable routine of life in confinement began to weigh heavily, but most of them, according to their prison records, continued to conduct themselves with the discipline that had marked their service as soldiers. Some of them also distinguished themselves in ways that brought them to the favorable attention of the prison authorities.

On December 5, 1921, Warden Biddle at Leavenworth wrote a letter to the Adjutant General of the Army to report an incident involving two of the Third Battalion prisoners. Isaac Deyo and Robert Tillman, Biddle said, "have performed commendable service in aiding and protecting Guard John Keneiry in the Tailor Shop." A prisoner assaulted the guard, who Biddle described as "an old man, in bad health," and prevented him from calling for help from the other guards. Deyo and Tillman physically restrained the violent man and protected the guard until other prison staff arrived on the scene. "In this," Biddle wrote, "they acted as the Houston Rioter prisoners always do for the protection of the officers of this institution." An official commendation was placed in each man's prison record. "This is submitted for your information, Biddle concluded, "as I know that you are always glad to learn of commendable service of this kind on behalf of well-disposed military prisoners."[27] Perhaps in recognition of this incident, on January 16, 1923, Tillman's life sentence was reduced to twenty years.

Warden Biddle continued to have a favorable impression of the Third Battalion men, so much so that he wrote to James Weldon Johnson at the NAACP to say, "I want to help the Houston Rioter prisoners in every way possible. I find them splendid prisoners and believe they are worthy of all the help you and other friends can give them."[28] That was not the only instance in which Biddle used his position as the Leavenworth warden to advocate for the Third Battalion prisoners. In October 1921 he sent a letter to the Adjutant General of the Army, and the file heading of his application sums up his view of their case. Warden Biddle, the file clerk wrote, "urges clemency for all ex-soldiers of the 24th Infantry . . . Reports that these prisoners are remarkably well behaved, uphold the prison authorities and should be granted clemency."[29]

The regular round of clemency reviews continued on a set schedule, and the prisoners very quickly understood what it meant when a standardized, formal letter went into their file, a letter that was addressed to the prison warden and consisted of only a single sentence: "Please inform the above-named general prisoner that, as a result of an investigation of his case, the Secretary of War has declined to grant clemency at this time." That meant their case could not be reviewed until another year had passed, another year spent waiting and hoping.

Some men did not live long enough to experience that cycle of hope and disappointment. Harrison Capers was one of the youngest of the prisoners, having begun his incarceration when he was twenty years old, but he arrived at Leavenworth suffering from tuberculosis and he died in the prison hospital on August 12, 1919, just one year and nine months after the court-martial that sent him there. Reuben Baxter had been Mike Company's bugler when the battalion was in Houston; he was sentenced to life imprisonment in the first court-martial but was released from Leavenworth in 1925 and died in Indiana a short time later. His release was based on the fact that the prison authorities knew that he, too, was dying of tuberculosis, and he was returned to his parents on compassionate grounds to die at home.

The men who remained incarcerated continued advocating for themselves, writing to anyone who might be able to help them. Several of them, perhaps surprisingly, wrote personal letters to the man who had sent them to prison—Colonel Hull. Roy Tyler was one of those who appealed to Hull for help. In a long letter in 1922, Tyler reminded Hull that he had an alibi that was never presented in court (he had been treated by the battalion medical officer and was on quarters at the time of the violence), and he named two additional witnesses who could alibi him, men who also had not been called to testify for the defense.

Hull replied to say he could do nothing for him. "I remember you quite well and am pleased to see that you are making a fine record as a prisoner," he wrote, with a degree of jocularity not altogether appropriate for a response to a man who was serving a life sentence for a crime he may not have committed.

As it turned out, Tyler's personal actions did more to help him regain his freedom than anything Hull could have ever done. On November 14, 1922, a civilian prisoner in the penitentiary named Joe Martinez used a smuggled knife to kill a captain of the guard and wounded six other guards by stabbing them. Warden Biddle reported that "Tyler voluntarily entered the underground coal bunker and took the dagger from Martinez. His conduct on this occasion met with the highest commendation of the prison officials. Anyone assisting Tyler will be aiding a worthy prisoner who possesses the full confidence and respect of the prison officials." Because of this incident, Tyler's life sentence was reduced to twenty years.

In 1924, the Clemency Review Board reported that Tyler would be eligible for parole later that year, provided that he was able to arrange for some verified employment to be waiting for him when released. He did, indeed, have a job lined up. During the years of his incarceration Tyler had begun playing baseball on the Booker T's baseball team that was part of the prison system's Inside League. Though he had never played baseball until he joined the Army, Tyler was a natural athlete who learned the game well enough to play at the semi-pro Inside League level. In 1921 Tyler met the famous Black heavyweight boxing champion Jack Johnson, who did a single-year stint in Leavenworth. Johnson provided him with an introduction to Rube Foster, owner of the Chicago American Giants, a team in the Negro National League. Foster was apparently impressed with Tyler's ability as a hitter and fielder, because when Tyler was released in August 1924, he was paroled directly to the Giants as his place of employment, and he went straight from prison to professional baseball.

Tyler might have thought himself a lucky man upon his release from prison, but unfortunately, his luck ran out quickly. He only played a few games as an outfielder in Chicago before transferring to Cleveland, where he played for the Elite Giants, one of the worst clubs in the league.

After some time in Cleveland Tyler drifted down to Fort Wayne, Indiana, where he got a job playing and managing a semipro team at a salary of $150 a week. Eventually that also fell through. When most of the other players went to Chicago, Tyler stayed in Indiana, and it was there that he got involved in an incident that would see him deprived of his freedom once more.

The landlady of the boardinghouse in which he roomed was apparently "on the game," sidelining as a prostitute, and one night she got into an argument with an aggressive white man. Tyler came on the scene as he returned from work, and at the landlady's urging he threw the man out. The next day the man lodged a complaint with the police and claimed that Tyler had stolen his wallet containing four dollars. Tyler was arrested and sentenced to ten years for robbery, of which he did three years in an Indiana prison. Because he had been on parole at the time of this civilian arrest, he was returned to Leavenworth to serve out the rest of his sentence.

On August 31, 1936, a JAG report stated, "Tyler, who is now about 36 years of age, has continued to maintain an excellent conduct record." The warden at Leavenworth believed Tyler had been unfairly treated in the Indiana incident and said that after having considerable opportunity to observe him, he found no fault with him. Therefore, the JAG report stated, "it is believed that the exercise of clemency is now warranted; and it is therefore recommended that so much of the sentence to confinement in Tyler's case as remains unexecuted be remitted."

Roy Tyler's sentence was finally commuted, and he was released from prison in 1936, when he was thirty-seven years old. Six years later, in 1942, America was at war again and the draft was reinstated. Tyler wrote to the JAG, "I would appreciate if you will inform me if I am eligible to inlist again as I have my dishonorable discharge according to the draft laws I am subject to military service. My age is 42 years old." He was informed that he was not eligible to reenlist, based on his age and his court-martial record. Tyler eventually settled in Michigan and worked as a caretaker at a Boy Scout camp until he died of a heart attack in 1983, at the age of eighty-four.

By 1926, others among the Third Battalion prisoners were beginning to become eligible for parole, and those men who were released from prison began the difficult process of trying to pick up lives that would never be the same as they had been before the Army sent them to Texas. Some of them were able to make a go of it. Isaac Deyo was paroled in 1924, one of the first men to be released, and he settled into a quiet life of relative anonymity. Gerald Dixon had originally run away from home in Indiana to join the Army, even though he was not old enough to enlist without his parents' permission. When his case came up for clemency review in 1924, the board reported that his life sentence had been reduced to twenty years, that his exemplary conduct had resulted in him being made an outside trusty, and that a petition on his behalf had been submitted by the citizens of Seymour, Indiana, his hometown.

Dixon was paroled in September 1924 and apparently made good on the second chance. In 1930 a JAG report was entered into his record to say that he had "maintained an exemplary record during the five-year period of his parole" and that he had "completely rehabilitated himself." Dixon was a success story, the report concluded, and it "recommended that the unexecuted portion of the period of confinement in Dixon's case be remitted." He was truly a free man at last.

Dean New was one of the prisoners declared eligible for parole in 1927, but by 1929 he was still behind bars. In November of that year, while he was assigned to work at the prison greenhouse, New slipped away from his work detail and swam across the Missouri River. He might have enjoyed a longer stint of freedom had he not decided to enter a general store in Beverly, Missouri, to buy a plug of chewing tobacco. The storekeeper recognized him as an escapee from the military prison and held him at gunpoint with a shotgun until the Army arrived to take him back into custody. Dean lost his eligibility for parole.

Henry Chenault was denied parole repeatedly and was still in prison in 1931. When he finally was paroled after fifteen years' incarceration, he moved west and eventually settled in Petaluma, California. His marriage failed, and he and his wife, Willie, divorced in 1937. He eventually remarried in 1944, to a woman named Bessie Thompson. As a small business owner, Chenault ran a popular shoeshine stand and was apparently well liked in the community, though for the next thirty years he was the only Black homeowner in Petaluma and his stepdaughter was the only Black student at the town's high school when she was growing up. Chenault died in 1969 at the age of seventy-four. He almost never spoke of the years he spent incarcerated at Leavenworth, and instead told people that he "worked on the railroads" during that time.[30]

Abner Davis, whose conviction Lieutenant Colonel Kreger had so thoroughly excoriated for its legal shortcomings, was still incarcerated in 1931, in no small part because of the JAG reviewer's concern that granting him clemency on the basis of wrongful conviction would "precipitate an avalanche of applications from the others." The Army thought it best to wait until "he has been sufficiently punished" before taking any action on his case. In the meantime, Davis taught his fellow prisoners in the penitentiary's night school and was repeatedly commended by the warden for "excellent service." When a fire broke out in the prison's steel shop he was noted to have rendered "meritorious service" in fighting the blaze. Still, he remained in prison long after separate reviews concluded that he never should have been convicted in the first place. His father and sister wrote regular letters asking the government to reconsider his case, without success. Davis was finally paroled in 1932.

As the years passed, men lost not just years of their lives but also family and friends. When a congressman wrote to the JAG to petition on behalf of prisoner Tom Bass, he wrote, "Since his confinement, his father has died, also an older sister, and his mother is practically without support."

Clemency was not considered appropriate for Bass, and he remained in Leavenworth. In its review of his case, the review board wrote that he was "apparently a fair average negro," once again making the racism of the day an undeniable part of the judicial process. The review of Bass's case also included the standard phrasing found in almost every one of the prisoner files when clemency was denied—the insistence that the prisoner "received a fair and impartial trial, during which his every legal right was carefully safeguarded." Bass was finally paroled and returned to his native Texas, where he married and tried to put the troubles behind him. He died of a heart attack in Trinity, Texas, in 1965, at the age of sixty-seven. On his death certificate, in response to the standard question "Was the deceased ever in the U.S. Armed Forces?" the answer was "No."

Several men who succeeded in being paroled wound up back in prison for parole violations, the most common of which was that they moved without informing their parole officers of their new locations. William Burnette was paroled in 1924 and took up residence in California. In 1928 his parole officer informed the Bureau of Prisons that "Burnette seems to have disappeared without a trace, leaving his clothes at his room. I fear foul play and have tried to locate him." In 1936, Burnette walked into a police station in Arizona, the state to which he had moved, and turned himself in, saying that he was tired of having the threat of arrest hanging over his head and just wanted to be done with it all. He was returned to Leavenworth to complete the last few years of his sentence.

William Dugan was not a model prisoner as far as the clemency review board was concerned—not because he violated the prison rules, but because they considered him insufficiently cooperative. When his case was reviewed in April 1924, the report stated, Dugan "says he does not care to talk about his case; claims he did not get justice; that the witnesses were coached; and he denies his guilt." When he was finally paroled, he promptly broke parole and the government lost track of him. Dugan was originally from Cleveland, Ohio, and the authorities might have expected to find him there, but he had instead gone to the most unlikely of places—he made his way back to Houston, where all his troubles had begun. Only one factor can usually exert that kind of pull on a man. It is entirely possible that Dugan had met a young woman in Houston that summer in 1917, and he went back for her.

His story was to have an unusual resolution. On January 13, 1958, the acting chief of the Correction Division at Leavenworth wrote him a letter, so the authorities had obviously managed to track him down in the intervening years. He was sixty-six years old by that time. The letter stated: "Dear Mr. Dugan: The records of the Department of the Army show that you escaped while on parole from the United States Disciplinary Barracks, Fort Leavenworth, Kansas, with an unsatisfied sentence to confinement. Inclosed is an official communication announcing remission of the unexecuted portion of your sentence to confinement. As a result of this action, you are no longer wanted by the military authorities." Dugan was finally a free man after nearly thirty years as a fugitive who was not really running and was never actually pursued.

The last of the Third Battalion prisoners was released from Leavenworth in July 1938: William Burnette, who had initially been released on parole in 1924, broke parole when he left California in 1928 without notifying the authorities, and turned himself in at the local Arizona police station in 1936. The unexpired part of his original sentence was finally remitted by President Franklin D. Roosevelt.

In a statement to the *Indianapolis Recorder* a week after his release, Burnette thanked "the NAACP, the churches, the press, and all friends" whose advocacy had helped secure his freedom. "I have served the country in the army during the best part of my life," he said, and spoke of his pride at having been a soldier for twenty-two years. "We were taught to be a 'man' in the army," he said, "and that is what we did in the so-called Houston riot."[31]

———

On May 17, 1937, a memo was issued by the headquarters of the Second Infantry Division at Fort Sam Houston. The old departmental system of Army organization had been done away with in the years since the Houston Incident, and the Second ID was now the senior military command on the post. The writer was Colonel G. W. Catts, the division's chief of staff, and he made it clear this was a document intended for internal dissemination only—it was not cleared for public release. The subject was an order to disinter the graves of the soldiers executed because of the three courts-martial, who had been buried down by Salado Creek since 1918. In the nearly twenty years since the first thirteen burials, the small grave plot had become something of a minor attraction in the San Antonio area, and it was now delineated by a metal fence, wooden markers bearing each man's name, and a large white sign bearing the words "In this plot of ground are buried . . . members of the 24th U.S. Infantry hanged near this site for mutiny at Houston Texas."

The memo stated that under the provisions of Army Regulation 210-500, "these soldiers should be buried in the Post Cemetery, that is, the Post Section of the National Cemetery, Fort Sam Houston." Nineteen men had been hanged on the temporary gallows erected out on the edge of the installation, but only seventeen graves remained for reinterment. The families of Corporal Larnon Brown and Private Joseph Smith had applied for permission to claim their remains, which had been disinterred and sent home for reburial. Additional requests had come from the families of Privates Albert Wright and Carlos Snodgrass for the repatriation of their soldiers' remains, "but this was never done."

"The Commanding General has this authority," the memo stated of the reinterment in the post cemetery, and raised the issue of headstones, because "the Government will not furnish headstones for dishonorably discharged soldiers." In an odd twist that again underscored the irregularities of the 1917–18 courts-martial, only Private First Class William Boone had actually been dishonorably discharged before he was hanged, as military regulations required. "The placing of headstones is not so important," the memo concluded, "as we could take care of that by wooden headstones or discarded stone ones."

An addendum at the bottom of this document stated the approval of the commanding general to the suggested reinterment. "Please have seventeen (17) wooden boxes (2 feet × 1 × 1) made for the remains," the memo directed. After nearly two decades, the remains were expected to be skeletal.

"Please arrange with Mr. Madigan to have the remains of the soldiers disinterred and reinterred in the Post Cemetery," the memo concluded. "The Commanding General wishes a few removed at a time, say three or four. Three headstones, for the time being, should be left in place" at the original burial site. After a decent interval, Colonel Catts said, the commanding general wanted all traces of the original burial site "entirely removed." Just as those men were executed in secrecy, so too would their reburial be conducted quietly, out of public view.

The reinterment was carried out over the next several weeks, until by the end of that summer a new row of seventeen graves was in place in the

Fort Sam Houston National Cemetery. Military cemeteries are striking in their carefully ordered uniformity, with rows on rows of marble headstones placed at exact intervals, stretching out across the grass in silent precision. What individuality each stone bears is visible only at close range, where one can see the name, dates of birth and death, and military service information of the person buried beneath it. At any distance greater than twenty feet, the white marble headstones of the Third Battalion soldiers looked like all the hundreds of others that surrounded them. The startling difference of their stones only became apparent when one stepped close enough to read them.

Their grave markers bore only their names and dates of death. Their birthdates, ranks, military unit, and campaign credits were missing. There was nothing on those stones to say that those men were soldiers of the U.S. Army, other than the fact that they are in a military cemetery. It was one final act of ignominy on the memory of men whose deaths were a shameful stain on the Army's record of honor and justice. In the end, though, those seventeen men rose above the circumstances of their deaths.

In 1937, the Fort Sam Houston National Cemetery was still racially segregated, just as most military cemeteries were in that era of institutionalized segregation. The cemetery map from that time shows one section of the burial ground conspicuously marked as the "Colored" section. When the men of 3-24 Infantry were reinterred, however, they were placed in what had until then been a section of the cemetery exclusively reserved for white soldiers. In effect, their burials integrated the entire cemetery. Today, their graves are surrounded by the headstones of other soldiers, from other eras and other wars, and here and there on the headstones arranged around them one can find other Buffalo Soldiers from the 25th Infantry and 9th and 10th Cavalry. Their stones are almost lost in the rows of white marble that impart a shared commonality and identity to men and women who wore the uniform and served their nation as they did.

In death, Jesse Moore, Charles Baltimore, William Nesbit, Thomas C. Hawkins, and the other men of 3-24 Infantry who lie at rest there among other soldiers achieved a measure of equality they were denied in life.

As the years became decades and the events of 1917 passed farther into the past, the details of the Houston Incident and its aftermath became matters of history rather than current events. Most of the information publicly available on the matter was in the form of newspaper stories, and those accounts were riddled with inaccuracies and misrepresentations of the facts. Any researchers seeking primary source information on the case, however, found their efforts stymied by the fact that the War Department had classified all records pertaining to the investigations, the three courts-martial, and the interdepartmental correspondence related to the incarceration of the Third Battalion men.

The first people to encounter this obstacle were private citizens who sought access to official files in support of clemency efforts on behalf of men then still in Leavenworth. Several times in the 1920s, Jules James, the brother of Captain Bartlett James, contacted the War Department to request information on the Houston courts-martial. Even though he had a very personal connection to the case through his deceased brother, and even though he was a senior officer in the U.S. Navy, the Army denied his request. The records were classified and not cleared for release.

In June 1949, a graduate student at the Texas Technological College, J. B. Lowrey, wrote to his congressman to ask for his help in "obtaining information, from the War Department, about the riot in Houston." Lowrey had not been able to learn much from publicly available sources—his limited understanding of the case was that "several soldiers (colored) were hanged and around 45–50 imprisoned for varying sentences."

Lowrey's request spelled out exactly what he was looking for. "I should like to get the names of all those charged with rioting, the names of those convicted and their respective sentences, the order convening the Court-Martial, the order approving the sentences," he wrote, "in fact all the data available in the case." He specifically asked for a copy of the trial transcript (he seemed unaware that there were actually three trials) as well as copies of all the reports of the Inspector General's office related to the case.

Lowrey's congressman passed his request on to the Department of the Army, where it eventually wound up on the desk of Major General Louis A. Craig, the Inspector General of the Army. Even though the pertinent records were by then collected in the National Archives, an agreement between the Army and the National Archives closely restricted access to those files. "Requests for access to or information from Inspector General Reports of Investigation," the policy declared, "will be referred directly to the Inspector General for consideration and return with indications as to whether the request will be granted." It was up to the Army to decide who could see that material, and the Army was under no obligation to allow access to any outsiders.

The IG rejected Lowrey's request and cited several reasons for the refusal, one of which was that "the contents of the report of investigation in question reflect discredit upon certain members of the military service at the time of the incident." Foremost on a list of such members, in the Army's view, would have been Ruckman, Snow, and Silvester. Thus, the IG stated, "It is the view of this office that the request of Mr. Lowrey should not be granted."

As a matter of established policy, the government never granted any requests for information on the Houston case in those days before the Freedom of Information Act was passed in 1966. "It has generally been deemed inadvisable by this office to make inspector general reports of investigation, relating to World War II or earlier wars, available to historians or researchers for historical purposes," the IG stated in 1949. The original reports and files were confidential, and the Army believed they should remain so. "This incident is perhaps without parallel in the military history of this country," the IG concluded, "and much of the information contained in the attached files is of a derogatory nature." Accordingly, Lowrey's request was denied. So, too, were the requests of every researcher well into the 1970s. When Robert Haynes was writing his important study of the Houston Incident, *A Night of Violence*, in 1975, he was unable to access any prison records of the Leavenworth inmates, files which were then held in the government archives at St. Louis, because the military classifications were still rigidly in place.[32]

The lives of the white officers responsible for the miscarriage of justice in the Houston case took different courses after 1918, but one thing they all had in common is that none of them ever had to account for their role in the tragedy.

John W. Ruckman, forcibly retired from the Army as a brigadier general, died at his home in Massachusetts on June 6, 1921, of a stroke. He remained stubbornly certain of the correctness of his handling of the three courts-martial, even as official condemnation of his decisions grew more definitive. He never explained his choice to execute the first thirteen men in such haste and secrecy, except for one indignant letter to the *Boston Globe* in which he defended the legality of his actions. It would have been fitting if the government had allowed his death to close his story, but in 1930 Congress posthumously awarded him the Distinguished Service Medal for "exceptionally meritorious and conspicuous service as Department Commander, Southern Department, between August 30, 1917, and May 9, 1918." The citation stated that Ruckman "handled many difficult problems arising in [that department] with rare judgment, tact, and great skill."[33] It was a characterization that senior officers in the JAG Corps and the War Department would have vehemently disagreed with, had they been consulted on the award.

Kneeland Snow, whose actions on August 23, 1917, had been thought deserving of a court-martial by two separate inspectors general, was never called to account for his failure of command. His court-martial for "conduct unbecoming" after the *Nesbit* trial did not derail his career, either, because he was promoted to lieutenant colonel in July 1918. He retired from the Army in 1921 and died in South Carolina in 1943. Lindsay Silvester also never faced a court-martial as the inspectors general had recommended, and he was promoted to the rank of major in 1918.

John Hull, the JAG prosecutor in the first two Houston Incident trials whose manipulation of the case sent seventy-three men to prison or the gallows, and who misrepresented the record when he reviewed the cases in 1921, went on to great success in the postwar Army. In 1924 President Calvin Coolidge appointed him to the position of the Judge Advocate General of the Army at the rank of major general. He retired from the Army in 1928, and later served as an associate justice of the Supreme Court of the Philippines, which at that time was an American territory. He died in April 1944 at the age of sixty-nine.

Haig Shekerjian's career also continued on an upward trajectory after the Houston Incident. He remained in the Army after the war ended, and served through the Second World War, retiring as a brigadier general in 1946. He died in San Francisco in 1966 when he was seventy-nine. Shekerjian chose to put his role in the Houston Incident trials, and his inexplicable defense of Kneeland Snow, as far in the past as he could—he never referred to it in his personal papers and did not mention it in his memoir.

The summer after *U.S. v. Nesbit* concluded, Harris County District Attorney John Crooker received a direct commission into the U.S. Army as a JAG officer. Those commissions were fiercely competitive at the height of the war, with thousands more applicants than available slots. It was his reward for assisting in the Army's prosecution of the accused Houston mutineers. That commission meant that Crooker was in the OTJAG in Washington D.C. when that office conducted the first clemency reviews of the prisoners' cases, a very small, close setting where everyone was likely to know everyone else's opinions on every issue, and he was far from an impartial party in that process. He went on to a career in private law practice and real estate development back in Houston and died a wealthy man in 1975.

The only men who were ever held responsible for the tragedy in Houston were the African American soldiers of 3-24 Infantry. The men who failed them in that crisis, and the men who railroaded them in a travesty of injustice, escaped any lasting accountability.

EPILOGUE

THE LONG ROAD TO CLEMENCY

It is rarely easy for people to admit to an error. Errors that they feel may adversely reflect on them, even peripherally, can cause people to throw up barriers. Social scientists refer to this as conservatism bias, a reluctance to change one's mind or position on a matter even when provided with new evidence that challenges previously held beliefs.

Institutions and organizations sometimes behave much the same way as individuals. During my military career, and frequently since then, I have sometimes felt the U.S. Army can be its own worst enemy when it comes to handling the sort of internal problems that might embarrass it. The Army has a manual for almost every conceivable task or operation that soldiers might have to undertake, and sometimes it seems there must be an unwritten manual for how to make a public affairs problem worse by handling it with astonishing ineptitude, or how to make a minor issue far worse by trying to cover it up, rather than confronting it head-on and openly. Part of this is an institutional mindset of self-protection, which is certainly not limited to the Army. Whatever the reason for it, it has some bearing on why more than a century passed before the Houston Incident case finally came to a point of full resolution.

I first became interested in this history when I moved to Fort Sam Houston in January 2018. My third book had just been published, and for my next project, I had an idea of writing a comprehensive history of the U.S. Army's use of capital punishment, from the American Revolution to the present day. I had heard of the 1917–18 trials related to the Houston "Mutiny," and I intended to cover them in a single chapter. My residence at the place where the courts-martial took place, where the executions were carried out, and where the executed men were buried offered an opportunity to do the research for that chapter.

An old truism among historians is that no research question survives its first foray into the archives, and that was definitely what happened for me. Within a couple of months of delving into the materials available in military, civilian, and private archives in Texas, two important facts became clear—I did not know nearly as much about the Houston case as I thought I did, and much of what I thought I knew was wrong. The only full study of the case at that time had been Robert Haynes's book *A Night of Violence* in 1976, and Haynes had not had access to a wealth of material that at that time was still classified by the military. With all that previously unreferenced information now available, a reconsideration of the case was appropriate.

Over the next eight months I contacted everyone I could trace who had some personal connection to or academic knowledge of this case. In November 2018, U.S. Army North, the senior military command headquartered at Fort Sam Houston, hosted a commemoration of the 1917 trial and executions. Army North's commanding general, Lieutenant General Jeffrey Buchanan, was determined that any statements coming from the military be historically accurate, so Major Jamie Dobson, the public affairs officer for U.S. Army North, contacted me to ask if I would serve as a consulting historian for the event.

At that time I did not know that important efforts had also begun to try to secure pardons for the thirteen men who were hanged in 1917. That campaign was undertaken by Professor Angela Holder, Jason Holt, Esq., and Charles Anderson, relatives of 3-24 Infantry soldiers Jesse Moore, Thomas C. Hawkins, and William Nesbit, respectively, and sponsored by the Houston chapter of the NAACP. Their petition for pardons was submitted to the Republican presidential administration then in office, but it was not filed with the correct recipient for disposition of military pardons, and nothing came of it.

In 2018 Professor Holder met with Geoff Corn, a retired JAG officer and law professor at South Texas College of Law (STCL) in Houston, to discuss the Houston "Mutiny," as it was commonly known. That conversation led, a few months later, to Corn asking another retired JAG officer, Dru Brenner-Beck, to examine the records to determine if there were any grounds for a clemency petition. Brenner-Beck agreed to undertake the investigation and lead the effort, pro bono.

In April 1919, Brenner-Beck and Corn met with attorney Clyde Lemon, a member of the Military Affairs Committee of the Houston branch of the NAACP, and regional officers of the Alpha Phi Alpha fraternity. They discussed Brenner-Beck's proposal to evaluate all 110 convictions from the three courts-martial to determine if there was any basis for seeking remedial action from the Army. The group agreed with her recommendation that any clemency action had to include all soldiers convicted in those trials. Her initial investigation had already determined that any due process flaws would have affected all the defendants. With that agreed as a course of action, Brenner-Beck continued with her research into more than 5,800 pages of courts-martial records and voluminous materials pertaining to the original incident and aftermath of the trials.

Brenner-Beck first contacted me in September 2020, and I shared my research with her, along with a copy of the executive summary of the case I had written for U.S. Army North two years earlier. I was initially hesitant about joining the clemency effort, however, because I still thought of the Houston Incident as a mutiny, and like almost everyone else who had spent time in the military, I had a visceral reaction to the idea of mutiny. For soldiers, mutiny is the unforgivable sin in action as well as in military law, and at that time I strongly felt that if those men had committed a mutiny then there was little way one could excuse or justify their actions. Brenner-Beck had experienced that reaction herself when she began her work, but as an expert in military law, she had quickly identified a salient point in the record that I had not yet realized—the Army never actually proved that a mutiny occurred in August 1917, even though it charged, convicted, and punished 110 men for participation in one. Once I had examined that assertion against the evidence—the records of trial of three courts-martial, the voluminous correspondence files, and the reports of numerous contemporary investigations—I was convinced as well. That September we began working together, Brenner-Beck as lead counsel and legal expert in the case, me as the principal historian. Over the next month we co-wrote the 130-page study in which we petitioned the Army to overturn the three courts-martial and extend clemency to the men of 3-24 Infantry.

Some people associated with the petition thought that asking the Army for clemency for all 110 men was asking for too much—we might have a better chance of success, they thought, if we limited our efforts to the nineteen men who were executed. Brenner-Beck and I disagreed. The judicial irregularities that denied justice to those men had also impacted every soldier convicted in those courts-martial, and they were all deserving of consideration. We also determined on seeking clemency, rather than pardons. Pardons are a more familiar concept to most people, but what is often overlooked is the fact that a pardon implies an admission of guilt. Clemency, on the other hand, addresses the errors in the judicial process that produced the convictions and can result in them being overturned or vacated, which was our goal.

We both understood, as military veterans ourselves, that any such petition would have to deal directly and forcefully with the institutional attitudes toward the alleged crime that lay at the heart of the entire case. As we wrote in the synopsis that opened the petition:

> Nothing strikes at the heart of military discipline quite as directly or egregiously as mutiny, and nothing is more anti-thetical to military professionalism. Mutiny is not just disobedi-ence of orders; it is the actual subversion of, and revolt against, lawful military authority. It is natural and entirely appropriate, then, that when soldiers today first encounter the history of the Houston Mutiny of 1917, their most common immediate reac-tion is to condemn the men who were accused of that crime. . . . Mutiny is not just a betrayal of the nation's trust in its soldiers, it is a betrayal of one's comrades and leaders.[1]

In the petition we showed the Army that there was far more to this story than simply the crime for which these soldiers were court-martialed and punished. We argued that in 1917 and 1918, the Army itself—the officers who served as the convening authorities, prosecutors, and judicial reviewers in the process—did not uphold the standards of justice guaran-teed to all soldiers under American military law. Military justice rightly demands that soldiers who violate their oaths and the laws that govern them should face appropriate punishment for their crimes. It is also an immutable fact that justice cannot be truly served if the law is violated in a headlong rush to judgment in a manner that perverts due process and fails to fully discern between the innocent and the truly guilty. In our petition, we stated it as an absolute—justice had not been served by the

Houston Incident courts-martial, and true justice was still owed to the soldiers of one of the Army's most storied African American regiments.

On October 27, 2020, we met with Michelle Pearce, who was then General Counsel of the Army, and her staff to formally present the petition requesting clemency on behalf of the men convicted in those trials. In that meeting we discussed the salient points developed by our exhaustive research, points that demanded a new evaluation of the case if the modern Army was going to abide by its own professed values. While the 1917–18 proceedings largely complied, at least in the formalist sense, with the requirements of the 1917 Manual for Courts-Martial, we showed that significant violations of military law occurred in the investigation and prosecution of the cases, raising grave doubts that justice or fairness was achieved in the trials, a truth that any impartial observer would have to consider. Those failures fall into three categories: (1) the inherent prejudice caused by a single defense counsel with minimal prior court-martial experience representing such a large number of defendants and the resulting conflict of interest; (2) the prosecution's violations of laws governing courts-martial; and (3) fundamental legal flaws that followed the courts-martial.

The rush to try the 118 soldiers of Third Battalion in joint trials, the immediate execution of the first thirteen soldiers sentenced to death without outside review or the opportunity to seek clemency, the joinder of so many defendants in a single trial, and the representation of all soldiers by a single officer, although permitted under the MCM, were deeply troubling and inconsistent with core principles of military law, even as they were understood in 1917. That was borne out by the Army's reaction to Ruckman's decisions in the aftermath of that first trial, and the speed with which the government moved to ensure that such injustice could never happen again. If there had been nothing wrong with Ruckman's actions, the Army would never have moved so quickly to change military law to prevent any repetition.

Compounding the doubts raised by these fundamental defects, we argued, were several instances of prosecutorial misconduct in the investigation and prosecution of the case that violated either the letter or the spirit of the prevailing law. These included illegalities in the investigation of the case by the Army that were accepted, directed, or furthered by the prosecuting judge advocates, the failure to prove the specific intent required for mutiny under military law for the vast majority of the accused soldiers, a reversal of the burden of proof requiring the accused soldiers to prove that they were not part of the mutiny, and, finally, the judge advocate's obstruction of mitigating evidence relating to the hostile racist environment into which the Army placed those soldiers. Finally, the record discloses that the Army did not meet its own standards when it failed to both review and act upon the soldiers' clemency requests in good faith and to apply its justice system in an even-handed way to ensure accountability for all those responsible for the Houston violence. Despite recommendations from two senior inspectors general, the Army did not prefer charges against Major Snow for his dereliction of duty on August 23, 1917.

These three courts-martial are unique, in both the nature of the allegations and the deprivation of justice. True justice in this case, we argued, would involve the modern Army's recognition of the injustices that tainted these courts-martial and an acknowledgment that the Army itself had not upheld the standards of justice to which all soldiers are entitled by American military law. The Army in the twenty-first century had the ability to restore those soldiers to the colors they served. Upgrading all 110 soldiers' discharges to honorable characterization, we believed, was an appropriate and long-overdue first step. We requested that the Army review the matter through the lens of its own core values, which are founded upon the ideals of honor, respect, integrity, and loyalty.

At the same time, Brenner-Beck and I both wanted anyone reading the petition to understand that it was not meant to excuse the deaths and injuries that occurred in the violence in Houston. Crimes were committed by soldiers that night and innocent people were killed in actions that were homicide, plain and simple. Other people were maimed for life. Families were left grieved and bereft. But punishment for any crimes committed by these soldiers had long been served by innocent men as well as by the guilty. Nobody was going to "get away with it," as some critics of the petition suggested. As a remedial action, our petition argued that the flaws in the judicial process resulted in the imposition of punishment on some soldiers who were not genuinely guilty or that the nature of the punishment was excessive, considering all the extenuating and mitigating factors associated with this tragedy. Because the Army did not ensure that these soldiers were accorded the full protections of military law and Army regulation to which the law entitled them, the ability of the military justice system to establish guilt beyond a reasonable doubt for those soldiers responsible for the deaths and serious injuries was irreparably lost. That represented a further injustice against the families of the people killed that night, because the Army failed to identify the men who were truly responsible for their murders. The rush to impose sweeping and severe penalties meant that just as some innocent men suffered along with the guilty, it is also possible that others more guilty may have escaped punishment altogether, and true justice was not delivered.

———

Immediately following announcement of the first thirteen executions in 1917, some commentators accused the army of carrying out "a military lynching." That view persists today in some circles, as we found when working on the petition. Although the sentiment is understandable, the characterization is inaccurate. Those executions were the result of a formal judicial process and carried out under the authority of law. Having said that, it is also important to not get distracted by legalities while missing the true nature of justice, or the failure to deliver justice. As a conflict historian, I believe that every word matters in history, and we must be very careful about the words we use to describe the events of the past.

Words like "genocide" or "massacre" can get tossed around far too casually or hyperbolically when feelings run high, and not everything that has been called a genocide or massacre truly was such. I would argue that the same applies to the word "lynching." Anyone who takes the time to read just a small portion of the extensive history of lynching in this country should come away from it appalled, disgusted, and frightened by the savagery inflicted on fellow humans. The fact that ordinary Americans could give themselves over to the sort of vicious barbarity that allowed them to carry out those kinds of atrocities—not just to commit murder but to engage in acts of horrific savagery, as were discussed earlier in this book—leaves one feeling that the veneer of enlightened, civilized behavior we like to believe we have achieved might be very thin indeed. If we today describe the military executions in 1917 as a lynching, we run the risk of reducing the sheer horror of what lynching really was, what it did, and the degree to which it remains an indelible stain on American history. The hanging of those thirteen soldiers was wrong and it was a terrible injustice, but it was not a lynching.

Brenner-Beck and I agreed on that point, as we also agreed that attempting to overturn the verdicts a century after the fact would probably open us up to accusations of revisionism, or of "wokism," a word beginning to enter the national vocabulary at the time. We felt that if we were to carry out this project fairly, we needed to show that all our criticisms of the Houston Incident trials were based on an evaluation of military law as it existed then, not by the standards that exist today. This could not be an exercise in revisionist history or revisionist law. Thus, the serious flaws we identified in the case were flaws because they violated Army law, regulations, and protocols in 1917 as stated in the Articles of War and Manual of Courts-Martial at that time, not the statutes of modern military law found in the Uniform Code of Military Justice, or the significant legal developments on due process protections that the U.S. Supreme Court developed in the following decades of the twentieth century.

We argued that virulent racism was an inextricable element of this entire case and the greatest cause of the outbreak of the events in Houston, even though the Articles of War themselves, the legal code under which these soldiers were prosecuted, was focused only on the legal identity of the accused as soldiers before the law, not on their race. Examination of the records quickly proves that racism permeated every aspect of the trials, the sentencing, and the Army's subsequent reviews of the case in the 1920s and 1930s. Racism was endemic in a military structure that segregated soldiers by race and denigrated them with the casual use of racist stereotypes in official documents—that was the reality of the Army in 1917. Lieutenant Colonel Ansell's outrage at Major General Ruckman's handling of the first case was not because the men involved were Black but was entirely based on his view that no American soldier should ever be denied due process of law and denied the chance of appeal, regardless of their racial identity. The Army's decision to send this battalion of Black soldiers into the Jim Crow South without taking any measures to insist on their fair treatment as U.S. soldiers directly contributed to the tragic events of the night of August 23, 1917, a fact the prosecution deliberately moved to eliminate from consideration in the trials. The law was formulistically followed in these courts-martial, but sometimes the law itself is the true source of an injustice, and that was an undeniable factor in this case.

The prosecution charged the accused with mutiny, but according to an essential tenet of military law, the crime of mutiny requires specific

intent. Mutiny is considered a crime of conspiracy, and once it is established that a soldier joined a mutiny he is criminally liable for all acts
committed by the participants in the mutiny, including any alleged acts of
murder and attempted murder committed during the mutiny. This liability
results regardless of a particular soldier's violent acts or even if he lacks any
knowledge of acts undertaken during the mutiny—it is a conspiratorial
liability. In the Houston courts-martial the prosecution bootstrapped the
remainder of its case—specifically the charges of murder and aggravated
assault with the intent to commit murder—on the joint liability resulting
from a finding of mutiny. Because no victim or witness was able to identify any particular soldier as committing an act of murder or assault, this
joint liability was critical to the prosecution of the case. Only by relying
on the concept of group complicity was prosecutor Colonel John Hull able
to prevail when he could not provide evidence beyond a reasonable doubt
that any particular soldier committed a criminal act.

Hull endeavored to show that a mutiny had occurred, because under
that theory of group liability, the prosecution was also excused from proving that a particular soldier had the necessary intent to be held criminally
liable for murder or assault. Hull premised his case on the theory that a
wide-ranging overt conspiracy took root among the soldiers of Third Battalion in the early afternoon of August 23, when false reports of Corporal
Baltimore's death at the hands of local police made their way back to camp,
and continued until the group marched out of the camp after the pandemonium that resulted when the cry that a mob was coming was raised.

Brenner-Beck and I believed that the evidence showed just the
opposite—the men of Third Battalion responded to what they believed
was an attack on their camp by a hostile mob, and some of them, responding
to the orders of their first sergeant, subsequently marched from the camp
in military formation to meet the perceived threat. Noncommissioned
officers were established as rear guards under the prevailing (and current)
military doctrine to prevent stragglers in the column. The evidence further showed that after its departure from camp, the column realized that
there was no mob to repel. This likely occurred after the group's initial
halt near Shepherd's Dam bridge on the edge of the San Felipe District.
Prior to that point, both criminal intent and the specific intent to join a
mutiny are absent for the majority of men in the column who were present
under the direct orders of their first sergeant in a fluid tactical situation.

After that halt, significant numbers of men in the column began to fall out and return to camp. By the time the column reached the corner of Arthur and San Felipe Streets, a witness counted only forty-nine soldiers in the column. Although actions later in the night did involve egregious criminal acts, particularly as the soldiers encountered police, the advancing column did not fire indiscriminately even when passing through white neighborhoods. They allowed several civilians, an ambulance, and two military officers to depart the street where they stopped them.

There was no evidence that the column departed the camp with the intent either to override military authority or to march on the city of Houston to harm its inhabitants. In fact, rather than following the most direct route into the city, the column instead marched to the historic Black district, which also would have been at risk from a mob attack, as events in East St. Louis seven weeks earlier had clearly shown. Neither did the soldiers march directly toward the nearest police station, as most contemporary accounts claimed— we proved that by walking the route the soldiers took that night, following the maps that the prosecution presented in *United States v. Nesbit*. While criminal intent for a specific crime such as murder may have developed later among some soldiers who remained in the diminished column, the departure from camp, particularly in the absence of any officer authority to the contrary, did not demonstrate the specific intent to join in a mutiny for all but possibly two of the participating soldiers, Sergeant Vida Henry and Corporal Larnon Brown. The prosecution never established the specific intent required to prove that the accused soldiers had "joined in a mutiny" to override or usurp military authority, as required under military law.

Because no victim or non-military witness could identify a single soldier as participating in the column that marched into Houston, the prosecutor was forced to rely on immunized witness testimony. Hull routinely led his witnesses in their frequently confused identification of soldiers allegedly involved and relied heavily on the unreliable and incomplete records of head counts made in the camp immediately prior to the shooting in town and on the skirmish line at various points over the night. Subsequent reviews of the records of trial conducted by Lieutenant Colonel Kreger in 1919 and other JAG officers in the 1920s repeatedly pointed out the unreliability of those witnesses' testimony, and yet the men convicted on that testimony remained in prison for years even after those legal reviews demonstrated a lack of sufficient evidence to sustain the convictions.

Even in the 1918 clemency petitions submitted to President Wilson for those soldiers who were condemned to death in the second and third trials, the Army stated that "commutation of the death sentences may not properly be recommended in any case in which the finding of guilty is supported by competent evidence showing actual participation in any such wounding or killing."[2] Yet, referring to the *Nesbit* case, the Army only stated that "thirteen of the accused have been hanged."[3] Given that the Army's own review of the *Nesbit* trial failed to identify any actual participation in any wounding or shooting by the original thirteen executed soldiers, with the possible exception of Private Pat McWhorter, this statement intimating that such evidence existed as to the guilt of those thirteen executed soldiers was at best misleading and at worst false. We also believed it was a demonstrable legal fact that Major General Ruckman's decision to immediately execute the sentence of the *Nesbit* court-martial upon his personal approval, without outside review, substantially impacted the ability of these thirteen soldiers to appeal, as was their right under long-standing military law. Although the 1916 Articles of War authorized immediate execution in time of war, it did not require it, nor was that provision ever intended to be applied within the limits of the continental United States. That, again, raised the distinction between legality and justice.

In support of our argument that the Third Battalion men were denied due process of law, we cited the War Department's report to Congress in December 1921 on the issue of clemency for the soldiers then incarcerated in Leavenworth. The Secretary of War, John Weeks, informed Congress, "The only reason clemency has not been extended and is not now recommended is that on account of the offenses of which these men were clearly guilty they are not entitled to any clemency."[4] That report, written by Hull, caused Congress to drop the matter of clemency altogether.

We argued that the War Department report illustrated three fundamental concerns. It disregarded the significant flaws identified by Lieutenant Colonel Kreger in his review, flaws that should have raised some concern about the lack of evidence supporting the convictions for a significant number of the accused soldiers. It falsely informed Congress that "in each of these three trials the defendants were represented by Major H. S. Grier, of Pennsylvania, Inspector General of the 36th Division, a lawyer of experience, specially assigned by the Government as counsel for the defendants," perpetuating the false claims about Grier's legal qualifications.

And it incorporated the comment from the January 29, 1918, written review of the *Nesbit* trial, "The evidence of guilt (of those sentenced to death) was overwhelming and stands without explanation or contradiction," a statement in the original that immediately followed the comment, "None of these men took the stand on his own behalf, neither did any of them make an unsworn statement as might have been done without being subject to cross examination."[5] The incorporation of this comment in the original reviews of the record of trial and in this report to Congress violated both the constitutional and military law privilege against self-incrimination. In other words, the court chose to regard the defendants' lack of testimony as admissions of guilt.

This was not the only example we cited of falsehoods being told to excuse or defend the trials of the Third Battalion men. In January 1919, General Ruckman, defensive about criticism of his handling of the case, published a statement in the *Boston Globe* in which he again falsely asserted that each of the thirteen men had been represented by qualified counsel. Colonel George M. Dunn, his staff judge advocate, falsely claimed that "each of the 13 men executed had confessed his guilt on the morning of the hanging."[6] That was an outright lie; all the executed men steadfastly asserted their innocence, including on the morning of the hanging. No witness accounts of the execution support Dunn's claim. Yet this false assertion entered the narrative as a tool to deny these soldiers their rights even after death. Contemporaneous eyewitness accounts described a completely different ending for the thirteen, one in which they maintained their dignity and unit cohesion to the end. And the condemned men insisted on their innocence in every letter they sent to their families. Such a deliberate distortion of the record by the two men responsible for the hasty execution speaks volumes about the intent of those involved.

The disregard of earlier identified flaws in the evidence supporting a significant number of convictions and the false assertions that the soldiers were represented by "a lawyer of experience" completely contradict claims that the Army ever conducted a dedicated good-faith assessment of clemency in the years after the trials. The sole rationale given for the denial of clemency after the trials and in the years that followed was the seriousness of the crimes, and we argued that the evidence on which that conclusion was based was thoroughly undermined by the facts we uncovered in our research. Because our review of the three courts-martial that followed the events in Houston opened substantial, evidence-based doubts that the Army ever fulfilled its duty a century ago, we urged the modern Army to overturn the courts-martial convictions and upgrade the characterization of the soldiers' discharges to reflect honorable service. That remedy, we concluded, would be a necessary step to achieve justice for all the convicted soldiers of the 3rd Battalion, 24th Infantry Regiment.

———

The term "revisionist history" tends to raise people's hackles, and rightly so. The idea that history might be constantly rewritten and altered to satisfy ever-shifting concepts of what later generations think is right or acceptable throws our ability to truly understand the past into perpetual uncertainty. There is a difference, though, between legitimate revisionism and illegitimate. It is entirely appropriate to revise our interpretations of history when new material comes to light, or when previously unknown evidence is presented, or when the discussion is broadened to include perspectives previously left out of the historical record, particularly the voices of marginalized or disenfranchised people. All of those elements were part of our clemency petition.

As the process went forward, we gained the support of a group of retired flag officers, generals and admirals from the Army, Navy, Marine Corps, and Air Force, all of whom had extensive experience with military justice. After reading our clemency petition with its extensive primary source evidence, thirty of them signed a letter asking the Army to grant clemency as requested in the petition. As the evidence in the petition and its addendum reached a wider audience, numerous other individuals and organizations joined in that chorus of support, including the City of Houston, which issued a statement in support of clemency.

The U.S. Army and the U.S. government are both bureaucratic entities, however, and a century's worth of established records and attitudes takes time to overturn. The Army has a formal system to deal with matters such as this, and it does not undertake such a process lightly. The General Counsel accepted our petition in October 2020, but that was just the start of a long, careful process of review, examination, and contention. With the national election in November that year, the presidential administration changed from Republican to Democratic, and that meant a new General Counsel, Secretary of the Army, and Under Secretary of the Army had to be appointed and confirmed by the Senate. We resubmitted the petition to the Army in December 2021. That second filing was even stronger than the first because Brenner-Beck and I had continued our research into the case in the interim.

American law, both civil and military, places a great deal of importance on precedents. A legal argument is bolstered by being able to show an established precedent in law. In November 2020 I discovered a case that provided clear precedent for our clemency petition. It was a fortuitous find, and completely inadvertent—I was researching something else when I stumbled across the precedent case.

In 1944, the Army court-martialed forty-three African American soldiers in the aftermath of a brawl between African American soldiers and Italian prisoners of war at Fort Lawton, Washington, which resulted in the death of one Italian. The trial, known as *United States v. Alston*, bore striking similarities with *United States v. Nesbit*. All forty-three defendants were tried jointly and represented by a single defense counsel (though in this later case the officer appointed to that duty was at least a fully qualified attorney), and the defense was not given access to the investigatory reports that the prosecution used to build its case. Three of the accused were also charged with murder and subsequently sentenced to death, though none were executed after the post-trial review process that was implemented as a result of the 1917 executions that followed the *Nesbit* trial. In 2007, the Army Board for the Correction of Military Records (ABCMR) recommended that the convictions in that court-martial be overturned, that the applicants be restored all rights, privileges, and property lost as a result of the conviction, and that the characterizations of discharge be upgraded to honorable. This recommendation was based on the board's determination that egregious errors in the trials rendered them fundamentally unfair and improper because "the Army failed to provide the applicant, and the 42 other Fort Lawton accused, with due process by the standards in place at the time of their trial."[7] The ABCMR found that the accused soldiers were not afforded a meaningful and full opportunity to exercise their right to counsel given the conflict of interest inherent in one counsel representing forty-three accused, that the limited opportunity for the defense to prepare for trial violated the soldiers' fundamental right to prepare for trial, that the defense was denied access to evidence to which the prosecutor had access, and that the decision to withhold that evidence from the defense deprived defense counsel of the opportunity to fully prepare for trial. All of those points were equally applicable to our petition in the Houston case. All convictions in the *Alston* court-martial were overturned in 2012, just as we were trying to do with the three Houston courts-martial.

The errors relied upon by the ABCMR in its recommendation to grant clemency in the *Alston* case not only were apparent in the three trials we were challenging but also were far more extreme and corrosive to any semblance of a fair adjudication of guilt and punishment, even under the standards of 1917. Although Major Grier was not an attorney, he was still required by the Manual for Courts-Martial to provide the same level of representation as a counsel in criminal cases in the civil courts.[8] The 118 soldiers tried in the three Houston Incident courts-marital, we argued, were entitled to conflict-free counsel, which they did not get. The deleterious effects on the ability of the defense representative to fully represent each soldier with individual roles in the events that night and potential defenses and alibis should be obvious to any impartial reviewer.

In *Alston*, the fact that the prosecution had access to confidential reports of investigation that the defense was not allowed to see was important to the ABCMR's decision to grant the request for clemency, particularly in light of the conflicted counsel and the short preparatory time; all of those factors were true of the *Nesbit, Washington,* and *Tillman* courts-martial as well. We were thus able to show that in both cases strong historical evidence existed as to improper and threatening questioning of the defendants in pretrial confinement, in violation of military law and the constitutional rights of the defendants.

Finally, in both cases, what is now known as cross-racial identification issues resulted in the inability of any non-immunized witness to identify any defendant. In fact, testimony in the Houston courts-martial is replete with misidentifications of the defendants even by prosecution witnesses.

Just as was determined in the *Alston* review, we argued, these errors, which were even more egregious in the three Houston courts-martial, collectively rose to the level of a "denial of due process in the proceedings amounting to fundamental unfairness." It is never too late to right a fundamental wrong, and in our December 5, 2021, addendum to the petition we asked the Secretary of the Army to review the three courts-martial with a view to both upgrade the characterization of discharges for all 110 convicted soldiers and to set aside their convictions and restore their rights, privileges and property as the Army did for the *Alston* defendants.

In February 2023, the Veterans Administration erected the first historical marker related to the Houston Incident at the Fort Sam Houston National Cemetery. The new Under Secretary of the Army, Gabe Camarillo, represented the Army at the ceremony, and we had the opportunity to make the case for our petition to him personally. That connection proved to be incredibly important to the outcome.

Our petition, in the normal process of such actions, had been submitted to the JAG Corps for its review. We were not particularly surprised when that JAG review stopped far short of endorsing our request for clemency. Yes, there were a few irregularities in the courts-martial proceedings, the JAG concluded, but not so much as would impact all 110 convictions. Some individual clemencies might be warranted, but not clemency for all of them. The OTJAG was reluctant to undertake a sweeping correction.

Brenner-Beck and I had each read the records of all three courts-martial in their entirety, along with all the associated hundreds of pages of interdepartmental correspondence related to the trials and the thousands of pages of IG investigations, but the JAG assigned a group of officers to its review—no single person at the JAG actually read the more than 5,800 pages of the records of trial in their entirety, which is absolutely necessary if one is to catch all the contradictions in prosecution witnesses' testimony from one trial to the next. The numerous instances of perjured testimony cannot be seen by people who are each reading different, limited sections of the record.

We were able to make that point quickly and effectively, but the TJAG then raised another objection to clemency. Awarding such a large clemency to so many individuals, he argued, would cause a veritable avalanche of appeals for clemency related to other historical cases, and where would it all end? The Army should not be quick to overturn decisions of past courts, he believed. Those decisions were made in accordance with the law of that time in accordance with legal practices of that era, and so they should be exempt from modern reinterpretation or challenge.

Our response to the OTJAG review was succinct. Every case, we said, must be examined on its own merits or lack thereof, and the Houston Incident convictions were truly unique in the history of American military law. If someone could find another case where the injustices were so egregious, and the irregularities in the trials so obvious and contrary to the Army's own laws, protocols, and regulations, then it absolutely ought to be challenged and overturned. Justice is a door that should never be closed and locked.

At that point in the process, perhaps because of gathering momentum or the increased involvement of supporters at senior levels of the Army, our petition was fast-tracked for quicker consideration by the ABCMR, by order of the Secretary of the Army. Once the opportunity to present evidence is concluded, that evaluative process is always a close hold while it is underway, and normally one has to settle in for a long period of silence while the matter is put through a strenuous and exhaustive examination. We did submit a letter of advocacy directly to the ABCMR during this process, however, and Brenner-Beck was able to confer with one of the board's attorneys early in the process. As weeks turned to months with no official word of which way the ABCMR might go on the petition, it was suggested that perhaps we should try to apply political pressure by getting members of Congress involved. Brenner-Beck and I disagreed with that idea, for two reasons.

The first was that as former soldiers ourselves, we understood the Army's culture and its prevailing mentalities, and we could work from that understanding to convince other soldiers of the fairness of what we were trying to do. Bringing pressure from Congress would just turn it into a partisan fight and an outside agitation, rather than a quest for justice. That was our practical concern.

The second was a philosophical point that had been made very clear to us by a young African American artist and community activist named Mich Stevenson when Brenner-Beck and I were in Houston in 2020 to give our petition to the Army's General Counsel. Stevenson met with us to show us where Sergeant Vida Henry and Private Bryant Watson were buried. When we explained our clemency effort, Stevenson thought it was long overdue. "If politicians fix this, that's just politics," he said. "But if the Army fixes this, that's justice." That was the philosophy that we absolutely agreed with, and he summarized our entire reason for taking on this project far better than I could ever have said it.

But in the spring of 2023, we had done everything we could up to that point. The full case as we had researched and written it, with all the supporting evidence and legal arguments we could muster, was now in the Army's hands, and there was nothing more to do but wait and see what could come of it. We had prepared the best case we could, exhaustively researched and with all due diligence, and we both believed that the Army, which was such a defining part of our own lives, would do the right thing for the right reason—because doing so would fulfill the values that are an inextricable part of its enduring identity and culture.

When the ABCMR finally completed its findings in May 2023, the result was everything we had hoped for—a unanimous decision that supported our petition in full, validated the claim that the Army had failed to provide the due process of law for those men, and came to the conclusion that restorative clemency was therefore warranted on their behalf. The board's recommendation then went to Christine Wormuth, Secretary of the Army, for her final decision.

Even at that late stage, efforts were made to stop the clemency process. An objection was raised on the grounds that if the courts-martial convictions were to be overturned, it could make the Army vulnerable to untold millions of dollars in reparation payments. Brenner-Beck and I disagreed with the idea that well-merited justice should be denied on the grounds of monetary cost. Her position on that matter was especially relevant as an attorney, since by that time she had committed thousands of hours of pro bono work to the entire petition process. Once again, though, we were able to show that a precedent already existed that answered the objection. The same issue had come up in the clemency appeal for the soldiers convicted in *United States v. Alston*, and in 2012 a law went into effect spelling out how reparations should be calculated when decades-old cases are overturned and honorable discharges restored to soldiers. Nobody was going to get rich off a clemency decision. Besides, we categorically rejected the idea that one can, or should, put a price on justice.

In October, Secretary Wormuth accepted the ABCMR's recommendation in full, and a short time later signed the order overturning all convictions in the Houston Incident courts-martial. In an emotional ceremony conducted at the Buffalo Soldiers National Museum in Houston on November 13, 2023, the 110 soldiers who had been denied the full measure of justice all those years ago were posthumously awarded honorable discharges. Jason Holt, Angela Holder, and Charles Anderson, who attended the ceremony as relatives of three of those men, spoke of what that long-awaited decision meant for them and their families. It was the largest act of clemency in the history of the U.S. Army.

From the beginning, this petition was an effort to secure a justice long denied, and it was based on the factual merits of the case, which showed that justice had not been served all those years ago. Nothing about it was an exercise in revisionist history or revisionist law. Those three courts-martial marked a salient turning point in the development of American military law, a fact that made correcting the injustices in the Houston Incident trials even more imperative. It is never too late to right a fundamental wrong. Those soldiers deserved no less from the Army and the nation they served, and in the end the Army did the right thing, as we truly believed it would once all the facts were presented to it.

The Army's decision generated national interest in a historic case that many people knew little about, or had never even heard of, but it also produced other, unexpected results that quickly affected other historic cases.

On July 17, 1944, a massive explosion at the Port Chicago ammunition-loading facility killed 320 men and injured more than 390, most of them African American sailors working as stevedores. In the aftermath of the disaster, other Black sailors refused to return to the dangerous work of loading munitions until the Navy addressed their concerns about training and safe working conditions. The Navy court-martialed 256 men in a case that became famous as the Port Chicago Mutiny. Fifty men were accused of mutiny and 208 were charged with disobeying orders. The 208 sailors convicted on the lesser charges were sentenced to bad-conduct discharges. The fifty convicted of mutiny were sentenced to fifteen years' imprisonment and dishonorable discharges.

After the Army announced its decision to award clemency in the Houston case in 2023, the Navy took a new look at its own racially tainted historic case of mass conviction for mutiny. If the Army's case deserved restorative justice, the Secretary of the Navy believed, then so too did the Port Chicago case. The general counsel of the Navy's review determined that significant legal errors existed, many of them similar to what we had identified in our clemency petition. On July 17, 2024, the Secretary of the Navy, Carlos Del Toro, signed the order restoring honorable characterizations of service to all 256 sailors convicted in the 1944 courts-martial.

Three months after the Army's clemency ceremony in Houston, another one took place at the Fort Sam Houston National Cemetery.

The seventeen headstones bearing only names and dates of death were removed and replaced by correct military markers. Now each Third Battalion soldier lies at rest under a marble stone inscribed with his name, rank, and regiment, restoring the seventeen of them to the full community and brotherhood of the other veterans whose graves surround them. One deeply moving element was included in that ceremony. A few weeks before, Brenner-Beck had pointed out that those soldiers had never had a funeral, and so on that cold February morning they were finally rendered full military honors. An Army bugler played the long, haunting notes of "Taps" over their graves, and their relatives were given the folded American flags that families receive at the graveside of the nation's honored dead.

At last, 106 years after the first thirteen of those soldiers were executed in secret and buried in ignominy in remote, unconsecrated ground, they and their comrades were given back their names, their service, and their honor.

Acknowledgments

Six years of research and writing went into this book, and along the way it became far more than the simple history project I envisioned in early 2018, especially after I joined the Clemency Project. None of it would have been possible without the involvement and the contributions of many people.

First on that list is Dru Brenner-Beck (U.S. Army, LTC, Ret.), who, more than any other single person, made the goal of achieving clemency for the soldiers of 3-24 Infantry a long-overdue reality. Dru not only did the lion's share of the work on the Clemency Project, putting in thousands of hours of pro bono work in researching, investigating, and co-writing the clemency petition, but also provided the essential expertise in military law and fact-checking of data that I needed as I wrote this book. She is a true and constant friend. At the time of this writing, she is adding a PhD in law to her LLM and JD degrees and her twenty years of experience as a U.S. Army JAG officer, and I wish her continued success in all her endeavors. When it comes to networking, Dru spiders better than anyone—she knows what that means.

I could never have started my work on this book without the generosity and assistance of other researchers who were working in this history long before I came to it. Professor Garna Christian of the University of Houston–Downtown; Bill Manchester (U.S. Army, CSM, Ret.) of the Airman History and Heritage Museum at Randolph Air Force Base in San Antonio; John Mancuso (U.S. Army, LTC, Ret.); Professor Bruce Glasrud; and Mike Kaliski all shared their research materials and insights with me in the early days, giving me a head start in my approach to this history.

Lieutenant Colonel Jamie Dobson was both a friend and an essential connection to the senior echelons of the Army throughout the process. Bob Naething (U.S. Army, COL, Ret.), deputy to the commanding general, U.S. Army North, at Fort Sam Houston, provided critical support in the project to create the first historical marker at the cemetery that Jamie helped to start. Jerry Cheathom (U.S. Army, LTC, Ret.), of the Bexar County chapter of the Buffalo Soldiers Association, provided both perspective and letters of support in my work. Dr. Chekita Hamilton, on the staff of the deputy director, Veterans Administration, helped me even more than I helped her.

Cliff Dickman (U.S. Army, COL, Ret.) generously gave many hours of his time to conduct archival research that Dru and I could not do ourselves. David Irvine (U.S. Army, BG, Ret.) helped coordinate the flag officers' letter of support that helped us get the petition across the line. Albert Sieber volunteered to help research the archived records at the Hoover Institute at Stanford. Adam Berenbak of the National Archives I in Washington, D.C., provided records that we could not access during the COVID shutdown. Archivist Eric Van Slander at the National Archives II assisted in numerous trips to that archive. Stephen Spence, archivist at the Kansas City National Archives, assisted us with research into the prisoner records. Erika Thompson, community liaison at the African American History Research Center of the Houston Public Library, helped us locate some of the historical photographs that appear in this book. Catherine Lemmer, legal librarian in Chicago, was indispensable in our search for archived African American newspapers. Ashley Cromika, a law student at South Texas College of Law, created a visual timeline of the Houston Incident that was a valuable contribution to the addendum of the clemency petition.

An invaluable part of the information and perspectives that went into this book came from relatives and descendants of men whose stories are part of this history. Charles Anderson, Jason Holt, Esq., and Professor Angela Holder are the relatives of Third Battalion soldiers William Nesbit, Thomas C. Hawkins, and Jesse Moore, respectively. Sandi Hajtman is the great-great-granddaughter of Houston police officer Ira Raney, Jules James is the great-nephew of Bartlett James. They all shared family records and photos, and I cannot thank them enough for their trust and generosity.

The friends who put up with me during the years of this project and who served as the best beta readers in the world are also a big part of this effort. Julee Vance and Mark Heideman (U.S. Army, SFC, Ret.) waded through early drafts of this text and gave me the benefit of their unvarnished feedback. Wendy Wilderwinters was much more than a dependable reader—she also gave me insights and perspectives on this story I could not acquire on my own, and her encouragement and support kept me at it through all the times when I was frustrated and despairing.

Anthony Ashton, deputy general counsel of the NAACP; Clive Lemon, Esq., of the Houston chapter of the NAACP; the East Texas Historical Society, which gave me an Ottis Locke Research Grant to further my research; the staff of the Houston Metropolitan Research Center; Dr. Michael Howard, of the Fort Sam Houston Museum; the personnel of the U.S. Army North Public Affairs Office; and Professor Geoff Corn, Dean Cathy Burnett, Monica Ortale, Heather Kushnerick, and students of the South Texas College of Law were all involved, and I very much appreciate the support of their organizations.

Mike Lacey (U.S. Army, COL, Ret.), the Army Deputy General Counsel (operations and personnel), provided more direct, impactful support to the clemency petition than almost anyone else as it worked its way through the Army's system. Mike and I served together in the same infantry battalion, 4-87 Infantry, longer ago than either of us care to admit, when he was a young officer and I was an even younger sergeant, and it is my privilege to count him as a friend. Catamounts, Mike!

Finally, my thanks to my agent, Andy Zack, who found the best publisher for this book, and George Gibson, executive editor at Grove Atlantic, who shepherded it through the entire process of its publication.

To all of them, I give my thanks for all their contributions and assistance. Any faults in this text are mine, not theirs, and the perspectives and views expressed in these pages are solely those of the author.

Appendix A

Casualties of the Houston Incident

Killed	Wounded
Ira D. Raney—Police officer	William J. Drucks—Civilian
Rufus Daniels—Police officer	W. H. Burkett—Civilian
E. J. Meineke—Police officer	Asa Bland—Civilian
Horace Moody—Police officer[a]	Zemmie Foreman—Civilian
D. R. Patten—Police officer[a]	James Lyon—Civilian
E. A. Thompson—Civilian[a]	T. A. Binford—Police officer
Eli Smith—Civilian	G. W. Butcher—Civilian
Senator Satton—Civilian	Alma Reichert—Civilian
Earl Findley—Civilian	Medora Miller—Civilian
A. R. Carsten—Civilian	Freddie Scofield—Civilian
Manuel Garedo—Civilian[b]	Charles Clayton—Police officer
Charles W. Wright	J. E. Richardson—Police officer
E. M. Jones—Civilian	W.A. Wise—Civilian
Fred Winkler—Civilian	
CPT J. W. Mattes—A Battery, 2nd FA, Illinois NG	
CPL M. D. Everton—E Battery, Texas NG	
SGT Vida Henry—I Company, 3rd BN, 24th IN	

(continued)

Killed	Wounded

PVT Bryant Watson—K Company,
3rd BN, 24th IN

PVT Wylie Strong—M Company,
3rd BN, 24th IN (wounded in
Third Battalion camp)[a]

PVT George Bivins—I Company,
3rd BN, 24th IN[a]

[a] These men later died of their wounds. Moody died on 24 August; Thompson died on 24 August; Strong died on 25 August; Bivens died on 28 August; Patten died on 8 September.

[b] The Army's investigation determined that Carstens, Butcher, Garedo, Thompson, Richert, and Miller were struck by bullets in the initial panicked firing in camp.

Sixteen people were killed the night of 23–24 August and thirteen were wounded. The number of deaths resulting from the violence can be counted as nineteen, if limited to those who died within five days of the incident, or twenty, if counting D. R. Patten who died nearly a month later.

Appendix B

The Three Courts-martial of the Houston Incident
(each trial was named for its lead defendant)

1. *United States v. Nesbit et al.*, 1–30 November 1917
   - Tried sixty-three soldiers on charges of mutiny, willful disobedience of orders, murder, and assault.
   - Convicted fifty-eight men; acquitted five.
   - Sentenced thirteen men to death by hanging; forty-five were sentenced to incarceration.
   - All thirteen condemned men were executed on 11 December 1917 at 7:17 a.m., within twelve hours of MG Ruckman approving the findings and sentence (based on the recommendation of his Staff Judge Advocate, Colonel Dunn), without the sentences being referred for outside review or opportunity to seek clemency.

2. *United States v. Washington et al.*, 17–21 December 1917
   - Tried fifteen soldiers of the Camp Logan guard detail on charges of murder and violations of the general article.
   - Convicted all fifteen men.
   - Sentenced five men to death by hanging, the others to terms of incarceration.
   - The issuance of General Orders No. 163 and No. 7 on 17 January 1918 required all sentences to be referred to the U.S. Army TJAG for legal review; death sentences now had to be approved by the president.
   - Five men were executed on 11 September 1918.

3. *United States v. Tillman et al.*, 18 February–27 March 1918
- Tried forty soldiers on charges of mutiny, willful disobedience, murder, and assault.
- Convicted thirty-seven men; acquitted two (charges against one soldier were dismissed because of insanity).
- Sentenced eleven men to death; ten of those death sentences were commuted to life imprisonment by President Wilson.
- One man was executed on 24 September 1918.

3-24 INFANTRY SOLDIERS EXECUTED 11 DECEMBER 1917 (*U.S. V. NESBIT*)

SGT William C. Nesbit

CPL Larnon J. Brown (Brown's body was later returned to his family for final burial)

CPL James Wheatley

CPL Jesse Moore (Ball)

CPL Charles W. Baltimore

PFC William Breckenridge

PFC Thomas C. Hawkins

PFC Carlos Snodgrass

PVT Ira B. Davis

PVT James Divins

PVT Frank Johnson

PVT Risley W. Young

PVT Pat McWhorter

3/24 INFANTRY SOLDIERS EXECUTED 11 SEPTEMBER 1918 (*U.S. V. WASHINGTON*)

PVT Babe Collier

PVT Thomas McDonald

PVT James Robinson

PVT Joseph Smith (Smith's body was later returned to his family for final burial)

PVT Albert D. Wright

3/24 INFANTRY SOLDIER EXECUTED 24 SEPTEMBER 1918
(*U.S. V. TILLMAN*)

PFC William D. Boone

APPENDIX C

Name and Rank	Unit	Findings	Adjudged Sentence
Court-martial: *United States v. Nesbit et al.*		Charge I, specification 1: disobeyed order to remain in camp Charge I, specification 2: disobeyed order to disarm Charge II: mutiny Charge III: premeditated murder of 14 persons Charge IV: assault with intent to murder	
SGT William Nesbit	Co I	Guilty as to specification 1 of charge I, not guilty as to specification 2, and guilty as to charges II–IV	Death (no dishonorable discharge, death alone) Executed December 11, 1917
CPL Larnon J. Brown	Co I	Same as above	Death (no dishonorable discharge, death alone) Executed December 11, 1917
CPL James Wheatley	Co I	Same as above	Death (no dishonorable discharge, death alone) Executed December 11, 1917
CPL Jesse Moore	Co I	Save as above	Death (no dishonorable discharge, death alone) Executed December 11, 1917
CPL Charles W. Baltimore	Co I	Same as above	Death (no dishonorable discharge, death alone) Executed December 11, 1917
Cook William Frazier	Co I	Same as above	Dishonorable discharge, total forfeiture, life at hard labor

(continued)

Name and Rank	Unit	Findings	Adjudged Sentence
Cook Nathan Humphries Jr.	Co I	Same as above	Dishonorable discharge, total forfeiture, life at hard labor
PFC William Breckenridge	Co I	Same as above	Death (no dishonorable discharge, death alone) Executed December 11, 1917
PFC Thomas C. Hawkins	Co I	Same as above	Death (no dishonorable discharge, death alone) Executed December 11, 1917
PFC John H. Hudson	Co I	Same as above	Dishonorable discharge, total forfeiture, life at hard labor
PFC James R. Johnson	Co I	Same as above	Dishonorable discharge, total forfeiture, life at hard labor
PFC Ben McDaniel	Co I	Same as above	Dishonorable discharge, total forfeiture, life at hard labor
PFC Stewart W. Philips	Co I	Same as above	Dishonorable discharge, total forfeiture, life at hard labor
PFC Carlos Snodgrass	Co I	Same as above	Death (no dishonorable discharge, death alone) Executed December 11, 1917
PVT William D. Beacoat	Co I	Not guilty of all charges and specifications	Acquitted
PVT Douglas T. Bolden	Co I	Guilty as to specification 1 of charge I, not guilty as to specification 2, and guilty as to charges II–IV	Dishonorable discharge, total forfeiture, life at hard labor
PVT Fred Brown	Co I	Same as above	Dishonorable discharge, total forfeiture, life at hard labor
PVT Robert Brownfield	Co I	Same as above	Dishonorable discharge, total forfeiture, life at hard labor
PVT Grover Burns	Co I	Not guilty of all charges and specifications	Acquitted

Name and Rank	Unit	Findings	Adjudged Sentence
PVT Harrison Capers	Co I	Guilty as to specification 1 of charge I, not guilty as to specification 2, and guilty as to charges II–IV	Dishonorable discharge, total forfeiture, life at hard labor
PVT Ben Cecil	Co I	Same as above	Dishonorable discharge, total forfeiture, life at hard labor
PVT Ira B. Davis	Co I	Same as above	Death (no dishonorable discharge, death alone) Executed December 11, 1917
PVT James Divins	Co I	Guilty as to all charges and specifications	Death (no dishonorable discharge, death alone) Executed December 11, 1917
PVT Gerald Dixon	Co I	Guilty as to specification 1 of charge I, not guilty as to specification 2, and guilty as to charges II–IV	Dishonorable discharge, total forfeiture, life at hard labor
PVT Henry Green	Co I	Same as above	Dishonorable discharge, total forfeiture, life at hard labor
PVT James R. Hawkins	Co I	Same as above	Dishonorable discharge, total forfeiture, life at hard labor
PVT George Hobbs	Co I	Same as above	Dishonorable discharge, total forfeiture, life at hard labor
PVT Norman B. Holland	Co I	Same as above	Dishonorable discharge, total forfeiture, life at hard labor
PVT Frank Johnson	Co I	Guilty as to all charges and specifications	Death (no dishonorable discharge, death alone) Executed December 11, 1917
PVT Richard Lewis	Co I	Guilty as to specification 1 of charge I, not guilty as to specification 2, and guilty as to charges II–IV	Dishonorable discharge, total forfeiture, life at hard labor

(continued)

Name and Rank	Unit	Findings	Adjudged Sentence
PVT Leroy Pinkett	Co I	Same as above	Dishonorable discharge, total forfeiture, life at hard labor
PVT Henry T. Walls	Co I	Same as above	Dishonorable discharge, total forfeiture, 2 years confinement at hard labor
PVT Joseph Wardlow	Co I	Same as above	Dishonorable discharge, total forfeiture, life at hard labor
PVT Risley W. Young	Co I	Same as above	Death (no dishonorable discharge, death alone) Executed December 11, 1917
PFC Alvin Pugh	Co I	Guilty only as to specification 1 of charge I, not guilty on all other charges	Dishonorable discharge, total forfeiture, 2 years confinement at hard labor
PVT William S. Kane	Co I	Guilty as to specification 1 of charge I, not guilty as to specification 2, and guilty as to charge II–IV	Dishonorable discharge, total forfeiture, life at hard labor
PVT Harry Richardson	Co I	Same as above	Dishonorable discharge, total forfeiture, life at hard labor
PVT Luther Rucker	Co I	Same as above	Dishonorable discharge, total forfeiture, life at hard labor
PVT Roy Tyler	Co I	Same as above	Dishonorable discharge, total forfeiture, life at hard labor
PVT Joseph Williams Jr.	Co I	Same as above	Dishonorable discharge, total forfeiture, life at hard labor
PVT Earnest E. Adams	Co K	Same as above	Dishonorable discharge, total forfeiture, life at hard labor
PVT John Adams	Co K	Same as above	Dishonorable discharge, total forfeiture, life at hard labor

Name and Rank	Unit	Findings	Adjudged Sentence
PVT Wash Adams	Co K	Same as above	Dishonorable discharge, total forfeiture, life at hard labor
PVT Douglass Lumpkins	Co K	Same as above	Dishonorable discharge, total forfeiture, life at hard labor
PVT Grant H. Mems	Co K	Not guilty of all charges and specifications	Acquitted
PVT Richard Brown	Co K	Guilty as to specification 1 of charge I, not guilty as to specification 2, and guilty as to charges II–IV	Dishonorable discharge, total forfeiture, life at hard labor
PVT Allie C. Buttler	Co L	Same as above	Dishonorable discharge, total forfeiture, life at hard labor
PVT Abner Davis	Co L	Same as above	Dishonorable discharge, total forfeiture, life at hard labor
PVT George H. Parham	Co L	Same as above	Dishonorable discharge, total forfeiture, life at hard labor
PVT Bursh L. Smith	Co L	Not guilty of all charges and specifications	Acquitted
Bugler Reuben W. Baxter	Co M	Guilty as to specification 1 of charge I, not guilty as to specification 2, and guilty as to charges II–IV	Dishonorable discharge, total forfeiture, life at hard labor
PVT William Burkett	Co M	Guilty of all charges and specifications	Dishonorable discharge, total forfeiture, life at hard labor
PVT James Coker	Co M	Guilty of all charges and specifications	Dishonorable discharge, total forfeiture, life at hard labor
PVT Oliver Fletcher	Co M	Guilty of both specifications, charge I; not guilty of all other charges	Dishonorable discharge, total forfeiture, 2 years 6 months confinement at hard labor

(continued)

Name and Rank	Unit	Findings	Adjudged Sentence
PVT Callie Glenn	Co M	Guilty as to specification 1 of charge I, not guilty as to specification 2, and guilty as to charge II–IV	Dishonorable discharge, total forfeiture, life at hard labor
PVT William J. Hough	Co M	Guilty of all charges and specifications	Dishonorable discharge, total forfeiture, life at hard labor
PVT Thomas Jackson	Co M	Guilty of all charges and specifications	Dishonorable discharge, total forfeiture, life at hard labor
PVT Walter T. Johnson	Co M	Guilty of all charges and specifications	Dishonorable discharge, total forfeiture, life at hard labor
PVT Pat McWhorter	Co M	Guilty of all charges and specifications	Death (no dishonorable discharge, death alone)
PVT Dean New	Co M	Guilty of all charges and specifications	Dishonorable discharge, total forfeiture, life at hard labor
PVT Terry Smith	Co M	Not guilty of all charges and specifications	Acquitted
PVT Jessie Sullivan	Co M	Guilty of all charges and specifications	Dishonorable discharge, total forfeiture, life at hard labor
PVT Walter B. Tucker	Co M	Guilty as to specification 1 of charge I, not guilty to all else	Dishonorable discharge, total forfeiture, 2 years confinement at hard labor
Court-martial: *United States v. Washington et al.*		Charge I, specification 2: premeditated murder of E. M. Jones Charge II, specification 1: marching out of camp Charge II, Specification 2: quitting post	
CPL John Washington	Co M	Not guilty of charge I Guilty of charge II, specification 1 Guilty with substitutions, specification 2	Dishonorable discharge, total forfeiture, 10 years confinement at hard labor

Name and Rank	Unit	Findings	Adjudged Sentence
CPL Robert B. Jones	Co M	Same as above	Dishonorable discharge, total forfeiture, 10 years confinement at hard labor
CPL Earl Clowers	Co M	Same as above	Dishonorable discharge, total forfeiture, 10 years confinement at hard labor
PVT Louie Oneal	Co I	Same as above	Dishonorable discharge, total forfeiture, 7 years confinement at hard labor
PVT Babe Collier	Co I	Guilty of all charges and specifications	Death (no dishonorable discharge, death alone) Executed September 16, 1918
PVT Thomas McDonald	Co I	Guilty of all charges and specifications	Death (no dishonorable discharge, death alone) Executed September 16, 1918
PVT Ed McKenney	Co I	Not guilty of charge I Guilty of charge II, specification 1 Guilty with substitutions, specification 2	Dishonorable discharge, total forfeiture, 7 years confinement at hard labor
PVT London Martin	Co I	Same as above	Dishonorable discharge, total forfeiture, 7 years confinement at hard labor
PVT Will Porter	Co I	Same as above	Dishonorable discharge, total forfeiture, 7 years confinement at hard labor
PVT James Robinson	Co I	Guilty of all charges and specifications	Death (no dishonorable discharge, death alone) Executed September 16, 1918
PVT John Smith	Co I	Not guilty of charge I Guilty of charge II, specification 1 Guilty with substitutions, specification 2	Dishonorable discharge, total forfeiture, 7 years confinement at hard labor
PVT Joseph Smith	Co I	Guilty of all charges and specifications	Death (no dishonorable discharge, death alone) Executed September 16, 1918

(*continued*)

Name and Rank	Unit	Findings	Adjudged Sentence
PVT Eugene B. Taylor	Co I	Not guilty of charge I Guilty of charge II, specification 1 Guilty with substitutions, specification 2	Dishonorable discharge, total forfeiture, 7 years confinement at hard labor
PVT Ernest Wilson	Co I	Same as above	Dishonorable discharge, total forfeiture, 7 years confinement at hard labor
PVT Albert D. Wright	Co I	Guilty of all charges and specifications	Death (no dishonorable discharge, death alone) Executed September 16, 1918
Court-martial: *United States v. Tillman et al.*		Charge I, Article 64: disobeyed order to remain in camp Charge II, Article 66: mutiny Charge III, Article 92: premeditated murder of same 14 persons Charge IV: assault with intent to commit murder	
CPL Robert Tillman	Co I	Guilty of all charges and specifications	Death (no dishonorable discharge, death alone) Commuted to life at hard labor
CPL John Geter	Co I	Guilty of all charges and specifications	Death (no dishonorable discharge, death alone) Commuted to life at hard labor
CPL James H. Mitchell	Co I	Guilty of all charges and specifications	Death (no dishonorable discharge, death alone) Commuted to life at hard labor
PFC William D. Boone	Co I	Guilty of all charges and specifications	Death (no dishonorable discharge, death alone) Executed September 24, 1918
PFC William Burnette	Co I	Guilty of all charges and specifications	Dishonorable discharge, total forfeiture, life at hard labor

Name and Rank	Unit	Findings	Adjudged Sentence
PFC James H. Gould	Co I	Guilty of all charges and specifications	Death (no dishonorable discharge, death alone) commuted to life at hard labor
PVT Fred Avery	Co I	Guilty of all charges and specifications	Dishonorable discharge, total forfeiture, life at hard labor
PVT Henry L. Chenault	Co I	Guilty of all charges and specifications	Death (no dishonorable discharge, death alone) commuted to life at hard labor
PVT Isaac A. Deyo	Co I	Guilty of all charges and specifications	Dishonorable discharge, total forfeiture, life at hard labor
PVT Charles J. Hattan	Co I	Guilty of all charges and specifications	Dishonorable discharge, total forfeiture, life at hard labor
PVT Albert D. Hunter	Co I	Guilty of all charges and specifications	Dishonorable discharge, total forfeiture, life at hard labor
PVT John Lanier	Co I	Guilty of all charges and specifications	Dishonorable discharge, total forfeiture, life at hard labor
PVT Edward Porter Jr.	Co I	Guilty of all charges and specifications	Death (no dishonorable discharge, death alone) commuted to life at hard labor
PVT Robert Smith	Co I	Guilty of all charges and specifications	Death (no dishonorable discharge, death alone) commuted to life at hard labor
PVT Hesekiah C. Turner	Co I	Guilty of all charges and specifications	Death (no dishonorable discharge, death alone) commuted to life at hard labor
PVT William Mance	Co I	Guilty of all charges and specifications	Dishonorable discharge, total forfeiture, life at hard labor

(*continued*)

Name and Rank	Unit	Findings	Adjudged Sentence
CPL Quiller Walker	Co K	Guilty of all charges and specifications	Death (no dishonorable discharge, death alone) commuted to life at hard labor
PVT Howard E. Bennett	Co K	Guilty of charges I and II, Not guilty of charges III and IV	Dishonorable discharge, total forfeiture, 15 years confinement at hard labor
PVT Grant Anderson	Co K	Guilty of all charges and specifications	Dishonorable discharge, total forfeiture, life at hard labor
PVT Wilder P. Baker	Co K	Charges dismissed, found not competent due to insanity	Committed to St. Elizabeth hospital
PVT James Gaffney	Co K	Guilty of all charges and specifications	Dishonorable discharge, total forfeiture, life at hard labor
PVT James E. Woodruff	Co K	Guilty of all charges and specifications	Dishonorable discharge, total forfeiture, life at hard labor
PVT David Wilson	Co K	Guilty of charge I Not guilty of charges II–IV	Dishonorable discharge, total forfeiture, 2 years confinement at hard labor
PVT Warsaw Lindsey	Co L	Guilty of charges I and II Not guilty of charges III and IV	Dishonorable discharge, total forfeiture, 15 years confinement at hard labor
PVT Joseph T. Tatums	Co L	Guilty of charge I Not guilty of charges II–IV	Dishonorable discharge, total forfeiture, 2 years confinement at hard labor
PVT Henry Thomas	Co L	Guilty of charges I and II Not guilty of charges III and IV	Dishonorable discharge, total forfeiture, 15 years confinement at hard labor
PVT Grant Wells	Co L	Guilty of charge I Not guilty of charges II–IV	Dishonorable discharge, total forfeiture, 2 years confinement at hard labor
PVT Charlie Banks	Co M	Guilty of all charges and specifications	Death (no dishonorable discharge, total forfeiture) Commuted to life at hard labor

Name and Rank	Unit	Findings	Adjudged Sentence
PVT Tom Bass	Co M	Guilty of charge I Not guilty of charges II–IV	Dishonorable discharge, total forfeiture, 15 years confinement at hard labor
PVT William L. Dugan	Co M	Guilty of all charges and specifications	Dishonorable discharge, total forfeiture, life at hard labor
PVT Glen L. Hedrick	Co M	Guilty of charges I and II Not guilty of charges III and IV	Dishonorable discharge, total forfeiture, 15 years confinement at hard labor
PVT John Jackson	Co M	Guilty of charge I Not guilty of charges II–IV	Dishonorable discharge, total forfeiture, 2 years confinement at hard labor
PVT William Lampkins	Co M	Not guilty of all charges and specifications	Acquitted
PVT Doyle Lindsay	Co M	Guilty of charges I and II Not guilty of charges III and IV	Dishonorable discharge, total forfeiture, 15 years confinement at hard labor
PVT Joe McAfee	Co M	Guilty of charge I Not guilty of charges II–IV	Dishonorable discharge, total forfeiture, 2 years confinement at hard labor
PVT Edie Maxwell	Co M	Guilty of charges I and II Not guilty of charges III and IV	Dishonorable discharge, total forfeiture, 15 years confinement at hard labor
PVT Levy V. McNeil	Co M	Not guilty of all charges and specifications	Acquitted
PVT Samuel O. Riddle	Co M	Guilty of charges I and II Not guilty of charges III and IV	Dishonorable discharge, total forfeiture, 15 years confinement at hard labor
PVT Sherman V. Vetelcer	Co M	Guilty of all charges and specifications	Dishonorable discharge, total forfeiture, life at hard labor
PVT James V. Wofford	Co M	Guilty of charges I and II Not guilty of charges III and IV	Dishonorable discharge, total forfeiture, 15 years confinement at hard labor

NOTES

1. HANGMAN'S SLOUGH

1 The details of the execution and quoted statements are from an article by C. E. Butzer published in the December 13, 1917, issue of the *Houston Post*. Butzer's is one of only a few known eyewitness accounts of the 1917 execution. Other details are drawn from a letter written to the parents of PFC Thomas C. Hawkins, one of the condemned men, by G. F. C. Curry, the Black clergyman who attended the soldiers at the hanging. Curry's letter is from the personal collection of Jason Holt, Esq., great-nephew of Thomas C. Hawkins.

2. LYNCH MOBS AND NIGHT RIDERS

1 The 1836 Constitution of the Republic of Texas stated in Section 9 of the General Provisions: "All persons of color who were slaves for life previous to their emigration to Texas, and who are now held in bondage, shall remain in the like state of servitude, provided the said slave shall be the bona fide property of the person so holding said slave as aforesaid. Congress shall pass no laws to prohibit emigrants from the United States of America from bringing their slaves into the Republic with them, and holding them by the same tenure by which such slaves were held in the United States; nor shall Congress have power to emancipate slaves; nor shall any slave-holder be allowed to emancipate his or her slave or slaves, without the consent of Congress, unless he or she shall send his or her slave or slaves without the limits of the Republic. No free person of African descent, either in whole or in part, shall be permitted to reside permanently in the Republic, without the consent of Congress, and the importation or admission of Africans or negroes into this Republic, excepting from the United States of America, is forever prohibited, and declared to be piracy." Section 10 expressly denied citizenship to "Africans, the descendants of Africans, and Indians."
2 Charles William Ramsdell, *Reconstruction in Texas* (New York: Columbia University Press, 1910), 302.
3 Bertram Doyle, *The Etiquette of Race Relations in the South: A Study in Social Control* (Chicago: University of Chicago Press, 1937), 21.
4 James Campbell, "'You Needn't Be Afraid Here; You're in a Civilized Country': Region, Racial Violence and Law Enforcement in Early Twentieth-Century New Jersey, New York and Pennsylvania," *Social History*, vol. 35, no. 3 (2010): 253–67.
5 Quoted in Grace Elizabeth Hale, *Making Whiteness: The Culture of Segregation in the South, 1890–1940* (New York: Pantheon Books, 1998).
6 Quoted in Leon F. Litwack, *Trouble in Mind: Black Southerners in the Age of Jim Crow* (New York: Alfred A. Knopf, 1998).
7 National Association for the Advancement of Colored People (NAACP), *Thirty Years of Lynching in the United States, 1889–1918* (New York: NAACP, 1919).
8 Ibid.

9 Litwack, *Trouble in Mind*.

10 NAACP, *Thirty Years of Lynching in the United States*.

11 *New York Tribune*, March 16, 1901.

12 W. E. B. Du Bois in *The Crisis*, March 13, 1912.

13 W. E. B. Du Bois in *The Crisis*, September 10, 1912.

14 James Weldon Johnson in the *New York Age*, June 3, 1915.

15 Quoted in Litwack, *Trouble in Mind*.

16 NAACP, *Thirty Years of Lynching in the United States*, 37.

17 *Waco Semi-Weekly Tribune*, May 16, 1916.

18 *San Antonio Express*, May 17, 1916.

19 *Houston Post*, May 15, 1916.

20 Ida B. Wells, *Crusade for Justice: The Autobiography of Ida B. Wells*, ed. Alfreda M. Duster (Chicago: University of Chicago Press, 1970), 154–55.

21 William R. Savage Papers, Southern Historical Collection, University of North Carolina; *Chicago Defender*, May 20, 1916.

22 Herbert Shapiro, *White Violence and Black Response: From Reconstruction to Montgomery* (Amherst: University of Massachusetts Press, 1988).

23 *St. Louis Post-Dispatch*, July 3, 1917.

24 "The Negro Silent Protest Parade Organized by the NAACP Fifth Ave., New York City July 28, 1917," National Humanities Center, Research Triangle Park, NC.

25 *St. Louis Post-Dispatch*, July 5, 1917.

26 Ibid.

27 Quoted in Litwack, *Trouble in Mind*.

3. SEMPER PARATUS

1 W. Thornton Parker, "The Evolution of the Colored Soldier," *North American Review* 168, no. 507 (February 1899): 223–28.

2 Stephen Bonsai, "The Negro Soldier in War and Peace," *North American Review* 185, no. 616 (June 7, 1907): 322.

3 Ibid.

4 Matthew F. Steele, "The 'Color Line' in the Army," *North American Review* 183, no. 605 (December 1906): 1287.

5 Ibid.

6 *The Colored American*, March 1898.

7 Ibid.

8 Quoted in Roger D. Cunningham, "The Black 'Immune' Regiments in the Spanish-American War," Army Historical Foundation, https://armyhistory.org/the-black-immune-regiments-in-the-spanish-american-war/, accessed November 14, 2024.

9 Piero Gleijeses, "African Americans and the War Against Spain," *North Carolina Historical Review* 73, no. 2 (April 1996).

10 Quoted in Willard B. Gatewood Jr., "Negro Troops in Florida, 1898," *Florida Historical Quarterly* 49, no. 1 (July 1970).

11 Quoted in Gleijeses, "African Americans and the War Against Spain," 195.

12 Quoted in Litwack, *Trouble in Mind*.

13 Ibid.

14 William Calvin Chase in the *Washington Bee*, March 5, 1898.

15 Matthew F. Steele, "The 'Color Line' in the Army," *North American Review* 183, no. 605 (December 21, 1906).

4. THE GHOSTS OF BROWNSVILLE

1 Herbert Shapiro, *White Violence and Black Response: From Reconstruction to Montgomery* (Amherst: University of Massachusetts Press, 1988).

2 Augustus Blockson, U.S. War Department, *The Brownsville Affray. Report of the Inspector General of the Army; Order of the President Discharging Enlisted Men of Companies B, C, and D, Twenty-fifth Infantry; Messages of the President to the Senate; and Majority and Minority Reports of the Senate Committee on Military Affairs* (Washington, DC: Government Printing Office, 1908).

3 William Calvin Chase in the *Washington Bee*, November 10, 1906.

4 Lewis, N. Wynne, "The Reaction of the Negro Press." *Phylon* 33, no. 2 (1972), 153–160.

5 "Affray at Brownsville, Texas," in *Hearings before the Committee on Military Affairs, United States Senate* (Washington, D.C.: Government Printing Office, 1907).

6 Francis J. Grimke, *The Works of Francis J. Grimke*, ed. Carter G. Woodson (Washington: The Associated Publishers, Inc., 1942).

7 William M. Donnelly, "The Root Reforms and the National Guard," May 2001, www .history.army.mil/documents/1901/Root-NG.htm, 1.

8 Nina Mjagkij, *Loyalty in Time of Trial: The African American Experience During World War I* (Lanham, MD: Rowman and Littlefield, 2011).

9 Southern IG Report, Box 1277, Houston 250.21.

10 Quoted in Robert Haynes, *A Night of Violence: The Houston Riot of 1917* (Baton Rouge: Louisiana State University Press, 1976), 52.

5. A NEST OF PREJUDICE

1 Martha Gruening, "Houston: An N.A.A.C.P. Investigation," *The Crisis*, November 1917, 14.

2 James M. Sorelle, "Race Relations in 'Heavenly Houston', 1917–1945," in *Black Dixie: Essays in Afro-Texas History in Houston*, edited by Howard Beeth and Cary D. Wintz (College Station: Texas A&M University Press, 1992).

3 Leon F. Litwack, *Trouble in Mind: Black Southerners in the Age of Jim Crow* (New York: Alfred A. Knopf, 1998).

4 Sorelle, "Race Relations Cary D. Wintz.

5 Lorenzo Greene, "Sidelights on Houston Negroes as Seen by an Associate of Dr. Carter G. Woodson in 1930," in *Black Dixie: Afro-Texan History and Culture in Houston*, edited by Howard Beeth and Cary D. Wintz (College Station: Texas A&M University Press, 1992).

6 Litwack, *Trouble in Mind.*

7 Frederick Douglass, *Narrative of the Life of Frederick Douglass* (Boston, 1849).

8 Quoted in Bertram Wilbur Doyle, *The Etiquette of Race Relations in the South: A Study in Social Control* (Chicago: University of Chicago Press, 1937).

9 Litwack, *Trouble in Mind.*

10 Thomas P. Bailey, *Race Orthodoxy in the South: And Other Aspects of the Negro Question* (New York: Neale, 1914).

11 Ibid.

12 *Waco Times-Herald*, July 23, 1905.

13 Garna Christian, *Black Soldiers in Jim Crow Texas, 1899–1917* (College Station: Texas A&M University Press, 1995).

14 Nina Mjagkij, *Loyalty in Time of Trial: The African American Experience During World War I* (Lanham, MD: Rowman and Littlefield, 2011).

15 William D. Carrigan, *The Making of a Lynching Culture: Violence and Vigilantism in Central Texas, 1836–1916* (Urbana: University of Illinois Press, 2004).

16 Sorrelle, "Race Relations."

17 Quoted in Gruening, "Houston: An N.A.A.C.P. Investigation," 18.

18 Elijah Clarence Branch, *Judge Lynch's Court in America: The Number of Negro Convicts in Prison in America and Other Injustice Done to the Negro in America* (Houston, 1913).

19 *Houston Daily Post*, August 15, 1917. Independence was (and remains) an unincorporated part of the Houston municipality. Caldwell is a small town about 107 miles from Houston.

20 Quoted in C. Calvin Smith, "The Houston Riot of 1917, Revisited," *Houston Review: History and Culture of the Gulf Coast* 13, no. 2 (1991).

21 Robert Haynes, *Night of Violence: The Houston Riot of 1917* (Baton Rouge: Louisiana State University Press, 1976).

22 Litwack, *Trouble in Mind*.

23 Bernard Nalty, *Strength for the Fight: A History of Black Americans in the Military* (New York: The Free Press, 1986).

6. Breaking Point

1 Albert Gallatin Forse, quoted in *Army and Navy Journal*, September 6, 1873. According to his entry in *Historical register and dictionary of the United States Army, from its organization, September 29, 1789, to March 2, 1903. By Francis B. Heitman. Published under act of Congress approved March 2, 1903*, v.1, Forse, who was commissioned into the army in June 1865, was killed in action at San Juan, Cuba, on July 1, 1898, during the Spanish-American War, as a major in the First Cavalry.

2 COL William Newman, September 20, 1917. Southern IG Report, Box 1277, Houston 250.21.

3 Thelma Bryant, quoted in Melissa Williams, "An Angry Encounter: The Camp Logan Riot," *Texas Historian* 53, no. 1 (September 1992): 1.

4 COL William Newman, September 20, 1917, Records of Inspector General, File 333.9, RG 159, Federal Records Center, hereafter FRC.

5 COL William Newman, Report to the Inspector General, Southern IG Report, Box 1277, Houston 250.21.

6 2LT John Jack, Southern IG Report, Box 1277, Houston 250.21.

7 COL William Newman, Southern IG Report, Box 1277, Houston 250.21.

8 Martha Gruening, "Houston: An N.A.A.C.P. Investigation," *The Crisis*, November 1917.

9 Robert Haynes, *Night of Violence: The Houston Riot of 1917* (Baton Rouge: Louisiana State University Press, 1976), 67.

10 COL William Newman, September 20, 1917, Records of Inspector General, File 333.9, RG 159, FRC.

11 Ibid.

12 COL George O. Cress, Inspector General, Southern Department, *Investigation of the Trouble at Houston, Texas, Between the Third Battalion, Twenty-fourth Infantry, and the Citizens of Houston, August 23, 1917*. Records of the United States Army Continental Commands, Southern Department, Headquarters File 370.61, Box 364, Records Group 393, NARA.

13 W. T. Patterson, Cress Report, RG 159, Box 80. Author's note: The Cress and Chamberlain Reports from 1917 are the most important primary sources in this history, as they contain all the personal interviews and sworn statements of the individuals involved in this event. They are archived as Southern Dept. General Correspondence File 370.61, Report of Col. G. O. Cress AIG to Commanding General, September 13,

1917; Cress Report RG 159, Box 802, File 333.9; and Chamberlain Report, Box 802, File 333.9. Unfortunately, these files are not organized, none of the contents are in sequential order, and elements of both reports are mixed in with each other. It is therefore impossible to apply page numbers to citations drawn from these records. Hereafter, these sources will be cited as "Cress Report" or "Chamberlain Report," with the particular file notation in which I found them.

14 CPT W. P. Rothrock, Cress Report, RG 159, Box 802.
15 Cress Report, RG 159, Box 802.
16 SGT William Nesbit, Cress Report, RG 159, Box 802.
17 W. C. Wilson, Cress Report, RG 159, Box 802.
18 CPT Haig Shekerjian, Cress Report, RG 159, Box 802.
19 *Houston Chronicle*, September 2, 1917.
20 PVT E. E. Fields, Cress Report, RG 159, Box 802.
21 Haynes, *Night of Violence*, 82.
22 All quotations in the following paragraphs about the events of the afternoon of August 20 are drawn from the statements of CPL Charles Baltimore, Records of the Office of the Inspector General (Army), RG 159, Box 801, p. 51), Sara Travers (Gruening, "Houston: An N.A.A.C.P. Investigation," 18), and Lee Sparks (Cress Report, RG 159, Box 802).
23 CPT Haig Shekerjian, Cress Report, RG 159, Box 802.
24 C. D. Waide, "When Psychology Failed," *Houston Gargoyle*, May 22, 1928.
25 E. F. Dougherty, Statement to BG Chamberlain, Cress Report, RG 159, Box 802.
26 William Johnson, Statement to BG Chamberlain, Cress Report, RG 159, Box 802.
27 E. E. Ammons, Cress Report, RG 159, Box 802.

7. THE CATACLYSM

1 MAJ Kneeland Snow, Cress Report, RG 159, Box 802.
2 All quotes by CPT Haig Shekerjian in this chapter come from Cress Report, RG 159, Box 802.
3 PVT Wiley L. Strong, statement made to Judge Advocate, 33rd Division, August 28, 1917, Records of the Office of the Inspector General, Correspondence Files, RG 159, Box 801.
4 CPT Haig Shekerjian, Cress Report, RG 159, Box 802.
5 CPT Bartlett James, Statement to BG John Chamberlain, Cress Report, RG 159, Box 802.
6 SGT Rhoden Bond, Cress Report, RG 159, Box 802.
7 Armstrong Emmott, quoted in Williams, "An Angry Encounter: The Camp Logan Riot," 1.
8 Glidden O'Connor, quoted in Williams, "An Angry Encounter: The Camp Logan Riot," 2.
9 H. G. Kniggs, *Houston Daily Post*, November 7, 1917.
10 R. R. McDaniel, Testimony Before the Houston Commission, August 1917, South Texas College of Law. Hereafter "Houston Commission."
11 F. B. Dwyer, September 20, 1917, Cress Report, RG 159, Box 802.
12 R. R. McDaniel, Houston Commission, August 1917.
13 CPT Haig Shekerjian, Cress Report, RG 159, Box 802. All following quotations by Shekerjian in this chapter come from the same source.
14 SGT Samuel Venters, Cress Report, RG 159, Box 802.
15 CPT Bartlett James, Cress Report, RG 159, Box 802.

16 SGT Rhoden Bond, Cress Report, RG 159, Box 802.
17 2LT Edward Hudson, Cress Report, RG 159, Box 802.
18 SGT Arthur Taylor, Cress Report, RG 159, Box 802.
19 Ibid.

8. THE KILLING

1   CPT Warren W. Morgan, Cress/Chamberlain Report, RG 159, Box 802.
2   *U.S. v. Tillman*, Record of Trial, p. 740.
3   William J. Drucks, sworn statement, August 24, 1917. Houston Commission.
4   *U.S. v. Tillman*, Record of Trial, p. 810.
5   J. D. Dixon, *U.S. v. Nesbit*, Record of Trial, 491–95.
6   CPT F. S. Haines, Cress Report, RG 159, Box 802.
7   CPT F. S. Haines, *U.S. v. Nesbit*, Record of Trial, 517–19.
8   C. W. Hahl, *U.S. v. Nesbit*, Record of Trial, 550–55.
9   W. C. Wilson. *U.S. v. Tillman*, Record of Trial, 841–47.
10 CPT L. A. Tuggle, Cress Report, RG 159, Box 802.
11 B. A. Calhoun, Cress Report, RG 159, Box 802.
12 PVT Isaac Deyo, Letter to Burris Jenkins, NAACP Archives, 001527-018-0751.
13 Henry Pratt, Cress Report, Box 159, Box 802.
14 Report of Special Board of Investigation in the Death of Captain Joseph Mattes to Commanding General, Camp Logan, August 27, 1917, Records of Inspector General, File 333.9, NARA, RG 159.
15 CPL Zemmie Foreman, *U.S. v. Tillman*, Record of Trial, 908–10; Private Alphens D. Jones, *U.S. v. Tillman*, Record of Trial, 894–95.
16 *U.S. v. Nesbit*, Record of Trial, 1219–1221; *U.S. v. Tillman*, Record of Trial, 1417-18 and 1322–23.
17 MAJ Kneeland Snow, telegram to CG Southern Department, 2:00 a.m., 24 August, Cress Report, RG 159, Box 802, p. 138.
18 1LT Louis Sauter, Cress Report, RG 159, Box 802.
19 Ibid.
20 COL Millard F. Waltz, Cress Report, RG 159, Box 802.
21 Ibid.

9. WHITEWASH

1   *Sunday Star*, August 30, 1917.
2   Dan Moody, Testimony before the Houston Commission, August 1917.
3   *Houston Post*, August 25, 1917.
4   Ibid.
5   Maude Potts, testimony before the Houston Commission, August 1917, Houston Riot File, Houston Metropolitan Research Center.
6   *Fort Wayne Sentinel*, August 24, 1917.
7   *Cleveland Gazette*, September 1, 1917.
8   *Broad Ax*, September 1, 1917.
9   John E. Green Jr., *Houston Post*, August 25, 1917.
10 *Bellville Times*, August 30, 1917.
11 Rep. Joe H. Eagle, Telegram to Newton Baker, Secretary of War, August 24, 1917.
12 *Fremont Eagle*, August 30, 1917.

13 *Houston Post*, August 25, 1917.

14 Ibid.

15 *Houston Post*, August 25, 1917.

16 *Houston Post*, August 26, 1917.

17 *Cleveland Gazette*, September 1, 1917.

18 James C. Waters Jr., Cress Report, NARA, RG 93e A-101, Southern Command, Box 364.

19 Correspondence File, NARA, RG 92e A-101, Southern Command, Box 364.

20 MG James Parker, telegram to BG John Hulen, August 24, 1917, Cress Report, RG 159, Box 802.

21 COL Millard F. Waltz, Cress Report, RG 159, Box 802.

22 Ibid.

23 A. L. Blesh, Cress Report, RG 159, Box 802.

24 *Escanaba Morning Press*, August 26, 1917.

25 Ed Stoermer, Cress Report, RG 159, Box 802.

26 CPT Haig Shekerjian, Cress Report, RG 159, Box 802.

27 1LT W. S. Chaffin, to BG Chamberlain, September 5, 1917, Cress/Chamberlain Report, RG 159, Box 802.

28 Kyle Paulus, Cress Report, RG 159, Box 802.

29 Cress Report, RG 159, Box 802.

30 J. W. Link, Joseph S. Cullinan Papers, University of Houston Libraries Special Collections, 2006-009, Box 55.

31 CPL Leonard Watkins and CPT Bartlett James, Sworn Statements, September 22, 1917, Southern IG Report, Box 1277, Houston 250.21.

32 ISG Samuel Venters, SGT Rhoden Bond, CPT Bartlett James, Sworn Statements, September 22, 1917, Southern IG Report, Box 1277, Houston 250.21.

33 Cress Report, RG 159, Box 802.

34 Ibid.

35 Dan M. Moody, Cress Report, RG 159, Box 802.

36 COL George Cress, Cress Report, RG 159, Box 802.

37 CPT Haig Shekerjian, Cress Report, RG 159, Box 802.

38 MAJ Kneeland Snow, Cress Report, RG 159, Box 802.

39 Ibid.

40 SGT Samuel Venters, Cress Report, RG 159, Box 802.

41 CPT Bartlett James, Sworn Statement, September 22, 1917, Southern IG Report, Box 1277, Houston 250.21.

42 COL William Newman, Report to the Inspector General, Southern IG Report, Box 1277, Houston 250.21.

43 BG John Chamberlain, Cress/Chamberlain Report, RG 159, Box 802.

44 COL William Newman, Report to the Inspector General, Southern IG Report, Box 1277, Houston 250.21.

45 CPT Haig Shekerjian, Cress/Chamberlain Report, RG 159, Box 802.

46 COL William Newman, Report to the Inspector General, Southern IG Report, Box 1277, Houston 250.21.

47 Inquest Reports of Harris County, Texas Records Center, Houston, Texas.

48 J. J. Hardeway, *Houston Chronicle*, August 1917 (specific day uncertain).

49 Cress Report, RG 159, Box 802.

50 CPT David E. VanNatta, Cress Report, RG 159, Box 802.

51 CPT Ralph C. Woodward, Cress Report, RG 159, Box 802.
52 Quoted in Martha Gruening, "Houston: An N.A.A.C.P. Investigation," *The Crisis,* November 1917.
53 MAJ Kneeland Snow, Cress Report, RG 159, Box 802.
54 C. L. Brock, Cress Report, RG 159, Box 802.
55 BG John A. Hulen, Cress Report, RG 159, Box 802.
56 COL John Hoover, Cress Report, RG 159, Box 802.
57 SGT Cecil Green, Cress Report, RG 159, Box 802.
58 Anonymous letter to Sec War Newton Baker, received at War Department September 7, 1917, Cress Report, RG 159, Box 802.

10. FAILURE OF COMMAND

1 LT William M. Nathan, Houston Riot File, Houston Metropolitan Research Center.
2 *Waco Morning News,* August 25, 1917.
3 MAJ Kneeland Snow, Cress Report, RG 159, Box 802.
4 Ibid.
5 MAJ Kneeland F. Snow, Cress/Chamberlain Report, RG 159, Box 802.
6 COL John Hoover, 5th Texas Infantry NG, to BG Chamberlain, Cress Report, RG 159, Box 802.
7 MAJ Kneeland Snow, Cress Report, RG 159, Box 802.
8 A. F. Butler, Cress Report, RG 159, Box 802.
9 CPT W. P. Rothrock, Cress/Chamberlain Report, RG 159, Box 802.
10 SGM William Washington, Cress Report, RG 159, Box 802.
11 SGT Rhoden Bond, Cress Report, RG 159, Box 802.
12 SGT William Fox, Cress Report, RG 159, Box 802.
13 COL William Newman, RG 92e A-101, Southern Command, Box 364.
14 CPT Lindsay Silvester, Cress/Chamberlain Report, RG 159, Box 802.
15 CPT Haig Shekerjian, Cress/Chamberlain Report, RG 159, Box 802.

11. INVESTIGATIONS

1 MG James Parker, Headquarters, Southern Dept., Cress Report, RG 159, Box 802.
2 Report to CG Southern Dept, August 27, 1917, Cress Report, RG 159, Box 802.
3 PVT Harry Richardson, *U.S. v. Nesbit,* Record of Trial, 1469–70; PVT Douglas Bolden, *U.S. v. Nesbit,* Record of Trial, 1829; PVT Grover Burns, *U.S. v. Nesbit,* Record of Trial, 1868.
4 SGT William Fox, Cress Report, RG 159, Box 802.
5 2LT Charles Snider, Cress Report, RG 159, Box 802.
6 CPT Bartlett James, Cress Report, RG 159, Box 802.
7 COL George Cress, Cress Report, RG 159, Box 802.
8 Chamberlain Report, NARA, RG 159, Box 802.
9 CPL Charles Baltimore, Cress Report, RG 159, Box 802.
10 COL George Cress, Chamberlain Report, Box 802, File 333.9.
11 2LT Charles Snider, Chamberlain Report, Box 802, File 333.9.
12 MAJ Kneeland Snow, Chamberlain Report, Box 802, File 333.9.
13 BG John Chamberlain, Chamberlain Report, Box 802, File 333.9.
14 *Broad Ax,* September 1, 1917.

15 W. E. B. Du Bois in *The Crisis*, October 1917, 10–12.
16 Dr. Charles Purvis, letter of August 31, 1917, "An Unpublished Letter from Dr. Charles B. Purvis to Judge Robert Heberton Terrell," *Journal of Negro History* 63, no. 3 (July 1978): 235–37.
17 Chamberlain Report, Box 802, File 333.9 Houston 4.
18 *Official Register of the Officers and Cadets of the U.S. Military Academy*, June 1879, and "Bureau Briefs," *Washington Post*, February 16, 1880.
19 COL George Cress, Cress Report, RG 92e A-101, Southern Command, Box 364.
20 BG John Chamberlain, Chamberlain Report, Box 802, File 333.9 Houston 4.
21 Ibid.

12. A MYSTERY WITHIN A TRAGEDY

1 Cress Report, RG 92e A-101, Southern Command, Box 364.
2 Minutes of the Meeting of the Board of Directors, NAACP, October 8, 1917, File 001527-018-05213.
3 BG John L. Chamberlain, Chamberlain Report, Box 802, File 333.9 Houston 4.
4 Ibid.
5 Correspondence File, NARA, RG 92e A-101, Southern Command, Box 364.
6 *Washington Evening Star*, September 1917.
7 James C. Waters Jr., Cress Report, RG 93e A-101, Southern Command, Box 364.
8 COL George Cress, Cress Report, RG 93e A-101, Southern Command Box 364.
9 Cress Report, RG 159, Box 802.
10 Ibid.
11 *San Antonio Light*, March 10, 1918.
12 Sixty-four soldiers were originally arraigned for trial. One man fell ill just before the trial convened and was not tried with the rest. Sixty-three men were tried in the first court-martial; the sixty-fourth man was subsequently tried in the third court-martial.

13. *UNITED STATES V. NESBIT*

1 *U.S. v. Nesbit et al.*, Record of Trial.
2 U.S. Department of Defense, OASD (Comptroller), Directorate for Information Operations and Control, Selected Manpower Statistics, May 1975, 23.
3 Manual for Courts-Martial, Corrected to April 15, 1917, Washington, DC: Govt Printing Office, 1917, para. 109.
4 COL Enoch Crowder, quoted in Dru Brenner-Beck and John A. Haymond, "Returning the 24th Infantry Soldiers to the Colors," December 2021, 22, South Texas College of Law, Houston, https://stexl.stcl.edu/search?/cKF7642+.R48+2020/ckf+7642+r48+2020/-3,-1,,E/browse.
5 Dru Brenner-Beck, email to author, July 14, 2024.
6 Ibid.
7 *Houston Daily Post*, November 2, 1917.
8 George C. Schnitzer in the *Houston Daily Post*, November 5, 1917.
9 Ibid.
10 *Houston Daily Post*, November 11, 1917.
11 A. J. Houston to James W. Johnson, NAACP Archives, File 001527-018-05213.
12 Dru Brenner-Beck, email to author, July 24, 2024.
13 *U.S. v. Nesbit*, Record of Trial, 2060.

14 American Bar Association, *Canon of Ethics*, 1908.

15 *U.S. v. Nesbit*, Record of Trial, 2122.

16 A. J. Houston to James W. Johnson, November 26, 1917, NAACP Archives, File 001527-018-05213.

17 Ibid.

14. GALLOWS

1 *Houston Daily Post*, December 1, 1917.

2 Corporal Charles Baltimore, *Chicago Defender*, January 1918.

15. OUTRAGE

1 MG John Ruckman, reproduced in *Official Bulletin*, Washington, D.C., December 12, 1917.

2 W. E. B. Du Bois, quoted in *San Antonio Express News*, August 29, 1976.

3 *New York Age*, quoted in C. Calvin Smith, "The Houston Riot of 1917, Revisited," *Houston Review: History and Culture of the Gulf Coast* 13, no. 2 (1991): 85–102.

4 James Weldon Johnson, *New York Age*, December 22, 1917.

5 *Afro-American*, December 22, 1917.

6 *Princeton Daily Democrat*, December 11, 1917.

7 LTC Samuel Ansell, Memorandum to TJAG, December 12, 1917, NARA, RG 153.

8 BG John Chamberlain, Chamberlain Report, Box 802, File 333.9 Houston 4.

9 General Orders Related to the Death Sentence, NARA, Box 539, File 250.47.

16. THE LAST COURT-MARTIAL

1 Andrew J. Houston to James W. Johnson, January 14, 1918, NAACP Archives, File 001527-018-05213.

2 Andrew J. Houston to James W. Johnson, February 8, 1918, NAACP Archives, File 001527-018-05213.

3 James W. Johnson to Andrew J. Houston, February 14, 1918, NAACP Archives, File 001527-018-05213.

4 MAJ Dudley Sutphin to MG John W. Ruckman, April 1, 1918, NARA, Box 801, Inspector General General Correspondence.

5 Colonel Wilson Chase to Major General John W. Ruckman, April 5, 1918, NARA, Box 801, Inspector General General Correspondence.

17. FAILURES OF JUSTICE

1 American Bar Association, *Canon of Professional Ethics*, 1908, Canon 5.

2 American Bar Association, *Canon of Professional Ethics*, 1908, Canon 6.

3 *Houston Post*, September 25, 1918.

4 Ibid.

18. THE PRISONERS

1 Warsaw Lindsey to W. E. B. Du Bois, October 28, 1920, NAACP Archives, Library of Congress.

2 PVT George Hobbs to Congressman James W. Wadsworth, April 17, 1919, South Texas College of Law.

3 PVT Isaac Deyo to Senator William S. Kenyon, August 24, 1920, South Texas College of Law.

4 PVT Isaac Deyo to Burris Jenkins, October 1920, South Texas College of Law.

5 John Sharp Williams to Ben McDaniel, October 14, 1919, NAACP File, Library of Congress, File 001527-018-05213.

6 PVT James R. Hawkins to LTC Samuel Ansell, May 1919, Records of the Judge Advocate General's Corps, NARA.

7 Memorandum, 4th Endorsement to Secretary of War, War Dep't, J.A.G.O. (July 16, 1919), from LTC E.A. Kreger to Secretary of War and handwritten note by COL King (12 September 1919), Records of the Judge Advocate General's Corps, NARA.

8 Record of Trial, *United States v. Nesbit, et al.*, January 29, 1918, available at https://digitalcollections.stcl.edu/digital/collection/p15568coll1/id/44/rec/2.

9 *United States v. Nesbit, et al.*; Review of Record of Trial, *United States v. Washington*, January 29, 1918, at 18, *available at* https://digitalcollections.stcl.edu/digital/collection/p15568coll1/id/2123/rec/3; Review of Record of Trial, *United States v. Tillman, et al.*, January 29, 1918, at 52, *available at* https://digitalcollections.stcl.edu/digital/collection/p15568coll1/id/2117/rec/4

10 Clemency file for Abner Davis (at Annex E), available at https://digitalcollections.stcl.edu/digital/collection/p15568coll1/id/679/rec/1.

11 Memorandum from Office of the Judge Advocate General to Secretary of War, "Subject: Commutation of death sentences in Houston Riot Cases," August 3, 1918, available at https://digitalcollections.stcl.edu/digital/collection/p15568coll1/id/1969/rec/3.

12 Ibid.

13 Letter of Secretary John Weeks, Secretary, War Dep't, to Representative Julius Kahn, December 6, 1921, at 5 ("Of the one hundred and ten accused who were convicted and sentenced as a result of the trials above mentioned, nineteen were executed; one was pardoned, apparently because following his conviction at the first trial he gave valuable testimony at a subsequent trial; six died in confinement, fifteen were restored to duty at the U.S. Disciplinary Barracks; the sentences to confinement of three were remitted by my predecessor on the recommendation of the Judge Advocate General; the sentence to confinement of one was reduced from seven years to three years, and as reduced subsequently expired; and two others were also released upon expiration of their terms of confinement of two years each, thus leaving in confinement at the present, sixty-three general prisoners, of whom fifty-eight are serving sentences to confinement for life and five for fifteen years each. These general prisoners, with the exception of one who has been transferred to St. Elizabeth's Hospital, Washington, D.C., on account of his mental condition are confined at the U.S. Penitentiary, Leavenworth, Kansas"), found at HR67A-F28.1, the file code assigned to the committee records of the House Military Affairs Committee from the 67th Congress.

14 Review Nesbit ROT, *supra* note 26, at 27.

15 "Ruckman Defends Texas Hangings," *Boston Globe*, January 5, 1919, 2.

16 NAACP communique, December 18, 1920, NAACP Archives, Library of Congress.

17 *Informer*, December 1, 1925, NAACP Archives, Library of Congress.

18 Congressman Hamilton Fish III to MG W. A. Bethel, TJAG, December 31, 1923, NAACP Archives, Library of Congress.

19 Henry J. Dannenbaum to Secretary, NAACP, December 27, 1923, NAACP Archives, Library of Congress.

20 James Coker to J. E. Spingarn, May 13, 1920, NAACP Archives, Library of Congress.

21 William Burnette to James Weldon Johnson, February 16, 1922, NAACP Archives, Library of Congress.

22 Gerald Dixon to James Weldon Johnson, March 22, 1922, NAACP Archives, Library of Congress.

23 Assistant Secretary, NAACP, to E. Harrison Fisher, January 21, 1920, NAACP Archives, Library of Congress.

24 Assistant Secretary, NAACP, to Negro Factories Corporation, October 23, 1920, NAACP Archives, Library of Congress.

25 George Hobbs to James Weldon Johnson, December 14, 1922, NAACP Archives, Library of Congress.

26 *Chicago Defender*, December 1, 1922.

27 W. I. Biddle to COL Julius A. Penn, December 5, 1921, Tillman File 13231, NARA.

28 W. I. Biddle to James Weldon Johnson, December 24, 1923, NAACP Archives, Library of Congress.

29 Office of the Adjutant General Archives, Box 549, File 253, War Department Correspondence to White House.

30 John Patrick Sheehy, *Argus-Courier*, September 9, 2021.

31 William Burnette, *Indianapolis Recorder*, July 30, 1938.

32 J. B. Lowrey, June 30, 1949, and Office of the Inspector General, July 20, 1949. Chamberlain Report, Box 802, File 333.9.

33 Congressional Act of June 21, 1930.

EPILOGUE

1 Dru Brenner-Beck and John A. Haymond, "Petition, Returning the 24th Infantry Regiment Soldiers to the Colors," October 27, 2020, and Dru Brenner-Beck and John A. Haymond, "Addendum to Petition, Returning the 24th Infantry Regiment Soldiers to the Colors," December 5, 2021, South Texas College of Law Houston Special Collections, https://digitalcollections.stcl.edu/digital/collection/p15568coll1.

2 Memorandum from Office of the Judge Advocate General to Secretary of War, Subject: Commutation of Death Sentences in Houston Riot Cases, August 3, 1918.

3 Ibid.

4 Secretary John Weeks to Representative Julius Kahn, December 6, 1921, Committee Records of the House Military Affairs Committee from the 67th Congress, NARA, HR67A-F28.1.

5 Review of *U.S. v. Nesbit*, Record of Trial, 27, https://digitalcollections.stcl.edu/digital/collection/p15568coll1/id/2025/rec/2.

6 "Ruckman Defends Texas Hangings," *Boston Globe*, January 5, 1919.

7 Army Board for Correction of Military Records, Record of Proceedings, October 18, 2007, Docket No. AR20070009496.

8 1917 Manual for Courts-Martial, para. 340, states: "An officer acting as counsel before a general or special court-martial should perform such duties as usually devolve upon the counsel for a defendant before civil courts in criminal cases. He should guard the interests of the accused by all honorable and legitimate means known to the law, but should not obstruct the proceedings with frivolous and manifestly useless objections or discussions."

BIBLIOGRAPHY

PRIMARY SOURCES

"Affray at Brownsville, Texas." *Hearings Before the Committee on Military Affairs, United States Senate.* 6 vols. Washington, DC: Government Printing Office, 1907.

Biennial Report of the Adjutant General of Texas, from January 1, 1917, to December 31, 1918, Texas State Archives, Austin, Texas.

Bivens, Private George, statement, August 25, 1917, Army Commands, Southern Department, Headquarters, RG 393, National Archives and Records Administration.

Chamberlain, Brig. Gen. John L. *Report of Investigation of Mutiny in 3d Battalion, 24th United States Infantry at Houston, Texas, on the Night of August 23, 1917.* Records of the Office of the Inspector General, General Correspondence, Records Group 159, Federal Records Center.

Chamberlain, Brig. Gen. John L., to George O. Cress, Memorandum, September 7, 1917, Army Commands, Southern Department, Headquarters, RG 393, National Archives and Records Administration.

Cress, Col. George O., Inspector General, Southern Department. *Investigation of the Trouble at Houston, Texas, Between the Third Battalion, Twenty-fourth Infantry, and the Citizens of Houston, August 23, 1917.* Records of the United States Army Continental Commands, Southern Department, Headquarters File 370.61, Box 364, Records Group 393; Box 802, Records Group 159, National Archives and Records Administration.

Edward Albert Kreger Papers, 1885–1968, Dolph Briscoe Center for American History, University of Texas at Austin.

Gruening, Martha. "Houston: An N.A.A.C.P. Investigation." *The Crisis,* November 1917, 19.

"Houston Riot Cases." House Report No. 503. 67th Congress, 2nd session, December 9, 1921. *Investigation of the Conduct of United States Troops Stationed at Fort Brown, Texas.* Washington, DC: Government Printing Office, 1906.

Judge Advocate General's Office. Record Group 153. National Archives and Records Service, Washington, DC.

Manual for Courts-Martial, Corrected to April 15, 1917. Washington, DC: Government Printing Office, 1917.

Manual for Courts-Martial, Courts of Inquiry, and of Other Procedure Under Military Law. New York: Military Publishing Co., 1917.

Newman, Lt. Col. William, statement, September 20, 1917. Records of Inspector General, File 333.9, RG 159, Federal Records Center.

Report of Inspector General to Secretary of War: Investigation of Controversies Pertaining to the Office of the Judge Advocate General. May 8, 1919. Records of the Inspector General, U.S. Army. Record Groups 153 and 393, Modern Military Records Branch, Textual Archives Services Division, National Archives Services Division, National Archives and Records Administration. [Incarceration and appeal records of the mutiny defendants.]

"Riot of United States Negro Soldiers at Houston, Texas." Senate Report No. 235. 66th Congress, 1st Session, October 1, 1919.

Snow, Major Kneeland, statement to Brig. Gen. John A. Hulen, "Report on Circumstances Attending the Mutiny," August 24, 1917. Record Group 393, U.S. Army, Southern Department, Box 364, National Archives and Records Administration.

United States v. Corporal Robert Tillman, et al, 24th Infantry. General Courts-Martial Case 109045, Records of the Judge Advocate General, General Courts-Martial, 1812–1938, Box 5384, RC 153, Federal Records Center.

United States v. Private James H. Johnson et al., General Courts-Martial Case 105553, Records of Judge Advocate General, RG 153, Federal Records Center.

United States v. Private Washington, et al, 24th Infantry. General Courts-Martial Case 109045, Records of the Judge Advocate General, General Courts-Martial, 1812–1938, Box 5384, RC 153, Federal Records Center.

United States v. Sergeant William C. Nesbit, et al, 24th Infantry. General Courts-Martial Case 109045, Records of the Judge Advocate General, General Courts-Martial, 1812–1938, Box 5384, RC 153, Federal Records Center.

United States Army. *Companies B, C, and D, Twenty-Fifth United States Infantry: Report of the Proceedings of the Court of Inquiry Relative to the Shooting Affray at Brownsville, Texas, August 13–14, 1906.* Washington, DC: Government Printing Office, 1911.

U.S. Congress. Senate. Committee on Military Affairs. *Affray at Brownsville, Texas: Proceedings of a General Court-Martial Convened at Headquarters Department of Texas, San Antonio, Tex., Apr. 15, 1907 in the Case of Capt. Edgar A. Macklin.* 66th Congress, 1st Session. Washington, DC: Government Printing Office, 1908.

U.S. War Department. *The Brownsville Affray: Report of the Inspector General.* Washington, DC: Government Printing Office, 1908.

U.S. War Department. *The Brownsville Affray. Report of the Inspector General of the Army; Order of the President Discharging Enlisted Men of Companies B, C, and D, Twenty-fifth Infantry; Messages of the President to the Senate; and Majority and Minority Reports of the Senate Committee on Military Affairs.* Washington, DC: Government Printing Office, 1908.

U.S. War Department. Inspector General's Office. *Affray at Brownsville, Texas, August 13 and 14, 1906: Investigation of the Conduct of United States Troops (Companies B, C, and D, Twenty-Fifth Infantry) Stationed at Fort Brown, Texas: Reports of Augustus P. Blocksom, Leonard A. Lovering, [and] Ernest A. Garlington (of the Inspector General's Dept.).* Washington, DC: Government Printing Office, 1906.

U.S. War Department. *Proceedings and Report of Special War Department Board on Courts-Martial and their Procedure.* Washington, DC: Government Printing Office, National Archives: Record Group 28, U.S. Postal Service Record Group 32, U.S. Shipping Board.

U.S. War Department. *Summary Discharge or Mustering Out of Regiments or Companies. Message from the President . . . Transmitting a Report from the Secretary of War, Together with Several Documents (and Additional Testimony in the Brownsville Case).* 2 vols. Washington, DC: Government Printing Office, 1906–7.

William R. Savage Papers, Southern Historical Collection, University of North Carolina, 1974–1987.

NEWSPAPERS

Afro-American, December 22, 1917.
———, May 23, 1924.

Bakersfield Californian, September 24, 1918.
Bellville Times, August 30, 1917.
Biloxi Daily Herald, February 14, 1918.
Broad Ax, September 1, 1917.
Brownsville Herald, August 28, 1917.
Bryan Weekly Eagle, August 30, 1917.
———, September 26, 1918.
Chicago Defender, January 1918.
———, December 1, 1922.
Cleveland Gazette, September 1, 1917.
———, September 15, 1917.
———, September 21, 1917.
———, December 15, 1917.
———, December 22, 1917.
———, January 5, 1918.
———, February 2, 1918.
———, March 2, 1918.
———, March 29, 1918.
———, May 2, 1918.
Escanaba Morning Press, Aug. 26, 1917.
Fort Wayne Sentinel, August 24, 1917.
Fremont Eagle, August 30, 1917.
Houston Chronicle, ca. October 15, 1917.
———, August 1917.
———, September 2, 1917.
———, December 13, 1917.
Houston Post, August 15, 1917.
———, August 22, 1917.
———, August 24, 1917.
———, August 25, 1917.
———, August 26, 1917.
———, August 27, 1917.
———, August 28, 1917.
———, August 29, 1917.
———, August 31, 1917.
———, November 2, 1917.
———, November 7, 1917.
———, November 11, 1917.
———, November 29, 1917.
———, December 1, 1917.
———, December 12, 1917.
———, September 25, 1918.
Hutchinson News, September 17, 1918.
Indianapolis Recorder, July 30, 1938.
Kokomo Daily Tribune, December 11, 1917.
Lincoln Daily Star, September 24, 1918.
Miami Daily, September 24, 1918.
Moulton Eagle, January 11, 1918.

————, October 4, 1918.
Mount Pleasant Daily News, August 28, 1917.
New York Age, December 22, 1917.
New York Times, August 25, 1917.
Philadelphia Tribune, March 2, 1918.
Princeton Daily Democrat, December 11, 1917.
San Antonio Evening News, June 19, 1920.
San Antonio Express, February 8, 1924.
————, November 1, 1927.
————, November 17, 1929.
San Antonio Express News, August 29, 1976.
San Antonio Light, August 24, 1917.
————, October 23, 1917.
————, October 30, 1917.
————, November 4, 1917.
————, November 6, 1917.
————, November 7, 1917.
————, November 8, 1917.
————, November 9, 1917.
————, November 11, 1917.
————, November 14, 1917.
————, November 21, 1917.
————, November 23, 1917.
————, December 11, 1917.
————, December 12, 1917.
————, December 20, 1917.
————, December 21, 1917.
————, December 23, 1917.
————, January 3, 1918.
————, January 4, 1918.
————, January 25, 1918.
————, February 5, 1918.
————, February 17, 1918.
————, February 21, 1918.
————, March 1, 1918.
————, March 10, 1918.
————, March 21, 1918.
————, March 26, 1918.
————, March 27, 1918.
————, April 1, 1918.
————, April 14, 1918.
————, April 23, 1918.
————, May 5, 1918.
————, June 5, 1918.
————, July 2, 1918.
————, September 4, 1918.
————, September 17, 1918.
————, December 10, 1921.

————, June 13, 1922.
————, November 27, 1924.
————, June 7, 1940.
————, December 7, 1975.
Sunday Star, August 30, 1917.
Topeka State Journal, July 30, 1917.
Waco Morning News, August 24, 1917.
————, August 25, 1917.
————, August 30, 1917.
Washington Evening Star, September 1917.
Washington Post, September 18, 1918.

SECONDARY SOURCES

Adams, S. B. "Lynching and Its Remedy." Paper read before the Georgia Bar Association at Tybee Island, Georgia, June 3, 1916. HathiTrust Digital Library.
Ashby, Lynn. "The Riot of '17." Pts. 1–4. *Houston Post,* August 22–25, 1978.
Astor, Gerald. *The Right to Fight: A History of African Americans in the Military.* Novato, CA: Presidio Press, 1998.
Bailey, Amy Kate, and Stewart E. Tolnay. *Lynched: The Victims of Southern Mob Violence.* Chapel Hill: University of North Carolina Press, 2015.
Bailey, Thomas P. *Race Orthodoxy in the South: And Other Aspects of the Negro Question.* New York: Neale, 1914.
Barbeau, Arthur E., and Florette Henri. *The Unknown Soldiers: Black American Troops in World War I.* Philadelphia: Temple University Press, 1974.
Barr, Alwyn. "The Black Militia of the New South: Texas as a Case Study." *Journal of Negro History* 63 (July 1979): 209–19.
Beaver, Daniel R. *Baker and the American War Effort: 1917–1919.* Lincoln: University of Nebraska Press, 1966.
Beck, E. M. and Stewart E. Tolnay. *A Festival of Violence: An Analysis of Southern Lynchings, 1882–1930.* Urbana: University of Illinois Press, 1995.
Beeth, Howard, and Cary D. Wintz, eds. *Black Dixie: Afro-Texan History and Culture in Houston.* College Station, TX: Texas A&M University Press, 1992.
Bernstein, Patricia. *The First Waco Horror: The Lynching of Jesse Washington and the Rise of the NAACP.* College Station: Texas A&M University Press, 2005.
Bluthardt, Robert F. "The Buffalo Soldiers at Fort Concho, 1869–1885." *Texas Heritage* (Spring 2002).
Bond, Horace Mann. "The Negro in the Armed Forces of the United States Prior to World War I." *Journal of Negro Education* 12, no. 3 (Summer 1943): 268–87.
Borch, Fred L. III. "The Largest Murder Trial in the History of the United States: The Houston Riots Courts-Martial of 1917." *Army Lawyer,* no. 2, 2011.
Bowers, W. J. *Legal Homicide: Death as Punishment in America, 1864–1982.* Boston: Northeastern University Press, 1984.
Brown, Richard Maxwell. "The Archives of Violence." *American Archivist* 41, no. 4 (October 1978): 431–43.
Brown, Terry W. "The Crowder-Ansell Dispute: The Emergence of General Samuel T. Ansell." *Military Law Review* 35, no.1 (1967).

Brundage, W. Fitzhugh, ed. *Under Sentence of Death: Lynching in the South.* Chapel Hill: University of North Carolina Press, 1997.

Buecker, Thomas R. "Prelude to Brownsville: The Twenty-Fifth Infantry at Fort Niobrara, Nebraska, 1902–06." *Great Plains Quarterly* 16, no. 2 (Spring 1996): 95–106.

Bullard, Robert Lee. "The Negro Volunteer: Some Characteristics." *Journal of the Military Service Institution of the United States* 29 (July 1901): 27–35.

Byrd, Alexander X. "Studying Lynching in the Jim Crow South." *OAH Magazine of History* 18, no. 2 (January 2004): 31–36.

Cade, John B. *Twenty-Two Months with "Uncle Sam": Being the Experiences and Observations of a Negro Student Who Volunteered for Military Service Against the Central Powers from June, 1917 to April, 1919.* Atlanta: Robinson-Cofer, 1929.

Carrigan, William D. *The Making of a Lynching Culture: Violence and Vigilantism in Central Texas, 1836–1916.* Urbana: University of Illinois Press, 2004.

Cecelski, David S., and Timothy B. Tyson. *Democracy Betrayed: The Wilmington Race Riot of 1898 and Its Legacy.* Chapel Hill: University of North Carolina Press, 1998.

Chandler, Susan Kerr. "'That Biting, Stinging Thing Which Ever Shadows Us': African-American Social Workers in France During World War I." *Social Service Review* 69, no. 3 (September 1995): 498–514.

Chase, Hal. S. "'Shelling the Citadel of Race Prejudice': William Calvin Chase and the Washington 'Bee.'" *Records of the Columbia Historical Society, Washington, D.C.* 49 (1973/1974): 371–91.

Christian, Garna L. *Black Soldiers in Jim Crow Texas, 1899–1917.* College Station: Texas A&M University Press, 1995.

———. "The Brownsville Raid's 168th Man: The Court-Martial of Corporal Knowles." *Southwestern Historical Quarterly* 93, no. 1 (July 1989): 45–59.

———. "The El Paso Racial Crisis of 1900." *Red River Historical Review* 6 (Spring 1981): 28–41.

———. "The Ordeal and the Prize: The 24th Infantry and Camp MacArthur." *Military Affairs* 50, no. 2 (April 1986): 65–70.

———. "The Twenty-fifth Regiment at Fort McIntosh: Precursor to Retaliatory Violence." *West Texas Historical Association Year Book* 55 (1979): 149–61.

———. "The Violent Possibility: The Tenth Cavalry at Texarkana." *East Texas Historical Journal* 23 (1985): 3–13.

Clarke, James W. "Without Fear or Shame: Lynching, Capital Punishment and the Subculture of Violence in the American South." *British Journal of Political Science* 28 (1998): 269–89.

Collins, Winfield H. *The Truth About Lynching and the Negro in the South: In Which the Author Pleads That the South Be Made Safe for the White Race.* New York: Neale, 1918.

Cortner, Richard C. *A Mob Intent on Death: The NAACP and the Arkansas Riot Cases.* Middletown, CT: Wesleyan University Press, 1988.

Cutler, James. *Lynch-Law: An Investigation into the History of Lynching in the United States.* New York: Longmans, Green, 1905.

Daily, Jane, Glenda Elizabeth Gilmore, and Bryant Simon, eds. *Jumpin' Jim Crow: Southern Politics from Civil War to Civil Rights.* Princeton, NJ: Princeton University Press, 2000.

Davis, David A. "Not Only War Is Hell: World War I and African American Lynching Narratives." *African American Review* 42, nos. 3/4 (Fall-Winter 2008): 477–91.

"The Death Detail." Edited by William Pickens. *The World Tomorrow*, 1930. Reprinted in *Reader's Digest*, June 1930. [An account of the hanging by an eyewitness, C. E. Butzer, was published in the *Houston Post* in the December 13, 1917 issue. Butzer was most likely the anonymous author of the *Reader's Digest* article, or it was closely based on his account.]

Dobak, William A., and Thomas D. Phillips. *The Black Regulars, 1866–1898*. Norman: University of Oklahoma Press, 2017.

Dollard, John. *Caste and Class in a Southern Town*. 3rd ed. Garden City, NY: Doubleday Anchor Books, 1957.

Dorau, Angela Armendariz. "Of Soldiers, Racism, and Mutiny: The 1917 Camp Logan Riot and Court Martial." *Heritage Magazine* (Texas Historical Foundation), Spring 1998.

Doyle, Bertram Wilbur. *The Etiquette of Race Relations in the South: A Study in Social Control*. Chicago: University of Chicago Press, 1937.

Du Bois, W. E. B. *The Crisis*, October 1917.

———. "Race Relations in the United States 1917–1947." *Phylon* 9, no. 3 (1948): 234–47.

———. *The Souls of Black Folk*. Greenwich, CT: Fawcett, 1961.

Ellis, Mark. "W. E. B. Du Bois and the Formation of Black Opinion in World War I: A Commentary on 'The Damnable Dilemma.'" *Journal of American History* 81, no. 4 (March 1995): 1584–90.

Foner, Jack D. *Blacks and the Military in American History*. New York: Praeger, 1974.

Foraker, Joseph B. *The Black Battalion: They Ask No Favors Because They Are Negroes, but Only for Justice Because They Are Men*. Washington, DC: Government Printing Office, 1909.

———. "A Review of the Testimony in the Brownsville Investigation." *North American Review*, April 1908.

Gatewood, Willard B., Jr. "Negro Troops in Florida, 1898." *Florida Historical Quarterly* 49, no. 1 (July 1970): 1–15.

———. *"Smoked Yankees" and the Struggle for Empire: Letters from Negro Soldiers, 1898–1902*. Urbana: University of Illinois Press, 1971.

Ginzburg, Ralph. *100 Years of Lynchings*. New York: Lancer Books, 1962.

Glasrud, Bruce A. *African Americans in Central Texas History: From Slavery to Civil Rights*. College Station: Texas A&M University Press, 2019.

———. *African Americans in South Texas History*. College Station: Texas A&M University Press, 2011.

———. *Anti-Black Violence in Twentieth Century Texas*. College Station: Texas A&M University Press, 2015.

———. *Blacks in East Texas History: Selections from the East Texas Historical Journal*. College Station: Texas A&M University, 2008.

———. *Buffalo Soldiers in the West: A Black Soldiers Anthology*. College Station: Texas A&M University Press, 2007.

———. "Child or Beast? White Texas' View of Blacks, 1900–1910." *East Texas Historical Journal* 15, no. 2 (1977): 38–44.

———. "Enforcing White Supremacy in Texas, 1900–1910." *Red River Valley Historical Review* 4, no. 4 (Fall 1979): 87–99.

———. *Exploring the Afro-Texas Experience: A Bibliography of Secondary Sources About Black Texans*. Alpine, TX: Sul Ross State University, 2000.

Greene, Lorenzo J. "Sidelights on Houston Negroes as Seen by an Associate of Dr. Carter G. Woodson in 1930." In *Black Dixie: Afro-Texan History and Culture in Houston*, edited by Howard Beeth and Cary D. Wintz, 144–68. College Station, TX: Texas A&M University Press, 1992.

Grimke, Francis J. *The Works of Francis J. Grimke.* Edited by Carter G. Woodson. Washington: The Associated Publishers, Inc.,1942.

Grimshaw, Allen D. "Actions of Police and the Military in American Race Riots." *Phylon* 24, no. 3 (1963): 271–89.

———. "Lawlessness and Violence in America and Their Special Manifestations in Changing Negro-White Relationships." *Journal of Negro History* 44, no. 1 (January 1959): 52–72.

———, ed. *Racial Violence in the United States.* Chicago: Aldine, 1969.

Guterl, Matthew Pratt. "The New Race Consciousness: Race, Nation, and Empire in American Culture, 1910–1925." *Journal of World History* 10, no. 2 (Fall 1999): 307–52.

Hackney, Sheldon. "Southern Violence." *American Historical Review* 74 (February 1969): 924–25.

Hair, William Ivy. *Carnival of Fury: Robert Charles and the New Orleans Race Riot of 1900.* Baton Rouge: Louisiana State University Press, 1976.

Hale, Grace Elizabeth. *Making Whiteness: The Culture of Segregation in the South, 1890–1940.* New York: Pantheon Books, 1998.

Hamann, Jack. *On American Soil: How Justice Became a Casualty of World War II.* Seattle: University of Washington Press, 2005.

Haynes, Robert V. "The Houston Mutiny and Riot of 1917." *Southwestern Historical Quarterly* 76, no. 4 (April 1973): 418–39.

———. *A Night of Violence: The Houston Riot of 1917.* Baton Rouge: Louisiana State University Press, 1976.

———. "Unrest at Home: Racial Conflict Between Civilians and Black Soldiers in 1917." *Journal of the American Studies Association of Texas* 6 (1975).

Hearings before the Committee on Military Affairs, "Affray at Brownsville, Texas." 6 volumes. Washington, DC, 1907.

Johnson, Charles, Jr. *African American Soldiers in the National Guard.* Westport, CT: Greenwood Press, 1992.

Jordan, Walker H. *With "Old Eph" in the Army (Not a History): A Simple Treatise on the Human Side of the Colored Soldier.* Baltimore: H. E. Houck, 1920.

Jordan, William G. *Black Newspapers and America's War for Democracy, 1914–1920.* Chapel Hill: University of North Carolina Press, 2001.

Knopf, Terry Ann. *Rumors, Race, and Riots.* Brunswick, NJ: Transaction Books, 1975.

Lane, Ann J. *The Brownsville Affair: National Crisis and Black Reaction.* Port Washington, NY: Kennikat Press, 1971.

Lanning, Michael Lee. *The African-American Soldier: From Crispus Attucks to Colin Powell.* Secaucus, NJ: Birch Lane Press, 1997.

Leiker, James N. *Racial Borders: Black Soldiers Along the Rio Grande.* College Station: Texas A&M University Press, 2002.

Lentz-Smith, Adriane. *Freedom Struggles: African Americans and World War I.* Cambridge, MA: Harvard University Press, 2009.

"Life, Liberty, and the Pursuit of Happiness": On our Own Side of the Border, 1916; Recent American History. New York: National Association for the Advancement of Colored People, 1916.

Littlejohn, Jeffrey L., et al. "The Cabiness Family Lynching: Race, War, and Memory in Walker County, Texas." *Southwestern Historical Quarterly* 122, no. 1 (July 2018): 1–30.

Litwack, Leon F. *Trouble in Mind: Black Southerners in the Age of Jim Crow*. New York: Alfred A. Knopf, 1998.

Marszalek, John F., Jr. "The Black Man in Military History." *Negro History Bulletin* 36, no. 6 (October 1973): 122–25.

McGhee, Fred Lee. *Two Texas Race Riots*. Austin, TX: Fidelitas, 2012.

Miller, Kelly. *The Disgrace of Democracy: Open Letter to President Woodrow Wilson*. Washington, DC: Howard University, 1917.

Minton, John. *The Houston Riot and Courts-Martial of 1917*. San Antonio, TX, n.d.

Mjagkij, Nina. *Loyalty in Time of Trial: The African American Experience During World War I*. Lanham, MD: Rowman and Littlefield, 2011.

Murray, Paul T. "Blacks and the Draft: A History of Institutional Racism." *Journal of Black Studies* 2 (September 1971).

Nalty, Bernard C. *Strength for the Fight: A History of Black Americans in the Military*. New York: Free Press, 1986.

Nalty, Bernard C., and Morris J. MacGregor, eds. *Blacks in the Military: Essential Documents*. Wilmington, DE: Scholarly Resources, 1981.

National Association for the Advancement of Colored People. *Thirty Years of Lynching in the United States, 1889–1918*. New York: NAACP, 1919.

Nevels, Cynthia S. *Lynching to Belong: Claiming Whiteness Through Racial Violence*. College Station: Texas A & M University Press, 2007.

Rabe, Elizabeth R. "African American Doughboys: Victory in France, Defeat in Dallas." *Texas Historian* 58, no. 1 (September 1997).

Rackleff, Robert B. "The Black Soldier in Popular American Magazines, 1900–1917." *Negro History Bulletin* 34, no. 8 (December 1971): 185–89.

Ramsdell, Charles William. *Reconstruction in Texas*. New York: Columbia University Press, 1910.

Reich, Steven A. "Soldiers of Democracy: Black Texans and the Fight for Citizenship, 1917–1927." *Journal of American History* 82 (March 1996): 1478–504.

Rudwick, Elliott M. *Race Riot at East St. Louis, July 2, 1917*. Carbondale, IL: Southern Illinois University Press, 1964.

Sayen, John. "Battalion: An Organizational Study of the United States Infantry." Working paper, Marine Corps Combat Development Command, 2001.

Schubert, Frank N. "Black Soldiers on the White Frontier: Some Factors Influencing Race Relations." *Journal of Negro History* 47 (July 1962): 169–81.

Schuler, Edgar A. "The Houston Race Riot, 1917." *Journal of Negro History* 3 (July 1944): 300–338.

Shapiro, Herbert. *White Violence and Black Response: From Reconstruction to Montgomery*. Amherst, MA: University of Massachusetts Press, 1988.

Smith, C. Calvin. "The Houston Riot of 1917, Revisited." *The Houston Review: History and Culture of the Gulf Coast* 13, no. 2 (1991): 85–102.

Sorelle, James Martin. "'The Darker Side of Heaven': The Black Community in Houston, Texas." Ph.D. dissertation, Kent State University, 1980.

———. "Race Relations in 'Heavenly Houston,' 1917–1945." In *Black Dixie: Essays in Afro-Texas History in Houston*, edited by Howard Beeth and Cary D. Wintz, 517–36. College Station: Texas A&M University Press, 1992.

———. "The Waco Horror: The Lynching of Jesse Washington." *Southwestern Historical Quarterly* 86, no. 4 (April 1983): 517–36.

Thirty Years of Lynching in the United States: 1889–1918. New York: National Association for the Advancement of Colored People, 1919.

Turner, Leo. *The Story of Fort Sam Houston, 1876–1936.* San Antonio: Leo Turner, 1936.

Tuttle, William M., Jr. *Race Riot: Chicago in the Red Summer of 1919.* New York: Atheneum, 1970.

Watson, Dwight D. "In the Name of Decency and Progress: The Response of Houston's Civic Leaders to the Lynching of Robert Powell in 1928." *Houston Review of History and Culture* 1, no. 2 (Summer 2004).

———. *Race and the Houston Police Department, 1930–1990: A Change Did Come.* College Station, TX: Texas A & M University Press, 2005.

Weaver, John D. *The Brownsville Raid.* New York: W. W. Norton, 1970.

Wells, Ida B. *Crusade for Justice: The Autobiography of Ida B. Wells.* Edited by Alfreda M. Duster. Chicago: University of Chicago Press, 1970.

Wiener, Frederick B. "The Seamy Side of the World War I Court-Martial Controversy." *Law Review* 123 (1989): 109–28.

Williams, Chad L. *Torchbearers of Democracy: African American Soldiers in the World War I Era.* Chapel Hill: University of North Carolina Press, 2010.

Williams, Melissa. "An Angry Encounter: The Camp Logan Riot." *Texas Historian* 53, no. 1 (September 1992).

Williamson, Joel. *The Crucible of Race: Black-White Relations in the American South Since Emancipation.* New York: Oxford University Press, 1984.

Wilson, Woodrow. "Lynching is Unpatriotic (July 26, 1918)." *Selected Addresses and Public Papers of Woodrow Wilson.* Albert Bushnell Hart, editor. New York: Modern Library, 1918.

Woodward, C. Vann. *The Strange Career of Jim Crow.* New York: Oxford University Press, 1974.

Wright, Richard. *Black Boy: A Record of Childhood and Youth.* New York: Harper Perennial Modern Classics, 2020.

Wynne, Lewis N. "The Reaction of the Negro Press." *Phylon* 33, No. 2 (1972).

Zangrando, Robert L. *The NAACP Crusade Against Lynching, 1909–1950.* Philadelphia: Temple University Press, 1980.

INDEX